DOCUMENTS

OF THE

CONVENTION

OF THE

STATE OF NEW YORK,

1867-'68.

VOL. I.

FROM NO. 1 TO NO. 39, INCLUSIVE.

ALBANY:
WEED, PARSONS AND COMPANY,
PRINTERS TO THE CONVENTION.
1868.

IN CONVENTION, *Feb.* 27, 1868.

Resolved, That there be printed, in addition to the number already printed, a sufficient number of copies of the debates, documents and journals, to furnish each of the members with three copies; and also one copy each to the Mayor and the members of the Common Council of the city of Albany, and one copy each to the State Law Libraries at Rochester and Syracuse, the law libraries of the several judicial districts, the Law Institute, the Astor Library, and the New York Historical Society in the city of New York, and the Young Men's Associations of the cities of Albany and Troy.

LUTHER CALDWELL, *Secretary.*

STATE OF NEW YORK.

No. 1.

OFFICIAL LIST

OF THE

DELEGATES TO CONVENTION.

Elected April 23, 1867.

A list of the names of the delegates elected in the State of New York, at an election held on the twenty-third day of April, 1867, pursuant to the act entitled "An act to provide for a Convention to revise and amend the Constitution," passed March twenty-nine, 1867, and the act entitled "An act to amend an act to provide for a Convention to revise and amend the Constitution," passed March 29, 1867, passed April 19, 1867, received from the respective county clerks.

FOR STATE AT LARGE.

Waldo Hutchins, William M. Evarts, George Opdyke, Augustine J. H. Duganne, George William Curtis, Horace Greeley, Joshua M. Van Cott, Ira Harris, Erastus Cooke, Martin I. Townsend, William A. Wheeler, Charles Andrews, Tracy Beadle, Charles J. Folger, Erastus S. Prosser, Augustus Frank, Augustus Schell, George Law, Henry C. Murphy, Homer A. Nelson, David L. Seymour, Jacob Hardenburgh, Smith M. Weed, Alonzo C. Paige, Francis Kernan, George F. Comstock, John Magee, Henry D. Barto, Sanford E Church, Henry O. Chesebro, Joseph G. Masten, Marshall B. Champlain.

BY SENATORIAL DISTRICTS.

First District.—Selah B. Strong, Solomon Townsend, William Wickham, Erastus Brooks.

Second District.—John P. Rolfe, Daniel P. Barnard, Charles Lowey Walter L. Livingston.

Third District.—Teunis G. Bergen, William D. Veeder, John G. Schumaker, Stephen I. Colahan.

Fourth District.—Charles P. Daly, Samuel B. Garvin, Abraham R. Lawrence, Jr., John E. Burrill.

Fifth District.—Nathaniel Jarvis, Jr., Elbridge T. Gerry, Henry Rogers, Norman Stratton.

Sixth District.—Frederick W. Loew, Gideon J. Tucker, Abraham D. Russell, Magnus Gross.

Seventh District.—Samuel J. Tilden, Anthony L. Robertson, Edwards Pierrepont, James Brooks.

Eighth District.—Richard L. Larremore, Claudius L. Monell, John E. Develin, William Hitchman.

Ninth District.—Abraham B. Conger, Abraham B. Tappen, Robert Cochran, William H. Morris.

Tenth District.—Stephen W. Fullerton, William H. Houston, Clinton V. R. Ludington, Gideon Wales.

Eleventh District.—B. Platt Carpenter, John Stanton Gould, Wilson B. Sheldon, Francis Silvester.

Twelfth District.—John M. Francis, Jonathan P. Armstrong, Cornelius L. Allen, Adolphus F. Hitchcock.

Thirteenth District.—Erastus Corning, William Cassidy, Amasa J. Parker, James Roy.

Fourteenth District.—Marius Schoonmaker, Solomon G. Young, Manly B. Mattice, Ezekiel P. Moore.

Fifteenth District.—Alembert Pond, Hezekiah Baker, Judson S. Landon, Horace E. Smith.

Sixteenth District.—George M. Beckwith, Matthew Hale, Nathan G. Axtell, Andrew J. Cheritree.

Seventeenth District.—William C. Brown, Edwin A. Merritt, Leslie W. Russell, Joel J. Seaver.

Eighteenth District.—Edward A. Brown, Marcus Bickford, James A. Bell, Milton H. Merwin.

Nineteenth District.—Richard U. Sherman, Theodore W. Dwight, Benjamin N. Huntington, George Williams.

Twentieth District.—Elijah E. Ferry, John Eddy, Ezra Graves, Oliver B. Beals.

Twenty-first District.—Elias Root, Lester M. Case, M. Lindley Lee, Loring Fowler.

Twenty-second District.—Thomas G. Alvord, L. Harris Hiscock, Patrick Corbett, Horatio Ballard.

Twenty-third District.—Elizur H. Prindle, John Grant, Samuel F. Miller, Hobart Krum.

Twenty-fourth District.—Stephen D. Hand, Charles E. Parker, Oliver H. P. Kinney, Milo Goodrich.

Twenty-fifth District.—George Rathbun, Charles C. Dwight, Leander S. Ketcham, Ornon Archer.

Twenty-sixth District.—Elbridge G. Lapham, Angus McDonald, Sterling G. Hadley, Melitiah H. Lawrence.

Twenty-seventh District.—Elijah P. Brooks, David Rumsey, Abraham Lawrence, George T. Spencer.

Twenty eighth District.—Jerome Fuller, Lorenzo D. Ely, William A. Reynolds, Freeman Clark.

Twenty-ninth District.—Seth Wakeman, Levi F. Bowen, Thomas T. Flagler, Ben Field.

Thirtieth District.—Edward J. Farnum, Isaac L. Endress, John M. Hammond, William H. Merrill.

Thirty-first District.—Israel T. Hatch, Isaac A. Verplanck, Allen Potter, George W. Clinton.

Thirty-second District.—George Barker, Augustus F. Allen, Norman M. Allen, George Van Campen.

STATE OF NEW YORK,
Secretary's Office.

I certify the preceding to be a true list of the names of the Delegates elected to the Convention, according to the returns received at this office, from the respective county clerks of the State.

[L. S.] In testimony whereof, I have hereunto affixed my seal of office, at the city of Albany, the 7th day of May, 1867.

FRANCIS C. BARLOW,
Secretary of State.

STATE OF NEW YORK.

No. 2.

IN CONVENTION

June 11. 1867.

REPORT OF THE COMMITTEE ON RULES.

MR. SHERMAN, from the Select Committee appointed to report a code of rules for the regulation of the proceedings of the Convention, reports the following, viz:

CHAPTER I.

Of the Powers and Duties of the President.

Rule 1. The President shall take the Chair each day at the hour appointed for the meeting of the session.

Rule 2. He shall possess the powers and perform the duties herein prescribed, viz:

1. He shall preserve order and decorum.

2. He shall decide all questions of order, subject to appeal to the Convention. On every appeal he shall have the right, in his place, to assign his reasons for his decision.

3. He shall appoint all committees except where the Convention shall otherwise order. .

4. He may substitute any member to perform the duties of the Chair for a period not exceeding two consecutive legislative days.

5. When the Convention shall be ready to go into Committee of the Whole, he shall name a Chairman to preside therein.

6. He shall designate the reporters for the public press, not

exceeding fifteen in number, and shall assign to them their respective seats.

CHAPTER II.

Of the Daily Order of Business.

Rule 3. The first business of each day's session shall be the reading of the Journal of the preceding day and the correction of any errors that may be found to exist therein. After which, except on days and at times set apart for the consideration of special orders, the order of business, which shall not be departed from except by unanimous consent, shall be as follows, viz:

1. *The presentation of memorials.* Under which head shall be included petitions, remonstrances and communications from individuals and from public bodies.
2. Messages from the Governor.
3. Communications from State officers. Under which head shall be embraced also, communications from public officers and from corporations, in response to calls for information.
4. Notices.
5. Reports of standing committees.
6. Reports of select committees.
7. Resolutions.
8. Unfinished business of the general orders.
9. Special orders.
10. General orders.

CHAPTER III.

Of the Rights and Duties of Members.

Rule 4. The President, or any member, when he shall be recognized in his place, may present, under the proper order of business, any paper of a respectful character, addressed to the Convention, and the same, unless the Convention shall otherwise order, shall be referred to the appropriate committee.

Rule 5. Every member presenting a paper shall endorse the same; if a petition, memorial, remonstrance, or communication in answer to a call for information, with a concise statement of its subject, adding his name; if a notice or resolution, with his name; if the report of a committee, with a statement of its subject, the name of the committee and of the member making the report; if a proposition of any other kind for the consideration of the Convention, with a statement of its subject, the proposer's name and the reference, if any, desired.

Rule 6. Every member who shall be within the bar of the Convention when a question shall be stated from the chair, shall vote thereon unless he be excused or be personally interested in the question. No member shall be obliged to vote on any question unless within the bar when the question shall be put, but in the case of a division by yeas and nays, may vote if present before the last name shall be called. The bar of the Convention shall be deemed to include only the floor of the Assembly Chamber, or of the open spaces adjacent thereto, within the doors.

Rule 7. Any member desiring to be excused from voting, must make his request before the roll-call shall be commenced. He may then state concisely, without argument his reasons for asking to be excused, and the question of excusing shall be taken without debate.

CHAPTER IV.

Of order and Decorum.

Rule 8. No member rising to debate, to give a notice, make a motion or present a paper of any kind, shall proceed until he shall have addressed the President, and been recognized by him as entitled to the floor.

Rule 9. Where a member shall have the floor for any purpose, no member shall entertain any private discourse or pass between him and the chair.

Rule 10. While the President shall be putting a question, or a division by counting shall be had, no member shall leave his place, or speak, unless to make a privileged motion or state a question of privilege demanding immediate attention.

Rule 11. When a motion to adjourn, or for a recess, shall be affirmatively determined, no member or officer shall leave his place till the adjournment or recess shall be declared by the President.

CHAPTER V.

Of Order in Debate.

Rule 12. No member shall speak more than once to the same question, without leave of the Convention, until every member desiring to speak on the question pending shall have spoken.

Rule 13. No remarks reflecting personally upon the charactei or action of any member shall be in order in debate.

Rule 14. If any member, in speaking, shall transgress the rules of the Convention, the President shall, or any member may call to order, in which case the member so called to order, shall not proceed, unless to explain or speak in order.

CHAPTER VI.

Of committees and their duties.

Rule 15. Standing Committees shall be appointed by the President to consider and report severally upon the following subjects, and such others as may be referred to them, viz.:

1. On the preamble and the bill of rights.

2. On the Legislature,—its organization and the number, apportionment, election, tenure of office, and compensation of its members.

3. On the powers and duties of the Legislature, except as to matters otherwise referred.

4. On the right of suffrage and the qualification to hold office.

5. On the Governor and Lieutenant-Governor, their election, tenure of office, compensation, powers and duties, except as otherwise referred.

6. On the Secretary of State, Comptroller, Treasurer, Attorney-General, and State Engineer and Surveyor, their election or appointment, tenure of office, compensation, powers and duties.

7. On town and county officers, other than judicial, their election or appointment, tenure of office, compensation, powers and duties.

8. On the Judiciary.

9. On the finances of the State, the canals, except their care and management, the public debt, revenues, expenditures and taxation, and restrictions on the powers of the Legislature in respect thereto.

10. On the superintendence and management of the canals, and the proper officers to be charged therewith, and the mode of their election or appointment.

11. On cities, their organization, government and powers.

12. On counties, towns and villages, their organization, government and powers.

13. On currency, banking and insurance.
14. On corporations other than municipal, banking and insurance.
15. On State prisons.
16. On the pardoning power.
17. On the militia and military officers.
18. On education and the funds relating thereto.
19. On future amendments and revisions to the Constitution.

Rule 16. All reports of Committees embracing propositions for constitutional alteration shall be referred as of course to the Committee of the whole for consideration therein before final action by the Convention.

CHAPTER VII.

Of General and Special Orders.

Rule 17. The matters referred to the Committee of the Whole shall constitute the General Orders, and shall be recorded by their titles or subjects in a calendar to be kept for that purpose by the Secretary, in the order in which they shall be referred respectively.

Rule 18. Any particular report or other matter on the General Orders may be made a Special Order for any particular day or from day to day, with the assent of two-thirds of the members voting, and no Special Order shall be postponed or rescinded except by a similar vote.

CHAPTER VIII.

Of the Committee of the Whole.

Rule 19. The same rules shall be observed in Committee of the Whole as in the Convention, as far as applicable, except that the previous question shall not apply nor shall the yeas and nays be taken on a division.

Rule 20. A motion to rise and report progress shall be in order at any stage, and shall be decided without debate.

Rule 21. Subjects shall be taken up in Committee of the Whole in the order in which they shall stand on the General Orders, unless the Committee, by a two-thirds vote, shall, in any case, otherwise direct. The paper under consideration shall be first read at length, unless the Committee shall otherwise order, and shall then be read and considered by sections. All amendments made in Committee of the whole shall be reported to the Convention for action,

Rule 22. If at any time, in the Committee of the Whole, it shall appear that no quorum be present, the Committee shall immediately rise, and the Chairman shall report the fact to the Convention.

CHAPTER IX.

Of Motions and their Precedence.

Rule 23. When a question shall be under consideration, no motion shall be received except as herein specified, and motions shall have precedence in the order stated, viz:

1. For an adjournment.
2. For a recess.
3. A call of the Convention.
4. For the previous question.
5. To lay on the table.
6. To postpone indefinitely.
7. To postpone to a day certain.
8. To commit to a Committee of the Whole.
9. To commit to a Standing Committee.
10. To commit to a Select Committee.
11. To amend.

Rule 24. The motion to adjourn for the day, for a recess, for the previous question and to lay on the table, shall be decided without amendment or debate. The respective motions to postpone or commit shall preclude debate on the main question.

Rule 25. Every motion or resolution shall, after presentation, be first stated by the President, or on his order read by the Clerk before debate, and again, if desired by any member, immediately before putting the question. And every resolution and amendment shall be reduced to writing if the President or any member desire it.

Rule 26. After a proposition shall have been stated by the President, it shall be deemed to be in possession of the Convention, but may be withdrawn at any time before it shall be decided or amended.

Rule 27. The motions to adjourn or to take a recess shall be always in order when made by a member entitled to the floor.

Rule 28. No motion for a reconsideration of any vote shall be in order unless made on the same day or the next following legislative day on which the decision proposed to be reconsidered shall have taken place; nor unless moved by one who shall have voted in the majority. After a motion for a reconsideration shall have been put and lost, it shall not be renewed without the unanimous consent of the Convention.

Rule 29. The previous question shall be, "*Shall the main question be now put;*" and if determined in the affirmative, no further debate or amendment shall be in order, and the main question shall be on the passage of the resolution or other matter under consideration; but when amendments shall be pending, the question shall be first taken on the amendments in their order; and when amendments shall have been recommended by the Committee of the Whole, and not acted on by the Convention, the question shall be taken upon such amendments in like order.

CHAPTER X.

Of Resolutions.

Rule 30. The following classes of resolutions shall lie over one day for consideration, after which they may be called up as of course, under their appropriate order of business:

1. Resolutions containing calls for information from any of the Executive Departments, from State, county or municipal officers, or from any incorporate bodies.
2. Resolutions giving rise to debate, except such as shall relate to the disposition of business immediately before the Convention, to the business of the day on which they may be offered, or to adjournments or recesses.

Rule 31. All resolutions for the printing of an extra number of documents, shall be referred, as of course, to the Standing Committee on Printing, for their report thereon before final action by the Convention.

Rule 32. All resolutions authorizing or contemplating expenditures for the purposes of the Convention, shall be referred to the Standing Committee on Contingent Expenses, for their report thereon before final action by the Convention.

CHAPTER XI.

Miscellaneous Provisions.

Rule 33. The privileges of admission to the floor of the Convention shall be confined to the following descriptions of persons, viz.:

1. The Governor and Lieutenant-Governor.
2. The Heads of the State Executive Departments and their Deputies.
3. Ex-Governors of the State.
4. Members of the United States Congress.
5. Officers of the Convention.
6. Reporters of the press, duly assigned as such by the President of the Convention.
7. Officers or ex-officers of the United States army or navy who have received the thanks of Congress.

Rule 34. In cases of the absence of a quorum at any session of the Convention, the members present may take such measures as they may deem necessary to secure the presence of a quorum, and may inflict such censure as they may deem just, on those who on being called on for that purpose shall render no sufficient excuse for their absence.

Rule 35. If any question contain several distinct propositions, it shall be divided by the President at the request of any member, provided each sub-division if left to itself, shall form a substantive proposition; but the motion to strike out and insert shall be indivisible.

Rule 36. The yeas and nays shall be taken and recorded in the journal on any question when demanded by one-fifth of the members present, except in cases where such a division shall have been already ordered on a pending question.

Rule 37. The journal of each day's proceedings shall be printed so that it shall be laid on the desks of members within two days after its approval.

Rule 38. Files of all documents ordered to be printed, shall be prepared and kept by the sergeant-at-arms, and one copy shall be placed upon the desk of each member of the Convention; one copy shall be supplied also to the secretary, one to each of his assistants, one to the stenographer, one to the librarian and one to each reporter for the press.

Rule 39. A similar allowance for stationery as is provided for the use of the members, shall be made to each officer of the Convention, except messengers, and a similar allowance shall also be made to each reporter.

Rule 40. No standing rule of the Convention shall be suspended, amended or rescinded, unless one day's notice of the motion therefor shall have been given; nor shall any amendment or repeal be then made, except by the vote of a majority of all the members elected to the Convention. But such notice shall not be required on the last day's session. The notice and motion for a suspension shall each state specifically the number of the rule and the object of the proposed suspension, and every suspension on such notice and motion shall be held to apply only to the particular object or objects specified therein.

Rule 41. All questions relating to the priority of business, that is, the priority of one subject matter over another under the same order of business, the postponement of any special order, or the suspension of any rule, shall be decided without debate.

Rule 42. There shall be printed, as of course, and without any special order, 800 copies of all reports of committees on the subject of Constitutional revision, and of all reports and communications made in pursuance of the order or request of the Convention; and 800 copies of the journal, which numbers shall be denominated the usual number.

Rule 43. The Governor and each head of the State Executive departments, shall be furnished by the printer with a copy of the official documents of the Convention out of the usual number printed.

Rule 44. The sergeant-at-arms shall receive from the printer all matter printed for the use of the Convention, and shall keep a record of the time of the reception of each document, and the number of copies received, and shall cause a copy of each to be placed on the desks of the members, officers and reporters entitled to receive them, immediately after their reception by him.

Rule 45. There shall be bound, out of the usual number printed, three hundred copies of the journal and three hundred copies of the reports and documents of the Convention, to be distributed as follows, viz: To each member of the Convention, one copy; State Library, five copies; the library of the Senate, sixteen copies; the library of the Assembly, fifty copies; the Counties and Public offices, sixty copies.

Rule 46. The Assistant Sergeant-at-Arms shall perform the duties of post-master of the Convention, and as such shall receive, distribute and dispatch such mail matter as may be deposited in his office, addressed to or by members of the Convention; and the Sergeant-at-Arms shall assign to the service of the acting postmaster such number of the messengers as he may need to aid him in the performance of his duty.

STATE OF NEW YORK.

No. 3.

IN CONVENTION

June 11, 1867.

REPORT OF COMMITTEE APPOINTED TO REPORT AS TO BEST MODE OF PROCEEDING IN REVISION OF CONSTITUTION.

The Committee appointed to consider and report to the Convention the best practicable mode of proceeding with the revision of the Constitution, respectfully

REPORT

That, while, in their opinion, there are some, perhaps many, parts of the Constitution which need no alteration, yet, as the whole fabric of the fundamental law of the State has been committed to this Convention, with instructions to examine it and propose for the consideration of the people such amendments as it may be thought to require, the Committee have deemed it their duty to recommend the examination of all the provisions of the Constitution by appropriate Committees. They therefore recommend the adoption of the following resolution:

Resolved, That Committees be appointed to consider and report on each of the following subjects, and that the several parts of the Constitution which relate to those subjects respectively, be referred to such Committees:

1. On the preamble and the bill of rights.
2. On the Legislature,—its organization and the number, apportionment, election, tenure of office, and compensation of its members.
3. On the powers and duties of the Legislature, except as to matters otherwise referred.

4. On the right of suffrage and the qualifications to hold office.

5. On the Governor and Lieutenant-Governor, their election, tenure of office, compensation, powers and duties, except as otherwise referred,

6. On the Secretary of State, Comptroller, Treasurer, Attorney-General, and State Engineer and Surveyor, their election or appointment, tenure of office, compensation, powers and duties.

7. On town and county officers, other than judicial, their election or appointment, tenure of office, compensation, powers and duties.

8. On the Judiciary.

9. On the finances of the State, the canals, except their care and management, the public debt, revenues, expenditures and taxation, and restrictions on the powers of the Legislature in respect thereto.

10. On the superintendence and management of the canals, and the proper officers to be charged therewith, and the mode of their election or appointment.

11. On cities, their organization, government and powers.

12. On counties, towns and villages, their organization, government and powers.

13. On currency, banking and insurance.

14. On corporations other than municipal, banking and insurance.

15. On State prisons.

16. On the pardoning power.

17. On the militia and military officers.

18. On education and the funds relating thereto.

19. On future amendments and revisions of the Constitution.

The Committee also recommend that Committee No. 9, on the "*Finances of the State*," consist of *sixteen* members; that Committee No. 8, on the "*Judiciary*," and Committee No. 11, "*on Cities*," consist of *fifteen* members each; and that the other Committees consist of *seven* members each.

The Committee further recommend that the committees, in making their reports, be allowed, at their option, to state briefly in writing the reasons in support of their conclusions.

All which is respectfully submitted.

IRA HARRIS, *Chairman.*

STATE OF NEW YORK.

No. 4.

IN CONVENTION

June 11, 1867.

RESOLUTIONS.

Mr. Graves offered the following resolution:

Resolved, That a committee of five be appointed by the Chair to report to this Convention, at as early a day as practicable, whether, in their opinion, a provision should be incorporated in the Constitution authorizing the women in this State to exercise the elective franchise, when they shall ask that right by a majority of all the votes given by citizen females over the age of twenty-one years, at an election called for that purpose, at which the women alone shall have the right to vote.

Mr. Colahan offered the following resolution:

Resolved, That a further committee of eight be appointed to take into consideration the educational interests of the State.

Mr. A. Lawrence offered the following resolution:

Resolved, That the Chair appoint a committee of seven whose duty it shall be to examine into and report to this Convention what offices, if any, may be abolished without detriment to the public service, and, especially, of those created by law since the revision of the Constitution in 1846.

Mr. Duganne offered the following resolution:

Resolved, That to the Permanent Committees, appointed by the Convention, shall be added a standing committee, to be known as the Committee on Industrial Interest, to which shall be referred all matters pertaining to the rights and claims of labor.

Mr. T. W. Dwight offered the following resolution:

Resolved, That one of the subjects upon which a standing committee shall be appointed shall be the creation, supervision and visitation of charities both public and private, especially of those which receive pecuniary aid from the State.

Mr. S. Townsend offered the following resolution:

Resolved, That it be referred to an appropriate committee to report to this Convention the policy of making Constitutional provision for the collection of all tolls, dues, and taxes authorized by the laws of this State, after the 1st of January, 1868, in *specie*, or its equivalent, and that *thereafter* the payments made by this State and the counties and towns thereof, shall be in like currency; *Provided*, That thereafter no salary of any office existing on the 1st of January, 1861, shall be greater than the one existing at that date, until otherwise changed by the Legislature.

Mr. Field offered the following resolution:

Resolved, That there be a committee of seven "on claims against the State and their adjudication."

Mr. Van Campen offered the following resolution:

Resolved, That a standing committee of seven be appointed on the subject of the relations of the State to Indian tribes remaining in the same.

Mr. Clark offered the following resolution.

Resolved, That the preamble of the Constitution be amended so as to read as follows:

"We, the people of the State of New York, grateful to Almighty God for our freedom, and humbly acknowledging Him as the ultimate source of all authority and power in civil government, and that states and nations, no less than individuals, are responsible to Him, and subject to His moral laws, in order to secure the blessings of liberty, justice and good government to ourselves and our posterity, do ordain and establish this Constitution."

Mr. McDonald offered the following resolution:

Resolved, That the Sergeant-at-Arms of this Convention be authorized to place on the files of each member a printed copy, in pamphlet form, of the verbatim report of the debates of this Convention, within two days after such debate, or portion of debate, shall have been had; and that the Sergeant at-Arms be also authorized, within the same time, to furnish and forward one such copy of debates to each editor, (or if there be more than one editor), then to the editor-in-chief of every newspaper issued and published within this State, to subscribers in intervals of one week or less. But in case the same persons shall be the editors of more than one such newspaper, then only one copy of such debates shall be furnished such editor or editors.

STATE OF NEW YORK.

No. 5.

IN CONVENTION

June 11, 1867.

COMMUNICATION.

STATE OF NEW YORK, COMPTROLLER'S OFFICE,
ALBANY, June 12, 1867.

HON. WILLIAM A. WHEELER, *President of the Constitutional Convention:*

SIR—I have the honor to acknowledge the receipt of a resolution of the Convention, adopted on the 11th inst., addressed to the Commissioners of the Canal Fund, and to state in reply, that it will be submitted for their consideration at the earliest day on which the Board can be convened.

Very respectfully yours,

THO. HILLHOUSE, *Comptroller*

STATE OF NEW YORK.

No. 6.

IN CONVENTION

June 14, 1867.

REPORT OF THE COMMITTEE ON RULES.

MR. SHERMAN, from the Select Committee appointed to report a code of rules for the regulation of the proceedings of the Convention, reports the following, viz:

CHAPTER I.

Of the Powers and Duties of the President.

Rule 1. The President shall take the Chair each day at the hour appointed for the meeting of the session.

Rule 2. He shall possess the powers and perform the duties herein prescribed, viz:

1. He shall preserve order and decorum.

2. He shall decide all questions of order, subject to appeal to the Convention. On every appeal he shall have the right, in his place, to assign his reasons for his decision.

3. He shall appoint all committees except where the Convention shall otherwise order.

4. He may substitute any member to perform the duties of the Chair for a period not exceeding two consecutive legislative days.

5. When the Convention shall be ready to go into Committee of the Whole, he shall name a Chairman to preside therein.

6. He shall designate the reporters for the public press, not exceeding fifteen in number, and shall assign to them their respective seats.

CHAPTER II.

Of the Daily Order of Business.

Rule 3. The first business of each day's session shall be the reading of the Journal of the preceding day and the correction of any errors that may be found to exist therein. After which, except on days and at times set apart for the consideration of special orders, the order of business, which shall not be departed from except by unanimous consent, shall be as follows, viz:

1. *The presentation of memorials.* Under which head shall be included petitions, remonstrances and communications from individuals and from public bodies.

2. Communications from the Governor.

3. Communications from State officers. Under which head shall be embraced also, communications from public officers and from corporations, in response to calls for information.

4. Notices.

5. Reports of standing committees.

6. Reports of select committees.

7. Resolutions.

8. Unfinished business of the general orders.

9. Special orders.

10. General orders.

CHAPTER III.

Of the Rights and Duties of Members.

Rule 4. The President, or any member, when he shall be recognized in his place, may present, under the proper order of business, any paper of a respectful character, addressed to the Convention, and the same, unless the Convention shall otherwise order, shall be referred to the appropriate committee.

Rule 5. Every member presenting a paper shall endorse the same; if a petition, memorial, remonstrance, or communication in answer to a call for information, with a concise statement of its subject, adding his name; if a notice or resolution, with his name; if the report of a committee, with a statement of its subject, the name of the committee and of the member making the report; if a proposition of any other kind for the consideration of the Convention, with a statement of its subject, the proposer's name and the reference, if any, desired.

Rule 6. Every member who shall be within the bar of the Convention when a question shall be stated from the chair, shall vote thereon unless he be excused or be personally interested in the question. No member shall be obliged to vote on any question unless within the bar when the question shall be put, but in the case of a division by yeas and nays, may vote if present before the last name shall be called. The bar of the Convention shall be deemed to include only the floor of the Assembly Chamber, and the open spaces adjacent thereto, within the doors.

Rule 7. Any member requesting to be excused from voting, may make, when his name is called, or immediately after the roll shall have been called, and before the result shall be announced, a brief statement of the reasons for making such request, not exceeding five minutes in time, and the question shall then be taken without bebate; and such request shall not be withdrawn without the consent of the Convention.

CHAPTER IV.

Of order and Decorum.

Rule 8. No member rising to debate, to give a notice, make a motion or present a paper of any kind, shall proceed until he shall have addressed the President, and been recognized by him as entitled to the floor.

Rule 9. Where a member shall have the floor for any purpose, no member shall entertain any private discourse or pass between him and the chair.

Rule 10. While the President shall be putting a question, or a division by counting shall be had, no member shall leave his place, or speak, unless to make a privileged motion or state a question of privilege demanding immediate attention.

Rule 11. When a motion to adjourn, or for a recess, shall be affirmatively determined, no member or officer shall leave his place till the adjournment or recess shall be declared by the President.

CHAPTER V.

Of Order in Debate.

Rule 12. No member shall speak more than once to the same question, without leave of the Convention, until every member desiring to speak on the question pending shall have spoken.

Rule 13. No remarks reflecting personally upon the character or action of any member shall be in order in debate.

Rule 14. If any member, in speaking, shall transgress the rules of the Convention, the President shall, or any member may call to order, in which case the member so called to order, shall not proceed, unless to explain or speak in order.

CHAPTER VI.

Of Committees and their duties.

Rule 15. Standing Committees shall be appointed by the President to consider and report severally upon the following subjects, and such others as may be referred to them, viz.:

To consist of seven members each.

1. On the preamble and the bill of rights.

2. On the Legislature,—its organization and the number, apportionment, election, tenure of office, and compensation of its members.

3. On the powers and duties of the Legislature, except as to matters otherwise referred.

4. On the right of suffrage and the qualifications to hold office.

5. On the Governor and Lieutenant-Governor, their election, tenure of office, compensation, powers and duties, except as otherwise referred.

6. On the Secretary of State, Comptroller, Treasurer, Attorney-General, and State Engineer and Surveyor, their election or appointment, tenure of office, compensation, powers and duties.

7. On town and county officers, other than judicial, their election or appointment, tenure of office, compensation, powers and duties.

To consist of fifteen members each.

8. On the Judiciary.

9. On the finances of the State, the public debt, revenues, expenditures and taxation, and restrictions on the powers of the Legislature in respect thereto.

10. On Canals.

11. On cities, their organization, government and powers.

To consist of seven members each.

12. On counties, towns and villages, their organization, government and powers.

13. On currency, banking and insurance.

14. On corporations other than municipal, banking and insurance.

15. On State prisons, and the prevention and punishment of crime.

16. On the pardoning power.

17. On the militia and military officers.

18. On education and funds relating thereto.

19. On charities and charitable institutions.

20. On industrial interests, except those already referred.

21. On the salt springs of the State.

22. On the relations of the State to the Indians residing therein.

23. On future amendments and revisions of the Constitution.

To consist of five members each.

24. Privileges and elections.

25. Printing.

26. Contingent expenses.

27. Engrossment and enrollment.

Rule 16. All reports of Committees embracing propositions for constitutional alteration shall be referred as of course to the Committee of the whole for consideration therein before final action by the Convention.

CHAPTER VII.

Of General and Special Orders.

Rule 17. The matters referred to the Committee of the Whole shall constitute the General Orders, and shall be recorded by their titles or subjects in a calendar to be kept for that purpose by the Secretary, in the order in which they shall be referred respectively.

Rule 18. Any particular report or other matter on the General Orders may be made a Special Order for any particular day or from day to day, with the assent of two-thirds of the members voting, and no Special Order shall be postponed or rescinded except by a similar vote.

CHAPTER VIII.

Of the Committee of the Whole.

Rule 19. The same rules shall be observed in Committee of the Whole as in the Convention, as far as applicable, except that the yeas and nays shall not be taken on a division.

Rule 20. A motion to rise and report progress shall be in order at any stage, and shall be decided without debate.

Rule 21. Subjects shall be taken up in Committee of the Whole in the order in which they shall stand on the General Orders, unless the Committee, by a two-thirds vote, shall, in any case, otherwise direct. The paper under consideration shall be first read at length, unless the Committee shall otherwise order, and shall then be read and considered by sections. All amendments made in Committee of the whole shall be reported to the Convention for action,

Rule 22. If at any time, in the Committee of the Whole, it shall appear that no quorum be present, the Committee shall immediately rise, and the Chairman shall report the fact to the Convention.

CHAPTER IX.

Of Motions and their Precedence.

Rule 23. When a question shall be under consideration, no motion shall be received except as herein specified, and motions shall have precedence in the order stated, viz:

1. For an adjournment.
2. For a recess.
3. A call of the Convention.
4. To lay on the table.
5. To postpone indefinitely.
6. To postpone to a day certain.
7. To commit to a Committee of the Whole.
8. To commit to a Standing Committee.
9. To commit to a Select Committee.
10. To amend.

Rule 24. The motion to adjourn for the day, for a recess, and to lay on the table, shall be decided without amendment or debate. The respective motions to postpone or commit shall preclude debate on the main question.

Rule 25. Every motion or resolution shall, after presentation, be first stated by the President, or on his order read by the Secretary before debate, and again, if desired by any member, immediately before putting the question. And every resolution and amendment shall be reduced to writing if the President or any member desire it.

Rule 26. After a proposition shall have been stated by the President, it shall be deemed to be in possession of the Convention, but may be withdrawn at any time before it shall be decided or amended.

Rule 27. The motions to adjourn or to take a recess shall be always in order when made by a member entitled to the floor.

Rule 28. A motion for reconsideration shall be in order at any time, and may be moved by any member of the Convention; but the question shall not be taken on the motion to reconsider on the same day on which the decision proposed to be reconsidered shall take place, unless by unanimous consent; and a motion to reconsider being once put and lost, shall not be renewed, nor shall any subject be a second time reconsidered without the consent of the Convention. If the motion to reconsider shall not be made on the same day or the day after that on which the decision proposed to be reconsidered was made, three days' notice of the intention to make the motion shall be given.

CHAPTER X.

Of Resolutions.

Rule 29. The following classes of resolutions shall lie over one day for consideration, after which they may be called up as of course, under their appropriate order of business:

1. Resolutions containing calls for information from any of the Executive Departments, from State, county or municipal officers, or from any incorporate bodies.

2. Resolutions giving rise to debate, except such as shall relate to the disposition of business immediately before the Convention, to the business of the day on which they may be offered, or to adjournments or recesses.

Rule 30. All resolutions for the printing of an extra number of documents, shall be referred, as of course, to the Standing Committee on Printing, for their report thereon before final action by the Convention.

Rule 31. All resolutions authorizing or contemplating expenditures for the purposes of the Convention, shall be referred to the Standing Committee on Contingent Expenses, for their report thereon before final action by the Convention.

CHAPTER XI.

Miscellaneous Provisions.

Rule 32. The privileges of admission to the floor of the Convention shall be confined to the following descriptions of persons, viz.:

1. The Governor and Lieutenant-Governor.

2. The Heads of the State Executive Departments and their Deputies.

3. Ex-Governors of the State.

4. Members of the United States Congress.

5. Officers of the Convention.

6. Reporters of the press, duly assigned as such by the President of the Convention.

7. Officers or ex-officers of the United States army or navy who have received the thanks of Congress by name on a special vote.

8. Judges and ex-Judges of the Court of Appeals, and the members of the two former Constitutional Conventions in this State.

Rule 33. In cases of the absence of a quorum at any session of the Convention, the members present may take such measures as they may deem necessary to secure the presence of a quorum, and may inflict such censure as they may deem just, on those who on being called on for that purpose shall render no sufficient excuse for their absence.

Rule 34. If any question contain several distinct propositions, it shall be divided by the President at the request of any member, provided each sub-division if left to itself, shall form a substantive proposition; but the motion to strike out and insert shall be indivisible.

Rule 35. The yeas and nays shall be taken and recorded in the journal on any question when demanded by fifteen members, except in cases where such a division shall have been already ordered on a pending question.

Rule 36. The journal of each day's proceedings shall be printed so that it shall be laid on the desks of members within one day after its approval.

Rule 37. Files of all documents ordered to be printed, shall be prepared and kept by the sergeant-at-arms, and one copy shall be placed upon the desk of each member of the Convention; one copy shall be supplied also to the secretary, one to each of his assistants, one to the stenographer, one to the librarian and one to each reporter for the press.

Rule 38. When a blank is to be filled and different sums or time shall be proposed, the question shall be first taken on the highest sum and the longest time.

Rule 39. No standing rule of the Convention shall be suspended, amended or rescinded, or additional rule or rules added, unless one day's notice of the motion therefor shall have been given; nor shall any such suspension, addition, amendment or repeal be then made, except by the vote of two-thirds of the members present, or that of a majority of all the members elected to the Convention. But such notice shall not be required on the last day's session. The notice and motion for a suspension, shall each state specifically the number of the rule and the object of the proposed suspension, and every suspension on such notice and motion shall be held to apply only to the particular object or objects specified therein.

Rule 40. All questions relating to the priority of business, that is, the priority of one subject matter over another under the same order of business, the postponement of any special order, or the suspension of any rule,. shall be decided without debate.

Rule 41. There shall be printed, as of course, and without any special order, 800 copies of all reports of committees on the subject of Constitutional revision, and of all reports and communications made in pursuance of the order or request of the Convention; and 800 copies of the journal, which numbers shall be denominated the usual number.

Rule 42. The Governor and each head of the State Executive departments, shall be furnished by the printer with a copy of the official documents of the Convention out of the usual number printed.

Rule 43. The sergeant-at-arms shall receive from the printer all matter printed for the use of the Convention, and shall keep a record of the time of the reception of each document, and the number of copies received, and shall cause a copy of each to be placed on the desks of the members, officers and reporters entitled to receive them, immediately after their reception by him.

Rule 44. There shall be bound, out of the usual number printed, three hundred copies of the journal and three hundred copies of the reports and documents of the Convention, to be distributed as follows, viz: To each member of the Convention, one copy; State Library, five copies; the library of the Senate, sixteen copies; the library of the Assembly, fifty copies; the Counties and Public offices, sixty copies.

Rule 45. The Assistant Sergeant-at-Arms shall perform the duties of post-master of the Convention, and as such shall receive, distribute and dispatch such mail matter as may be deposited in his office, addressed to or by members of the Convention; and the Sergeant-at-Arms shall assign to the service of the acting post-master such number of the messengers as he may need to aid him in the performance of his duty.

STATE OF NEW YORK.

No. 7.

IN CONVENTION

June 14, 1867.

PREAMBLE AND RESOLUTION

Offered by Mr. Graves.

Whereas, the use of adulterated, intoxicating liquors has become an alarming evil, increasing domestic sorrow, creating pauperism and crime, thereby adding to the burdens of taxation, therefore

Resolved, That a committee of one from each judicial district be appointed to report

1. Whether, in their opinion, under our republican form of government, any authority should be granted to sell or any prohibition enacted against the sale of intoxicating liquors either by a legislative or organic law of the State.

2. Whether, in their opinion, the sale of intoxicating liquors should be denied to all except such as shall receive a certificate under the hand and official seal of a person properly qualified and duly appointed showing that the liquor offered for sale had been carefully analyzed and was unadulterated, pure, and contained no poisonous drug.

3. Whether, in their opinion, any law authorizing or prohibiting the sale should not be organic instead of legislative, thereby creating a rule controling and regulating public opinion, and relieving each successive Legislature from the pressing importunities of those in favor of or opposed to the sale of intoxicating drinks.

STATE OF NEW YORK.

No. 8.

IN CONVENTION

June 19, 1867.

REPORT OF SPECIAL COMMITTEE ON PUBLISHING PROCEEDINGS AND DEBATES.

Your Committee, to whom was referred a resolution of inquiry as to the terms upon which verbatim reports of the proceedings of this Convention can be published in two or more newspapers of this city, have had the subject under consideration, and respectfully

REPORT.

It first became necessary to ascertain whether the power to contract for the performance of such work as was contemplated by the resolution was conferred by the terms of the law which created the Convention. Under the eighth section of the law referred to, the Comptroller and Secretary of State are "authorized and required "to receive proposals and make contract for all the printing neces- "sary for the said Convention."

Under this provision, a contract was made with Weed, Parsons & Co., of the date of May 16th, 1867, for the printing of *Documents* at a compensation of $11 for each 800 copies of 8 pages, to include all charges, and for each additional 100 copies of 8 pages, 66 cents; for *Journals*, each 800 copies of 8 pages, to include all charges, $12.75, and for each additional 100 copies of 8 pages, 40 cents; for *Debates*, each 800 copies of 8 pages, each page to contain not less than 3000 ems of brevier and nonpareil type, to include all charges, $5.88, and for each additional 100 copies of 8 pages, $1. The following paragraph appears in the advertisement for proposals issued by the Secretary of State and Comptroller, and in the opinion of the latter officer, becomes a part of the contract with the Convention Printers by virtue of the official acceptance of their proposals:

"Miscellaneous printing not coming under above heads, will be "paid for at the rates current in the city of Albany, at the time of "the execution thereof."

These are all the provisions of the contract with the Convention Printers bearing upon the subject of printing its proceedings and debates. The law is silent with reference to *newspaper* publication of this matter, and under its express authority, such publication could only be secured by an arrangement with the Convention Printers at the terms agreed upon with them for miscellaneous printing. But this would involve a compensation at "the rates current at Albany," in this case regulated by the charges for transient advertising—an expense much larger than is necessary to be incurred for the service. This plan being considered impracticable, the next question that arose was, whether parties proposing for the work would be willing to go forward and perform it under direction of the Convention, without any fund from which their remuneration could be drawn, relying upon future action by the Legislature to secure payment for their service.

Propositions have been made to the Committee by the publishers of the Evening *Journal* and of the Albany *Argus*, the proprietors of other newspapers here declining to offer terms, for the reason that they did not care to undertake the work. The *Journal* and *Argus* publishers respectively are willing to print the stenographic reports of the debates and proceedings, from day to day, in the regular editions of their papers, and at prices which your Committee consider liberal to the State—being considerably less than half the legal rates for publishing,—to wit: six dollars and a half per column for such publication in each paper, and to include the daily delivery of two copies of all the issues of their papers containing the proceedings and debates to each member of the Convention without further charge.

In this connection, your Committee have given attention to a proposition germane to the subject-matter referred to them—that the proceedings and debates be published in pamphlet form under the contract with the Convention Printers, and distributed by the Convention. This method, while involving a larger cost, if estimated upon the basis of an equal circulation to be obtained by the newspaper publication, as proposed, would also be attended with much additional labor, and fail to accomplish the ends desired. A pamphlet does not go into general circulation; it lacks the freshness, and does not secure the interest that attaches to the newspaper. It would be read by comparatively few persons.

A newspaper, on the other hand, is received everywhere, and comes under the observation of all classes. Circulate as many of the pamphlets as you may, still you will fail to reach the people and instruct them in the work of this Convention, as may be done by the newspaper publication of the full stenographic reports of its daily proceedings and debates.

The *Evening Journal* and the *Argus* are in a sense representative organs of the two great political parties, and the Convention debates published in their columns from day to day, would be brought to the attention of a very large number of people, of a class interested in public questions, and would also be placed sooner than otherwise could be done, in the hands of newspaper editors throughout the State, who would be certain to make such excerpts from and comments upon them as would attract the attention of the people to questions upon which they will be called upon to decide.

The inquiry is pertinent here, whether the advantages derivable from the publication as proposed, would be sufficient to justify the expense to be incurred. Your Committee assume that the sessions of the Convention will continue many weeks. Perhaps, when it adjourns, but a short time will elapse, as was the case in 1846, before the period when its work is to be submitted to the people for approval or rejection. In that brief intervening time there will be little opportunity for stating and discussing the questions which have arisen and received attention here. But if the proceedings and debates are published *in extenso* as they transpire, and in a manner to secure their largest reading and study, discussions will begin with them at the outset, and when we adjourn, the public will have a full and accurate understanding of what we have accomplished. Certainly it is of the first importance in connection with the great work committed to this Convention, that the people should be fully informed of its doings and the reasons in detail for all action taken here.

But an object, perhaps quite as important, will be accomplished by the proposed newspaper publication, in placing upon the tables of members daily the verbatim reports of the discussions which occur. An opportunity will thus be furnished to members to deliberately review the arguments advanced in the Convention while subjects are still under discussion, and while the measures proposed are still within their control. Relying upon the pamphlet publication of the debates, experience shows that there would be a much greater delay, thus in a measure depriving the Convention of the important advantages named.

Your Committee, therefore, are of opinion that the publication referred to is both feasible and proper, and in their opinion the advantages that would result therefrom fully justify the expenditure necessary for the purpose. They recommend the adoption of the following resolution:

Resolved, That the Albany *Evening Journal* and the Albany *Argus* be authorized to publish the daily reports of the proceedings and debates of this Convention, as furnished by the stenographer, and to furnish two copies to each member of the Convention, for the compensation of six dollars and fifty cents per column of solid brevier and nonpareil type for such publication in each paper named —said reports to be printed in the regular editions of said papers— and that the next Legislature be requested to make the requisite appropriations for payment of the service.

J. M. FRANCIS, *Chairman*.

STATE OF NEW YORK.

No. 9.

IN CONVENTION

June 19, 1867.

STANDING COMMITTEES OF THE CONVENTION.

1. *On the preamble and the bill of rights.*

Mr. Evarts,
Mr. Spencer,
Mr. A. R. Lawrence,
Mr. Bowen,
Mr. Paige,
Mr. Frank,
Mr. Hardenburgh.

2. *On the Legislature,—its organization and the number, apportionment, election, tenure of office, and compensation of its members.*

Mr. Merritt,
Mr. Cooke,
Mr. Sherman,
Mr. Monell,
Mr. Barker,
Mr. J. Brooks,
Mr. Merwin.

3. *On the powers and duties of the Legislature, except as to matters otherwise referred.*

Mr. Rathbun,
Mr. Rumsey,
Mr. Robertson,
Mr. E. A. Brown,
Mr. Fields,
Mr. M. H. Lawrence,
Mr. Burrill.

4. *On the right of suffrage and the qualification to hold office.*

Mr. Greeley,
Mr. Endress,
Mr. Cassidy,
Mr. Merrill,
Mr. Williams,
Mr. L. W. Russell,
Mr. Schumaker.

5. *On the Governor and Lieutenant-Governor, their election, tenure of office, compensation, powers and duties, except as otherwise referred.*

Mr. C. L. Allen,
Mr. E. P. Brooks,
Mr. A. J. Parker,
Mr. Flagler,
Mr. Wakeman,
Mr. Miller,
Mr. Garvin.

6. *On the Secretary of State, Comptroller, Treasurer, Attorney-General and State Engineer and Surveyor, their election or appointment, tenure of office, compensation, powers and duties.*

Mr. Tucker,
Mr. Baker,
Mr. Duganne,
Mr. Fuller,
Mr. Hand,
Mr. Ketcham,
Mr. A. R. Lawrence.

7. *On town and county officers, other than judicial, their election or appointment, tenure of office, compensation, powers and duties.*

Mr. Smith,
Mr. Bickford,
Mr. Rolfe,
Mr. A. Lawrence,
Mr. Kinney,
Mr. Sheldon,
Mr. Roy.

8. *On the Judiciary.*

Mr. Folger,
Mr. Evarts,
Mr. Comstock,
Mr. Van Cott,
Mr. Daly,
Mr. Barker,
Mr. Kernan,
Mr. Hutchins,
Mr. Masten,
Mr. T. W. Dwight,
Mr. A. J. Parker
Mr. Andrews,
Mr. Hale,
Mr. Goodrich,
Mr. Pierrepont.

9. *On the finances of the State, the public debt, revenues, expenditures, and taxation, and restrictions on the powers of the Legislature in respect thereto.*

Mr. Church,
Mr. Frank,
Mr. Corning,
Mr. Opdyke,
Mr. Tilden,
Mr. Clark,
Mr. Van Cott,
Mr. Schell,
Mr. W. C. Brown,
Mr. Nelson,
Mr. A. F. Allen,
Mr. Hatch,
Mr. Carpenter,
Mr. Barto,
Mr. Hardenburgh.

10. *On canals.*

Mr. Lapham,
Mr. Alvord,
Mr. Clinton,
Mr. Prosser,
Mr. Seymour,
Mr. Beckwith,
Mr. Schoonmaker,
Mr. Hutchins,
Mr. Champlain,
Mr. Root,
Mr. Bell,
Mr. Magee,
Mr. Prindle,
Mr. Bergen,
Mr. Tappen.

11. *On cities, their organization, government and powers.*

Mr. Harris,
Mr. Opdyke,
Mr. Murphy,
Mr. Francis,
Mr. Paige,
Mr. Alvord,
Mr. Verplanck,
Mr. Bowen,
Mr. Law,
Mr. Fullerton,
Mr. E. Brooks,
Mr. Graves,
Mr. Weed,
Mr. Hand,
Mr. Chesebro.

12. *On counties, towns and villages, their organization, government and powers.*

Mr. Hadley,
Mr. N. M. Allen,
Mr. Lowrey,
Mr. Ferry,
Mr. Fowler,
Mr. Corbett,
Mr. Wickham.

13. *On currency, banking and insurance.*

Mr. Beadle,
Mr. Huntington,
Mr. Veeder,
Mr. Eddy,
Mr. Armstrong,
Mr. Ludington,
Mr. Hitchman.

14. *On corporations other than municipal, banking and insurance.*

Mr. Ballard,
Mr. Stratton,
Mr. S. Townsend,
Mr. Krum,
Mr. L. W. Russell,
Mr. Hitchcock,
Mr. Barnard.

15. *On State prisons, and the prevention and punishment of crime.*

Mr. Gould,
Mr. C. C. Dwight,
Mr. A. D. Russell,
Mr. Cochran,
Mr. Lee,
Mr. Axtell,
Mr. Conger.

16. *On the pardoning power.*

Mr. M. I. Townsend,
Mr. Pond,
Mr. Develin,
Mr. Landon,
Mr. Prindle,
Mr. Lee,
Mr. Gerry.

17. *On the militia and military officers.*

Mr. Morris,
Mr. Seaver,
Mr. Barto,
Mr. C. C. Dwight,
Mr. Cheritree,
Mr. Stratton,
Mr. Hammond.

18. *On education and funds relating thereto.*

Mr. Curtis,
Mr. Archer,
Mr. Conger,
Mr. Gould,
Mr. Beals,
Mr. Clinton,
Mr. Larremore.

19. *On charities and charitable institutions.*

Mr. E. Brooks,
Mr. T. W. Dwight,
Mr. Strong,
Mr. Spencer,
Mr. Ludington,
Mr. Silvester,
Mr. Livingston.

20. *On industrial interests, except those already referred.*

Mr. Duganne,
Mr. Gross,
Mr. Farnum,
Mr. Armstrong,
Mr. Wales,
Mr. Case,
Mr. More.

21. *On the salt springs of the State.*

Mr. Bell,
Mr. Comstock
Mr. C. E. Parker,
Mr. McDonald,
Mr. Rolfe,
Mr. Houston,
Mr. Young.

22. *On the relations of the State to the Indians residing therein.*

Mr. Van Campen,
Mr. Silvester,
Mr. Bergen,
Mr. Axtell,
Mr. S. Townsend,
Mr. McDonald,
Mr. Colahan.

23. *On future amendments and revisions of the Constitution.*

Mr. E. A. Brown,
Mr. Greeley,
Mr. Robertson,
Mr. Flagler,
Mr. Murphy,
Mr. Grant,
Mr. J Brooks.

24. *Privileges and elections.*

Mr. Landon,
Mr. Endress,
Mr. Loew,
Mr. Lowrey,
Mr. Mattice.

25. *Printing.*

Mr. Seaver,
Mr. Francis,
Mr. Potter,
Mr. Merrill,
Mr. Jarvis.

26. *Contingent expenses.*

Mr. Ferry,
Mr. Williams,
Mr. Cochran,
Mr. Reynolds,
Mr. Rogers.

27. *Engrossment and enrollment.*

Mr. Sherman,
Mr. Archer,
Mr. Cassidy,
Mr. Cheritree,
Mr. Mattice.

STATE OF NEW YORK.

No. 10.

IN CONVENTION

June 19, 1867.

REPORT OF THE COMMISSIONERS OF THE CANAL FUND.

CANAL DEPARTMENT.
ALBANY, June 19, 1867.

HON. WILLIAM A. WHEELER, *President of the Constitutional Convention:*

SIR—The Commissioners of the Canal Fund respectfully report, that they have had under consideration the resolution of the Convention adopted on the 11th inst., requesting the said Commissioners to prepare and communicate to the Convention a statement showing

"1. The original cost of the several canals of this State, including that of any enlargement or extension thereof."

"2. The aggregate cost of each canal as aforesaid, including superintendence, repairs and legal interest on the cost of construction, up to the close of the last fiscal year."

"3. The aggregate receipts or income from each canal up to the close of the last fiscal year."

"4. The net cost (or profit) of each canal up to the close of the fiscal year."

"5. The annual receipts or income of the State from each canal, with the annual cost of the superintendence and repairs, respectively, of such canal up to the close of the last fiscal year."

"6. And a table which will show with how much each so-called lateral canal should be credited for its contributions to the revenues which, in the yearly official tables and reports, are credited to the Erie canal."

"7. And also the amount of outstanding canal debt, and when due, and when the same would be paid, assuming as a basis of calculation for the future revenue of the toll receipts, the revenue from the same source for the last seven years."

"Provided said information is not already prepared by the Canal Department for the Convention."

If the Commissioners correctly understand the import of the several subdivisions of the resolution, they require answers to the following questions:

1st. The cost of the several canals of the State in three forms: first, the cost of construction and enlargement; second the cost including superintendence and repairs, and interest on such cost; third, the net loss or profit of each canal.

2d. The aggregate amount of the receipts or income of each canal up to the close of the last fiscal year, and the net income after deducting the expenses of repairs and superintendence, the statements in each case to be brought down to the close of the last fiscal year.

3d. The amount of tolls credited to the Erie canal which should properly be credited to the lateral canals.

4th. The outstanding debt chargeable on the canal revenues, and the period in which it will be extinguished by the application of the surplus revenues to that object.

The Commissioners understand that the net cost or profit of the several canals is to be established by a comparison of the aggregate expenditures, including interest, with the aggregate receipts, and they assume that it was the intention to state an interest account on receipts as well as payments, although the language of the resolution fails to express it.

On this construction of the scope and purpose of the resolution, the Commissioners conclude that the exigency under which, in accordance with the proviso, they are required to report, has not arisen, as the information called for will be given substantially in the detailed statements of the Auditor of the Canal Department, included in the Manual prepared for the use of the Convention. Such of the statements as have not already been published will be included in following pages of the volume devoted to Statistics, and laid on the tables of members in a few days.

As an additional reason for this conclusion, it may be stated that the records from which the information sought for must be derived, are not in the possession of the Commissioners or under their control. By the act, chapter 162, Laws of 1848, creating the office of Auditor, that officer was invested with some of the most important powers that had previously been exercised by the Commissioners of the Canal Fund, from the organization of the Board in 1817.

By section 4 it was provided that all books and papers pertaining to the duties of said Auditor, or to the duties of the Commissioners of the Canal Fund, or of the Canal Board, should be deposited in the Canal Department, and be securely and safely kept by said Auditor.

By section 6, the power given by law to the Commissioners of the Canal Fund to employ and pay the necessary clerks in the Canal Department, was vested in the said Auditor.

By section 13, the accounts of receipts and payments on account of the canals and canal fund and debt, before kept by the Commissioners of the Canal Fund, were directed to be kept by the Auditor from the 1st day of October, 1848, from which date, neither the Commissioners of the Canal Fund, nor the Comptroller, as a member of the Board, have had charge of them.

This transfer of authority and of records, render the Commissioners of the Canal Fund no longer the official channel for the communication of information of the character of that required in the first six subdivisions of the resolution of the Convention, and restricts their powers and duties more particularly to the care and supervision of the surplus revenues, carried to the credit of the sinking funds at the close of each fiscal year.

The Commissioners of the Canal Fund respectfully submit these facts to the Convention, with the assurance that they have no wish to withhold any information that can be drawn from any records under their control, but on the contrary earnestly desire to afford to the important labors of the Convention every aid in their power.

Respectfully submitted,

THOS. HILLHOUSE, Comptroller,

FRANCIS C. BARLOW, Sec'y of State,

JOSEPH HOWLAND, Treasurer,

JOHN H. MARTINDALE, Att'y Gen'l,

Commissioners of the Canal Fund.

STATE OF NEW YORK.

No. 11.

IN CONVENTION

June 19, 1867.

RESOLUTION

Offered by Mr. Smith.

Resolved, That the Committee on the Right of Suffrage and qualifications to hold office be instructed to inquire into the expediency of reporting a constitutional provision permanently excluding from the rights of the elective frauchise all persons who may be convicted by a court of record of having received, or who have paid or offered to pay money or other valuable thing to influence or reward their vote; and to make the offense, with or without such conviction, a cause of disfranchisement at the polls.

Which was laid on the table and ordered printed.

No. 1

MEMBERS, OFFICERS AND REPORTERS OF THE CONSTITUTIONAL CONVENTION OF 1867.

WITH THEIR RESPECTIVE COUNTIES, NEAREST POST-OFFICE, AND RESIDENCE IN ALBANY.

HON. WILLIAM A. WHEELER, President, (Malone, Franklin County,) No. 7 Park Place.

NAME.	COUNTY.	POST-OFFICE ADDRESS.	BOARDING HOUSE.
Allen, Augustus F.,	Chautauqua,	Jamestown,	7 Park Place.
Allen, Cornelius L.,	Washington,	Salem,	Congress Hall.
Allen, Norman M.,	Cattaraugus,	Dayton,	
Alvord, Thomas G.,	Onondaga,	Syracuse,	87 Columbia street.
Andrews, Charles,	Onondaga,	Syracuse,	
Archer, Ornon,	Wayne,	Palmyra,	Merchants' Hotel.
Armstrong, Jonathan P.,	Rensselaer,	Hoosick,	Hoosick.
Axtell, Nathan G.,	Clinton,	Peru,	126 State street.
Baker, Hezekiah,	Montgomery,	St. Johnsville,	Stanwix Hall.
Ballard, Horatio,	Cortland,	Cortland Village,	Stanwix Hall.
Barker, George,	Chautauqua,	Fredonia,	7 Park Place.
Barnard, Daniel P.,	New York,	New York,	12 Jay street.
Barto, Henry D.,	Tompkins,	Trumansburgh,	Delavan House.
Beadle, Tracy,	Chemung,	Elmira,	Delavan House.
Beals, Oliver B.,	Herkimer,	Cedarville,	Rensselaer House.

MEMBERS, OFFICERS, &c.—Continued.

Name.	County.	Post-Office Address.	Boarding House.
Beckwith, George M.,	Clinton,	Plattsburgh,	136 State street.
Bell, James A.,	Jefferson,	Dexter,	7 Park Place.
Bergen, Teunis G.,	Kings,	Brooklyn,	Congress Hall.
Bickford, Marcus,	Jefferson,	Carthage,	71 Eagle street.
Bowen, Levi F.,	Niagara,	Lockport,	Delavan House.
Brooks, Erastus,	New York,	New York,	Delavan House.
Brooks, Elijah P.,	Chemung,	Elmira,	Stanwix Hall.
Brooks, James,	New York,	New York,	Delavan House.
Brown, Edward A.,	Lewis,	Lowville,	Stanwix Hall.
Brown, William C.,	St. Lawrence,	Ogdensburgh,	Congress Hall.
Burrill, John E.,	New York,	New York,	Congress Hall.
Carpenter B. Platt,	Dutchess,	Poughkeepsie,	Congress Hall.
Case, Lester M.,	Madison,	Cazenovia,	Avenue House.
Cassidy, William,	Albany,	Albany,	5 Clinton Square.
Champlain, Marshall B.,	Allegany,	Cuba,	Delavan House.
Cheritree, Andrew J.,	Warren,	Luzerne,	677 Broadway.
Chesebro, Henry O.,	Ontario,	Canandaigua,	Congress Hall.
Church, Sanford E.,	Orleans,	Albion,	
Clarke, Freeman,	Monroe,	Rochester,	Congress Hall.
Clinton, George W.,	Erie,	Buffalo,	Delavan House.
Cochran, Robert,	Westchester,	White Plains,	Delavan House.
Colahan, Stephen I.,	Kings,	Brooklyn,	73 Eagle street.
Comstock, George F.,	Onondaga,	Syracuse,	Congress Hall.

Conger, Abraham B.,	Rockland,	Haverstraw,	Congress Hall.
Cooke, Erastus,	Ulster,	Kingston,	American Hotel.
Corbett, Patrick,	Onondaga,	Syracuse,	87 Columbia street.
Corning, Erastus,	Albany,	Albany,	102 State street.
Curtis, George William,	New York,	New York,	92 Columbia street.
Daley, Charles P.,	New York,	New York,	Congress Hall.
Develin, John E.,	New York,	New York,	Congress Hall.
Duganne, Augustine J. H.,	New York,	New York,	Congress Hall.
Dwight, Charles C.,	Cayuga,	Auburn,	Congress Hall.
Dwight, Theodore W.,	New York,	New York,	104 State street.
Eddy, John,	Otsego,	Milford,	
Ely, Lorenzo D.,	Monroe,	Rochester,	Congress Hall.
Endress. Isaac L.,	Livingston,	Dansville,	Delavan House.
Evarts, William M.,	New York,	New York,	
Farnum, Edward J.,	Allegany,	Wellsville,	Delavan House.
Ferry, Elijah E.,	Otsego,	Schenevus,	American Hotel.
Field, Ben.,	Orleans,	Albion,	Congress Hall.
Flagler, Thomas T.,	Niagara,	Lockport,	Delavan House.
Folger, Charles J.,	Ontario,	Geneva,	
Fowler, Loring,	Madison,	Canastota,	Avenue House.
Francis, John M.,	Rensselaer,	Troy,	Troy.
Frank, Augustus,	Wyoming,	Warsaw,	7 Park Place.
Fuller, Jerome,	Monroe,	Brockport,	51 North Pearl.
Fullerton, Stephen W.,	Orange,	Newburgh,	
Garvin, Samuel B.,	New York,	New York,	Congress Hall.
Gerry, Elbridge T.,	New York,	New York,	Congress Hall.
Goodrich, Milo,	Tompkins,	Dryden,	51 North Pearl street.
Gould, John Stanton,	Columbia,	Hudson,	American Hotel.
Grant, John,	Delaware,	Margaretville,	

MEMBERS, OFFICERS, &c.—Continued.

NAME.	COUNTY.	POST-OFFICE ADDRESS.	BOARDING HOUSE.
Graves, Ezra,	Herkimer,	Herkimer,	Rensselaer House.
Greeley, Horace,	Westchester,	New York,	Delavan House.
Gross, Magnus,	New York,	New York,	93 Green street.
Hadley, Sterling G.,	Seneca,	Waterloo,	Congress Hall.
Hale, Matthew,	Essex,	Elizabethtown,	185 State street.
Hammond, John M.,	Allegany,	Filmore,	
Hand, Stephen D.,	Broome,	Binghamton,	104 State street.
Hardenburgh, Jacob,	Ulster,	Kingston,	83 Hawk street.
Harris, Ira,	Albany,	Albany,	28 Eagle street.
Hatch, Israel T.,	Erie,	Buffalo,	Congress Hall.
Hitchcock, Adolphus F.,	Washington,	Kingsbury,	27 Dove street.
Hitchman, William,	New York,	New York,	Delavan House.
Houston, William H.,	Orange,	Florida,	Congress Hall.
Huntington, Benjamin H.,	Oneida,	Rome,	Delavan House.
Hutchins, Waldo,	New York,	New York,	Congress Hall.
Jarvis, Nathaniel, Jr.,	New York,	New York,	Congress Hall.
Kernan, Francis,	Oneida,	Utica,	Congress Hall.
Ketcham, Leander S.,	Wayne,	Clyde,	Delavan House.
Kinney, Oliver H. P.,	Tioga,	Waverly,	71 Eagle street.
Krum, Hobart,	Schoharie,	Schoharie C. H.,	Stanwix Hall.
Landon, Judson S.,	Schenectady,	Schenectady,	
Lapham, Elbridge G.,	Ontario,	Canandaigua,	Congress Hall.
Larremore, Richard L.,	New York,	New York,	Delavan House.

Law, George,	New York,	New York,	Delavan House.
Lawrence, Abraham,	Schuyler,	Havana,	Delavan House.
Lawrence, Abraham R. Jr.,	New York,	New York,	Congress Hall.
Lawrence, Melatiah H.,	Yates,	Penn Yan,	American Hotel.
Lee, M. Lindley,	Oswego,	Fulton,	7 Park Place.
Livingston, Walter L.,	New York,	New York,	Congress Hall.
Loew, Frederick W.,	New York,	New York,	Delavan House.
Lowrey, Charles,	New York,	New York,	Congress Hall.
Luddington, Clinton V. R.,	Sullivan,	Monticello,	Congress Hall.
Magee, John,	Schuyler,	Watkins,	
Masten, Joseph G.,	Erie,	Buffalo,	Stanwix Hall.
Mattice, Manley B.,	Greene,	Durham,	76 Eagle street.
McDonald, Angus,	Ontario,	Geneva,	
Merrill, William H.,	Wyoming,	Warsaw,	7 Park Place.
Merritt, Edwin A.,	St. Lawrence,	Potsdam,	Congress Hall.
Merwin, Milton H.,	Jefferson,	Watertown,	7 Park Place.
Miller, Samuel F.,	Delaware,	Franklin,	
Monell, Claudius L.,	New York,	New York,	Congress Hall.
Moore, Ezekiel P.,	Greene,	Prattsville,	76 Eagle street.
Morris, William H.,	Putnam,	Cold Spring,	198 South Swan street.
Murphy, Henry C.,	Kings,	Brooklyn,	Delavan House.
Nelson, Homer A.,	Dutchess,	Poughkeepsie,	Delavan House.
Opdyke, George,	New York,	New York,	Delavan House.
Paige, Alonzo C.,	Schenectady,	Schenectady,	Congress Hall.
Parker, Amasa J.,	Albany,	Albany,	143 Washington Av.
Parker, Charles E.,	Tioga,	Owego,	
Pierrepont, Edwards,	New York,	New York,	
Pond, Alembert,	Saratoga,	Saratoga Spa,	Stanwix Hall.
Potter, Allen,	Erie,	Buffalo,	136 State street.

MEMBERS, OFFICERS, &c.—Continued.

NAME.	COUNTY.	POST-OFFICE ADDRESS.	BOARDING HOUSE.
Prindle, Elizur H.,	Chenango,	Norwich,	3 Washington Av.
Prosser, Erastus S.,	Erie,	Buffalo,	Congress Hall.
Rathbun, George,	Cayuga,	Auburn,	Congress Hall.
Reynolds, William A.,	Monroe,	Rochester,	Congress Hall.
Robertson, Anthony L.,	Westchester,	Peekskill,	Congress Hall.
Rogers, Henry,	New York,	New York,	25 Jay street.
Rolfe, John P.,	New York,	New York,	Congress Hall.
Root, Elias,	Oswego,	Oswego,	7 Park Place.
Roy, James,	Albany,	West Troy,	West Troy.
Rumsey, David,	Steuben,	Bath,	Congress Hall.
Russell, Abraham D.,	New York,	New York,	Congress Hall.
Russell, Leslie W.,	St. Lawrence,	Canton,	188 State street.
Schell, Augustus,	New York,	New York,	Congress Hall.
Schoonmaker, Marius,	Ulster,	Kingston,	Congress Hall.
Schumaker, John G.,	Kings,	Brooklyn,	Delavan House.
Seaver, Joel J.,	Franklin,	Malone,	7 Park Place.
Seymour, David L.,	Rensselaer,	Troy,	Troy.
Silvester, Francis,	Columbia,	Kinderhook,	136 State street.
Sheldon, William B.,	Dutchess,	Green Haven,	Congress Hall.
Sherman, Richard U.,	Oneida,	Utica,	Stanwix Hall.
Smith, Horace E.,	Fulton,	Johnstown,	188 State street.
Spencer, George T.,	Steuben,	Corning,	Congress Hall.
Stratton, Norman,	New York,	New York,	48 Steuben street.

Strong, Selah B.,	Suffolk,	Setauket,	Congress Hall.
Tappen, Abraham B.,	Westchester,	Fordham,	72 Eagle street.
Tilden, Samuel J.,	New York,	New York,	Congress Hall.
Townsend, Martin I.,	Rensselaer,	Troy,	Troy.
Townsend, Solomon,	Queens,	Oyster Bay,	Delavan House.
Tucker, Gideon J.,	New York,	New York,	584 Broadway.
Van Campen, George,	Cattaragus,	Allegany,	51 North Pearl.
Van Cott, Joshua M.,	Kings,	Brooklyn,	Congress Hall.
Veeder, William D.,	Kings,	Brooklyn,	Congress Hall.
Verplanck, Isaac A.,	Erie,	Buffalo,	Stanwix Hall.
Wakeman, Seth,	Genesee,	Batavia,	Stanwix Hall.
Wales, Gideon,	Sullivan,	Pike Pond,	Congress Hall.
Weed, Smith M.,	Clinton,	Plattsburgh,	Delavan House.
Wickham, William,	Suffolk,	Cutchogue,	Congress Hall.
Williams, George,	Oneida,	Delta,	Stanwix Hall.
Young, Solomon G.,	Ulster,	Highland,	49 Eagle street.

OFFICERS.

Name.	Name of Office.	County.	Post Office.	Boarding House.
Luther Caldwell,	Secretary,	Chemung,	Elmira,	Stanwix Hall.
Cornelius S. Underwood,	Asst. Secretary,	Cayuga,	Auburn,	51 North Pearl st.
Henry A. Glidden,	Asst. Secretary,	Orleans,	Albion,	136 State street.
Edward W. Simmons,	Asst. Secretary,	Dutchess,	Millerton,	
Edward F. Underhill,	Stenographer,	New York,	New York,	Congress Hall.
Charles S. Pierce,	Sergt.-at-arms.	Monroe,	Rochester,	51 North Pearl st.
John H. Kemper,	Asst. Sergt.-at-arms.	Wayne,	Arcade,	2 Jefferson street.
Ferdinand De Wigne,	Librarian,	Schenectady,	Schenectady,	Stanwix Hall.
Nathaniel Goodwin,	Janitor,	Albany,	Albany,	134 Spring street.
James Armstrong,	Doorkeeper,	New York,	New York,	Avenue House.
James Tanner,	do	Schoharie,	Richmondville,	45 Congress street.
E. V. Schram,	do	Oneida,	Utica,	Avenue House.
David L. Shields,	do	Wyoming,	Eagle Village,	Mansion House.
Hermon Rulison,	do	Jefferson,	Carthage,	71 Eagle street.
Eugene L. Demers,	do	Rensselaer,	Troy,	Troy.
John Peart,	do	Saratoga,	Hadley,	73 Eagle street.
William McManus,	do	Rensselaer,	Troy,	Troy.
Byron Andrus,	Bank Messenger.	Monroe,	Penfield,	24 Jay street.
James K. Van Campen,	Secy's Messenger,	Cattaraugus,	Allegany,	51 North Pearl st.
John T. McDonald,	Prest's Messenger,	Albany,	Albany,	183 Spring street.

REPORTERS.

9

NAME.	PAPER.	COUNTY.	POST-OFFICE.	BOARDING HOUSE.
George W. Demers,	Albany Eve. Jour.,	Rensselaer,	Troy,	Troy.
J. Wesley Smith,	Albany Argus,	Albany,	Albany,	Delavan House.
J. F. Mills,	N. Y. Tribune,	Westchester,	Mott Haven,	Delavan House.
Nathan Comstock,	N. Y. Times,	New York,	New York,	Delavan House.
J. C. Fitzpatrick,	N. Y. Herald,	New York,	New York,	Delavan House.
Hiram Calkins,	The World,	New York,	New York,	Delavan House.
H. J. Hastings,	Albany Knick'er,	Albany,	Albany,	178 State street.
Charles E. Smith,	Albany Express,	Albany,	Albany,	74 Eagle street.
George W. Bull,	N. Y. Com. Adv.,	Erie,	Buffalo,	Congress Hall.
Alexander Wilder,	Evening Post,	New York,	New York,	Mansion House.
M. H. Northrup,	N. Y. Express,	Onondaga,	Syracuse,	7 Lafayette street.
A. G. Johnson,	Troy Budget,	Rensselaer,	Troy,	Troy.
C. B. Martin,	Newburgh Journal,	Orange,	Newburgh.	

STATE OF NEW YORK.

No. 13.

IN CONVENTION

June 25, 1867.

COMMUNICATION

FROM THE NEW YORK COMMISSIONERS OF TAXES AND ASSESSMENTS.

OFFICE OF THE COMMISSIONERS OF TAXES AND ASSESSMENTS,
NEW YORK, *June* 22, 1867.

To the Constitutional Convention of the State of New York:

GENTLEMEN: In accordance with the resolution received by us requesting a statement to be furnished your honorable body "of the number of tax-payers in the city of New York, as the same appears from the records and documents in that office; distinguishing, as far as practicable, between those assessed for real estate and those assessed for personal property," we have caused an examination to be made of the records of the department, and respectfully submit the following statement therefrom:

Number of persons assessed for real estate,	44,153
Number of persons assessed for personal estate,	11,653
Number of persons assessed as shareholders of banks,	25,388
Making an aggregate of,	81,194

The records do not show whether the same name may not in some instances be duplicated in the different classes of assessments.

All of which is respectfully submitted,

J. W. ALLEN,

IRA O. MILLER,

Commissioners of Taxes and Assessments.

STATE OF NEW YORK.

No. 14.

IN CONVENTION

June 25, 1867.

REPORT

ON INDIAN TRIBES IN THE STATE.

OFFICE OF THE SECRETARY OF STATE
OF THE STATE OF NEW YORK,
ALBANY, *June* 25, 1867.

To Hon. WILLIAM A. WHEELER, *President of the Constitutional Convention:*

In response to the resolution of Hon. George T. Spencer, the Secretary of State communicates the following.

INDIAN TRIBES.

A few remnants of the native races still reside in the State, mostly occupying reservations of land in common, and receiving annuities under treaties by which their original territory was ceded to the State. The reservations are as follows:

Allegany Reservation, chiefly of Senecas, lying in the towns of South Valley, Cold Spring, Bucktooth, Great Valley and Carrolton, in Cattaraugus county. The tract extends 35 miles along both sides of the Allegany river, is about half a mile wide, and contains about 42 square miles, or 26,680 acres. Population in 1865, 825 being an increase of 71 in ten years.

Cattaraugus Reservation, on both sides of Cattaraugus creek, in the towns of Perrysburgh, Cattaraugus county, Collins, Erie county, and Hanover, Chautauqua county, including 21,680 acres of excellent land, and mostly under improvement. A council house is owned by the tribe, and three churches are maintained. Population in 1865, 1,347, being an increase of 168 in ten years. The Thomas Orphan Asylum, hitherto aided by the State, is located here.

The *Cayugas* have no reservation. Many have removed west of the Mississippi river, and 64 persons, in 1865, received $1,093.50 annuities from the sale of their former reservation. Others have received the principal of their annuities, and a few reside among the Senecas at Cattaraugus.

The *Oneidas*, now reduced to 155 persons (in 1865), reside on farms owned as individual freeholds, in the towns of Lenox, Madison county, and Vernon, Oneida county. The greater part of these people emigrated, over thirty years since, to the neighborhood of Green Bay, Wisconsin, where they own about 800 acres of land, and now reside.

Onondaga Reservation, on Onondaga creek, in the towns of Fayette and Onondaga, in Onondaga county. Population, in 1865, 360, an increase of 11 in ten years. They receive annuities from the State amounting to about $1,550 annually. About two-thirds of their lands are leased to the State.

St. Regis Reservation, bordering upon the St. Lawrence river and the Province line of Canada. The tribe were originally Mohawks and other tribes of the Five Nations, who were induced to emigrate in the French Colonial period of Canada, and who settled at their present location about 1760. Population living south of the boundary line in 1865, 426, being an increase of 13 in ten years. The number of this tribe living on the Canada side is about 760. Some of these draw annuities from this State by virtue of treaties of cession. In 1864, the number who shared in the State annuities was 648, and the amount paid was $2,396.60. This reservation includes about 14,000 acres.

The division of this tribe into British and American parties, which determines from which government they shall receive their annuities or presents, originated in the war of 1812–'15, and according as they or their ancestors declared their preferences at that time. The distinction is kept up by inheritance from mother to child, according to the Indian custom. Each party is governed by a separate class of trustees or chiefs, and their domestic affairs are generally managed harmoniously. Although tenants in common, it is customary for them to buy and sell improvements among themselves, and the conventional titles thus acquired are respected by common consent.

Shinnecock Reservation. This is a tract of land held in common by a remnant of the native tribes of Long Island, numbering, in 1865, 147 persons. Many of these people show traces of African blood. They have lost all traces of their native language and customs, are generally industrious, and support one or two small churches. They receive no annuities from the State.

The Shinnecock lands are supposed to contain about 630 acres.

Tonawanda Reservation, in Alabama and Pembroke, in Genesee county, Newstead, Erie county, and Royalton, Niagara county. This reservation lies on the Tonawanda creek, and contains about 45,440 acres. Population, in 1865, 509, a decrease of 93 in ten years.

Tuscarora Reservation, in Lewiston, Niagara county, embracing 6,249 acres of land purchased with moneys received from the sale of lands in North Carolina, and given by the Holland Land Company and the Senecas. They receive no annuities. Population, in 1865, 370, an increase of 54 in ten years.

These people anciently emigrated from North Carolina and settled near the Oneidas. They were removed to their present location through the influence of British agents, during the revolutionary war.

On all the Indian Reservations, schools are maintained by the State. The number of schools, by latest reports, was 25; children between 5 and 16, 1,175; number of children attending schools, 866. These schools are under the immediate care of the Superintendent of Public Instruction.

AGRICULTURAL AND OTHER INDUSTRIAL STATISTICS OF THE INDIAN TRIBES,

Called for by the Resolution of Mr. Spencer.

RESERVATION.	Acres of improved land 1865	Acres of unimpro'd land 1865	Cash value of lands 1865	Cash value of stock 1865	Cash value of tools 1865	WHEAT. Acres sown 1864	WHEAT. Bushels harvested 1864	OATS. Acres sown 1864	OATS. Acres sown 1865
Allegany	2436	8317	$36,175	$18,371	$5,272	8	50	164¾	144
Cattaraugus......	4962½	5263½	225,603	54,081	17,586	216¾	3,082	458⅜	553¼
Oneida	225½	....	17,890	1,825	645	21	264	25½	10½
Onondaga	569	....	....	11,956	3,096	88	1,107	84½	93
St. Regis	1826½	736	64,655	12,589	3,308	92	831	163	208½
Tonawanda	2006	....	108,104	15,113	5,688	153½	200	149½	174
Tuscarora........	3372½	....	47,021	25,062	4,926	456¼	3,471½	178½	205
	15,398¼	14,316½	$499,448	$138,997	$40,521	1,035	9,005½	1,224¼	1,388⅕

AGRICULTURE OF THE INDIAN TRIBES—*Continued.*

RESERVATION.	OATS.	RYE.			BARLEY.			BUCKWHEAT.			CORN.
	Bushels harvested. 1864	Acres sown 1864	Acres sown 1865	Bushels harvested 1864	Acres sown 1864	Acres sown 1865	Bushels harvested 1864	Acres sown 1864	Acres sown 1865	Bushels harvested 1864	Acres planted 1864
Allegany,	3,384	22½	13	329	......	1½	....	147¾	75	2,031½	269½
Cattaraugus,	11,266	......	3	......	15	12½	82	32¼	....	623	626¼
Oneida,	381	......	......	......	38½	46¾	725	5	9¼	....	92½
Onondaga,	1,655	......	......	......	......	......	....	....	....	....	209
St. Regis,	2,534½	......	......	......	26	36	280	66½	2½	596	92½
Tonawanda,	3,086	4	......	50	......	......	....	1½	....	30	177¼
Tuscarora,	3,654	3	......	......	......	......	....	35½	12	391	208
	25,960½	29½	16	379	79½	96¾	1,087	288½	98¾	3,671½	1,674¾

AGRICULTURE OF THE INDIAN TRIBES—*Continued.*

RESERVATION.	CORN.		POTATOES.			PEAS.			BEANS.			TURNIPS.
	Acres planted 1865	Bushels harvested 1864	Acres planted 1864	Acres planted 1865	Bushels harvested 1864	Acres sown 1864	Acres sown 1865	Bushels harvested 1864	Acres planted 1864	Acres planted 1865	Bushels harvested 1864	Acres sown 1864
Allegany, ...	292	6,260	75½	99¾	4,770	10½	13½	178	13	13¾	132¼	2
Cattaraugus, ...	716	12,363	124¼	159¼	11,104	4½	4½	61½	......	......	190¼	......
Oneida, ...	102¾	100	15¼	16	40	5	3½	......	17⅛	13¼	......	......
Onondaga, ...	231½	3,219	4	5	1,217	......	......	......	......	......	69	......
St. Regis,..........	142½	1,528½	55½	78½	3,760	46	46½	486	6¾	13¼	104	......
Tonawanda,........	200½	8,145	29⅞	35½	3,161	2½	3½	40	2	1½	20	......
Tuscarora, ...	230½	4,184	27½	26⅜	1,468	½	1½	5	6¾	1¼	59¼	½
	1,915¾	35,799½	331⅞	420⅜	25,520	69	72¾	770½	45⅝	43	574¾	2½

AGRICULTURE OF THE INDIAN TRIBES—*Continued.*

RESERVATION.	TURNIPS.		APPLE ORCHARDS.		MEADOWS.				ACRES IN PASTURE.		ACRES PLOWED.	
	Acres sown. 1865	Bushels harvested 1864	Bushels of Apples. 1864	Barrels of cider. 1864	Acres. 1864	Acres. 1865	Tons of hay 1864	Bushels of grass seed 1864	1864	1865	1864	1865
Allegany, ...	11½	47	3,462½	24⅛	443	463¾	434½	5	252½	303½	828½	799¼
Cattaraugus .	......	......	3,405	106	647½	757	759	......	1,252½	1,328½	1,400¼	1,506¾
Oneida	......	......	2,857	......	22	22	55½	......	22	22	107½	115½
Onondaga, ..	......	......	265	20	80¾	89¾	96½	......	......	......	443	408½
St. Regis, ...	......	......	....	......	1,660	1,801	773½	......	385	444	627½	716½
Tonawanda, .	......	......	1,162	6	179¾	162¼	261½	......	263	279	578	473½
Tuscarora, ..	......	4	1,237	10	581½	706½	591	......	518	450	849½	694½
	11½	51	12,388½	166⅛	3,614½	4,002¼	2,921½	5	2,693	2,827	4,834¼	4,714½

AGRICULTURE OF THE INDIAN TRIBES—*Continued.*

RESERVATION.	ACRES IN FALLOW.		Total number of neat cattle.	Neat cattle over 1 year old, exclusive of working oxen and cows.	Working oxen.	NUMBER OF COWS MILKED.		Pounds of butter.	Pounds of cheese made.	WOOL.		Total No. of swine kept in	Pork, pounds of.
										Pounds shorn in	Pounds shorn in		
	1864.	1865.	1865.	1865.	1865,	1864.	1865.	1865.	1864.	1864.	1865.	1865.	1864.
Allegany, ...	161	92¼	377	63	54	108	90	8,525	....	62	127	289	15,422
Cattaraugus,.	184	10	907	255	136	206	231	1,855	....	48	15	424	21,745
Oneida, ...	3	......	332	5	....	276	264	5,400	75,056	841	417	73	14,492
Onondaga, ...	......	......	137	42	22	44	48	4,465	....	57	......	246	11,440
St. Regis,........	140	154	188	17	2	71	72	5,141	....	......	......	181	14,460
Tonawanda,......	114	23	223	50	7	64	56	2,175	....	349	469	295	23,040
Tuscarora, ...	143½	46½	308	37	17	91	93	9,080	....	125	130	317	15,020
	745½	325¾	2,472	469	238	860	854	36,641	75,056	1,482	1,158	1,825	115,619

All of which is respectfully submitted,

FRANCIS C. BARLOW,
Secretary of State.

STATE OF NEW YORK.

No. 15.

IN CONVENTION

June 28, 1867.

REPORT

OF THE COMMITTEE ON THE RIGHT OF SUFFRAGE AND QUALIFICATIONS TO HOLD OFFICE.

Mr. Greeley, from the above standing committee, reports as follows:

Your committee, having given careful attention to the subject referred to them, have prepared as a substitute for Article II, of the present constitution, the following:

ARTICLE —.

SEC. 1. Every man of the age of twenty-one years who shall have been an inhabitant of this State for one year next preceding an election, and for the last thirty days a citizen of the United States, and a resident of the election district where he may offer his vote, shall be entitled to vote at such election, in said district, and not elsewhere, for all officers elected by the people.

Provided, That idiots, lunatics, persons under guardianship, felons and persons convicted of bribery, unless pardoned or otherwise restored to civil rights, shall not be entitled to vote. No person who shall at any time within thirty days next preceding, have been a public pauper, shall vote at any election. No person who shall receive, expect to receive, pay, or offer to pay any money or other valuable thing to influence or reward a vote to be given at an election, shall vote at such election; and, upon challenge for such cause, the person so challenged shall, before the inspectors receive his vote, swear or affirm before such inspectors that he has not received, does not expect to receive, has not paid nor offered to pay, any money or other valuable thing to influence or reward a vote to be given at such election. Laws may be passed excluding from voting at an election every person who shall have made, or who shall be interested in, a bet or wager depending upon the result thereof.

SEC. 2. For the purpose of voting, no person shall be deemed to have gained or lost a residence by reason of his presence or absence while employed in the service of the United States, nor while engaged in the navigation of the waters of this State, of the United States, or of the high seas, nor while kept in any almshouse or other asylum, at the public expense, nor while confined in any public prison. And the Legislature shall prescribe the manner in which electors absent from their homes in time of war, in the actual military or naval service of this State, or of the United States, may vote, and shall provide for the canvass and return of their votes.

SEC. 3. Laws shall be made for ascertaining by proper proofs the citizens who shall be entitled to the right of suffrage hereby established. And the Legislature shall provide that a register of all citizens entitled to the right of suffrage in each election district shall be made and completed at least six days before any election; and no person shall vote at such election who shall not have been registered according to law; but such laws shall be uniform in their requirements throughout the State.

SEC. 4. All elections by the citizens shall be by ballot, except for such town officers as may by law be directed to be otherwise chosen.

SEC. 5. No person who is not, at the time of taking the oath of office, an elector, shall hold any office under this Constitution. All officers shall, before they enter on the duties of their respective offices, take and subscribe the following oath or affirmation:

"I do solemnly swear (or affirm) that I will support the Constitution of the United States, and the Constitution of the State of New York; and that I will faithfully discharge the duties of (the office he is to hold) according to the best of my ability."

EXPLANATIONS.

It will be seen that the existing article has been retained by us in substance, and that the qualifications of a legal voter proposed by us be:

1. Adult rational manhood.

2. Citizenship of the United States of not less than thirty days' standing.

3. Residence in the State for the year preceding.

4. Residence in the election district for the last thirty days.

5. Freedom from crime.

6. Exemption from dependence on others, through pauperism or guardianship.

The material changes we recommend are these:

1st. Strike out all discriminations based on color. Slavery, the vital source and only plausible ground of such invidious discrimination, being dead, not only in this State, but throughout the Union, as it is soon to be, we trust, throughout this hemisphere, we can imagine no tolerable excuse for perpetuating the existing proscription. Whites and blacks are required to render like obedience to our laws, and are punished in like measure for their violation. Whites and blacks were indiscriminately drafted and held to service to fill our State's quotas in the war whereby the Republic was saved from disruption. We trust that we are henceforth to deal with men according to their conduct, without regard to their color. If so, the fact should be embodied in the Constitution.

We ask you to abolish the present requirement of four months' residence in a county as a pre-requisite to voting. This exaction bears hardly on such residents of cities as spend their summer mainly in the country, and cannot afford to maintain a double residence. Thousands of intelligent and patriotic young mechanics, employed as carpenters, bricklayers, painters, plumbers, gas-fitters, &c., by masters located in our great cities, are sent out to work in neighboring counties for periods over which they have no control, and in

November find their right to vote anywhere questionable, if not invalid. Hundreds of Methodist and other clergymen who are assigned to new charges in summer, find themselves disfranchised when our State election comes around. Under circumstances which impel doubt as to the right of a citizen to vote, the conscientious refrain, while the unscrupulous insist. We hold it wise to abolish a requirement which debars thousands of capable and worthy citizens, while it is a constant incitement to distortion or suppression of truth, to dissimulation and perjury.

At present, a resident in any county for four months is allowed to vote at the poll of any district wherein he actually resides on the day of election, though he may be a total stranger in that district, and does not pretend to have resided in it two days, only he must vote to fill an office he could not have voted to fill before his change of residence. But how are inspectors to know the contents of his folded ballot? And how are frauds to be prevented in districts where the preponderance of one party is overwhelming? It seems advisable to your committee to require an absolute residence by the voter of thirty days in the district where he tenders his ballot. This will give time for proper scrutiny, and will, when accompanied by an efficient registry, afford a substantial barrier against fraud. And the cases must be few indeed where the requirement of a thirty days' residence before voting will work individual hardship or affect the result of an important election.

Our present Constitution requires that naturalization shall precede voting by at least ten days; a memorial referred to us asks that this interval be extended to sixty days. We have fixed on thirty days as the proper time. We would stop the hunting out and dragging up before courts of indifferent and often reluctant immigrants in order to crowd them into citizenship, in order to affect by their votes the result of a pending election. This is the object of the present requirement of ten days' interval, and it will be far more completely accomplished by extending the prescribed term to thirty days. It is well, moreover, that the terms of citizenship and residence in the election district should be identical, so as to avoid complexity and possible misapprehension. Should we extend the interval between naturalization and voting to sixty days, the change would be inveighed against as impelled by a spirit of hostility to adopted citizens, or by a desire to impede naturalization. We trust the Convention will assent to our proposition.

As to disfranchisement of criminals and law-breakers, what we propose is very nearly identical with what is now prescribed, partly by the Constitution, partly by statute. It has seemed to us advisable to make the qualifications of voters as specific and unambiguous as possible, and to fix them, so far as may be, in the Constitution.

We propose that public paupers shall not be voters. We hold that to allow the inmates of almshouses, subsisting upon the charity of the public, to vote, is to accord an excessive influence and power over the results of our elections to the keepers of those establishments, whose retention in office is often at stake, each of whom can appeal with effect to his boarders not to vote him out of house and home. The end is now awkwardly contemplated in the provision that no pauper shall gain or lose a residence by reason of his stay in an almshouse; but it is evaded by sending the paupers, under watchful keepers, just prior to an important election, to the towns or wards whence they came, there to be registered and vote, when they are welcomed back to their old haunts as patriots who have been absent in their country's and their keeper's service. Specific disfranchisement will add to the wholesome horror of pauperism now cherished by most Americans, and there seems to be no good reason for allowing paupers to govern by their votes the policy of our country and State, and at the same time enabling them to supersede a keeper who may have been so cruel as to require the able-bodied among them to work. At all events, let this matter be dealt with frankly.

Having thus briefly set forth the considerations which seem to us decisive in favor of the few and moderate changes proposed above, we proceed to indicate our controlling reasons for declining to recommend other and, in some respects, more important innovations.

Your committee does not recommend an extension of the elective franchise to women. However defensible in theory, we are satisfied that public sentiment does not demand, and would not sustain, an innovation so revolutionary and sweeping, so openly at war with a distribution of duties and functions between the sexes as venerable and pervading as government itself, and involving transformations so radical in society and domestic life. Should we prove to be in error on this head, the Convention may overrule us by changing a few words in the first section of our proposed article.

Nor have we seen fit to propose the enfranchisement of boys above the age of eighteen years. The current of ideas and usages in our day, but especially in this country, seems already to set quite too strongly in favor of the relaxation, if not total overthrow of parental authority, especially over half grown boys. With the sincerest good-will for the class in question, we submit that they may spend the hours which they can spare from their labors and their lessons more usefully and profitably in mastering the wisdom of the sages and philosophers who have elucidated the science of government, than in attendance on midnight caucuses or in wrangling around the polls.

The proposition that a tax should be assessed on and collected from voters, is commended, like some others by plausible analogies. The rightful and intimate connection between taxation and representation was a potent watchword of our Revolutionary fathers; yet we cannot ignore the fact that the Constitution of 1821 having, like its predecessors, embodied this principle, an amendment striking out this qualification, and thus establishing manhood suffrage, was adopted by the Legislature of 1825, and ratified by an overwhelming popular vote in 1826; yeas, 127,077; nays, 3,215. We do not feel called upon to appeal from their judgment.

Nor have we chosen to adopt any of the schemes of disfranchising illiterate persons which have been referred to us. We freely admit that ignorance is a public evil and peril, as well as a personal misfortune, and we are ready to march abreast with the foremost in limiting its baleful influence. But men's relative capacity is not absolutely measured by their literary acquirements; and the State requires the illiterate, equally with others, to be taxed for their support, and to shed their blood in her defense. We prefer that she shall persist in her noble efforts to instruct and enlighten all her sons by means less invidious and more genial than disfranchisement. Were there no other consideration impelling to this decision, we should rest on and defer to the forcible truths, that ability to read and write is not absolute, but comparative; that inspectors of election are fallible and swayed by like passions with other men—and that they might be tempted, in an exciting and closely contested election, to regard with a partial fondness, almost parental, the literary acquirements of those claimants of the franchise who were notoriously desirous of voting the ticket of those inspectors' own party, while applying a far sterner and more critical rule to those who should proffer the opposite ballots.

Our present Constitution authorizes the Legislature to pass laws designed to ascertain, by proper proofs, the persons entitled to exercise the right of suffrage. We recommend that those laws shall provide for a registration of all the legal voters, to be completed at least six days before each State election, and that none other than registered electors shall vote. Your committee are confident that the experience of our State and of the civilized world, fully justifies these requirements. Unless the ballot-box is to be regarded and treated as a spittoon, no person should be allowed to vote whose right to do so is not fully ascertained and unquestionable. In a rural neighborhood where every one who approaches the ballot-box is known to dozens of either party, the frauds of unregistered voting may be mainly confined to those districts where the ascendancy of one party is practically unchecked; but in any densely peopled districts where hundreds offer to vote who are known only to their few cronies, the case is totally different. Not to register the names of the voters, so as to give time for deliberate and general scrutiny, not merely by the few who may chance to be present when a particular vote is tendered is to stimulate knavery and offer a premium on fraud. It is to proclaim the right of suffrage worthless and proffer to each vagrant or felon half a dozen votes at every election which he may condescend to patronize. To uphold a registration of deeds, yet oppose a registration of voters, is virtually to assert a higher value, a more precious importance in our lands than in our liberties. Doubtless, some frauds will be committed where suffrage is so nearly universal, no matter what safeguards may be thrown around the elective franchise; but to maintain that registration, while it does afford protection to the titles whereby we hold our lands, will give none to our right of suffrage is to defy reason and insult our common sense. Your committee would urge that this precious right, so fundamental to all others, be carefully shielded from corruption, and that the main safeguards against its abuse should not be left to unstable and fluctuating statutes, but should be firmly imbedded in the Constitution.

Your committee, having thus fulfilled the duty imposed on them, ask to be discharged from the further consideration of the memorials referred to them, and that these, with this report, be committed to a Committee of the Whole.

HORACE GREELEY,
Chairman,
LESLIE W. RUSSELL,
WM. H. MERRILL,
GEO. WILLIAMS.

ALBANY, *June* 28*th*, 1867

STATE OF NEWYORK.

No. 16.

IN CONVENTION

June 28, 1867.

MINORITY REPORT

OF THE COMMITTEE ON THE RIGHT OF SUFFRAGE AND THE QUALIFICATIONS TO HOLD OFFICE.

The undersigned, while cordially concurring in many of the objects sought to be accomplished by the majority of the committee of which they are members, differ as to several of the conclusions reached by them. The undersigned would prefer to preserve, as far as possible, the language of the existing Constitution, on the subject of the elective franchise, to which usage and the decisions of the courts have given definite interpretations. They would prefer, also, to retain most of the provisions of the present article in regard to the pre-requisites of residence, etc., and especially that which exacts of a naturalized citizen that he shall have perfected his citizenship ten days before election, instead of requiring, as the article proposed by the committee does, a term of thirty days.

The inevitable effect of the change is to deprive of their votes, in the elections of 1868 and 1869, all that numerous class, who on the faith of existing regulations, may have declared their purpose to become citizens, on or about the tenth day, antecedent to the elections of 1866 and 1867, and who expected to perfect their citizenship in the prescribed two years from that date. If the change shall thus operate to the disfranchisement of many thousand citizens, in two important elections, one of which involves a contest for the Presidency of these United States, that injustice will more than counterbalance any supposed good to be obtained by the change. The ten days interposed by the Constitution of 1846 give ample time for the inspection of the registry, and of the rolls of the courts; and afford all the opportunity that either party may need to take measures against the parties to a fraud. Let us not commence the work of reforming our Constitution by practically disfranchising so large a class of our most useful citizens.

The provision which makes the giving or the taking of a bribe a ground of challenge and a disqualification to vote, though it may exclude many from the suffrage, is liable to no such objection. It aims at a great and growing evil, and it strikes only at the criminal. Corruption is the leprosy of political society, and the taint is infectious. The venality of the elector is the source of the corruption of the official. The representative who secures his seat by the expenditure of money only reimburses himself for his outlay, when he sells his vote or barters his legislative influence. No penal enactment has yet sufficed to check this evil; but in making it a ground of challenge at the polls, we call the vigilance of parties to our aid; diminish their temptation to corrupt practices; and find in their natural rivalries the machinery of a self-executing law.

While the undersigned believe that all Registry Laws are expensive, vexatious and onerous, more often depriving the honest voter of a right than closing the opportunity of fraud against a dishonest one, and while the history of political contest shows that they have served as the agency for many of the great conspiracies against the elective franchise, yet they regard the promise of the Committee "that all such laws shall be uniform in their requirements in every part of the State," as a compensation for many of the evils of the system, and a most valuable safeguard against abuse. It will effectually prevent the Legislature from imposing restrictions upon one community and awarding license to another; and we shall no longer have to endure the existence of three or four separate systems of election imposed on different parts of the State by the caprice or jealousy of sectional majorities. If a registration of voters is necessary before election, let every citizen be made to conform to its requirements. The law will be more likely to be respected by all when it is equal in its requirements in regard to all.

As respects the extension of suffrage to colored the same as to white citizens of the State, the undersigned submit that if the regeneration of political society is to be sought in the incorporation of this element into the constituency, it must be done by the direct and explicit vote of the electors. We are foreclosed from any other course by the repeated action of the State. In 1846 this question was submitted in a separate article to be voted on, at the same time with the Constitution itself; and was negatived by a vote of 223,884 to 85,306. It was again exhibited in 1850, and was again defeated by a vote of 337,984 to 197,503. A similar submission was provided by a concurrent resolution of the Legislature of 1859, which, by the neglect of the State officers to provide for its publication, was defeated; but its fate may fairly be regarded as further evidence of the indifference of the public towards a change.

The undersigned are of opinion that the Convention will depart from its representative character if, after these repeated manifestations of the popular will, it should enact this extension of the suffrage without such a separate submission. It would be unfair to the people to declare: that, whereas, they have again and again refused to accept this change, therefore we will incorporate it into the Constitution and compel them either to repeal that instrument or to accept this measure. If the reform is an organic one, and if other changes in our political system involve this also; and if, under new influences, popular opinion has been modified, let us meet the question and decide it upon its simple merits. To make it dependent upon the fate of financial articles or of changes in the judicial structure, or of innovation of doubtful popularity, would be unjust to the class who solicit this extension of privilege. To force its acceptance against the convictions of the main body of the constituency, by relaxing severe but just restrictions upon delegated power, or by concessions to local or moneyed interest, would be an obvious wrong of which this body could not be consciously guilty.

The submission of the question by itself is so direct and honest, as to tend to disarm the jealousy with which this question has been regarded by the people. It is without embarrassment or difficulty in practice, and whether the mode of separate submission be extended to allow articles or not, the popular will may be conceded in regard to this without trouble or expense.

For the sake, therefore, of disembarassing the Convention from the further consideration of this subject, and of relieving the wise and salutary reforms to be secured by the Revised Constitution, from an unnecessary complication, the undersigned beg leave to offer the following resolution as an amendment to the report of the majority:

Resolved, That a proposition further to extend the elective franchise to colored men be submitted, to be voted on separately from the rest of the Constitution.

As to the extension of suffrage to women, the undersigned reserve, for the present, any expression of opinion.

All of which is respectfully submitted.

WILLIAM CASSIDY,
JOHN G. SCHUMAKER.

STATE OF NEW YORK.

No. 17.

IN CONVENTION

June 25, 1867.

STANDING COMMITTEES OF THE CONVENTION.

1. *On the preamble and the bill of rights.*

Mr. Evarts, New York.
Mr. Spencer, Steuben.
Mr. A. R. Lawrence, N. Y.
Mr. Bowen, Niagara.
Mr. Paige, Schenectady.
Mr. Frank, Wyoming.
Mr. Hardenburgh, Ulster.

2. *On the Legislature,—its organization and the number, apportionment, election, tenure of office, and compensation of its members.*

Mr. Merritt, St. Lawrence.
Mr. Cooke, Ulster.
Mr. Sherman, Oneida.
Mr. Monell, New York.
Mr. Barker, Chautauqua.
Mr. J. Brooks, New York.
Mr. Merwin, Jefferson.

3. *On the powers and duties of the Legislature, except as to matters otherwise referred.*

Mr. Rathbun, Cayuga.
Mr. Rumsey, Steuben.
Mr. Robertson, New York.
Mr. E. A. Brown, Lewis.
Mr. Fields, Orleans.
Mr. M. H. Lawrence, Yates.
Mr. Burrill, New York.

4. *On the right of suffrage and the qualification to hold office.*

Mr. Greeley, Westchester.
Mr. Endress, Livingston.
Mr. Cassidy, Albany.
Mr. Merrill, Wyoming.
Mr. Williams, Oneida.
Mr. L. W. Russell, St. Lawrence.
Mr. Schumaker, Kings.

5. *On the Governor and Lieutenant-Governor, their election, tenure of office, compensation, powers and duties, except as otherwise referred.*

Mr. C. L. Allen, Washington.
Mr. E. P. Brooks, Chemung.
Mr. A. J. Parker, Albany.
Mr. Flagler, Niagara.
Mr. Wakeman, Genesee.
Mr. Miller, Delaware.
Mr. Garvin, New York.

6. *On the Secretary of State, Comptroller, Treasurer, Attorney-General and State Engineer and Surveyor, their election or appointment, tenure of office, compensation, powers and duties.*

Mr. Tucker, New York.
Mr. Baker, Montgomery.
Mr. Duganne, New York.
Mr. Fuller, Monroe.
Mr. Ely, Monroe.
Mr. Ketcham, Wayne.
Mr. A. R. Lawrence, N. Y.

7. *On town and county officers, other than judicial, their election or appointment, tenure of office, compensation, powers and duties.*

Mr. Smith, Fulton.
Mr. Bickford, Jefferson.
Mr. Rolfe, Kings.
Mr. A. Lawrence, Schuyler.
Mr. Kinney, Tioga.
Mr. Sheldon, Dutchess.
Mr. Roy, Albany.

8. *On the Judiciary.*

Mr. Folger, Ontario.
Mr. Evarts, New York.
Mr. Comstock, Onondaga.
Mr. Van Cott, Kings.
Mr. Daly, New York.
Mr. Barker, Chautauqua.
Mr. Kernan, Oneida.
Mr. Hutchins, New York.
Mr. Masten, Erie.
Mr. T. W. Dwight, Ontario.
Mr. A. J. Parker, Albany.
Mr. Andrews, Onondaga.
Mr. Hale, Essex.
Mr. Goodrich, Tompkins.
Mr. Pierrepont, New York.

9. *On the finances of the State, the public debt, revenues, expenditures, and taxation, and restrictions on the powers of the Legislature in respect thereto.*

Mr. Church, Orleans.
Mr. Frank, Wyoming.
Mr. Corning, Albany.
Mr. Opdyke, New York.
Mr. Tilden, New York.
Mr. Clarke, Monroe.
Mr. Van Cott, Kings.
Mr. Schell, New York.
Mr. W. C. Brown, St. Lawrence.
Mr. Nelson, Dutchess.
Mr. A. F. Allen, Chautauqua.
Mr. Hatch, Erie.
Mr. Carpenter, Dutchess.
Mr. Barto, Tompkins.
Mr. Hardenburgh, Ulster.

10. *On canals.*

Mr. Lapham, Ontario.
Mr. Alvord, Onondaga.
Mr. Clinton, Erie.
Mr. Prosser, Erie.
Mr. Seymour, Rensselaer.
Mr. Beckwith, Washington.
Mr. Schoonmaker, Ulster.
Mr. Hutchins, New York.
Mr. Champlain, Allegany.
Mr. Root, Oswego.
Mr. Bell, Jefferson.
Mr. Magee, Schuyler.
Mr. Prindle, Chenango.
Mr. Bergen, Kings.
Mr. Tappen, Westchester.

11. *On cities, their organization, government and powers.*

Mr. Harris, Albany.
Mr. Opdyke, New York.
Mr. Murphy, Kings.
Mr. Francis, Rensselaer.
Mr. Paige, Schenectady.
Mr. Alvord, Onondaga.
Mr. Verplanck, Erie.
Mr. Bowen, Niagara.
Mr. Law, New York.
Mr. Fullerton, Orange.
Mr. E. Brooks, Richmond.
Mr. Graves, Herkimer.
Mr. Weed, Clinton.
Mr. Hand, Broome.
Mr. Chesebro, Ontario.

12. *On counties, towns and villages, their organization, government and powers.*

Mr. Hadley, Seneca.
Mr. N. M. Allen, Cattaraugus.
Mr. Lowrey, Kings.
Mr. Ferry, Otsego.
Mr. Fowler, Madison.
Mr. Corbett, Onondaga.
Mr. Wickham, Suffolk.

13. *On currency, banking and insurance.*

Mr. Beadle, Chemung.
Mr. Huntington, Oneida.
Mr. Veeder, Kings.
Mr. Eddy, Otsego.
Mr. Armstrong, Rensselaer.
Mr. Ludington, Sullivan.
Mr. Hitchman. New York.

14. *On corporations other than municipal, banking and insurance.*

Mr. Ballard, Cortland.
Mr. Stratton, New York.
Mr. S. Townsend, Queens.
Mr. Krum, Schoharie.
Mr. L. W. Russell, St. Lawrence.
Mr. Hitchcock, Washington.
Mr. Barnard, Kings.

15. *On State prisons, and the prevention and punishment of crime.*

Mr. Gould, Columbia.
Mr. C. C. Dwight, Cayuga.
Mr. A. D. Russell, New York.
Mr. Cochran, Westchester.
Mr. Lee, Oswego.
Mr. Axtell, Clinton.
Mr Conger, Rockland.

16. *On the pardoning power.*

Mr. M. I. Townsend, Rensselaer.
Mr. Pond, Saratoga.
Mr. Develin, New York.
Mr. Landon, Schenectady.
Mr. Prindle, Chenango.
Mr. Lee, Oswego.
Mr. Gerry, New York.

17. *On the militia and military officers.*

Mr. Morris, Putnam.
Mr. Seaver, Franklin.
Mr. Barto, Tompkins.
Mr. C. C. Dwight, Cayuga.
Mr. Cheritree, Warren.
Mr. Stratton, New York.
Mr. Hammond, Allegany.

18. *On education and funds relating thereto.*

Mr. Curtis, New York.
Mr. Archer, Wayne.
Mr. Conger, Rockland.
Mr. Gould, Columbia.
Mr. Beals, Herkimer.
Mr. Clinton, Erie.
Mr. Larremore, New York.

19. *On charities and charitable institutions.*

Mr. E. Brooks, Richmond.
Mr. T. W. Dwight, Oneida.
Mr. Strong, Suffolk.
Mr. Spencer, Steuben.
Mr. Ludington, Sullivan.
Mr. Silvester, Columbia.
Mr. Livingston, Kings.

20. *On industrial interests, except those already referred.*

Mr. Duganne, New York.
Mr. Gross, New York.
Mr. Farnum, Allegany.
Mr. Armstrong, Rensselaer.
Mr. Wales, Sullivan.
Mr. Case, Madison.
Mr. More, Greene.

21. *On the salt springs of the State.*

Mr. Bell, Jefferson.
Mr. Comstock, Onondaga.
Mr. C. E. Parker, Tioga.
Mr. McDonald, Ontario.
Mr. Rolfe, Kings.
Mr. Houston, Orange.
Mr. Young, Ulster.

22. *On the relations of the State to the Indians residing therein.*

Mr. Van Campen, Cattara'gus.
Mr. Silvester, Columbia.
Mr. Bergen, Kings.
Mr. Axtell, Clinton.
Mr. S. Townsend, Queens.
Mr. McDonald, Ontario.
Mr. Colahan, Kings.

23. *On future amendments and revisions of the Constitution.*

Mr. E. A. Brown, Lewis.
Mr. Greeley, Westchester.
Mr. Robertson, New York.
Mr. Flagler, Niagara.
Mr. Murphy, Kings.
Mr. Grant, Delaware.
Mr. J. Brooks, New York.

24. *Privileges and elections.*

Mr. Landon, Schenectady.
Mr, Endress, Livingston.
Mr. Loew, New York.
Mr. Lowrey, Kings.
Mr. Mattice, Greene.

25. *Printing.*

Mr. Seaver, Franklin.
Mr. Francis, Rensselaer.
Mr. Potter, Erie.
Mr. Merrill, Wyoming.
Mr. Jarvis, New York.

26. *Contingent expenses.*

Mr. Ferry, Otsego.
Mr. Williams, Oneida.
Mr. Cochran, Westchester.
Mr. Reynolds, Monroe.
Mr. Rogers, New York.

27. *Engrossment and enrollment.*

Mr. Sherman, Oneida.
Mr. Archer, Wayne.
Mr. Cassidy, Albany.
Mr. Cheritree, Warren.
Mr. Mattice, Greene.

Select committee on the adulteration or sale of intoxicating liquors.

Mr. Graves,
Mr. Livingston,
Mr. Ely,
Mr. Cochran,
Mr. Landon,
Mr. Hand,
Mr. Ray,
Mr. Verplanck.

STATE OF NEW YORK.

No. 18.

IN CONVENTION

July 9, 1867.

COMMUNICATION

FROM CLERK OF COURT OF APPEALS.

STATE OF NEW YORK.
COURT OF APPEALS CLERK'S OFFICE,
ALBANY, *July 8th*, 1867.

HON. WILLIAM A. WHEELER, *President of the Convention to revise the Constitution and to amend the same:*

SIR: I have the honor to forward herewith, in response to the resolution of the Convention dated June 21st, 1867, a statement of the number of appeals now pending in this court, distinguishing the years in which said appeals were brought; the court from which such appeals were taken, the number of causes disposed of during the five years immediately preceding, including also the number of preferred causes disposed of by the court during the said years.

Very respectfully,

PATRICK H. JONES,
Clerk Court of Appeals.

STATEMENT.

TABLE

Showing the number of Causes brought into the Court of Appeals from each Judicial District, and what Court appealed from, from January first, 1856, *to January first,* 1867. *Also the number of Causes on Preferred Calendar for the years* 1862, 1863, 1864, 1865, 1866, *and number of Causes determined in said years respectively:*

YEAR.	DISTRICTS.								TOTAL.	COURT APPEALED FROM.				Number Causes determined.	Number Causes on Preferred Calendar.
	1	2	3	4	5	6	7	8		Supreme.	Superior, N. Y.	Superior, Buffalo.	Common Pleas.		
1856..	123	20	25	27	26	13	22	46	302	216	53	15	18		
1857..	127	25	38	16	28	42	46	46	368	275	50	25	18		
1858..	177	20	65	40	40	37	35	61	475	379	57	12	27		
1859..	142	53	37	36	36	37	47	66	454	365	46	19	24		
1860..	118	45	56	40	28	37	66	55	445	357	54	18	16		
1861..	162	42	37	30	27	33	59	55	445	364	46	6	29		
1862..	184	53	59	27	33	29	50	57	492	403	54	16	19	287	115
1863..	146	54	55	18	13	26	35	34	381	315	41	7	18	287	124
1864..	137	49	28	30	23	24	34	36	361	296	35	13	17	273	109
1865..	124	45	30	34	11	17	25	27	313	259	32	5	17	296	135
1866..	110	61	51	18	16	28	43	56	383	338	23	10	12	327	127

Previous to the year 1856 the Registers of the court do not show in every instance the district or court from which causes were brought into this court.

STATE OF NEW YORK.

No. 19.

IN CONVENTION

July 10, 1867.

COMMUNICATION.

FROM THE SUPERINTENDENT OF ONONDAGA SALT SPRINGS, IN REPLY TO FOURTEEN INTERROGATORIES OF THE CONSTITUTIONAL CONVENTION.

OFFICE OF THE SUPERINTENDENT OF ONONDAGA SALT SPRINGS, SYRACUSE, *July 9th*, 1867.

Hon. WILLIAM A. WHEELER, *President of the Constitutional Contion:*

SIR: I have received from the Clerk of the Constitutional Convention fourteen interrogatories "in regard to the Salt Springs and the manufacture of salt," to which I respectfully submit the following answers:

First Interrogatory.—"The whole number of salt wells on the Reservation."

I presume this question was framed with the view of determining the total number of wells that have been sunk for salt water from the earliest use of these salines. There are no records in this office that furnish the information necessary to answer with any approximation to accuracy. In the early history of the manufacture of salt, wells were sunk at Salina (now first ward of the city of Syracuse), at Geddes, at Liverpool and at Syracuse, that from time to time failed to yield water of any value. Other wells were sunk, many of them of no value, and some of them were of some value for a few years, and then became useless. Various localities were tested, and now the expectation of finding good salt water is nearly confined to two localities—one near the pump house, in the third ward of Syracuse, and the other at the mouth of Onondaga creek, in the first ward.

Between these points, which are about one mile apart, there is a section which has not been tested fully, and in which it is probable good wells may be had. The wells at Geddes and Liverpool have all been abandoned as worthless, and these two villages now manufacture salt from water that is pumped from the localities stated, and sent from there to the places of consumption in conduits. There are now five wells on the Reservation, that within a few years have been sunk by individuals, that are not used.

Second Interrogatory.—"The number owned and now in use by the State."

There are now fifteen wells owned by the State and in use.

Third Interrogatory.—"The quantity of salt, in bushels of 56 pounds each, said wells are capable of producing annually."

This question is best answered by making an extract from my last annual report. "The water in the wells now used is of different degrees of strength, ranging, when pumping from them all the water they can be made to yield, from 52° to 74° of the salometer. One of these wells was brought into use on the 20th of June, 1866, yielding about the same amount and quality of water as the other wells in that locality, and stronger brine than any other well except in that locality.

The amount of brine that can be pumped from all these fifteen wells, is about 1,400 gallons per minute, of which 900 gallons will give an average strength of 66° salometer, or 16½ per cent. salt. The remaining 500 gallons will have an average strength of about 54° salometer, or 13½ per cent. salt. By mixing the weaker with the stronger, we get about 62° or 15½ per cent. salt." If 1,400 gallons of water is pumped in one minute, we have 2,016,000 gallons for every twenty-four hours. Making proper allowances for unavoidable waste of water in conveying to the works, and from other causes, it is probable that not less than fifty gallons must be pumped from the wells for every bushel of salt made." Taking fifty gallons as necessary for one bushel, we have the ability of furnishing the water to make 40,320 bushels of salt in one day. The law prohibits the Superintendent from furnishing the boiling works with water during the months of December, January, February and March, and during those months the solar works cannot make salt, so that the season is restricted to eight months. The power used for pumping the water is taken from the canals, and during the month of April the water is generally drawn from the canals for repairs, so that it is not until the canal opens in May that the pumps can be put in operation ; thus another month (April) must be deducted from the manufacturing season, leaving only seven—or say 210 days.

Furnishing water for these 210 days sufficient to make 40,320 bushels of salt per day, we have 8,467,200 bushels for the season. To this should be added about 400,000 bushels that can be made from the water that is, during the winter, pumped into an earth reservoir.

This calculation is based on the expectation that all the machinery will work without accident or delay during the entire period of 210 days. This never, in fact, happens, and the unavoidable delays that come of breaks should be taken into the account, as perhaps sufficient to balance the advantages derived from the water stored in the earth reservoir.

The necessity of a larger supply of the strongest water to meet the demands of the manufacturers, is apparent, and measures are now being taken to sink more wells, as fast as the money placed by the Legislature at the disposal of the Superintendent will warrant.

Fourth Interrogatory.—"The least, greatest and average quantity of salt of the different kinds produced therefrom."

Reports have been made annually by the Superintendent to the Legislature since the year 1797, of the quantity of salt made. I submit, in answer to this interrogatory, a table taken from my last report of the quantity of salt made in each year.

Since 1841, inclusive, the solar salt has been reported separately, but is included in the aggregate quantity stated for each year. The total amount of salt made is 175,857,072 bushels. I have inserted in the table the solar salt produced each year, which, in the aggregate amounts to 22,554,153 bushels. This deducted from the total salt, leaves 153,302,919 bushels as the number of bushels of fine or boiled salt that has been made. This table is submitted as not only containing the information asked for, but as giving a full history of the annual production of salt.

The following is a statement of the number of bushels of salt made at the Onondaga Salt Springs, since June 20, 1797, which is the date of the first leases of the lots.

DATE.	NO. OF BUSHELS,	SOLAR.	SUPERINTENDENT.
1797......	25,474.....	....	William Stevens.
1798......	59,928.....	....	do
1799......	42,704.....	....	do
1800......	50,000.....	....	do
1801......	62,000.....	....	Sheldon Logan.
1802......	75,000.....	....	Asa Danforth.
1803......	90,000.....	....	do
1804......	100,000.....	....	do
1805......	154,071.....	....	do
1806......	122,577.....	....	Wm. Kirkpatrick.
1807......	165,448.....	....	do
1808......	319,618.....	....	P. H. Ransom.
1809......	128,282.....	....	Nathan Stewart.
1810......	450,000.....	....	John Richardson.
1811......	200,000.....	....	Wm. Kirkpatrick.
1812......	221,011.....	....	do
1813......	226,000.....	....	do
1814......	295,000.....	....	do
1815......	322,058.....	....	do
1816......	348,665.....	....	do
1817......	408,665.....	....	do
1818......	406,540.....	....	do
1819......	548,374.....	....	do
1820......	558,329.....	....	do
1821......	526,049.....	....	do

Date.	No. of Bushels.	Solar.	Superintendent.
1822......	481,562.....	....	Wm. Kirkpatrick.
1823......	726,988.....	....	do
1824......	816,634.....	....	do
1825......	757,203.....	....	do
1826......	811,023.....	....	do
1827......	983,410.....	....	do
1828......	1,160,888.....	....	do
1829......	1,129,280.....	....	do
1830......	1,435,446.....	....	do
1831......	1,514,037.....	....	N. H. Earll.
1832......	1,652,985.....	....	do
1833......	1,838,646.....	....	do
1834......	1,943,252.....	....	do
1835......	2,209,867.....	....	do
1836......	1,912,858.....	....	Rial Wright.
1837......	2,167,287.....	....	do
1838......	2,575,033.....	....	do
1839......	2,864,718.....	....	do
1840......	2,622,305.....	....	Thomas Spencer.
1841......	3,340,767.....	220,247....	do
1842......	2,291,903.....	163,021....	do
1843......	3,127,500.....	318,105....	Rial Wright.
1844......	4,300,554.....	332,418....	do
1845......	3,762,358.....	353,455....	Enoch Marks.
1846......	3,838,851.....	331,705....	do
1847......	3,951,355.....	262,879....	do
1848......	4,737,126.....	342,497....	Robert Gere.
1849......	5,083,569.....	377,735....	do
1850......	4,268,919.....	374,732....	do
1851......	4,614,117.....	378,967....	do
1852......	4,922,533.....	633,595....	Hervey Rhoades.
1853......	5,404,524.....	577,947....	do
1854......	5,803,347.....	734,474....	do
1855......	6,082,885.....	498,124....	Vivus W. Smith.
1856......	5,966,810.....	709,391....	do
1857......	4,312,126.....	481,280....	do
1858......	7,033,219.....	1,514,554....	do
1859......	6,894,272.....	1,345,022....	do
1860......	5,593,247.....	1,462,565....	do

DATE.	NO. OF BUSHELS.	SOLAR.	SUPERINTENDENT.
1861......	7,200,391.....	1,884,697....	Vivus W. Smith.
1862......	9,053,874.....	10,983,22....	do
1863......	7,942,383.....	1,437,656....	do
1864......	7,378,834.....	1,971,122....	do
1865......	6,385,930.....	1,886,760....	George Geddes.
1866......	7,158,503.....	1,978,183....	do
Total,	175,857,072	22,554,153	

Fifth Interrogatory.—"The annual ratio of increase and diminution of production."

By reference to the table given under the fourth interrogatory, a satisfactory answer, I think, will be had.

Sixth Interrogatory.—"The principal causes which operate to produce an increase or diminution of the yearly production of salt."

The demands of the consumers of salt tend greatly to regulate the production. By reference to the table of production given under the fourth interrogatory, it will appear that in 1857, which was the year of bank suspension, the demand so fell off that there was less salt sold that year than had been in any one year since 1850; and by reference to 1858, it will be seen that the demand was greatly increased to supply salt that in ordinary times would have been taken in 1857. This fluctuation is fully explained by the state of the finances of the country, and was exceptional. So in 1862, the production of salt was greatly stimulated by the closing of the Mississippi river, by the rebellion, against the importation of foreign salt to the markets bordering on the upper part of that river.

Generally it will appear from the table, that as population has increased in the localities supplied by our salt, that the demand has grown from decade to decade. The last ten years does not show the usual ratio of increase, as during that period the salines of the State of Michigan have been developed, and have sent a large quantity of salt to markets that formerly were supplied by our salt. The following table gives the average annual production in each period of ten years, from 1797 to 1867.

				Bushels.
From 1797 to 1806 the average annual production was				78,000
1807 to 1816	do	do	do	267,000
1817 to 1826	do	do	do	608,000
1827 to 1836	do	do	do	1,594,000
1837 to 1846	do	do	do	3,058,000
1847 to 1856	do	do	do	5,083,000
1857 to 1866	do	do	do	6,895,277

(See Report 1861, Assembly Doc. 26, page 17.)

During the year 1866, it is believed that two millions and three quarters of bushels of Michigan salt was sent to markets that before the discovery of salt water in the Saginaw Valley, were supplied from our salines. This competition has made the cost of fuel and labor, and the strength and supply of water at such times as the manufacturer can most advantageously make salt, of much greater importance than these things were when there was no competition except from imported salt.

Seventh Interrogatory—"The facilities, such as wells, pumps, reservoirs, aqueducts, machinery, labor or otherwise, which the State furnish in the manufacture of salt; showing the share of the cost per barrel borne by the State in proportion to the whole expense thereof."

The State sinks the wells, pumps water into reservoirs, and conveys it in conduits to the works of the manufacturers, who have to connect their cisterns by pipes with the main conduits that the State lays along side. The pumps are mostly driven by water power, taken from the Erie and Oswego canals; one 16 horse power steam engine, being all the steam power now used.

The machinery is adequate to pump and distribute all the water the present wells produce. The reservoirs now in use consist of one large earth reservoir near the Syracuse pump-house, that holds over 20,000,000 of gallons, and a reservoir constructed of timber at the same pump-house.

At Salina (1st ward of Syracuse) there are six (6) reservoirs made of timber; at Liverpool, two of timber, and at Geddes, two of timber. All these except the one of earth, are mere distributing reservoirs.

The aqueducts have been estimated to equal forty miles in length for distributing the salt water to the various manufacturers.

The present value of the wells, pumps, reservoirs, aqueducts and machinery, has been estimated as follows:

15 salt wells now in use, $3,000 each,.................	$45,000
6 Rotary pumps, $250 each,..........................	1,500
1 Pump-house and machinery, at Geddes,.............	15,000
1 do do Syracuse, 3d ward,...	30,000
1 do do 1st do......	35,000
Old pump-house, at Syracuse, worn out, probably cost,...	15,000
3 high reservoirs, 1 in 3d ward, 1 in 1st ward, Syracuse, and 1 at Geddes, at $5,000 each,...............	15,000
8 reservoirs at Syracuse, Geddes and Liverpool, $2,500 each,	20,000
1 earth storage reservoir, at Syracuse, 3d ward,.........	20,000
40 miles of aqueducts, now worth 55c., as estimated, per lineal foot,.................................	116,160
1 dressed stone office, 3d ward, Syracuse,..............	7,500
1 brick office in 1st ward, one-half of it used for Canal Collector's office,..................................	4,000
1 brick office at Liverpool,..........................	800
1 do Geddes, ...	800
1 barrel stand, at 1st ward,...........................	350
1 do Liverpool, ...	250
1 do Geddes, ...	350
	$311,710

As to the "share of cost per barrel borne by the State," the only answer I can make is to say that since 1846, when the duties were fixed at one cent a bushel, there has been made 123,726,815 bushels of salt, which has paid in duties $1,237,268.15, of which three has gone into the treasury of the State, over and above the sums disbursed through this office on account of expenses of the salt springs, $421,582.55, leaving $815,685.60, as the amount paid through this office.

To this sum should be added $7,000 paid by the Comptroller for debts contracted previous to the first day of March, 1865, as directed by law; this sum being added, gives $822,685.60 as the total sum expended by the State on account of the salt springs, for the twenty-one years that include 1846 and 1866. This divided by the number of bushels made, gives less than seven mills (6.65) that has been expended by the State for each bushel of salt produced. This, reduced to barrels, as in the interrogatory, is three cents, three mills and a quarter per barrel.

This sum has paid all the salaries of the officers that have superintended the manufacture, and inspected, weighed and branded all this salt, and that have inspected all the barrels used, and has paid for all the labor and material employed in laying and keeping in order the conduits, buildings and machinery, and has constructed the earth reservoir at an expense of over $20,000, and has constructed a stone three story pump-house in the first district, which with the machinery in it, cost as near as can now be ascertained $30,000. Another stone pump-house in the fourth district (Geddes), that with its machinery cost about $15,000, and the central office of dressed stone, that is estimated to have cost $7,500. These are leading items, but there are many more improvements that have been made to the works within this period of twenty-one years.

The cost of salt to the manufacturer is now, as near as I can determine ($2.03) two dollars and three cents a barrel for boiled salt, and for solar salt ($1.46) one dollar and forty-six cents per barrel.

Eighth Interrogatory.—"The minimum, maximum and average price at which salt has been sold at the works during the last twenty years."

To answer this interrogatory, the books of Timothy R. Porter, Esq., a well-known and large manufacturer of salt, have been carefully examined, and taken as a guide from 1847 to 1859 inclusive. From 1859 to this time the books of the salt Company of Onondaga have been taken, as that company during this period has sold most of the salt made here.

Date.	Maximum Price.	Minimum Price.	Average Price.	Date.	Maximum Price.	Minimum Price.	Average Price.
1847,..	$1 56	$0 87½	$1 17	1858,..	$1 33	$1 25	$1 27
1848,..	1 06	75	93	1859,..	1 00	83	90
1849,..	80	70	77	1860,..	1 25	1 25	1 25
1850,..	1 50	1 25	1 19	1861,..	1 25	1 25	1 25
1851,..	1 25	1 25	1 25	1862,..	1 50	1 25	1 40
1852,..	1 00	1 00	1 00	1863,..	2 45	1 70	1 99
1853,..	1 50	1 12½	1 18	1864,..	3 25	2 00	2 70
1854,..	1 40	1 30	1 34	1865,..	2 50	2 10	2 26
1855,..	1 30	1 30	1 30	1866,..	2 35	2 35	2 35
1856,..	1 60	1 25	1 41	1867,..	2 35	2 35	2 35
1857,..	1 25	1 25	1 25				

Ninth Interrogatory.—"The present price of salt." Two dollars and thirty-five cents a barrel.

Tenth Interrogatory.—"The whole number of fine salt manufactories or blocks, and the capacity, and the value thereof, now on the reservation, and by whom owned."

There are now on the reservation, entitled to an equal participation in the use of salt water, 316 salt blocks, or the remains of blocks, as stated in the following schedule.

The capacity of the blocks to make salt, if all were put in operation and kept supplied with water, would be not less than the production of from 12 to 15 millions of bushels during the season of eight months.

The names of the owners of these blocks appear in the schedule. The value of blocks is not certainly determined, but taking the sales of the two or three years last past for a guide, they may be divided into classes as follows:

1st class, of which there are	215,	valued at $8,000.....	$1,720,000
2d " " "	66,	" " 5,500.....	363,000
3d " " "	35,	" " 3,500.....	122,500
Total number of Blocks,...	316	Total value, ...	$2,205,500

In connection with the salt manufactories are six mills for grinding salt, owned and valued as follows:

James P. Haskin's mill, estimated to be worth,			....	$40,000
John W. Barker & Co.,	"	" "	....	40,000
Henry B. & Wilmot E. Burton,		" "	....	16,000
Timothy R. Porter,	"	" "	....	16,000
Ashton Salt Company,	"	" "	....	16,000
H. White,	"	" "	....	10,000
				$138,000

In this estimate of the value of salt blocks, is included the advantages the owner has in the use of the lot, which is leased to him by the State, and the right to participate in the use of the salt water. The present cost of construction of a first class block, with the necessary cisterns and appurtenances, would be from seven to eight thousand dollars, according to location.

Besides the blocks enumerated in the schedule, there is a triple block, owned by James P. Haskin, and two blocks, owned by James Spencer, situated on private lands, and constructed since the passage of the law of 1859, and that are not entitled to salt water until the 316, above enumerated, are supplied.

Schedule of Owners of Salt Blocks in the Onondaga Salt Springs Reservation.

Owners of Blocks.	Nos. of Blocks.	No. of Inspection District.	
J. H. Parker,...........	1	1	On leased land.
P. Hall,................	2	1	" "
I. S. Auburn,...........	3, 4	1	" "
S. Stafford,............	5	1	" "
S. Kent,................	6	1	" "
L. Hulin,...............	7	1	" "
J. H. Sweet,............	8	1	" "
J. Ryan,................	9	1	" "
H. Huntley,.............	10	1	" "
D. Reigle,..............	11	1	" "
E. Ryan,................	12	1	" "
John White,.............	13, 14	1	" "
P. Hall,................	15	1	" "

Owners of Blocks.	Nos. of Blocks.	No. of Inspection District.	
Crowell & Baker, ...	16	1	On leased land.
P. Hall, ...	17	1	" "
W W. Fairfield, ...	18	1	" "
B. Yorkey, ...	19	1	" "
P. Miller, ...	20	1	" "
H. Ackerman, ...	21, 22	1	" "
P. Wood, ...	23	1	" "
P. Reese, ...	24	1	" "
R. Maley, ...	25	1	" "
M. Brown, ...	26	1	" "
A. Listman, ...	27, 28	1	" "
T. R. Porter, ...	29	1	" "
F. Schneider, ...	30	1	" "
A. J. Lynch, ...	31	1	" "
J. D. P. Douw, ...	32, 33, 34	1	" "
J. Lynch, ...	35	1	" "
L. Power, ...	36, 37	1	" "
R. Ryan, ...	38	1	" "
J. Fitzgerald, ...	39	1	" "
J. Pfohl, ...	40	1	" "
J. Lynch, ...	41	1	" "
F. Schneider, ...	42	1	" "
C. Franchot & Co., ...	43, 44, 45, 46	1	On private land, or on coarse salt land.
Wood & Spencer, ...	47	1	On leased land.
New York Cen. R. R. Co.,*	48, 49, 50	1	On private land.
M. Beardslee, ...	51, 52	1	" "
John Stacey, ...	1, 2	2	" "
John Shannahan, ...	3	2	" "
W. Rubell, ...	4	2	" "
J. Dolphin, ...	5	2	" "
J. Lynch, ...	6	2	" "
G. Zimmerman, ...	7	2	" "
P. Fitzgerald, ...	8	2	" "
J. Prendergast & Co., ...	9	2	" "
J. Fitzgerald, ...	10, 11	2	" "

* Blocks 48, 49 and 50 have been taken down, and the ground is unused as yet.

Owners of Blocks.	Nos. of Blocks.	No. of Inspection District.	
T. R. Porter, ...	12, 13, 14, 15	2	On private land.
"	16, 16½, 17, 17½	2	" "
N. M. Childs, ...	18, 19, 20	2	" "
M. E. Lynch, ...	21	2	" "
G. A. Clark, ...	22	2	" "
F. Morrell, ...	23	2	" "
J. Cawley, ...	24	2	" "
R. Mara, ...	25	2	" "
N. M. Childs, ...	26, 27	2	" "
J. & M. Salmon, ...	28, 29	2	" "
A. H. Nutting, ...	30	2	" "
W. Barnes, ...	31, 32	2	" "
J. P. Haskin, ...	32½	2	" "
T. Cullivan, ...	33	2	On leased land.
Ford & Slattery, ...	34, 35, 36	2	" "
J. Cawley, ...	37	2	" "
Jas. Lynch, ...	38, 39, 40	2	" "
"	41, 42, 43	2	" "
T. & J. Comerford, ...	44, 45, 46	2	" "
E. B. Lynch, ...	47	2	" "
J. Ryan & others, ...	48	2	" "
R. Mara & J. Cawley, ...	49	2	" "
J. F. Barnes, ...	50, 50½	2	" "
J. W. Kellogg, ...	51	2	" "
G. J. & T. G. Doyle, ...	52	2	" "
R. Mara, ...	53	2	" "
M. Murray, ...	54, 55	2	" "
C. B. Williams, ...	56	2	" "
P. Cawley, ...	57	2	" "
M. McKeever, ...	58	2	" "
J. Shannon, ...	59	2	" "
J. Griffin, ...	60	2	On private land.
M. Cooney, ...	61, 62	2	On leased land.
C. Cooney, ...	63	2	" "
M. McKeever, ...	64, 65	2	" "
J. Keeffe, ...	66	2	" "
J. Griffin, ...	67	2	" "

Owners of Blocks.	Nos. of Blocks.	No. of Inspection District.	
J. Spencer,	68	2	On leased land.
O. W. Clark,	69	2	" "
D. S. Clark,	70	2	" "
P. Molloy,	71	2	" "
R. Farrell & Co.,	72, 73	2	" "
J. Shannon,	74	2	" "
M. Shannon,	75	2	" "
P. Molloy,	76, 77	2	" "
J. Lynch,	78	2	" "
D. Keeffe,	79	2	" "
D. Dwyer,	80	2	" "
F. McChesney,	81	2	On private land.
D. S. Clark,	82	2	" "
Mrs. A. Clark,	83, 84	2	" "
C. H. Usenbentz,	85, 86	2	" "
R. Farrell & Co.,	87	2	" "
Mrs. A. Clark,	88	2	On leased land 1 half.
Wm. Butler,	89, 90	2	" "
J. P. Babcock,	91	2	" "
D. Luther,	92	2	On leased land.
G. A. & D. S. Clark,	93	2	" "
J. Harvey,	94	2	" "
Burr Burton Estate,	95, 95½, 96	2	" "
P. S. Avery,	97	2	" "
M. Cooney,	98	2	On private land.
J. Hartshorn,	99	2	On leased land.
D. & J. Murray,	100, 101	2	" "
P. Cooney, Jr.,	102	2	" "
W. Dunn,	103	2	" "
M. Murray,	104, 105, 106	2	On private land.
A. Blake,	107	2	" "
G. Doyle,	108	2	" "
M. R. Avery,	109	2	" "
P. Cooney,	110, 111	2	" "
J. P. Haskin,	112, 113, 114	2	" "
do	115, 116, 117	2	" "
do	118, 119	2	" "
J. H. Childs,	120	2	" "

Owners of Blocks.	Nos. of Blocks.	No. of Inspection District.	
J. Griffin, ...	121	2	On private land.
T. G. & J. Doyle, ...	122, 123	2	" "
P. Lynch, ...	124	2	" "
J. Scott, ...	125	2	On leased land.
G. L. Avery, ...	126, 127	2	" "
J. Spencer, ...	128	2	" "
A. Crippen, ...	129, 130, 131	2	" "
A. L. Mason, ...	132	2	" "
O. W. Clark, ...	133, 134	2	" "
A. L., Mason, ...	135	2	" "
D. & J. Murray, ...	136	2	" "
J. P. Haskin, ...	137	2	On private land.
P. S. Avery, ...	138	2	On leased land.
T. R. Porter, ...	139	2	" "
W. H. Hoyt, ...	140	2	On private land.
The Salina C. & F. S. Co.,	141, 142, 143	2	" "
J. Scott, ...	144	2	On leased land.
C. P. Kingsley, ...	145	2	" "
J. McCann, ...	146	2	On private land.
J. Lynch, ...	147	2	" "
J. O. S. & T. P. Lynch, ..	148	2	" "
J. Spencer, ...	149	2	" "
T. G. & J. Doyle, ...	150	2	" "
P. Ford, ...	151	2	" "
S. Jaqueth, ...	1	3	" "
L. Gleason, ...	2	3	" "
Frank Alvord, ...	3	3	On leased land.
L. Gleason, ...	4	3	" "
James Scott, ...	5	3	" "
Justus Corbin, ...	6, 7	3	" "
Warner & Rowan, ...	8, 9	3	" "
John Nelson, ...	10	3	" "
A. & J. Downie, ...	11, 12	3	" "
P. Hutchins, ...	13	3	" "
Wm. Manly, ...	14, 15	3	" "
T. Hinckley, ...	16, 17	3	" "
Frank Alvord, ...	18	3	" "
S. Seward, ...	19	3	" "

Owners of Blocks.	Nos. of Blocks.	No. of Inspection District.	
W. J. Machan, ...	20	3	On leased land.
W. H. Seymour, ...	21	3	" "
D. P. Wood, ...	22	3	" "
Bonta & Son, ...	23, 24	3	" "
H. L. Packer, ...	25	3	On private land.
Lucius Larkin, ...	26	3	" "
W. H. Slocum, ...	27	3	" "
J. Olmsted, ...	28	3	" "
Mrs. H. J. Beggs, ...	29	3	" "
J. Bassett, ...	30	3	" "
Peter Smith, ...	31	3	" "
Pettilon, Mentz & J., ...	32	3	" "
R. Savage, ...	33, 34	3	" "
Bassett & Cornell, ...	35	3	" "
James Hardy, ...	36	3	" "
J. Bassett, ...	37	3	" "
L. Gleason, ...	38	3	" "
D. P. Wood, ...	39, 40	3	" "
Liverpool C. S. Co., ...	41	3	" "
L. Gleason, ...	42	3	" "
Mrs. H. J. Beggs, ...	43	3	" "
H. W. Slocum, ...	44	3	" "
Henry Wyker, ...	½ of 45	3	" "
John Paddock, ...	½ of 45	3	" "
L. Gleason, ...	46, 47	3	46 Private land. 47 Leased land.
C. Warner, ...	48	3	On leased land.
J. Van Alstyne, ...	49	3	" "
Jesse McKinley, ...	50, 51	4	" "
E. Pierce, ...	52, 53	3	" "
P. Hutchins, ...	54	3	" "
R. Savage, ...	55	3	" "
S. Jaqueth, ...	56	3	" "
Dual & Alvord, ...	57	3	On Private land.
A. & J. Downie, ...	58	3	" "
A. McKinley, ...	59	3	" "
Mrs. E. A. Sitterly, ...	½ of 60	3	" "
Geo. Everson, ...	½ of 60, 61	3	On leased land.

Owners of Blocks.	Nos. of Blocks.	No. of Inspection District.	
L. H. Ward,.............	62	3	On private land.
M. M. Willey, ...	1	4	" "
G. Woodson,............	½ of 2	4	" "
Wm. F. Gere,...........	½ of 2	4	" "
J. D. & W. E. Rose,......	3, 4	4	" "
Woolson & Pratt,........	5, 6	4	On leased land.
Harvey Stewart, ...	7, 8	4	" "
J. W. Barker,...........	9	4	" "
H. Duncan,......... ...	10	4	" "
John White,............	11	4	" "
W. F. Gere, ...	12	4	" "
Henry Vroman,.........	13	4	" "
H. Stewart,.............	14	4	" "
G. F. Comstock,.........	15, 16, 17, 18	4	" "
I. R. Pharis, ...	19	4	" "
Pharis & Nye, ...	20	4	" "
H. Stewart,.............	21	4	" "
I. R. & C. E. Pharis,.....	22, 23	4	" "
F. H. Nye,.............	24	4	" "
J. W. Sammons, ...	25	4	" "
A. S. Avery,............	26	4	" "
H. H. Pratt,............	27	4	" "
I. R. Pharis, ...	28	4	" "
H. Stewart,.............	29, 30	4	" "
D. Driscoll, Jr., ...	31	4	" "
The Salt Co. of Onon.,...	32, 33	4	" "
Burgess & Nye, ...	34, 35	4	" "
A. Woolson,............	36	4	" "
J. J. Peck, ...	37	4	" "
S. C. Brewster,..........	38	4	" "
D. &. P. Coykendall,.....	39, 40, 41,	4	" "
" "	42, 43	4	" "
D. Coykendall,..........	44	4	" "
Wm. Dunn, ...	45, 46	4	" "

Eleventh Interrogatory.—"The number of coarse or solar vats or covers, by whom owned, and the value thereof."

Some confusion has heretofore existed in regard to what was meant by a "Solar vat or cover," as they are not all of the same dimensions. By common consent, a section that measures sixteen by eighteen feet (16x18 feet), of one of the vats, is now considered as the standard. I report a table giving the names of the individuals or companies owning, and the number of covers owned by each. From this table it appears that by count, the total number of covers is 44,083, and that reduced to standard covers of 16 by 18 feet, there are only 41,781.

These vats, 16 by 18 feet, with the store-houses, roads, and neces sary conveniences, are now worth $57 each, making an aggregate of $2,381,517. (See report for 1866, Assembly, *Doc.* 19, page 7).

These vats are estimated as capable of producing fifty (50) bushels of salt to the cover, during an average season. This would give 2,089,050 bushels in a year, but this quantity has never yet been equaled. The greatest production was in the year 1862, and amounted to 1,983,022 bushels.

SCHEDULE of owners of Coarse Salt Fields.

OWNERS.	Whole No. of covers by count.	Reduced to 16x18 standard.
Western Coarse Salt Co.,	2,545	2,497
James M. Gere,	416	416
Draper & Porter,	454	430
J. A. Robinson & Co.,	809	808
Turk's Island Coarse Salt Co.,	1,080	1,053
Geddes Coarse Salt Co.,	2,526	2,379
W. & G. Kirkpatrick,	1,502	1,335
S. C. Brewster,	517	517
J. F. Paige,	485	466
Union Coarse Salt Co.,	3,387	3,379
Cape Cod Coarse Salt Co.,	1,831	1,831
John White & Co.,	1,057	1,057
L. Stevens & Co.,	1,035	1,033
Onondaga Solar Salt Co.,	1,765	1,765
Syracuse Solar Salt Co.,	3,132	3,132
C. Franchot & Co.,	220	220
Empire Coarse Salt Co.,	1.913	1,700
Salt Springs Solar Coarse Salt Co.,	4,333	3,852
Salina Coarse and Fine Salt Co.,	999	916
Salina Solar Coarse Salt Co.,	3,609	3,208
Thomas Gale,	1,967	1,897
Soule, Wright & Doyle,	999	888
Highland Coarse Salt Co.,	2,059	2,054
Liverpool Coarse Salt Co.,	963	859
John Paddock,	354	316
R. N. & N. S. Gere,	509	509
Heacock & Berry,	1,251	1,112
D. S. Earll,	703	655
Thomas Gale,	988	897
S. Stevens & Sons,	675	600
	44,083	41,781

Twelfth Interrogatory.—"The quantity of salt lands leased, to whom, at what rent, and for what term of time."

Thirty-three acres of marsh land at the mouth of Onondaga creek, a large part of it covered with water and flags, and on it six salt wells now in use, and running across it several lines of salt water logs, and having on it a pump-house, with a steam-engine in it. The pasturage on this land is leased to Jabez Hungerford for this year for $15.

Another piece of land containing one acre and 26-100 of land, known as the "Chlorine spring lot," is leased to Julio H. Rae, under a special act, chap. 204, Laws of 1866. Lease runs to 1889, at an annual rent of $25, to 1868, and after that $60, to the end of the term.

Another piece known as city lots 15 and 16, of block 423, leased to Edwin Miles for one year at $10.

These are all the pieces of land that the State receives rent for directly. The other lands being leased for manufacturing salt, pay no rent except in the form of duties on the salt made.

It is not practicable for me to state the exact quantity of land that the salt blocks occupy, without consuming more time than I suppose should be given to this matter. There are maps in this office, giving all the particulars of each lot by its boundaries. It would take a long time to transcribe and compute the contents.

The lots are of no uniform shape or size, but from computing several of them, I think they average about one-fourth of an acre each

Nearly one-third of these blocks are on private land, as will appear from the schedule. There are about 216 on State leased land; this would give, as used for boiling works, 54 acres of State land.

Blocks 1, 2, 3, 4, 5, 6, 7, and 8, situated in the first district, have leases for five years, from 1859, renewable in periods of not more than five years; all the other blocks have leases, or are entitled to them, that run to 1889. By reference to the schedule under the tenth interrogatory, the names of the persons to whom these lots are leased, will appear.

The grants of lands for the manufacture of Solar salt, are made by the Commissioners of the Land Office (and are perpetual for salt purposes), and in that office the only official record is to be found. I have taken from a large map, owned by the Salt Company of Onondaga, such information as it contained, and by consulting the grantees, procured other information that I thought would be of value, and submit the same in the following schedule, giving the number of acres of State land granted to each grantee, the number of acres used by the grantee for making solar salt; that is not the land of the State, but belongs to the party using it, and the total acres used by each party.

Although this schedule is not made up from official information, it is believed to be substantially correct; and so far as relates to the land owned by the State, it is probably within a few acres of being correct.

SCHEDULE of State land granted, &c.

Occupants.	Number of Acres in grant or used.	Number of Acres owned by State.	No. of Acres owned by o'rs than State.
Western Coarse Salt Co.,	61.15	60.15	1.00
James M. Gere,	9.45	9.45	
Draper & Porter,	7.37	7.37	
J. A. Robinson & Co.,	14.26	14.26	
Turks Island Coarse Salt Co.,	20.00	20.00	
Geddes Coarse Salt Co.,	46.83	46.83	
W. & D. Kirkpatrick,	25.00	15.00	10.00
S. C. Brewster,	10.00	10.00	
J. F. Paige,	10.00	10.00	
Union Coarse Salt Co.,	99.12	99.12	
Cape Cod Coarse Salt Co.,	30.50	30.50	
John White & Co.,	19.40	19.40	
L. Stevens & Co.,	24.00	24.00	
Onondaga Solar Salt Co.,	31.00	31.00	
Syracuse Solar Salt Co.,	55.58	28.85	26.73
C. Franchot & Co.,	3.54	3.54	
Empire Coarse Salt Co.,	29.45	....	29.45
Salt Springs Coarse Salt Co.,	66.12	25.00	41.12
Salina Coarse Salt Co.,	60.00	40.00	20.00
Heacock & Berry,	25.00	18.82	6.18
Salina Coarse and Fine Salt Co.,	36.00	36.00	
Thos. Gale,	40.00	38.00	2.00
Soule, Wright & Doyle,	21.50	21.50	
D. S. Earll,	23.00	23.00	
Thos. Gale,	57.00	57.00	
Highland Coarse Salt Co.,	38.75	38.75	
Liverpool Coarse Salt Co.,	22.79	22.79	
John Paddock,	16.82	....	16.82
R. N. & N. S. Gere,	4.55	4.55	
Jerome J. Briggs,	20.00	....	20.00
	928.18	754.88	173.30

Thirteenth Interrogatory.—"The amount of money received for duties on coarse or solar salt since 1845:"

Two hundred and fifteen thousand, two hundred and three dollars and sixty-two cents ($215,203.62).

Fourteenth Interrogatory.—"The cost to the State of its pro rata share thereof for expenses incurred in the manufacture of coarse or solar salt, during the same period:"

There is no reason to suppose that it costs the State any more or less to furnish water for solar than for boiled salt—therefore, the answer is, three cents, three mills and a quarter per barrel.

In replying to the foregoing interrogatories, I have aimed to answer, as well as I could, not only to the exact question asked, but to give such further information as was in my possession, that I supposed would aid the committee and the Convention, in arriving at the whole facts in regard to the interests that the State has in the Onondaga Salt Springs.

Such are the interests of the State and of the manufacturers, and so interwoven are they, that I will venture to take the liberty of suggesting that the committee would derive much valuable information, by visiting and personally inspecting the property of the State, and of the persons who have embarked their capital in the manufacture of salt.

I cannot doubt but that many things would suggest themselves, that nothing but such an examination would be likely to bring to the mind of a person drawing up interrogatories, or to a person answering them. Respectfully submitted by,

GEO. GEDDES,

Superintendent of Onondaga Salt Springs.

STATE OF NEW YORK.

No. 20.

IN CONVENTION

July 9, 1867.

MEMORIAL

TO THE CONSTITUTIONAL CONVENTION OF NEW YORK IN REFERENCE TO THE GENESEE VALLEY CANAL.

To the Honorable the Constitutional Convention for the State of New York, assembled at Albany.

The memorial of the undersigned citizens of the county of McKean, and commonwealth of Pennsylvania, respectfully represents:

We have learned, with sorrow and surprise, a proposition is now pending before your honorable body for a discontinuance or abandonment of the Genesee Valley canal.

We feel confident such a proposition would not for a moment be entertained if the people of your State and the members of your Convention were fully advised of its certain prospective financial value, its importance as a feeder to the Erie canal, and as affording the means of supply to your mechanical and manufacturing interests.

You cannot correctly judge of it by what it has done or to this time has failed to do.

Its incomplete condition and small capacity for transportation has deterred parties who would desire to employ it, from making the considerable outlays for placing freight on it which would otherwise have been done, and which would at once be done, if they could be assured it would be made a reliable means of transportation.

We beg leave respectfully to call your attention to a few facts.

The Genesee Valley Canal terminates at the Allegany River, with which it is united by a lock at Millgrove, one mile from the south line of your State. It practically terminates in Pennsylvania, ten miles south of the line of your State, as the river is navigable for boats for that distance and has been constantly used for their transportation since the canal has been built. A steam tug is now making daily trips from the southern terminus of the canal ten miles up the Allegany river.

The county of McKean in Pennsylvania, which lies immediately adjoining Cattaraugus and Allegany, in your own State, contains extensive deposits of bituminous coal of superiour quality for the forge, for gas, fuel and generating steam.

Its quantity and quality have been fully demonstrated, and though some parties who have made investments in coal lands in McKean county, have been disappointed and deceived in the character of the lands they purchased; all who are at all conversant with this region, admit the large extent and good quality of the coal. With the reasonable price afforded by water transportation, the demand for it in western New York and southern Canada, will be only measured by the supply.

It will be reached in ample quantities at the distance of fourteen to twenty-two miles from the G. V. canal.

A charter was procured from the Legislature of Pennsylvania at its last session, authorizing the improvement of the Allegany river, from the terminus of the Genesee Valley canal and the construction of a canal or railroad thence to the coal mines. It is confidently expected work will soon commence on this improvement, particularly if the capitalists, who have it in contemplation, can be assured the Genesee Valley canal will be held and maintained in a condition to render it a reliable means of transportation for the heavy freight which will thus be thrown upon it. It will be safe to say this improvement will give the G. V. canal in coal alone, one thousand tons per day during the season of canal navigation, from the Bunker Hill mines, near Bishop's summit. Immediately south of this lie the extensive coal fields of Elk and Cameron counties.

There are now in full working operation, not less than ten companies, who are shipping by the P. & E. R. R., all of whom are earnestly desirous of sending their coal North to market, and would do so via the Genesee Valley canal, if it could be relied on. From these and the anthracite and bituminous coal regions further south, vast quantities will also be thrown upon this canal, by the Buffalo and Washington Railroad, which is to be immediately constructed.

This railroad is now under contract, and work will commence on it in this State as soon as the proper surveys can be made, engineers now being engaged in completing its location. It will connect with the P. & E. R. R., at Emporium, in Cameron county, and run north, crossing the Genesee Valley canal at Portville or Olean.

In addition to this freight, there will be afforded millions upon millions of lumber annually, this whole region being heavily covered with valuable timber. The country also abounds in iron ore, which, at no distant day, will be extensively worked, and will look to your State for a market.

There is now constructed and fully equipped, a first class railroad, running from the Erie Railway at Carrolton, to the Lafayette coal mines in this county, a distance of twenty-five miles.

By this road, and using the Erie Railway for the distance of eleven miles, the Genesee Valley canal is reached at Olean.

There are now organized at Lafayette, six coal companies, to wit: The McKean Co., bituminous, with a present capacity for producing and delivering by their lateral railroads one hundred tons per day, and have prepared a place at Cuba for the transhipment of their coal from the cars to the boats of the Genesee Valley canal. The Lafayette Coal Company are now shipping one hundred and fifty tons per day via Dunkirk to Buffalo and Rochester. This Company shipped last year by the Genesee Valley canal, one thousand five hundred tons, and would have shipped one hundred tons per day if the canal had been in good order, and would now ship three hundred tons per day if they had the means of cheap water communication.

They also have a chute at Dunkirk for transhipment to boats on the lake.

The Bond Vein Coal Company are shipping fifty tons per day. The Kinzua Coal Company are prepared to ship seventy-five tons per day. The Longwood Coal Company are shipping fifty tons per day. The Tunungwunt Coal Company have their mines opened and are prepared to ship seventy-five tons per day.

It has been estimated by persons competent to judge, that from the Lafayette Coal field alone, there could be delivered, next season, two thousand tons per day, and much the greater part, would seek a market by this canal if it could be relied on.

Connected with this memorial, we send a map showing very accurately the true position of this mineral region to your State, and its public improvements, with distances, elevations, &c., to a careful examination of which we respectfully beg your attention.

SMITHPORT, *July* 5, 1867.

SETH A. BACKUS,
and 39 *others.*

STATE OF NEW YORK.

No. 21.

IN CONVENTION

July 9, 1867.

COMMUNICATION

FROM STATE ENGINEER AND SURVEYOR RELATIVE TO FREIGHT ON RAILROADS.

OFFICE OF THE STATE ENGINEER AND SURVEYOR,
ALBANY, *July* 9, 1867.

Hon. WILLIAM A. WHEELER, *President of the Constitutional Convention:*

SIR: I have the honor to transmit herewith a report in answer to a resolution of the Convention, adopted June 26, 1867.

Very respectfully,

J. P. GOODSELL,

State Engineer and Surveyor.

REPORT.

Sir—In reply to the following:

On motion of Mr. Van Campen,

"*Resolved*, That the State Engineer and Surveyor be requested, at his earliest convenience, to furnish in a tabular form, from the reports of the railroad companies of the State, from the 30th day of September, 1850, to the 30th day of September, 1866, made in pursuance of Section 31, of chapter 140, of the laws of 1850, for the use of this House of Delegates; the total amount of freight in tons of 2,000 lbs. carried over each road—the number of tons carried one mile, with the amount of each kind of freight classified."

By order,

LUTHER CALDWELL, *Secretary*.

The State Engineer and Surveyor has the honor to submit the following tables:

Table "A" shows the total amount of freight carried over each railroad; the number of tons carried one mile, with the amount of each kind of freight classified, in each year from the 30th day of September, 1850, to the 30th day of September, 1866.

Table "B" shows the aggregate number of tons of freight carried in each year during the above-mentioned period, over all of the railroads of the State which reported to the State Engineer and Surveyor; with the number of tons carried one mile, and the amount of each kind of freight, classified.

Table "C" exhibits the amount of freight carried in successive years on some of the principal railroads, and the number of tons carried one mile, classified as in the preceding tables.

Respectfully submitted,

J. P. GOODSELL,

State Engineer and Surveyor.

TABLE A,—*Showing the total amount of Freight in Tons of 2000 lbs. carried over each Railroad, the number of tons carried one mile, with the amount of each kind of Freight classified. For the year ending September 30, 1851.*

NAME OF ROAD.	Am't of freight in tons of 2000 pounds.	Number of tons carried one mile.	AMOUNT OF EACH KIND OF FREIGHT IN TONS, CLASSIFIED.						
			Products of the forest.	Of animals.	Vegetable food.	Other agricultural products.	Manufactures.	Merchandise.	Other articles.
Albany and Schenectady	92,058	1,564,986	1,880	29,415	8,873	1,124	4,800	32,240	13,726
Albany and West Stockbridge.	185,119	6,479,165	7,032	19,853	84,824	3,772	33,288	8,364	27,986
Buffalo and Niagara Falls	3,402	74,844	165	385	353	288	798	796	617
Buffalo and Rochester	48,880	3,010,730	2,972	11,238	7,034	1,063	8,003	14,122	4,448
Cayuga and Susquehanna	13,897	395,162	4,408	2,703	2,088	109	1,957	1,046	1,586
Hudson River	12,915	516,600	357	2,585	334	1,539	4,865	1,624	1,611
Hudson and Berkshire........	37,145	851,158	6,943	1,595	6,209	1,160	9,907	2,749	8,582
Long Island	32,000	....	....	....	....	......	....	....	....
New York and Erie	250,096	34,790,480	58,357	53,991	26,125	1,374	45,562	37,917	26,770
New York and Harlem,.......	47,904	2,399,435	255	18,194	6,665	1,659	1,800	19,020	321
New York and New Haven ...	60,525	Not given.	3,288	7,158	197	5,193	17,750	15,354	11,585
Northern (Ogdensburgh)	109,700	8,319,042	37,064	3,982	41,187	6,595	3,957	8,617	8,298
Oswego and Syracuse	19,992	426,748	12,609	408	3,864	113	444	1,599	955
Rensselaer and Saratoga	27,194	744,883	1,908	839	1,567	452	2,470	6,051	13,907
Rochester and Syracuse... ...	83,569	5,416,084	2,146	21,275	12,604	2,954	9,590	23,042	11,958
Washington and Saratoga.....	23,906	674,918	397	2,035	33	116	2,088	4,455	14,782
Schenectady and Troy........	15,898	325,909	417	6,010	3,524	293	1,610	2,735	1,309
Syracuse and Utica	86,849	3,734,507	5,130	33,972	17,574	1,389	6,203	9,566	13,015
Troy and Greenbush	29,449	176,697	2,021	6,581	8,354	74	3,567	481	8,371
Utica and Schenectady	115,750	5,579,150	4,848	44,105	16,527	1,459	7,922	30,552	10,233
Watertown and Rome........	34,307	1,062,166	21,652	2,708	900	91	1,633	7,030	291
Totals	1,330,555	76,542,664	173,849	269,032	248,826	30,817	168,214	227,360	180,351

TABLE A — (*Continued*) — *For the year ending September* 30, 1852.

NAME OF ROAD.	Am't of freight in tons of 2,000 pounds.	Number of tons carried one mile.	AMOUNT OF EACH KIND OF FREIGHT IN TONS, CLASSIFIED.						
			Products of the forest.	Of animals.	Vegetable food.	Other agricultural products.	Manufactures.	Merchandize.	Other articles.
Albany & Schenectady.	162,178	....	3,230	55,531	32,752	2,815	12,108	29,776	25,966
Albany & W. Stockbr'ge	158,323	5,933,777	7,342	21,703	81,418	5,474	25 985	6,163	10,238
Buffalo, Corning & N. Y.	10,155	174,917	6,482	160	360	90	2,498	346	219
Buffalo & Niag. Falls...	3,514	77,290	245	290	366	361	596	1,199	457
Buffalo & Rochester....	81,364	5,981,865	7,975	25,291	17,000	3,275	4,849	18,185	4,789
Buffalo & State Line ...	13,351	577,431	1,265	3,773	1,765	98	851	2,106	3,493
Canandaigua & Elmira.	16,331	751,226	1,381	4,238	5,020	846	1,466	2,429	951
Cayuga & Susquehanna.	65,498	2,021,211	9,853	1,839	5,696	238	2,804	981	44,087
Hudson River.........	65,046	7,643,678	1,018	22,248	3,497	9,820	10,630	14,078	3,755
Hudson & Berkshire...	38,560	800,118	2,351	1,581	5,087	1,864	7,270	2,440	17,967
Long Island,..........	49,549	1,610,321	19,886	518	3,819	778	537	2,583	21,428
New York & Erie	456,460	96,697,695	76,908	75,943	56,929	2,419	74,847	50,687	118,727
New York & Harlem...	68,248	....	2,438	34,124	15,250	853	6,824	3,400	5,359
New York & N. Haven.	65,064	....	7,263	10,420	6,183	10,169	12,459	11,326	7,244
Northern (Ogdensburgh)	181,809	16,594,139	46,311	7,412	83,863	14,344	7,712	17,682	4,485
Oswego & Syracuse....	23,117	614,491	14,495	464	4,443	130	510	1,839	1,236
Rensselaer & Saratoga..	50,215	1,326,357	2,536	2,638	5,297	1,639	4,313	9,689	24,103
Rochester & Syracuse ..	207,644	12,458,640	6,781	72,132	67,394	3,218	14,327	26,467	17,325
Roch. Lockp't & N. Falls	1,268	....	237	159	423	......	57	225	167
Saratoga & Washington	49,996	1,709,211	1,984	4,926	5,499	1,445	11,549	7,832	16,761
Schenectady & Troy...	32,080	657,640	3,169	10,226	8,335	2,083	2,027	3,041	3,199

Syracuse & Utica......	147,367	6,493,350	6,971	41,982	46,550	2,567	15,288	24,786	9,223
Troy & Boston........	13,582	369,882	100	800	500	50	150	11,900	82
Troy & Greenbush	62,483	374,900	3,196	9,598	7,407	937	6,439	623	34,283
Utica & Schenectady...	190,719	14,579,422	6,799	70,143	43,021	5,499	14,135	33,853	17,269
Watertown & Rome...	60,949	3,604,084	30,499	9,480	6,833	305	5,373	6,854	1,875
Totals	2,274,870	181,051,645	270,715	487,619	514,707	71,317	245,604	290,220	394,688

TABLE A—(*Continued*)—*For the year ending September* 30, 1853.

NAME OF ROAD.	Am't of freight in tons of 2000 pounds.	Number of tons carried one mile.	AMOUNT OF EACH KIND OF FREIGHT IN TONS, CLASSIFIED.						
			Products of the forest.	Of animals.	Vegetable food.	Other agricultural products.	Manufactures.	Merchandise.	Other articles.
†Albany & Schenect'dy	205,886	2,500,062	7,339	67,317	48,148	6,344	22,169	47,029	7,540
Alb'y & W. Stockb'dge	192,051	6,673,152	11,000	30,298	91,563	11,899	24,889	6,392	16,010
Buffalo, Cor'ng & N. Y.	24,189	672,177	12,744	499	4,601	84	3,631	1,577	1,023
Buffalo & N. Y. City	28,569	1,799,212	3,563	8,341	560	7,936	1,008	6,111	1,050
Buffalo & N. Falls	8,468	186,296	960	728	1,016	1,421	1,583	1,503	1,257
Buffalo & State Line	53,073	1,872,422	7,433	14,367	3,322	2,501	5,007	5,551	14,892
†Buffalo & Rochester	119,548	7,209,290	6,489	34,360	36,162	1,866	6,615	20,528	13,528
Cayuga & Susquehanna	69,774	2,147,057	10,305	1,631	4,689	312	3,410	2,634	46,793
Canandaigua & Elmira	36,501	1,760,092	4,534	6,472	13,195	426	4,068	4,483	3,323
Canandaigua & N. Falls	20,748	380,646	3,475	202	9,286	90	6,463	437	972
Hudson River	114,953	12,874,736	3,284	43,348	11,834	5,714	30,136	8,716	11,921
Long Island	52,603	2,322,990	10,632	1,202	4,185	1,503	1,055	5,049	28,977
N. Y. Central (2 mo's)	73,140	10,861,290	2,438	25,723	18,587	3,464	6,235	12,846	3,847
N. Y. & Harlem	101,197	....	8,851	38,659	10,076	2,764	15,181	3,966	21,700
N. Y. & Erie	631,039	101,626,522	124,087	99,755	80,868	9,849	112,281	68,742	135,457
North'rn (Ogdensb'rgh)	204,814	19,596,143	45,027	11,708	68,275	28,060	9,370	26,874	15,496
Oswego & Syracuse	39,489	1,039,515	24,550	831	7,787	227	892	3,226	1,976
Rens'laer & Saratoga & Saratoga & Scht'y	53,890	1,370,751	3,123	4,165	8,707	116	7,034	9,517	21,228
†Roch'str, L. & N. Falls	92,317	2,861,837	9,269	16,650	39,945	4,117	3,705	5,651	12,980
‡Rochester & Syracuse	82,749	4,964,940	4,774	19,359	31,683	1,741	8,253	3,534	13,405

Rutland & Washington	56,277	1,008,255	3,337	4,181	11,315	1,200	5,786	5,409	25,006
Saratoga & Washington	63,107	1,793,165	3,267	3,284	8,845	2,871	7,935	5,706	29,196
Sack'ts H'r & Ellisburg	1,715	25,525	1,067	33	342	17	156	80	20
†Schenectady & Troy .	39,497	809,703	5,049	6,796	10,934	855	4,206	4,501	7,156
†Syracuse & Utica....	185,588	8,177,466	31,048	62,492	39,364	7,144	25,916	3,192	16,432
*Troy & Boston......	49,578	1,528,281	2,595	6,498	6,914	843	4,149	9,514	18,965
Troy & Greenbush ...	69,299	415,798	4,020	13,291	13,862	652	12,665	5,109	19,700
†Utica & Schenectady.	211,906	16,316,762	7,555	77,936	47,801	6,111	15,705	37,610	19,188
Watertown & Rome ..	107,801	6,683,662	41,868	11,950	19,425	4,142	10,570	12,748	7,098
Totals,..........	2,989,766	219,477,747	403,723	612,076	653,291	114,269	360,073	328,235	516,136

* Includes Troy and Bennington.
† Includes only ten months.

TABLE A — (*Continued*) — *For the year ending September* 30, 1854.

NAME OF ROAD.	Am't of freight in tons of 2000 pounds.	Number of tons carried one mile.	AMOUNT OF EACH KIND OF FREIGHT IN TONS, CLASSIFIED.						
			Products of the forest.	Of animals.	Vegetable food.	Other agricultural products.	Manufactures	Merchandise.	Other articles.
Albany & W. Stockb'e	206,268	7,179,492	14,788	1,467	140,910	3,837	26,537	13,004	5,725
Blossburgh & Corning	72,202	1,067,149	29,792	....	....	....	....	1,374	41,036
Buffalo, Corning & N.Y	44,460	1,825,768	21,702	1,104	8,168	227	2,742	2,179	8,338
Buffalo & N. Y. City.	51,430	4,113,637	151	9,785	123	21,864	7,001	10,344	2,162
Buffalo & State Line..	81,042	4,807,946	4,570	43,783	3,796	436	4,490	7,521	16,446
Canandaigua & Elmira	38,359	1,855,347	2,142	10,478	12,245	1,432	3,978	2,876	5,208
Cayuga & Susquehanna	86,765	2,684,793	9,223	1,702	3,514	244	5,241	845	65,996
Flushing	40	200	....	....	....	....	....	....	40
Hudson River	156,715	18,141,520	4,203	32,038	19,301	12,632	35,525	18,859	34,158
Long Island	56,432	2,483,008	12,942	3,114	5,756	5,802	1,986	5,582	21,250
New York Central ...	549,805	81,168,080	45,530	115,417	156,204	10,935	52,244	94,643	74,832
New York & Erie	743,250	130,808,034	135,757	136,500	99,293	12,237	110,443	79,014	170,006
New York & Harlem .	114,180	9,988,096	9,258	43,022	10,848	2,156	15,899	5,089	27,908
New York & N. Haven	80,376	....	355	6,008	1,529	6,718	31,670	33,363	733
Northern (Ogdensburg)	219,250	19,684,332	66,720	8,228	71,007	11,550	8,367	31,766	21,612
Oswego & Syracuse...	35,198	1,112,445	2,345	1,079	21,093	101	4,199	4,034	2,347
*Rensselaer & Saratoga	68,661	1,690,383	3,635	8,281	15,470	350	7,072	10,523	23,330

Sac. Harbor & Ellisb'h	7,422	179,000	3,000	300	1,200	2,400	100	300	122
Saratoga & Washing'n	70,518	1,987,324	5,712	4,141	10,139	7,813	5,348	6,941	30,424
†Troy & Boston......	61,243	1,725,056	6,618	4,925	7,901	2,854	2,190	10,914	25,841
Troy & Greenbush....	79,913	479,479	5,905	8,110	18,759	1,468	15,773	4,658	25,240
Watertown & Rome..	132,859	8,200,388	54,379	14,368	30,129	432	....	18,108	3,754
Totals	2,956,389	301,181,477	438,727	453,850	637,385	105,488	352,494	361,937	606,508

* Includes Saratoga and Schenectady.
† Includes Troy and Bennington.

TABLE A—(*Continued*)—*For the year ending September* 30, 1855.

NAME OF ROAD.	Am't of freight in tons of 2,000 pounds.	Number of tons carried one mile.	AMOUNT OF EACH KIND OF FREIGHT IN TONS, CLASSIFIED.						
			Products of the forest.	Of animals.	Vegetable food.	Other agricultural products.	Manufactures.	Merchandize.	Other articles.
*Albany Northern	45,289	1,200,523	2,987	3,730	3,216	12,182	4,822	12,524	5,828
Albany & W. Stockb'ge	226,228	8,103,048	13,982	1,472	147,920	2,929	27,126	22,089	10,710
Black River & Utica ..	7,403	105,110	4,749	840	472	139	339	526	338
Blossburgh & Corning .	126,479	1,824,055	50,307	....	....	......	....	4,543	71,629
Buffalo & N. Y. city...	62,162	4,972,960	....	....	....	......	....	....	....
Buffalo & State Line ..	179,451	10,936,790	7,504	96,429	13,696	1,073	9,428	48,151	3,166
Buffalo, Corning & N. Y.	49,056	2,371,866	17,925	2,189	17,283	692	4,138	2,696	4,137
†Canandaigua & Elmira	31,036	1,634,303	752	8,221	12,355	1,474	3,421	2,297	2,516
Canandaigua & N. Falls	7,352	287,838	933	739	8	2,759	780	491	1,634
Cayuga & Susquehanna.	127,516	4,190,445	11,095	2,428	6,733	149	3,599	1,072	102,440
Flushing	800	5,780	....	....	....	......	....	....	....
Hudson & Boston	56,035	929,875	888	822	1,121	985	3,788	2,241	46,198
Hudson River	139,968	15,221,956	2,620	35,417	29,611	6,761	22,196	22,507	20,856
Long Island	62,768	2,665,518	8,347	3,060	6,798	2,611	4,069	8,039	29,844
New York & Erie.....	842,054	150,673,997	118,434	155,595	116,092	8,070	96,494	106,508	240,855
New York Central	670,073	99,605,836	37,971	131,224	244,605	9,792	60,140	105,312	81,029
New York & N. Haven	74,625	4,067,062	....	....	....	......	....	....	....
New York & Harlem ..	123,256	[a]10,879,200	10,640	45,378	10,015	2,584	11,776	7,653	35,206
Northern (Ogdensburgh)	162,013	14,690,910	50,559	8,179	53,996	1,557	5,558	38,206	3,954
Oswego & Syracuse....	40,848	1,287,461	1,310	1,135	27,779	440	4,709	3,855	1,620
Potsdam & Watertown.	22,825	[a]350,650	14,654	31	....	2,491	2,860	2,568	209

‡Rensselaer & Saratoga.	52,695	1,322,697	4,460	2,125	9,480	2,969	9,304	8,550	15,807
Roch. & Genesee Valley	18,022	315,860	1,493	174	10,957	387	1,959	1,402	1,643
Sacketts H'r & Ellisb'gh	5,886	58,860	1,382	353	2,220	20	396	532	983
Saratoga & Whitehall..	18,019	438,384	1,116	1,099	995	298	1,068	2,031	11,412
Syracuse & Binghamton	41,578	2,273,588	1,250	3,714	5,394	992	3,533	2,951	23,684
‖Troy & Boston	62,536	1,937,064	3,523	2,817	14,210	2,299	7,462	11,798	20,427
Troy & Greenbush	79,751	478,506	3,104	8,690	34,361	1,306	11,341	4,022	16,927
Watertown & Rome...	132,676	8,360,432	44,809	14,932	42,356	1,350	13,450	12,651	3,128
Totals	3,468,400	351,190,574	416,794	530,794	811,673	66,309	313,756	435,215	756,180

* Includes "Troy & Rutland."
† Includes "Chemung."

a Estimated.

‡ Includes "Saratoga & Schenectady."
‖ Includes "Troy & Bennington."

TABLE A — (*Continued*) — *For the year ending September* 30, 1856.

NAME OF ROAD.	Am't of freight in tons of 2000 pounds.	Number of tons carried one mile.	AMOUNT OF EACH KIND OF FREIGHT IN TONS, CLASSIFIED.						
			Products of the forest.	Of animals.	Vegetable food.	Other agricultural products.	Manufactures	Merchandise.	Other articles.
*Albany, Vt. & Canada	27,703	742,030	714	2,105	5,025	4,693	3,903	6,600	4,663
Albany & W. Stockb'e.	235,682	7,852,627	9,263	3,923	150,107	6,027	11,127	55,235	....
Black River & Utica...	11,865	271,222	4,452	2,342	598	486	1,188	2,009	577
Blossburgh & Corning..	115,834	1,709,186	40,261	....	....	......	....	3,653	71,920
Buffalo, Corning & N.Y.	127,161	6,501,899	41,300	4,843	48,071	936	8,800	8,621	15,580
Buffalo & State Line...	247,586	12,752,720	9,435	137,755	24,416	3,524	22,710	29,682	20,064
Canandaigua & Elmira.	39,992	2,332,326	1,586	11,144	12,160	191	4,191	5,383	5,337
Canandaigua & N. Falls	36,621	2,522,303	2,879	10,589	2,103	9,957	7,723	1,578	1,774
Cayuga & Susquehanna.	85,556	2,674,875	8,491	1,960	3,383	207	1,659	2,133	67,723
Flushing	1,460	8,356	....	....	....	......	....	....	....
Hudson & Boston......	78,983	1,885,666	1,132	976	5,953	3,464	16,158	7,378	43,922
Hudson River.........	165,312	20,116,030	2,743	49,405	26,183	9,334	36,818	24,189	16,640
Long Island...........	61,037	2,879,806	11,275	14,984	12,872	180	3,527	5,031	13,168
New York Central.....	776,112	145,733,678	29,547	161,807	283,027	20,068	72,732	127,231	81,700
New York & Erie......	933,221	183,458,046	116,378	170,099	148,943	13,556	110,769	155,473	218,003
New York & Harlem...	164,516	8,799,957	3,730	48,308	11,140	3,300	17,729	6,736	68,563
New York & N. Haven.	81,834	4,232,744	....	....	....	......	....	....	....
Northern (Ogdensburgh)	160,839	14,604,687	41,240	11,051	52,400	4,226	7,968	33,640	10,314
Oswego and Syracuse...	54,484	1,724,431	1,843	1,624	35,650	325	7,614	5,473	1,955
Potsdam & Watertown.	26,697	390,112	11,426	2,255	3,211	154	6,786	2,210	655
Rensselaer & Saratoga..	60,813	1,567,813	3,820	6,870	10,534	1,047	14,848	5,773	17,921

Rochester & Gen. Valley	26,281	448,512	3,473	855	13,297	348	3,115	2,272	3,897
Saratoga & Whitehall ..	61,828	1,941,105	2,023	5,808	8,950	1,850	6,315	6,500	30,382
S. Harbor & Ellisburgh	8,342	74,692	....	....	....	......	....	....	....
Troy & Boston	69,469	1,883,126	6,961	3,846	10,220	3,880	8,444	12,648	23,470
Watertown & Rome ...	143,172	9,574,474	39,579	14,473	50,682	969	14,725	18,217	2,004
Totals	3,802,400	436,682,423	393,569	667,022	918,925	88,722	388,849	527,665	720,232

* Late "Albany Northern."

TABLE A — (*Continued*) — *For the year ending September* 30, 1857.

NAME OF ROAD.	Am't of freight in tons of 2000 pounds.	Number of tons carried one mile.	AMOUNT OF EACH KIND OF FREIGHT, IN TONS, CLASSIFIED.						
			Products of the forest.	Of animals.	Vegetable food.	Other agricultural products.	Manufactures.	Merchandize.	Other articles.
Albany & W. Stockb'dge	273,156	8,932,030	8,700	3,612	140,103	507	10,276	109,958	....
Albany, Vt. & Canada.	34,124	818,976	3,846	1,320	3,412	6,735	5,116	6,830	6,865
Black River & Utica...	12,277	279,579	3,776	2,760	1,527	126	1,065	2,077	945
Blossburgh & Corning .	133,772	1,928,544	43,386	....	....	......	....	3,965	86,421
Buffalo & State Line...	367,460	16,454,465	35,945	181,241	41,313	5,901	40,633	59,998	2,429
Elmira, C. & N. Falls..	8,408	465,835	597	372	2,479	120	1,550	1,275	2,015
Hudson River	176,798	19,642,158	3,476	58,604	21,828	6,366	34,250	40,786	11,488
Long Island	81,320	2,033,000	13,348	8,606	10,056	246	2,428	6,273	40,360
New York & Erie.....	978,069	165,100,850	126,093	145,957	120,617	13,909	143,338	143,716	284,436
New York Central	838,791	145,873,776	31,468	180,852	275,941	18,989	75,731	177,708	78,102
New York & Harlem ..	150,863	9,333,743	10,088	60,698	13,718	2,545	24,265	3,824	1,066
New York & New Haven	86,391	4,470,747	1,156	2,322	1,340	1,390	39,049	40,065	35,722
Northern (Ogdensburgh)	177,528	16,242,825	38,839	7,899	71,852	3,626	6,121	34,324	12,867
Oswego & Syracuse....	59,236	1,900,710	1,394	2,037	40,211	482	9,052	4,256	1,804
Potsdam & Watertown.	28,661	554,233	11,368	4,391	2,957	338	5,325	2,330	1,952
Rensselaer & Saratoga .	65,186	1,689,560	2,602	8,469	13,072	1,037	14,042	8,190	17,774
Roch. & Genesee Valley	39,841	2,270,965	9,339	380	13,558	176	1,591	2,290	12,505

Saratoga & Whitehall..	72,431	2,146,820	3,412	7,011	9,698	2,075	9,287	6,373	34,573
Syracuse, B. & N. Y...	51,008	2,876,981	2,512	3,730	6,930	254	5,783	1,323	30,476
Troy & Boston........	76,547	1,753,441	9,165	2,921	9,110	4,323	8,191	12,525	30,309
Watertown & Rome...	116,012	11,253,164	36,429	11,894	34,398	1,896	10,091	14,019	7,375
Totals	3,827,879	416,022,402	394,939	697,076	834,030	71,041	447,184	682,105	699,484

TABLE A—(*Continued*)—*For the year ending September* 30, 1858.

NAME OF ROAD.	Am't of freight in tons of 2000 pounds.	Number of tons carried one mile.	AMOUNT OF EACH KIND OF FREIGHT IN TONS, CLASSIFIED.						
			Products of the forest.	Of animals.	Vegetable food.	Other agricultural products.	Manufactures.	Merchandise.	Other articles.
Albany, Vt. and Canada	34,918	698,360	2,793	4,190	5,237	6,984	4,842	5,738	5,134
Albany & W. Stockb'ge	226,035	7,511,341	8,250	2,610	139,290	493	9,927	65,465	....
Black River & Utica...	13,135	316,660	3,180	3,638	1,280	175	1,064	2,089	1,709
Blossburgh & Corning..	73,904	831,679	31,040	....	....	......	....	3,013	39,851
Buffalo, N. Y. & Erie..	143,709	14,360,000	4,281	38,140	49,620	3,157	9,265	26,790	12,456
Buffalo & State Line...	290,532	19,809,225	10,500	165,134	32,849	9,018	24,062	42,344	6,625
Canandaigua & Elmira.	4,293	175,969	174	219	1,991	6	151	734	1,018
Cayuga & Susquehanna	52,175	1,615,012	7,703	1,639	3,157	110	1,877	1,461	36,228
Hudson & Boston	50,806	880,466	2,311	2,196	567	2,046	5,268	4,792	33,626
Hudson River.........	160,197	18,416,865	3,443	59,786	17,274	9,403	24,986	32,299	13,006
Long Island..........	89,480	2,236,990	11,482	9,740	5,690	1,620	1,846	10,839	48,262
New York Central.....	765,407	142,691,178	24,368	172,076	301,507	18,373	47,939	134,482	66,662
New York & Erie.....	816,964	165,895,635	92,550	178,076	154,534	10,885	88,976	128,709	163,234
New York & Harlem..	122,371	7,446,561	8,170	52,478	11,177	2,898	17,576	4,302	25,770
New York & N. Haven.	64,058	3,715,364	890	2,058	1,384	882	31,426	26,476	942
Northern (Ogdensburgh)	150,432	13,210,757	31,773	8,156	76,616	3,003	5,295	22,523	3,066
Oswego & Syracuse....	42,810	1,375,557	1,214	1,162	26,453	211	8,938	3,642	1,190
Potsdam & Watertown.	21,142	699,023	6,406	3,988	2,372	142	4,120	3,576	538
Rensselaer & Saratoga..	59,903	1,550,757	2,197	7,084	12,552	805	11,590	6,926	18,749

Rochester & Gen. Valley	27,700	470,900	8,150	300	9,150	100	1,100	2,100	6,800
Saratoga & Whitehall..	62,868	1,871,411	3,244	6,449	9,415	1,070	6,697	5,705	30,288
Syracuse, Bing'n & N. Y.	73,410	5,058,890	4,914	3,923	5,806	275	4,296	1,432	52,764
Troy & Boston........	56,049	1,482,292	5,607	2,395	2,377	4,137	8,077	14,659	18,797
Watertown & Rome...	123,599	9,899,128	36,299	11,196	47,065	1,490	8,154	13,743	5,652
Totals	3,525,897	422,219,620	310,939	736,633	917,363	77,283	327,472	563,839	592,367

TABLE A — (*Continued*) — *For the year ending September* 30, 1859.

NAME OF ROAD.	Am't of freight in tons of 2,000 pounds.	Number of tons carried one mile.	AMOUNT OF EACH KIND OF FREIGHT IN TONS, CLASSIFIED.						
			Products of the forest.	Of animals.	Vegetable food.	Other agricultural products.	Manufactures.	Merchandize.	Other articles.
Alb'y & W. Stockb'dge	246,983	7,616,839	7,390	3,100	147,090	6,220	19,725	63,458	....
Black River & Utica..	15,253	375,762	5,414	3,266	1,601	37	1,139	3,048	1,018
Blossburgh & Corning.	88,730	1,293,641	35,349	....	....	....	....	4,554	48,827
Buffalo, N. Y. & Erie.	181,565	18,156,500	15,448	31,160	45,376	5,320	24,980	52,324	6,957
Buffalo & State Line..	289,985	19,703,894	11,478	137,662	25,531	11,209	20,543	69,452	14,110
Cayuga & Susquehanna	49,146	1,534,766	5,586	1,998	3,857	115	2,199	1,384	34,007
Hudson & Boston,....	76,400	1,247,975	4,470	3,304	1,832	3,088	8,414	6,708	48,584
*Hudson River	258,965	30,155,130	7,497	104,832	22,766	13,773	43,284	53,444	13,369
Long Island	78,186	1,954,675	13,784	26,424	11,332	115	3,247	6,093	17,191
†New York Central ..	834,319	157,136,000	35,154	204,167	249,751	30,096	57,036	178,782	79,333
‡New York & Erie ...	869,072	147,127,039	97,754	170,322	112,727	15,107	94,266	179,050	199,846
New York & Harlem .	145,577	9,131,851	9,485	52,332	12,486	4,206	20,422	6,698	39,948
New York & N. Haven	85,383	4,233,430	423	6,340	1,606	7,016	33,303	35,933	762
North'rn (Ogdensb'rgh)	137,427	11,477,361	39,575	10,125	53,434	1,354	6,642	22,915	3,382
Oswego & Syracuse...	32,998	1,037,765	2,163	1,977	17,161	266	3,312	6,904	1,215
Potsdam & Watertown	22,302	733,974	6,825	4,695	2,197	112	4,442	3,174	857
‖Rensselaer & Saratoga	72,402	1,908,314	3,081	7,362	12,456	410	19,144	8,004	21,945

Roch. & Genesee Vall'y	23,939	408,000	5,862	1,125	3,821	1,023	5,368	3,289	3,451
Saratoga & Whitehall.	67,594	2,069,095	4,347	5,770	8,343	1,325	8,770	6,958	32,081
Syracuse, Bing. & N. Y.	96,671	6,334,269	6,919	4,461	5,287	226	3,984	1,236	74,558
**Troy & Boston.....	74,107	2,267,747	2,545	2,731	2,653	5,340	18,239	15,001	27,598
Watertown & Rome..	112,009	7,520,604	43,601	13,785	25,110	1,335	8,472	13,023	6,683
Totals	3,859,283	433,425,441	364,150	796,938	766,417	107,693	406,931	741,432	675,722

* Includes "Troy and Greenbush."
† Includes "Niagara Bridge and Canandaigua."
‡ Includes "Chemung," and "Elmira, Jefferson and Canandaigua."
‖ Includes "Saratoga and Schenectady."
** Includes "Troy and Bennington."

TABLE A — (*Continued*) — *For the year ending September* 30, 1860.

NAME OF ROAD.	Am't of freight in tons of 2000 pounds.	Number of tons carried one mile.	AMOUNT OF EACH KIND OF FREIGHT IN TONS, CLASSIFIED.						
			Products of the forest.	Of animals.	Vegetable food.	Other agricultural products.	Manufactures.	Merchandise.	Other articles.
Albany & W. Stockb'ge	280,816	9,412,864	8,710	9,270	221,710	8,640	7,410	25,076	
Avon, G. & Mt. Morris.	550	8,250	50	60	20	150	40	190	40
Black River & Utica,..	19,743	475,400	7,928	3,937	1,604	26	1,221	4,163	864
Blossburgh & Corning.	113,741	1,693,300	24,547	....	....	....	....	4,144	85,050
Buffalo, N. Y. & Erie..	227,713	22,771,300	18,920	32,465	43,628	7,210	28,908	50,421	46,161
Buffalo & State Line..	342,761	16,577,071	12,302	151,998	41,521	20,074	38,949	71,920	5,997
Cayuga & Susquehanna	45,187	1,377,785	7,415	2,242	5,445	203	2,280	1,330	26,272
Hudson & Boston.....	86,878	....	1,918	2,386	1,935	2,586	8,691	3,258	66,104
*Hudson River.......	337,852	40,187,539	8,093	124,224	36,389	15,784	66,106	68,672	18,584
Long Island	102,413	2,560,325	13,944	33,929	11,049	43	1,888	16,209	25,351
†New York Central...	1,028,183	199,231,392	42,305	223,362	343,872	39,169	77,256	201,587	100,632
‡New York & Erie....	1,139,554	214,084,396	118,890	201,823	197,233	19,909	113,948	198,610	289,141
New York & Harlem..	153,511	9,382,119	8,271	53,773	14,115	4,186	22,113	9,809	41,244
New York & N. Haven	78,691	3,909,502	383	5,862	1,547	6,475	30,785	32,962	677
Northern	166,675	15,611,653	40,384	9,605	80,303	2,155	5,810	26,237	2,181
Oswego & Syracuse...	53,720	1,722,438	1,827	2,427	32,380	740	6,462	7,565	2,319
Potsdam & Watertown	17,051	620,566	4,054	4,149	1,798	30	2,998	3,086	936
‖Rensselaer & Saratoga	93,135	1,947,849	2,074	4,600	14,218	1,155	36,352	8,657	26,079
Roch. & Genesee Valley	25,489	425,000	5,720	1,220	3,940	1,225	5,246	3,321	4,817
Sacketts H., R. & N. Y.	136	1,448	19	....	29	40	16	22	10
Saratoga & Whitehall.	76,423	2,321,986	3,976	4,792	11,067	1,314	16,090	8,601	30,583

Staten Island	40	....	....	....	....	....	....	40	
Syracuse, B. & N. Y...	132,679	9,331,032	7,565	5,112	5,347	279	4,667	1,310	108,399
**Troy & Boston.....	110,539	4,109,745	3,331	4,459	3,126	9,432	26,756	22,300	41,135
Watertown & Rome..	108,293	6,287,545	30,798	13,824	31,364	2,394	7,924	14,321	7,668
Totals	4,741,773	564,050,505	373,424	895,519	1,103,640	143,219	511,916	783,811	930,244

*Includes "Troy and Greenbush."
†Includes "Niagara Bridge and Canandaigua."
‡Includes "Chemung & Elmira," "Jefferson and Canandaigua."
‖Includes the "Albany and Vermont," and "Saratoga and Schenectady."
**Includes "Troy and Bennington."

TABLE A—(*Continued*)—*For the year ending September* 30, 1861.

NAME OF ROAD.	Am't of freight in tons of 2000 pounds.	Number of tons carried one mile.	AMOUNT OF EACH KIND OF FREIGHT IN TONS, CLASSIFIED.						
			Products of the forest.	Of animals.	Vegetable food.	Other agricultural products.	Manufactures	Merchandise.	Other articles.
Albany & W. Stockb'e	328,286	10,472,279	18,760	91,992	122,764	31,843	18,760	44,167	....
Avon, Gen. & Mt. Mor	1,300	20,150	150	70	200	500	60	270	50
Blossburgh & Corning.	125,384	1,866,473	20,930	....	....	....	....	3,363	101,091
Buffalo, N. Y. & Erie.	237,409	23,740,900	19,626	33,581	44,860	19,165	30,187	40,897	49,093
Buffalo & State Line..	600,031	20,111,585	180,085	197,567	65,776	30,852	53,844	43,568	28,339
Cayuga & Susquehanna	53,146	1,659,642	6,752	1,767	6,492	213	2,527	1,367	34,028
Elmira & Williamsport	131,441	9,314,555	12,380	5,580	18,851	664	20,157	5,189	68,620
Hudson & Boston	79,052	1,293,741	669	1,001	804	3,178	9,381	2,647	61,372
Hudson River........	370,098	42,834,771	7,033	150,793	54,822	18,844	54,607	71,487	12,512
Long Island..........	92,741	2,318,332	17,929	6,710	10,633	1,134	1,636	7,850	46,849
New York Central....	1,167,302	237,392,974	39,310	251,964	441,562	47,341	80,597	192,583	113,945
New York & Erie	1,253,419	251,350,127	108,685	209,757	243,959	26,920	145,672	167,245	351,181
New York & Harlem..	168,527	11,032,070	7,369	62,053	17,410	2,496	29,043	12,210	37,946
New York & N. Haven	51,824	2,573,925	251	3,850	1,003	4,387	19,123	22,732	478
Northern (Ogdensburg)	166,530	15,559,949	34,713	7,506	88,345	4,041	5,954	24,200	1,771
Oswego & Syracuse...	44,529	1,569,283	1,107	2,626	20,321	1,977	6,887	8,207	3,404
Potsdam & Watertown	19,575	753,330	3,742	4,903	2,884	412	2,907	3,399	1,328
Rensselaer & Saratoga.	92,282	2,072,121	2,918	2,095	20,073	2,760	31,048	11,129	22,259
Rochester & G. Valley	24,521	416,580	5,692	1,329	3,894	1,429	4,986	4,260	2,931
S. Harbor, Rome & N.Y	2,167	42,298	589	214	360	58	293	292	361
Saratoga & Whitehall.	63,438	1,942,303	3,811	3,679	10,861	812	13,492	10,803	19,980

Staten Island	320	....	....	....	....	....	....	....	320
Syracuse, Bing. & N. Y.	153,596	11,083,577	6,873	5,802	5,150	350	4,196	1,348	129,877
Troy & Boston	108,335	4,361,960	2,976	5,222	3,480	10,162	24,530	25,250	36,715
Utica & Black River ..	18,551	458,091	6,969	4,141	1,612	247	1,633	2,864	1,085
Watertown & Rome ..	106,605	6,315,859	30,760	12,868	34,216	1,424	7,171	11,690	8,476
Totals	5,460,409	660,556,875	540,079	1,067,070	1,220,332	211,209	568,691	719,017	1,134,011

TABLE A — (*Continued*) — *For the year ending September* 30, 1862.

NAME OF ROAD.	Am't of freight in tons of 2,000 pounds.	Number of tons carried one mile.	AMOUNT OF EACH KIND OF FREIGHT IN TONS, CLASSIFIED.						
			Products of the forest.	Of animals.	Vegetable food.	Other agricultural products.	Manufactures.	Merchandize.	Other articles.
Alb'y & W. Stockb'dge	382,958	12,286,943	36,892	72,610	219,906	7,625	21,993	13,932	10,000
Atl'c & G. W. in N. Y.	75,565	....	1,280	4,605	1,082	164	53,890	5,916	8,628
Avon, Gen. & Mt. Morris	1,500	18,000	100	125	220	575	100	300	80
Blossburgh & Corning.	189,916	2,827,212	28,063	....	....	....	....	3,228	158,625
Buffalo, N. Y. & Erie.	301,234	30,123,400	20,420	35,828	45,217	20,128	40,868	50,729	88,044
Buffalo & State Line ..	653,717	32,468,454	37,018	222,921	124,469	38,538	65,192	114,029	51,550
Cayuga & Susquehanna	72,646	2,284,950	9,665	2,318	10,526	271	1,177	3,375	45,314
Elmira & Williamsport	149,538	....	16,086	4,000	....	21,608	2,556	4,077	101,211
Erie Railway	1,632,955	351,092,285	99,677	299,715	261,824	44,067	236,909	220,499	470,264
Hudson & Boston	73,123	1,164,973	830	1,997	2,873	3,744	9,840	3,576	50,263
Hudson River........	517,740	60,375,643	7,104	238,895	61,287	33,211	68,900	93,109	15,234
Long Island,.........	96,893	2,906,790	19,379	7,047	11,744	1,164	1,919	8,430	47,210
New York Central ...	1,387,433	296,963,492	39,479	359,020	469,885	45,245	92,123	243,105	138,576
New York & Harlem..	198,667	15,322,994	9,086	74,844	16,242	9,833	34,861	10,845	42,956
New York & N. Haven	70,782	3,652,168	304	5,283	1,393	5,987	26,096	31,079	640
North'n (Ogdensburgh)	187,647	19,157,715	35,610	10,840	62,042	45,401	5,999	25,684	2,071
Oswego & Syracuse...	66,680	2,095,022	1,113	2,738	40,301	2,370	9,027	8,177	2,954

*Rensselaer & Saratoga	....	....	....	....	....	....	....	....	....
Roch.& Genesee Valley	27,423	411,345	6,022	1,580	4,096	1,823	5,048	5,681	3,173
†Rome, Wat'n & Ogd'h	129,639	7,727,942	35,215	19,600	36,600	6,453	8,294	15,592	7,885
Saratoga & Whitehall.	55,486	1,816,072	3,740	2,984	9,036	712	10,980	8,621	19,413
Syr., Bingh'n & N. Y..	211,342	15,257,380	8,331	5,824	8,508	251	4,200	1,375	182,853
Utica & Black River..	17,860	449,821	5,972	4,823	1,960	132	1,949	1,618	1,406
Warwick Valley......	5,391	....	1,357	322	27	1,861	500	389	925
Totals	6,506,135	858,402,601	422,743	1,377,929	1,389,238	291,163	702,421	873,366	1,449,275

* No report. Books destroyed at great fire in Troy.
† Late "Watertown and Rome."

TABLE A — (*Continued*)— *For the year ending September* 30, 1863.

NAME OF ROAD.	Am't of freight in tons of 2000 pounds.	Number of tons carried one mile.	AMOUNT OF EACH KIND OF FREIGHT IN TONS, CLASSIFIED.						
			Products of the forest.	Of animals.	Vegetable food.	Other agricultural products.	Manufactures.	Merchandise.	Other articles.
Albany & W. Stockb'e	448,158	14,632,882	44,633	84,150	256,180	8,563	25,589	15,744	13,299
*Atlantic & G't West'n	133,333	5,910,377	5,729	4,286	4,445	709	95,994	9,115	13,055
Avon, G. & Mt. Morris	2,566	33,370	230	36	240	735	200	822	303
Buffalo, N. Y. & Erie.	369,246	40,113,979	33,309	41,563	81,175	18,830	49,491	71,421	73,457
Buffalo & State Line.	733,181	53,295,500	41,376	261,076	81,891	52,566	78,850	146,639	70,783
Cayuga & Susquehanna	87,203	2,732,712	10,715	2,507	16,777	169	880	3,757	52,398
†Erie Railway	1,815,096	403,670,861	102,008	338,551	228,632	65,171	270,952	296,998	512,784
Hudson & Boston	111,985	1,774,285	725	1,665	2,810	2,881	13,110	3,583	87,211
‡Hudson River	656,967	75,191,270	7,759	307,757	33,384	79,182	105,714	106,836	16,335
Long Island	106,996	3,098,410	22,695	9,642	13,804	1,365	2,714	8,692	48,084
New York Central....	1,449,604	312,195,796	52,829	395,876	405,380	72,467	88,965	310,275	123,812
New York & Harlem.	233,981	18,201,839	12,078	70,365	20,570	15,918	40,353	16,620	58,077
New York & N. Haven	79,177	4,354,292	340	5,933	1,578	6,734	29,303	34,835	454
North'n (Ogdensburgh)	211,024	19,815,427	48,650	12,668	51,551	48,911	5,768	41,061	2,415
Oswego & Syracuse...	61,905	1,916,445	2,400	2,976	35,646	1,398	6,411	9,028	4,046
‖Rensselaer & Saratoga	95,654	1,984,489	2,341	7,575	13,379	1,640	37,218	9,365	24,136
Rome, W. & Ogdensb'h	137,561	9,668,547	45,192	22,254	31,842	4,969	11,699	10,351	11,254

Saratoga & Whitehall.	69,041	2,540,971	4,862	3,071	14,849	1,388	13,943	12,394	18,534
Syracuse, B. & N. Y...	208,576	15,040,156	11,778	6,712	9,710	334	7,479	3,469	169,094
**Troy & Boston.....	156,296	7,363,215	5,053	8,967	4,360	16,473	34,796	40,231	46,416
Union & Black River.	19,247	504,679	5,493	5,172	2,944	201	2,115	1,536	1,786
Warwick Valley	11,007	....	1,910	5,310	368	181	264	814	2,160
Totals	7,197,804	994,039,502	462,105	1,598,112	1,311,515	400,785	921,808	1,153,586	1,349,893

* Includes the business of the Atlantic & Gt. Western R. R. in Penna. and Ohio.
† Includes "Chemung" and "Rochester & Genesee Valley."
‡ Includes "Troy & Greenbush."
‖ Includes "Saratoga & Schenectady."
** Includes "Troy & Bennington."

TABLE A.—(*Continued*)—*For the year ending September* 30, 1864.

NAME OF ROAD.	Am't of freight in tons of 2000 pounds.	Number of tons carried one mile.	AMOUNT OF EACH KIND OF FREIGHT IN TONS, CLASSIFIED.						
			Products of the forest.	Of animals.	Vegetable food.	Other agricultural products.	Manufactures.	Merchandise.	Other articles.
Albany & Susquehanna	17,370	569,885	423	2,926	2,300	5,970	1,375	3,918	458
Albany & W. Stock'be.	489,724	15,266,328	33,762	83,230	251,471	8,371	25,806	10,236	76,848
Atlantic & G't West'rn	247,527	11,492,868	10,714	33,015	15,175	11,735	74,048	32,982	69,858
Avon, Geneseo & Mt. M.	2,791	35,620	230	....	325	813	250	850	323
Buffalo, N. Y. & Erie.	369,245	34,718,139	30,025	69,216	93,052	11,362	48,506	40,833	76,251
Buffalo & State Line..	685,732	34,620,339	46,846	222,205	58,283	89,622	62,136	121,299	85,341
Cayuga & Susquehanna	82,401	2,584,965	5,693	3,041	17,169	157	1,675	4,506	50,460
Elmira & Williamsport	156,280	10,992,480	14,824	4,057	12,317	17,972	20,655	8,245	78,210
Erie Railway	2,170,798	422,013,644	104,069	280,723	215,986	260,902	116,681	362,767	829,670
Hudson & Boston	135,792	2,172,672	815	1,580	2,930	3,087	17,123	3,720	106,537
Hudson River........	601,824	72,720,351	12,042	237,901	41,241	68,416	114,165	107,344	20,715
Long Island	128,395	3,718,092	27,234	11,570	16,565	1,638	3,257	10,430	57,701
New York Central....	1,557,148	314,081,410	87,584	383,000	461,511	57,150	112,267	287,804	167,832
New York & Harlem .	236,467	15,571,828	12,233	81,384	17,488	23,901	19,479	14,123	67,859
New York & N. Haven	114,357	6,201,435	573	8,572	2,287	9,716	42,310	50,214	685
Northern (Ogdensb'gh)	230,201	21,154,384	59,597	13,533	55,281	41,338	6,194	51,500	2,758
Oswego & Syracuse...	79,834	2,451,432	3,345	3,446	47,382	1,891	11,183	8,296	4,291
Rensselaer & Saratoga	108,186	2,232,550	5,454	6,715	16,344	3,420	40,350	10,220	25,683
Rome, Wat'n & Ogd'h.	197,865	11,766,254	98,456	20,082	32,445	2,864	13,616	17,015	13,387
Saratoga & Whitehall.	51,771	1,604,901	6,402	2,371	1,893	3,332	14,158	5,707	17,908
Syracuse, Bing. & N. Y.	253,634	18,293,256	8,761	7,368	8,971	836	9,374	1,907	216,419

Troy & Boston	188,828	8,223,589	6,157	10,265	5,045	19,384	41,691	48,516	57,770
Utica & Black River .	23,614	640,542	8,193	5,684	3,791	188	2,565	1,433	1,760
Warwick Valley	13,776	....	1,064	7,606	486	326	469	616	3,209
Totals	8,143,562	1,013,126,964	584,496	1,499,490	1,379,738	644,391	799,033	1,204,481	2,031,933

TABLE A — (*Continued*) — *For the year ending September* 30, 1865.

NAME OF ROAD.	Am't of freight in tons of 2000 pounds.	Number of tons carried one mile.	AMOUNT OF EACH KIND OF FREIGHT IN TONS, CLASSIFIED.						
			Products of the forest.	Of animals.	Vegetable food.	Other agricultural products.	Manufactures.	Merchandise.	Other articles.
Albany & Susquehanna	20,348	790,633	1,065	3,044	3,636	3,958	2,585	5,344	716
Albany & W. Stockb'ge	430,380	12,774,664	29,279	49,207	290,609	12,106	25,762	13,201	10,216
Atl'c & G. W. in N. Y..	233,380	....	10,567	23,212	17,928	9,025	21,858	78,302	72,488
Avon, Gen. & Mt. Morris	2,500	30,000	200	....	300	800	200	800	200
Buffalo, N. Y. & Erie..	278,807	16,297,937	23,373	67,955	77,572	5,574	31,358	24,105	48,870
Buffalo & State Line..	620,329	31,668,398	41,215	202,530	52,845	84,440	57,346	108,696	73,257
Cayuga & Susquehanna	58,853	1,959,801	2,372	2,671	11,422	580	1,150	3,415	37,243
Elmira & Williamsport	137,132	9,143,889	15,680	3,989	6,475	17,185	10,328	2,289	81,186
Erie Railway	2,234,350	388,557,213	99,865	249,220	212,677	75,344	226,298	327,328	1,043,618
Hudson & Boston	109,595	1,753,957	520	980	2,227	1,887	10,125	2,221	91,635
Hudson River........	491,850	53,738,444	9,380	174,979	31,287	46,618	102,876	88,112	38,498
Long Island	154,072	4,647,615	32,680	13,884	19,878	1,965	3,908	12,516	69,241
New York Central....	1,275,299	264,993,626	55,718	348,661	349,103	32,099	71,484	258,043	160,191
New York & Harlem .	239,603	17,153,978	13,597	106,407	16,920	11,877	24,617	11,603	55,122
New York & N. Haven	107,818	6,200,750	478	8,103	2,051	9,088	40,160	47,331	598
*Ogden'h & L. Champ'n	203,781	18,834,478	47,133	16,918	38,707	46,807	6,077	45,711	2,428
Oswego & Syracuse...	72,705	2,236,346	13,060	8,999	20,126	5,481	10,104	9,173	5,762

Rensselaer & Saratoga.	139,097	4,702,143	8,877	7,754	12,759	8,760	29,459	51,282	20,206
Rome, Watert'n & Og'h	210,760	10,841,749	105,505	30,985	35,457	2,105	12,576	13,939	10,193
Syr., Bingh'n & N. Y..	182,441	13,158,384	6,197	7,322	9,152	468	8,278	1,682	149,342
Troy & Boston.......	150,711	6,616,997	4,502	4,727	4,630	15,193	33,169	39,876	48,614
Utica & Black River..	20,543	546,538	4,980	6,479	3,984	147	1,930	1,096	1,927
Warwick Valley	14,498	....	1,047	7,335	655	530	1,013	761	3,157
Totals	7,388,852	866,647,540	527,299	1,345,361	1,220,500	392,037	732,661	1,146,286	2,024,708

* Formerly "Northern."

TABLE A — (*Continued*) — *For the year ending September* 30, 1866.

NAME OF ROAD.	Amount of freight in tons of 2000 pounds.	Number of tons carried one mile.	AMOUNT OF EACH KIND OF FREIGHT IN TONS, CLASSIFIED.						
			Products of the forest.	Of animals.	Vegetable food.	Other agricultural products.	Manufactures	Merchandise.	Other articles.
Adirondack Company.	4,711	73,559	3,594	....	52	....	216	849	....
Albany & Susquehanna	39,509	2,310,397	4,471	5,963	6,216	5,348	5,072	10,463	1,976
Albany & W. Stockb'ge	641,968	20,040,507	35,764	52,792	357,902	35,762	26,709	30,207	102,832
Atlantic & G't West'rn	171,801	....	4,230	1,709	1,604	1,285	19,517	79,353	64,103
Avon, G. & Mt. Morris	3,500	42,000	280	....	420	620	780	1,120	280
Buffalo & State Line..	794,882	39,425,940	50,981	244,003	104,976	104,122	68,473	132,231	90,096
Cayuga & Susquehanna	96,774	3,096,628	6,298	2,119	15,143	....	1,280	4,139	67,785
Elmira & Williamsport	198,719	13,974,845	24,119	915	6,416	22,304	19,000	6,309	119,656
Erie Railway,........	3,242,792	478,485,772	173,410	314,468	397,963	72,554	458,026	356,316	1,470,065
Hudson & Boston	136,289	2,194,658	567	938	3,324	4,002	14,222	2,932	110,304
Hudson River........	497,307	57,545,439	12,041	132,202	62,408	45,578	117,942	92,034	35,102
Long Island	160,915	4,980,850	33,790	14,120	19,900	1,975	3,980	12,892	74,258
New York Central ...	1,602,197	331,075,547	77,443	366,516	453,663	31,620	94,426	342,767	235,762
New York & Harlem .	298,206	22,107,033	30,151	111,287	8,382	22,862	29,920	16,189	79,415
New York & N. Haven	128,041	7,130,052	578	9,627	2,436	10,793	47,690	56,206	711
Northern (of N. Jersey)	17,688	428,492	6,218	328	1,622	1,925	1,850	5,328	417

Ogdn'h & Lake Cham'n	266,268	22,373,866	73,601	13,284	39,337	59,220	7,873	65,751	7,202
Oswego & Syracuse...	66,214	2,014,556	9,660	8,481	19,205	4,233	10,388	8,537	5,710
Rensselaer & Saratoga.	273,039	9,234,863	17,240	14,930	24,727	16,901	58,625	100,510	40,106
Rome, W. & Ogdensb'h	266,896	14,577,032	120,517	23,629	60,156	5,217	20,751	18,318	18,308
Sterling Mountain....	62,350	451,000	59,020	....	....	....	3,308	22	....
Syracuse, B. & N. Y...	361,913	21,213,908	10,639	6,959	11,057	559	9,920	3,035	319,744
Utica & Black River..	21,832	577,121	6,307	5,016	3,795	250	2,374	1,474	2,616
Warwick Valley	17,590	....	3,476	7,604	981	335	1,020	678	3,496
Totals	9,371,401	1,053,344,075	764,395	1,336,890	1,601,685	447,455	1,023,362	1,347,660	2,849,954

TABLE B,

Showing the total amount of Freight, in tons of 2000 pounds, carried over all of the Railroads in the State, which reported to the State Engineer and Surveyor, in each year from the 30th day of September, 1850, to the 30th day of September, 1866; the number of tons carried one mile, with the amount of each kind of freight, classified.

FOR THE YEAR ENDING	Am't of freight in tons of 2000 pounds.	Number of tons carried one mile.	AMOUNT OF EACH KIND OF FREIGHT IN TONS, CLASSIFIED.						
			Products of the forest.	Of animals.	Vegetable food.	Other agricultural products.	Manufactures.	Merchandise.	Other articles.
Sept. 30, 1851..	1,330,555	76,542,664	173,849	269,032	248,826	30,817	168,214	227,360	180,351
do 1852..	2,274,870	181,051,645	270,715	487,619	514,707	71,317	245,604	290,220	394,688
do 1853..	2,989,766	219,477,747	403,723	612,076	653,291	114,269	360,073	328,235	516,136
do 1854..	2,956,389	301,181,477	438,727	453,850	637,385	105,488	352,494	361,937	606,508
do 1855..	3,468,400	351,190,574	416,794	530,794	811,673	66,309	313,756	435,215	756,180
do 1856..	3,802,400	436,682,423	393,569	667,022	918,925	88,722	388,849	527,665	720,232
do 1857..	3,827,879	416,022,402	394,939	697,076	834,030	71,041	447,184	682,105	699,484
do 1858..	3,525,897	422,219,620	310,939	736,633	917,363	77,283	327,472	563,839	592,367
do 1859..	3,859,283	433,425,441	364,150	796,938	766,417	107,693	406,931	741,432	675,722
do 1860..	4,741,773	564,050,505	373,424	895,519	1,103,640	143,219	511,916	783,811	930,244
do 1861..	5,460,409	660,556,875	540,079	1,067,070	1,220,332	211,209	568,691	719,017	1,134,011
do 1862..	6,506,135	858,402,601	422,743	1,377,929	1,389,238	291,163	702,421	873,366	1,449,275
do 1863..	7,197,804	994,039,502	462,105	1,598,112	1,311,515	400,785	921,808	1,153,586	1,349,893
do 1864..	8,143,562	1,013,126,964	584,496	1,499,490	1,379,738	644,391	799,033	1,204,481	2,031,933
do 1865..	7,388,852	866,647,540	527,299	1,345,361	1,220,500	392,037	732,661	1,146,286	2,024,708
do 1866..	9,371,401	1,053,344,075	764,395	1,336,890	1,601,685	447,455	1,023,362	1,347,660	2,849,954

TABLE C,

Showing the amount of Freight, in tons of 2000 pounds, carried in successive years on some of the principal railroads, and classified as in the preceding tables.

NEW YORK CENTRAL RAILROAD.

FOR THE YEAR ENDING	Am't of freight in tons of 2,000 pounds.	Number of tons carried one mile.	AMOUNT OF EACH KIND OF FREIGHT IN TONS, CLASSIFIED.						
			Products of the forest.	Of animals.	Vegetable food.	Other agricultural products.	Manufactures	Merchandise.	Other articles.
Sept. 30, 1854.......	549,805	81,168,080	45,530	115,417	156,204	10,935	52,244	94,643	74,832
do 1855.......	670,073	99,605,836	37,971	131,224	244,605	9,792	60,140	105,312	81,029
do 1856.......	776,112	145,733,678	29,547	161,807	283,027	20,068	72,732	127,231	81,700
do 1857.......	838,791	145,873,776	31,468	180,852	275,941	18,989	75,731	177,708	78,102
do 1858.......	765,407	142,691,178	24,368	172,076	301,507	18,373	47,939	134,482	66,662
do 1859.......	834,319	157,136,000	35,154	204,167	249,751	30,096	57,036	178,782	79,333
do 1860.......	1,028,183	199,231,392	42,305	223,362	343,872	39,169	77,256	201,587	100,632
do 1861.......	1,167,302	237,392,974	39,310	251,964	441,562	47,341	80,597	192,583	113,945
do 1862.......	1,387,433	296,963,492	39,479	359,020	469,885	45,245	92,123	243,105	138,576
do 1863.......	1,449,604	312,195,796	52,829	395,876	405,380	72,467	88,965	310,275	123,812
do 1864.......	1,557,148	314,081,410	87,584	383,000	461,511	57,150	112,267	287,804	167,832
do 1865.......	1,275,299	264,993,626	55,718	348,661	349,103	32,099	71,484	258,043	160,191
do 1866.......	1,602,197	331,075,547	77,443	366,516	453,663	31,620	94,426	342,767	235,762

TABLE C — *Continued.*

ERIE RAILWAY.

FOR THE YEAR ENDING	Am't of freight in tons of 2000 pounds.	Number of tons carried one mile.	AMOUNT OF EACH KIND OF FREIGHT IN TONS, CLASSIFIED.						
			Products of the forest.	Of animals.	Vegetable food.	Other agricultural products.	Manufactures	Merchandise.	Other articles.
Sept. 30, 1851.......	250,096	34,790,480	58,357	53,991	26,125	1,374	45,562	37,917	26,770
do 1852.......	456,460	96,697,695	76,908	75,943	56,929	2,419	74,847	50,687	118,727
do 1853.......	631,039	101,626,522	124,087	99,755	80,868	9,849	112,281	68,742	135,457
do 1854.......	743,250	130,808,034	135,757	136,500	99,293	12,237	110,443	79,014	170,006
do 1855.......	842,054	150,673,997	118,434	155,595	116,092	8,070	96,494	106,508	240,855
do 1856.......	933,221	183,458,046	116,378	170,099	148,943	13,556	110,769	155,473	218,003
do 1857.......	978,069	165,100,850	126,093	145,957	120,617	13,909	143,338	143,716	284,436
do 1858.......	816,964	165,895,635	92,550	178,076	154,534	10,885	88,976	128,709	163,234
do 1859.......	869,072	147,127,039	97,754	170,322	112,727	15,107	94,266	179,050	199,846
do 1860.......	1,139,554	214,084,396	118,890	201,823	197,233	19,909	113,948	198,610	289,141
do 1861.......	1,253,419	251,350,127	108,685	209,757	243,959	26,920	145,672	167,245	351,181
do 1862.......	1,632,955	351,092,285	99,677	299,715	261,824	44,067	236,909	220,499	470,264
do 1863.......	1,815,096	403,670,861	102,008	338,551	228,632	65,171	270,952	296,998	512,784
do 1864.......	2,170,798	422,013,644	104,069	280,723	215,986	260,902	116,681	362,767	829,670
do 1865.......	2,234,350	388,557,213	99,865	249,220	212,677	75,344	226,298	327,328	1,043,618
do 1866.......	3,242,792	478,485,772	173,410	314,468	397,963	72,554	458,026	356,316	1,470,065

TABLE C — *Continued.*

BUFFALO AND STATE LINE.

FOR THE YEAR ENDING	Am't of freight in tons of 2000 pounds.	Number of tons carried one mile.	AMOUNT OF EACH KIND OF FREIGHT IN TONS, CLASSIFIED.						
			Products of the forest.	Of animals.	Vegetable food.	Other agricultural products.	Manufactures.	Merchandise.	Other articles.
Sept. 30, 1852	13,351	577,431	1,265	3,773	1,765	98	851	2,106	3,493
do 1853	53,073	1,872,422	7,433	14,367	3,322	2,501	5,007	5,551	14,892
do 1854	81,042	4,807,946	4,570	43,783	3,796	436	4,490	7,521	16,446
do 1855	179,451	10,936,790	7,504	96,429	13,696	1,073	9,428	48,151	3,166
do 1856	247,586	12,752,720	9,435	137,755	24,416	3,524	22,710	29,682	20,064
do 1857	367,460	16,454,465	35,945	181,241	41,313	5,901	40,633	59,998	2,429
do 1858	290,532	19,809,225	10,500	165,134	32,849	9,018	24,062	42,344	6,625
do 1859	289,985	19,703,894	11,478	137,662	25,531	11,209	20,543	69,452	14,110
do 1860	342,761	16,577,071	12,302	151,998	41,521	20,074	38,949	71,920	5,997
do 1861	600,031	20,111,585	180,085	197,567	65,776	30,852	53,844	43,568	28,339
do 1862	653,717	32,468,454	37,018	222,921	124,469	38,538	65,192	114,029	51,550
do 1863	733,181	53,295,500	41,376	261,076	81,891	52,566	78,850	146,639	70,783
do 1864	685,732	34,620,339	46,846	222,205	58,283	89,622	62,136	121,299	85,341
do 1865	620,329	31,668,398	41,215	202,530	52,845	84,440	57,346	108,696	73,257
do 1866	794,882	39,425,940	50,981	244,003	104,976	104,122	68,473	132,231	90,096

TABLE C — *Continued.*

HUDSON RIVER RAILROAD.

FOR THE YEAR ENDING	Am't of freight in tons of 2000 pounds.	Number of tons carried one mile.	AMOUNT OF EACH KIND OF FREIGHT IN TONS, CLASSIFIED.						
			Products of the forest.	Of animals.	Vegetable food.	Other agricultural products.	Manufactures.	Merchandise.	Other articles.
Sept. 30, 1851.......	12,915	516,600	357	2,585	334	1,539	4,865	1,624	1,611
do 1852.......	65,046	7,643,678	1,018	22,248	3,497	9,820	10,630	14,078	3,755
do 1853.......	114,953	12,874,736	3,284	43,348	11,834	5,714	30,136	8,716	11,921
do 1854.......	156,716	18,141,520	4,203	32,038	19,301	12,632	35,525	18,859	34,158
do 1855.......	139,968	15,221,956	2,620	35,417	29,611	6,761	22,196	22,507	20,856
do 1856.......	165,312	20,116,030	2,743	49,405	26,183	9,334	36,818	24,189	16,640
do 1857.......	176,798	19,642,158	3,476	58,604	21,828	6,366	34,250	40,786	11,488
do 1858.......	160,197	18,416,865	3,443	59,786	17,274	9,403	24,986	32,299	13,006
do 1859.......	258,965	30,155,130	7,497	104,832	22,766	13,773	43,284	53,444	13,369
do 1860.......	337,852	40,187,539	8,093	124,224	36,389	15,784	66,106	68,672	18,584
do 1861.......	370,098	42,834,771	7,033	150,793	54,822	18,844	54,607	71,487	12,512
do 1862.......	517,740	60,375,643	7,104	238,895	61,287	33,211	68,900	93,109	15,234
do 1863.......	656,967	75,191,270	7,759	307,757	33,384	79,182	105,714	106,836	16,335
do 1864.......	601,824	72,720,351	12,042	237,901	41,241	68,416	114,165	107,344	20,715
do 1865.......	491,850	53,738,444	9,380	174,979	31,387	46,618	102,876	88,112	38,498
do 1866.......	497,307	57,545,439	12,041	132,202	62,408	45,578	117,942	92,034	35,102

TABLE C—*Continued.*

SYRACUSE, BINGHAMTON & NEW YORK.

FOR THE YEAR ENDING	Am't of freight in tons of 2000 pounds.	Number of tons carried one mile.	AMOUNT OF EACH KIND OF FREIGHT IN TONS, CLASSIFIED.						
			Products of the forest.	Of animals.	Vegetable food.	Other agricultural products.	Manufactures.	Merchandise.	Other articles.
Sept. 30, 1855.......	41,578	2,273,588	1,250	3,714	5,394	992	3,533	2,951	23,684
do 1856.......	(No report.)								
do 1857.......	51,008	2,876,981	2,512	3,730	6,930	254	5,783	1,323	30,476
do 1858.	73,410	5,058,890	4,914	3,923	5,806	275	4,296	1,432	52,764
do 1859.......	96,671	6,334,269	6,919	4,461	5,287	226	3,984	1,236	74,558
do 1860.......	132,679	9,331,032	7,565	5,112	5,347	279	4,667	1,310	108,399
do 1861.......	153,596	11,083,577	6,873	5,802	5,150	350	4,196	1,348	129,877
do 1862.......	211,342	15,257,380	8,331	5,824	8,508	251	4,200	1,375	182,853
do 1863.......	208,576	15,040,156	11,778	6,712	9,710	334	7,479	3,469	169,094
do 1864.......	253,634	18,293,256	8,761	7,368	8,971	836	9,374	1,907	216,419
do 1865.......	182,441	13,158,384	6,197	7,322	9,152	468	8,278	1,682	149,342
do 1866.......	361,913	21,213,908	10,639	6,959	11,057	559	9,920	3,035	319,744

TABLE C— *Continued.*

ROME, WATERTOWN AND OGDENSBURGH RAILROAD.

FOR THE YEAR ENDING	Am't of freight in tons of 2000 pounds.	Number of tons carried one mile.	AMOUNT OF EACH KIND OF FREIGHT IN TONS, CLASSIFIED.						
			Products of the forest.	Of animals.	Vegetable food.	Other agricultural products.	Manufactures.	Merchandise.	Other articles.
Sept. 30, 1851*	34,307	1,062,166	21,652	2,708	900	91	1,633	7,030	291
do 1852*	60,949	3,604,084	30,499	9,480	6,833	305	5,373	6,584	1,875
do 1853*	107,801	6,683,662	41,868	11,950	19,425	4,142	10,570	12,748	7,098
do 1854*	132,859	8,200,388	54,379	14,368	30,129	432	11,689	18,108	3,754
do 1855*	132,676	8,360,432	44,809	14,932	42,356	1,350	13,450	12,651	3,128
do 1856*	143,172	9,574,474	39,579	14,473	50,682	969	14,725	18,217	2,004
do 1857*	116,012	11,253,164	36,429	11,894	34,398	1,896	10,091	14,019	7,375
do 1858*	123,599	9,899,128	36,299	11,196	47,065	1,490	8,154	13,743	5,652
do 1859*	112,009	7,520,604	43,601	13,785	25,110	1,335	8,472	13,023	6,683
do 1860*	108,293	6,287,545	30,798	13,824	31,364	2,394	7,924	14,321	7,668
do 1861*	106,605	6,315,859	30,760	12,868	34,216	1,424	7,171	11,690	8,476
do 1862	129,639	7,727,942	35,215	19,600	36,600	6,453	8,294	15,592	7,885
do 1863	137,561	9,668,547	45,192	22,254	31,842	4,969	11,699	10,351	11,254
do 1864	197,865	11,766,254	98,456	20,082	32,445	2,864	13,616	17,015	13,387
do 1865	210,760	10,841,749	105,505	30,985	35,457	2,105	12,576	13,939	10,193
do 1866	266,896	14,577,032	120,517	23,629	60,156	5,217	20,751	18,318	18,308

* "Watertown and Rome Railroad."

TABLE C—*Continued.*

OGDENSBURGH & LAKE CHAMPLAIN RAILROAD.

FOR THE YEAR ENDING	Am't of freight in tons of 2,000 pounds.	Number of tons carried one mile.	AMOUNT OF EACH KIND OF FREIGHT IN TONS, CLASSIFIED.						
			Products of the forest.	Of animals.	Vegetable food.	Other agricultural products.	Manufactures.	Merchandise.	Other articles.
Sept. 30, 1851*	109,700	8,319,042	37,064	3,982	41,187	6,595	3,957	8,617	8,298
do 1852*	181,809	16,594,139	46,311	7,412	83,863	14,344	7,712	17,682	4,485
do 1853*	204,814	19,596,143	45,027	11,708	68,275	28,060	9,370	26,874	15,496
do 1854*	219,250	19,684,332	66,720	8,228	71,007	11,550	8,367	31,766	21,612
do 1855*	162,013	14,690,910	50,559	8,179	53,996	1,557	5,558	38,206	3,954
do 1856*	160,839	14,604,687	41,240	11,051	52,400	4,226	7,968	33,640	10,314
do 1857*	177,528	16,242,825	38,839	7,899	71,852	3,626	6,121	34,324	12,867
do 1858*	150,432	13,210,357	31,773	8,156	76,616	3,003	5,295	22,523	3,066
do 1859*	137,427	11,477,361	39,575	10,125	53,434	1,354	6,642	22,915	3,382
do 1860*	166,675	15,611,653	40,384	9,605	80,303	2,155	5,810	26,237	2,181
do 1861*	166,530	15,559,949	34,713	7,506	88,345	4,041	5,954	24,200	1,771
do 1862*	187,647	19,157,715	35,610	10,840	62,042	45,401	5,999	25,684	2,071
do 1863*	211,024	19,815,427	48,650	12,668	51,551	48,911	5,768	41,061	2,415
do 1864*	230,201	21,154,384	59,597	13,533	55,281	41,338	6,194	51,500	2,758
do 1865	203,781	18,834,478	47,133	16,918	38,707	46,807	6,077	45,711	2,428
do 1866	266,268	22,373,866	73,601	13,284	39,307	59,220	7,873	65,751	7,202

* "Northern Railroad."

STATE OF NEW YORK.

No. 22.

IN CONVENTION

July 11, 1867.

REPORT

OF CLERK OF COURT OF APPEALS, AS TO CERTAIN FUNDS HELD BY HIM.

STATE OF NEW YORK.

COURT OF APPEALS CLERK'S OFFICE,
ALBANY, *July* 4, 1867.

Hon. WILLIAM A. WHEELER, *President Convention to revise the Constitution and amend the same.*

SIR: In compliance with the resolution of the Convention, dated June 30, 1867, calling upon the Clerk of the Court of Appeals for information concerning the funds held by him in trust, and the manner of the investment of said funds, &c., I have the honor to

REPORT:

That on the 4th day of June, 1849, the fund known as the "Library Fund" of the Court of Appeals, amounting to the sum of $56,342.87 passed into the hands of the clerk of this court.

The principal sum of this fund has not since increased or diminished, the same being invested in the name of the clerk of this court, and the interest accruing thereon only being subject to draft, prescribed in section 5, of chapter 300, of the Laws of 1849.

The principal sum of this fund is invested in bond and mortgage, and United States government securities, and the interest accruing thereon is set apart for the use of the several libraries of the Court of Appeals as follows:

One-fourth for the replenishment of the libraries of the four judges of the court, elected as such directly by the people of the State at large, and by them turned over to their successors in office, the remaining three-fourths is divided between the libraries of the court, situated at Binghamton, Rochester and Syracuse.

There is in the possession of the clerk, at the date of this report, in securities belonging to this fund, the sum of $56,643.04, and of accrued interest thereon and principal, recently paid in and awaiting investment, in the bank designated by the court as the depository of its funds, the sum of $2,605.63.

The amount belonging to the "Chancery Fund," which passed into the hands of the clerk, at the time of the establishment of this office, was $93,808.73. On the first day of August, 1854, an additional sum was received from the New York Life Insurance & Trust Company, amounting to $3,622.02, and incorporated with this fund.

This fund being held in trust for infants, idiots and lunatics, wards of the late Court of Chancery, and various classes of litigants who have died, or whose heirs and their places of residences were then unknown, the original sum has been actually and nominally reduced by drafts, made upon the clerk at various times, upon the order of the Supreme Court, pursuant to chap. 28, of the Laws of 1847, sec. 71, as these persons or their heirs were discovered and adjudged entitled to receive the same.

At the date of this report, there is in the hands of the clerk securities belonging to this fund, the sum of $70,802.89, and there is in the designated depository—the National Commercial Bank of Albany—the sum of $4,298.84, awaiting investment or the order of the Supreme Court.

Schedule "A" embraces a list of the securities belonging to the

Library Fund, and Schedule "B" a list of those belonging to the Chancery Fund, together with a statement of the amount of interest reserved upon the same respectively.

Schedules "C" and "D" contain a full and complete exposition of the state of these respective funds, annually, since they came into the hands of the Clerk of the Court of Appeals: Schedule "C" relating to the Library Fund, and Schedule "D" to the Chancery Fund.

Schedule "E" is a verified statement of the Cashier of the National Commercial Bank of Albany, relating to the moneys in his possession belonging to the above mentioned funds respectively.

All of which is respectfully submitted,

P. H. JONES,

Clerk of the Court of Appeals of the State of New York.

SCHEDULE "A"—*Of Securities in the Library Fund of the Court of Appeals, January* 1, 1867.

DATE.	Name of debtor.	Amount.	Nature of security.	Rate of interest.	Remarks.
Nov. 27, 1865,	Aldrich, Stephen,	$3,000 00	Bond & M.,	.07	Interest paid.
Dec. 31, 1862,	Ayers, Daniel,	1,087 75	do	.07	Int. paid to Dec. 31, 1862, in foreclo'e.
June 16, 1864,	Alexander, O. C.,	2,400 00	do	.07	Interest paid.
Nov. 9, 1866,	Bartlett, Daniel,	1,500 00	do	.07	New mortgage.
Aug. 20, 1866,	Bamberg, Wm.,	250 00	do	.07	New mortgage.
June 14, 1854,	Briscoe, Isaac,	500 00	do	.07	Interest paid.
Jan. 19, 1858,	Billings, C. O.,	3,500 00	do	.07	Interest paid.
May 21, 1866,	Caguin, Peter,	1,000 00	do	.07	New mortgage—interest paid.
Oct. 10, 1849,	Campbell, H.,	2,000 00	do	.07	Interest paid.
Mar. 5, 1867,	Canfield, Roswell,	1,000 00	do	.07	New mortgage.
Aug. 1, 1858,	Collier, and Meesic,	2,000 00	do	.07	Interest paid.
Jan. 5, 1857,	Carrington, Joel,	2,300 00	do	.07	Interest due from March 19, 1866.
June 17, 1859,	Cramp, John,	500 00	do	.07	Interest due from December 17, 1863.
July 11, 1859,	Champine, Charles,	500 00	do	.07	Interest paid.
April 3, 1863,	Eagle, George,	1,500 00	do	.07	Interest due from April 3, 1864.
Jan. 25, 1864,	Edwards, James,	5,000 00	do	.07	Interest paid.
Nov. 29, 1866,	Evans, Sarah,	600 00	do	.07	New mortgage.
May 6, 1867,	Evans, D. M.,	500 00	do	.07	New mortgage.
June 9, 1862,	Doubleday, D.,	1,000 00	do	.07	Interest due from June 9, 1863.
Aug. 1, 1858,	Hoffman, Jacob,	500 00	do	.07	Interest paid.
June 22, 1859,	Hoffman, Wm. L.,	400 00	do	.07	Interest paid.
Feb. 11, 1864,	Hill, George,	2,500 00	do	.07	Interest paid.
Jan. 28, 1861,	Lozier, A. V.,	1,215 69	Judgment,	.07	Judgment.

May 21, 1867,.	Oaks, Leonard L., ...	1,000 00	Bond & M.,.	.07	New mortgage.
Feb. 11, 1856,.	Rathbone, Chauncey,	1,100 00	do	.07	Interest paid.
April 11, 1859,.	Rice and Jenks,.....	1,800 00	do	.07	Interest paid.
Jan. 24, 1865,.	Sourbeer, Casper,....	250 00	do	.07	Interest paid.
June 7, 1850,.	Steele, Frederick,....	300 00	do	.07	Interest due from July 1, 1865.
May 29, 1861,.	Smith, A. and F.,....	1,515 20	Judgment, .	.07	Judgment.
Dec. 10, 1864,.	Sprague, J. N. & A. M.,	2,500 00	Bond & M.,.	.07	Interest due from December 10, 1864.
Aug. 10, 1865,.	Stuart, John, ...	2,500 00	do	.07	Interest paid.
April 24, 1867,.	Starks, George, ...	700 00	do	.07	New mortgage.
April 24, 1867,.	Starks, S. F., ...	300 00	do	.07	New mortgage.
May 21, 1867,.	Stebbins, Anson G.,..	1,200 00	do	.07	New mortgage.
Dec. 15, 1865,.	United States, ...	7,000 00	Treas. notes,	.07	Interest paid.
Aug. 1, 1858,.	White, Luther,......	1,000 00	Bond & M.,.	.07	Interest paid.

SCHEDULE "B"—*Of Securities in the Chancery Fund of the Court of Appeals, January* 1, 1867.

DATE.	Name of debtor.	Amount.	Nature of security.	Rate of interest.	Remarks.
April 23, 1859,.	Adams, J. Q.,.......	$500 00	Bond & M.,.	.07	Interest paid.
Nov. 8, 1860,.	Bamberg, William,..	500 00	do	.07	Interest paid.
April 17, 1860,.	Babcock, E.,........	1,148 59	do	.07	Interest paid.
Oct. 8, 1856,.	Abell, D. H.,.......	2,374 33	do	.05	Interest paid.
Jan. 4, 1859,.	Berry, C. A., ...	400 00	do	.07	Interest due from July 4, 1864.
Jan. 20, 1864,.	Bleecker, W. E.,....	8,000 00	do	.07	Interest paid.
April 10, 1862,.	Ballou, W. P.,......	725 95	Judgment, .	.07	Judgment.
April 10, 1862,.	do	481 58	do	.07	Judgment.
April 10, 1862,.	do	453 36	do	.07	Judgment.
April 23, 1859,.	Bunte, J., ...	400 00	Bond & M.,.	.07	Interest paid.
Nov. 10, 1866,.	Bartlett, D. E., ...	600 00	do	.07	Interest paid.
Jan. 30, 1866,.	Bank stock, Oneida, .	827 00	Bank stock,.	....	Dividends paid.
Aug. 1, 1858,.	Bank stock, Union,..	5 59	....	....	
Aug. 1, 1858,.	Bank of Albany,....	1 17	....	....	
April 23, 1859,.	Castle, F. W., ...	600 00	Bond & M.,.	.07	Interest paid.
July 19, 1861,.	Eldrer & Russ,......	1,351 22	Judgment, .	.07	Judgment.
Feb. 6, 1867,.	Fisher, H. G.,.......	1,700 00	Bond & M.,.	.07	Interest paid.
June 9, 1866,.	Frank, P. J., ...	300 00	do	.07	New mortgage.
March 1, 1860,.	Foung, F., ...	350 00	do	.07	Interest due from Sept. 1, 1862.
Dec. 26, 1862,.	French, S., ...	789 62	Judgment, .	.07	Judgment.
Dec. 26, 1862,.	do	400 00	Bond & M.,.	.07	Foreclosed.

Dec. 26, 1862,	do	800 00	do	.07	Foreclosed.
Dec. 26, 1862,	do	400 00	do	.07	Interest due from June 26, 1863.
Aug. 6, 1853,	Goodwin, S. A.,	3,831 29	do	.07	Interest paid.
Sept. 15, 1864,	Gladding, H. L.,	3,500 00	do	.07	Interest paid.
July 11, 1859,	Gibbons, F. F.,	371 47	do	.07	Foreclosed.
Oct. 1, 1860,	do	400 00	do	.07	Interest due from February 16, 1866.
Nov. 14, 1859,	do	600 00	do	.07	Interest due from Nov. 15, 1862.
Aug. 4, 1860,	do	2,000 00	do	.07	Interest due from Feb. 4, 1863.
May 6, 1865,	Hill, G.,	3,000 00	do	.07	Interest paid.
March 1, 1860,	Houghtuk, J.,	350 00	do	.07	Interest paid.
Oct. 10, 1860,	Hendrick, J. H.,	900 00	do	.07	Interest paid.
Nov. 1, 1847,	Howard, N., Jr.,	336 08	Bond,	.07	Interest due from Nov. 1, 1862.
Feb. 2, 1855,	King, N. G.,	120 00	Note,	.07	Interest due from Aug. 1, 1858.
March 1, 1860,	Klump, J.,	3,000 00	Judgment,	.07	Judgment.
Nov. 8, 1860,	Kirkpatrick, T.,	500 00	Bond & M.,	.07	Interest paid.
Aug. 1, 1858,	L. F. Temp. Associa'n,	1,789 00	Mortgage,	.07	Interest paid.
June 11, 1866,	Lynch, P.,	300 00	Bond & M.,	.07	New mortgage.
Sept. 24, 1860,	Minton, C.,	500 00	do	.07	Interest paid.
July 9, 1860,	Mackay, J.,	3,000 00	Judgment,	.07	Judgment.
July 9, 1860,	Moore, S. J.,	423 96	do	.07	Judgment.
June 26, 1843,	Paige, J. K.,	374 00	Bond & M.,	.07	Interest paid.
Nov. 1, 1859,	Richards, L. I.,	3,500 00	do	.07	Interest paid.
June 21, 1866,	Ryan, Catharine,	300 00	do	.07	New mortgage.
Mar. 29, 1861,	Smith, F. & A.,	3,754 00	Judgment,	.07	Judgment.
July 31, 1862,	Straight, W. C.,	5,551 25	do	.07	Judgment.
Aug. 10, 1865,	Stuart, John,	2,500 00	Bond & M.,	.07	Interest paid.
Sept. 9, 1861,	Swayne, W. D.,	692 93	Judgment,	.07	Judgment.
Dec. 10, 1864,	Sprague, J. A.,	2,500 00	Bond & M.,	.07	Interest due from Dec. 10, 1864.

SCHEDULE "B"—*Of Securities in the Chancery Fund of the Court of Appeals, January* 1, 1867—(Continued).

DATE.	Name of debtor.	Amount.	Nature of security.	Rate of interest.	Remarks.
April 23, 1859,.	Vedder, I. A.,.......	$500 00	Bond & M.,.	.07	Interest due from March 1, 1865.
Nov. 8, 1860,.	Walker, J. B.,.......	650 00	do	.07	Interest due from Sept. 8, 1866.
Dec. 31, 1859,.	Wiley, John, ...	1,200 00	do	.07	Interest due from Jan. 1, 1864.
Jan. 10, 1867,.	Rhodes, Edward,....	800 00	do	.07	New mortgage.

SCHEDULE "C."—*Statement of the Library Fund of the Court of Appeals.*

1849. Dr.		
To securities discharged and deducted,...	$32,649 43	
To amount paid for new securities,......		$26,100 00
To amount to librarians,................		633 32
To amount to libraries,.................		315 00
To amount to judges,....................		5,250 00
To balance of securities,...............	44,108 23	
To balance of cash,.....................		8,535 37
	$76,757 66	$40,833 69

1849. Cr.		
By amount of securities on hand,.......	$50 657 66	
By amount of cash on hand, principal,..		
By amount of cash on hand, interest,....		$5,685 21
By amount received for discharged securities,..............................		32,311 93
By amount of interest received, ...		2,836 55
By new securities added, ...	26,100 00	
	$76,757 66	$40,833 69

1850. Dr.		
To securities discharged and deducted,...	$16,710 86	
To amount paid for new securities,......		$21,900 00
To amount disbursed to librarians,......		502 06
To amount disbursed to libraries,.......		107 97
To amount disbursed to judges,.........		3,645 13
To balance of securities,...............	49,297 37	
To balance of cash,.....................		3,239 39
	$66,008 23	$29,394 55

1850. Cr.		
By balance of securities brought down,..	$44,108 23	
By balance of cash brought down,......		$8,535 37
By amount received for discharged securities,............................		6,710 86
By amount of interest received, ...		4,148 32
By new securities added, ...	21,900 00	
	$66,008 23	$29,394 55

1851. Dr.		
To securities discharged and deducted,...	$1,550 00	
To amount paid for new securities,......		$2,400 00
To amount disbursed to librarians,......		379 75
To amount disbursed to libraries, ...		50 35
To amount disbursed to judges, ...		2,056 70
To balance securities, ...	50,147 37	
To balance cash, ...		2,135 62
	$51,916 37	$7,022 42

1851. Cr.		
To balance of securities brought down,..	$49,297 37	
By balance of cash brought down,......		$3,239 39
By amount received for discharged securities, ...		1,550 00
By amount of interest received, ...		2,233 03
By new securities added,...............	2,400 00	
	$51,697 37	$7,022 42

1852. Dr.		
To securities discharged and deducted,..	$7,097 37	
To amount paid for new securities,......		$4,030 00
To amount disbursed to librarians,......		626 00
To amount disbursed to libraries, ...		2,235 52
To amount disbursed to judges, ...		3,247 29
To balance securities, ...	47,080 00	
To balance cash, ...		3,447 13
	$54,177 37	$13,585 94

1852. Cr.		
By balance of securities brought down,..	$50,147 37	
By balance of cash brought down,......		$2,135 62
By amount received for discharged securities,..............................		7,097 37
By amount of interest received, ...		4,352 95
By new securities added, ...	4,030 00	
	$54,177 37	$13,585 94

1853. Dr.		
To securities discharged and deducted,..	$2,600 00	
To amount paid for new securities,......		$2,450 00
To amount disbursed to librarians,......		612 75
To amount disbursed to libraries,.......		592 31
To amount disbursed to judges, ...		1,915 83
To balance securities,.................	46,930 00	
To balance cash, ...		2,991 12
	$49,530 00	$8,562 01

1853. Cr.		
By balance of securities brought down,..	$47,080 00	
By balance of cash brought down,......		$3,447 13
By amount received for discharged securities,..............................		2,600 00
By amount of interest received,........		2,514 88
By new securities added, ...	2,450 00	
	$49,530 00	$8,562 01

1854. Dr.		
To securities discharged and deducted,..	$9,530 75	
To amount paid for new securities,......		$11,102 53
To amount disbursed to librarians,......		619 62
To amount disbursed to libraries,.......		1,080 26
To amount disbursed to judges,........		595 56
To balance securities, ...	48,501 78	
To balance cash, ...		2,752 75
	$58,032 53	$16,150 72

1854. Cr.		
By balance of securities brought down,..	$46,930 00	
By balance of cash brought down,......		$2,991 12
By amount received for discharged securities, ...		9,530 75
By amount of interest received, ...		3,628 85
By new securities added, ...	11,102 53	
	$58,032 53	$16,150 72

1855—1856. Dr.		
To securities discharged and deducted,..	$6,419 45	
To amount paid for new securities,......		$5,586 27
To amount disbursed to librarians,......		3,047 31
To amount disbursed to libraries, ...		1,758 10
To amount disbursed to judges, ...		641 00
To balance securities, ...	47,668 69	
To balance cash, ...		2,588 94
	$54,088 05	$13,621 62

1855—1856. Cr.		
By balance securities brought down, ...	$48,501 78	
By balance cash brought down,.........		$2,752 75
By amount received for discharged securities,............................		6,419 45
By amount of interest received, ...		4,449 42
By new securities added, ...	5,586 27	
	$54,088 05	$13,621 62

1857. Dr.		
To securities discharged and deducted,...	$8,252 33	
To amount paid for new securities,......		$5,942 31
To amount disbursed to librarians,......		390 25
To amount disbursed to libraries,.......		798 91
To amount disbursed to judges,........		658 27
To balance securities,.................	45,358 58	
To balance cash, ...		5,357 95
	$53,610 91	$13,147 69

1857. Cr.		
By balance securities brought down,....	$47,668 60	
By balance cash brought down,.........		$5,588 94
By amount received for discharged securities,...........................		8,252 33
By amount of interest received, ...		2,306 42
By new securities added,..............	5,942 31	
	$53,610 91	$13,147 69

1858. Dr.		
To securities discharged and deducted,..	$11,132 91	
To amount paid for new securities,......		$14,524 33
To amount disbursed to librarians,......		370 25
To amount disbursed to libraries, ...		1,471 75
To amount disbursed to judges, ...		845 53
To balance securities, ...	48,750 00	
To balance cash, ...		874 53
To expenses for search, foreclosure, &c.,..		667 65
	$59,882 91	$18,754 04

1858. Cr.		
By balance of securities brought down,..	$45,358 58	
By balance of cash brought down,......		$5,357 95
By amount received for discharged securities, ...	11,132 91	
By amount of interest received, ...		2,263 18
By new securities added, ...	14,524 33	
	$59,882 91	$18,754 04

1859. Dr.		
To securities discharged and deducted,..	$13,350 00	
To amount paid for new securities,......		$5,500 00
To amount disbursed to librarians,......		673 41
To amount disbursed to libraries,.......		949 23
To amount disbursed to judges, ...		191 93
To disbursements for cost of search, &c.,.		431 52
To balance securities, ...	52,598 33	
To balance cash, ...		247 07
	$65,948 33	$7,993 16

1859. Cr.		
By balance of securities brought down,..	$48,750 00	
By balance of cash brought down,......		$874 53
By amount received for discharged securities, ...		5,380 00
By amount of interest received, ...		1,690 40
By new securities added, ...	17,198 33	
By extra charge, ...		48 23
	$65,948 33	$7,993 16

1860. Dr.		
To securities discharged and deducted,..	$3,441 60	
To amount paid for new securities,......		$3,100 00
To amount disbursed to librarians,......		790 63
To amount disbursed to libraries,.......		1,518 16
To amount disbursed to judges, ...		404 23
To balance securities, ...	52,256 73	
To balance cash, ...		2,103 64
	$55,698 33	$7,916 66

1860. Cr.		
By balance of securities brought down,..	$52,598 33	
By balance of cash brought down,......		$247 07
By amount received for discharged securities, ...		3,441 60
By amount of interest received, ...		4,227 99
By new securities added, ...	3,100 00	
	$55,698 33	$7,916 66

1861. Dr.		
To securities discharged and deducted,..	$4,605 00	
*To amount paid for new securities,.....		$1,400 00
To amount disbursed to librarians,......		703 25

* Upon examination of the ledger accounts of the books of this office, an entry appears under date of May 2, 1861, which seems to be an error. It deducts $1,000 (one thousand dollars) from the amount received without paying any charge against the fund, or adding to it any new securities, and is therefore a loss to that amount. The item so charged is embraced in the account of 1861 above, and should be deducted from the amount of money disbursed for new securities in that year.

To amount disbursed to libraries,.......		$1,636 13
To amount disbursed to judges, ...		664 06
To disbursements for costs of search, &c.,		299 67
To balance securities, ...	$50,004 14	
To balance cash, ...		3,252 26
	$54,609 14	$7,955 37

1861. Cr.		
By balance of securities brought down,..	$52,256 73	
By balance of cash brought down,......		$2,103 64
By amount received for discharged securities,...........................		2,605 00
By amount of interest received, ...		3,246 73
By new securities added, ...	2,352 41	
	$54,609 14	$7,955 37

1862. Dr.		
To securities discharged and deducted,..	$4,205 00	
To amount paid for new securities,......		$2,400 00
To amount disbursed to librarians,......		438 75
To amount disbursed to libraries, ...		1,225 56
To amount disbursed to judges, ...		418 07
To disbursements for costs of search, &c.,		46 88
To balance securities,..................	49,719 34	
To balance cash, ...		6,023 68
	$53,919 34	$10,552 94

1862. Cr.		
By balance of securities brought down,..	$50,004 14	
By balance of cash brought down,......		$3,252 26
By amount received for discharged securities, ...		4,200 00
By amount of interest received, ...		3,100 68
By new securities added, ...	3,915 20	
	$53,319 34	$10,552 94

1863. Dr.		
To securities discharged and deducted,..	$9,650 00	
To amount paid for new securities,......		$11,087 75
To amount disbursed to librarians,......		792 75
To amount disbursed to libraries,.......		697 51
To amount disbursed to judges,........		530 60
To disbursements for costs of search, &c.,		54 65
To balance of securities,...............	51,157 09	
To balance of cash,....................		5,193 61
	$60,807 09	$18,356 87

1863. Cr.		
By balance of securities brought down,..	$49,719 34	
By balance of cash brought down,......		$6,023 68
By amount received for discharged securities, ...		9,650 00
By amount of interest received,........		2,683 19
By new securities added,..............	11,087 75	
	$60,807 09	$18,356 87

1864. Dr.		
To securities discharged and deducted,..	$9,220 00	
To amount paid for new securities,......		$12,400 00
To amount disbursed to librarians,......		789 25
To amount disbursed to libraries,.......		1,121 18
To amount disbursed to judges, ...		259 16
To balance securities, ...	54,339 09	
To balance cash, ...		3,183 24
	$63,557 09	$17,752 83

1864. Cr.		
By balance of securities brought down,..	$5,157 09	
By balance of cash brought down,......		$5,193 61
By amount received for discharged securities, ...		9,220 00
By amount of interest received, ...		3,339 22
By new securities added, ...	12,400 00	
	$63,557 09	$17,752 83

1865. Dr.		
To securities discharged and deducted,...	$4,766 00	
To amount paid for new securities,......		$4,388 48
To amount disbursed to librarians,......		617 50
To amount disbursed to libraries, ...		376 15
To amount disbursed to judges, ...		471 75
*To deficit securities, ...	672 48	
To deficit cash, ...		
To balance securities, ...	53,287 09	
To balance cash, ...		3,350 64
	$58,725 57	$9,204 52

1865. Cr.		
By balance of securities brought down,..	$54,337 09	
By balance of cash brought down,......		$3,183 22
By amount received for discharged securities, ...		4,766 00
By amount of interest received, ...		1,255 28
By new securities added, ...	4,388 48	
	$58,725 57	$9,204 52

1866. Dr.		
To securities discharged and deducted,..	$8,241 30	
To amount paid for new securities,......		$10,350 00
To amount paid to librarians, ...		702 89
To amount paid to libraries, ...		1,489 50
To amount paid to judges, ...		1,901 66
To miscellaneous disbursements,........		629 29
To balance securities, ...	55,395 79	
To balance cash, ...		3,279 71
	$63,637 09	$18,353 05

1866. Cr.		
By balance securities brought down, ...	$53,287 09	
By balance cash brought down,.........		$3,350 64
By amount received for discharged securities, ...		8,913 78

* Since made good.

By amount of interest received, ...		6,088 63
By new securities added,...............	10,350 00	
	$63,637 09	$18,353 05

1867. Dr.		
To securities discharged and deducted,...	$5,577 15	
To amount paid for new securities,......		$6,400 00
To amount to librarians, ...		350 00
To amount to libraries,................		1,300 13
To amount to judges,.........		120 87
To balance of securities, ...	56,218 64	
To balance of cash,..................		2,694 17
	$61,795 79	$10,865 17

1867. Cr.		
By amount of securities on hand,.......	$55,395 79	
By amount of cash on hand, principal, ..		$1,248 19
By amount of cash on hand, interest,....		2,031 52
By amount received for discharged securities, ...		5,577 15
By amount of interest received, ...		2,008 31
By new securities added, ...	6,400 00	
	$61,795 79	$10,865 17

RECAPITULATION.

To securities discharged and deducted,.	$158,984 15	
To amount paid for new securities,....		$151,001 67
To amount disbursed to librarians,....		13,039 74
To amount disbursed to libraries, ...		18,723 59
To amount disbursed to judges, ...		23,799 64
To amount disbursed for cost of search, &c., ...		2,129 66
To deficit securities Dec. 31, 1865, ...	672 48	
To balance securities, ...	56,218 64	
To balance cash, ...		2,694 17
	$215,875 27	$211,388 47

RECAPITULATION.

By amount of securities on hand in 1849, ...	$50,657 66	
By amount of cash, principal, same date, ...		$5,685 21
By amount of cash, interest, same date,.		
By amount received for discharged securities, ...		149,349 00
By amount of interest received, ...		56,306 03
By extra charge in 1860, ...		48 23
By new securities added, ...	165,217 61	
	$265,875 27	$211,288 47

SCHEDULE "D."—*Statement of the Chancery Fund of the Court of Appeals.*

DR.

To accounts paid on order of the court from 1847 to Aug. 1, 1858, ...	$53,324 63	
To balance on hand Aug. 1, 1858, ...	70,448 14	
	$123,772 77	

CR.

By amount in court at its organization,	$93,808 73	
By interest on this sum to Aug. 1, 1858,	25,652 25	
By moneys of litigants received in 1854,		$3,622 02
By interest to August 1, 1858, ...		689 77
	$123,772 77	

1858. DR.

To balance on hand, ...	$70,501 49
	$70,501 49

1858. CR.

By balance on hand brought down, ...	$70,448 14
By interest received, ...	53 35
	$70,501 49

1859. DR.		
To disbursements on order of court,...	$4,460 92	
To balance on hand,................	69,005 88	
	$73,466 80	
1859. CR.		
By balance on hand brought down,....	$70,501 49	
By interest received,................	2,965 31	
	$73,466 80	
1860. DR.		
To disbursements on order of court,...	$12,954 30	
To balance on hand,................	60,526 66	
	$73,480 96	
1860. CR.		
By balance brought down, ...	$69,005 88	
By interest received,................	4,475 08	
	$73,480 96	
1861. DR.		
To disbursements on order of the court,		$300 00
To balance on hand, securities,.......	$60,526 66	
To balance on hand, cash,...........		854 52
	$60,526 66	$1,154 52
1861. CR.		
By balance on hand brought down,...	$60,526 66	
By interest received,...............		$1,154 52
	$60,526 66	$1,154 52
1862. DR.		
To securities discharged and deducted,	$6,666 00	
To disbursements on order of the court,		$2,688 23
To amount paid for new securities,....		2,672 11
To balance on hand, securities,.......	66,789 74	
To balance on hand, cash, ...		1,730 25
	$73,455 74	$7,090 59

1862. Cr.		
By balance securities brought down,..	$60,526 66	
By balance cash brought down, ...		$854 52
By amount received for discharged securities,..........................		2,400 00
By interest received,................		3,836 07
By new securities added, ...	12,929 08	
	$73,455 74	$7,090 59

1863. Dr.		
To securities discharged and deducted,.	$3,234 11	
To amount paid for new securities,....		$6,000 00
To balance on hand, securities, ...	69,628 44	
To balance on hand, cash, ...		834 17
	$72,862 55	$6,834 17

1863. Cr.		
By balance securities brought down, ..	$66,789 74	
By balance cash brought down, ...		$1,730 25
By amount received for discharged securities, ...		2,400 00
By interest received,................		2,703 92
By new securities added,............	6,072 81	
	$72,862 55	$6,834 17

1864. Dr.		
To securities discharged and deducted,.	$12,481 65	
To disbursements on order of court, ..		$126 48
To amount paid for new securities,....		14,000 00
To balance on hand, securities, ...	71,146 79	
To balance on hand, cash, ...		1,626 15
	$83,628 44	$15,752 63

1864. Cr.		
By balance securities on hand, ...	$69,628 44	
By balance cash on hand, ...		$834 17
By amount received for discharged securities, ...		12,050 00

	Securities	Cash
By interest received, ...		$2,868 46
By new securities added, ...	$14,000 00	
	$83,628 44	$15,752 63

1865. DR.		
To securities discharged and deducted,.	$830 00	
To disbursements on order of court,...		$153 30
To amount paid for new securities, ...		5,500 00
To balance on hand, securities,.......	75,986 79	
To balance on hand, cash,............		263 97
	$76,816 79	$5,916 27

1865. CR.		
By balance securities on hand,.........	$71,146 79	
By balance cash on hand,.............		$1,626 15
By amount received for discharged securities,.........................		800 00
By interest received,................		3,490 12
By new securities added, ...	5,670 00	
	$76,816 79	$5,916 27

1866. DR.		
To securities discharged and deducted,.	$11,919 99	
To disbursements on order of court,...		$4,642 96
To amount paid for new securities,....		2,200 00
To balance on hand, securities, ...	70,134 20	
To balance on hand, cash, ...		2,037 98
	$82,054 19	$8,880 94

1866. CR.		
By balance of securities on hand, ...	$75,986 79	
By balance of cash on hand,.........		$263 97
By amount received for discharged securities,.........................		5,936 73
By amount of interest received,.......		2,680 24
By new securities added, ...	6,067 40	
	$82,054 19	$8,880 94

1867. Dr.		
To securities discharged and deducted,	$2,731 31	
To disbursements on order of court,..		$390 97
To amount paid for new securities,....		3,400 00
To balance on hand, securities,.......	70,802 89	
To balance on hand, cash,...........		4,318 84
	$73,534 20	$8,109 81

1867. Cr.		
By balance securities brought down,..	$70,134 20	
By balance cash brought down, ...		$2,037 98
By amount received for discharged securities,..		2,701 31
By interest received,.................		3,370 52
By new securities added,............	3,400 00	
	$73,534 20	$8,109 81

Recapitulation.

To securities discharged and deducted,	$37,862 96	
To disbursements on order of court,...	70,739 85	$8,300 89
To amount paid for new securities,....		33,772 11
To balance on hand, securities,.......	70,802 89	
To balance on hand, cash,...........		4,318 84
	$179,405 70	$46,391 84

Recapitulation.

By amount on hand in 1847,........	$93,808 73	
By amount received in 1854,..........	3,622 02	
By interest to January 1, 1860,.......	33,835 66	
By interest to July 1st, 1867,........		$20,103 82
By amount for discharged securities,..		26,288 02
By new securities added, ...	48,139 29	
	$179 405 70	$46,391 84

SCHEDULE "E."

ALBANY, *July* 10, 1867.

On the morning of July 4, 1867, there stood to the credit of P. H. Jones, clerk, &c., "Chancery Fund," in the National Commercial Bank of Albany, four thousand two hundred and ninety-eight dollars and eighty-four cents ($4,298.84); and at the same time, to the credit of P. H. Jones, clerk, &c., "Library Fund," two thousand six hundred and five dollars and sixty-three cents ($2,605.63).

JOHN VAN DYCK, *Bookkeeper.*

STATE OF NEW YORK.

No. 23.

IN CONVENTION

July 12, 1867.

COMMUNICATION

FROM AUDITOR OF CANAL DEPARTMENT AS TO COST AND REVENUE OF CANALS.

STATE OF NEW YORK.

CANAL DEPARTMENT,
ALBANY, *July* 12, 1867.

Hon. WILLIAM A. WHEELER, *President of the Convention.*

SIR: I herewith transmit the report from this department, in answer to the resolution of the Convention of the 26th of June last.

At the suggestion of several members of the Convention, during the late recess of that body, and with a view to the early printing of the same, the tables referred to in the report, were sent to the printer, in whose hands they now are.

I am very respectfully, yours, &c.,

N. S. BENTON,
Auditor.

REPORT.

CANAL DEPARTMENT,
ALBANY, *July* 1*st*, 1867.

To the Covention:

The Auditor of the Canal Department, in answer to the following resolution of the Convention, viz:

IN CONSTITUTIONAL CONVENTION,
ALBANY, N. Y., *June* 26*th*, 1867.

On motion of Mr. M. I. Townsend,

Resolved, That the Auditor of the Canal Department be requested to prepare and communicate to this Convention a tabular statement showing:

1. The original cost of the several canals of the State, including that of any enlargement or extension thereof.

2. The aggregate cost of each canal, as aforesaid, including superintendence, repairs and legal interest on the cost of construction up to the close of the last fiscal year.

3. The aggregate receipts or income from each canal, completed in like manner, with interest thereon, to the close of the last fiscal year.

4. The annual receipts or income of the State from each canal, with the annual cost of superintendence and repairs respectively of such canals, up to the close of the last fiscal year.

6. Also a table which will show with how much each so called lateral canal should be credited for its contributions to the revenues, which in the yearly official tables are credited to the Erie canal.

7. The amount of outstanding canal debt and when due, and when the same would be paid, assuming as a basis of calculation for the future revenue of the toll receipts, the revenue from the same source for the last seven years.

And that the Auditor be requested to report upon the several propositions of inquiry in the order, and as soon as each answer can be completed.

By order,

LUTHER CALDWELL, *Secretary.*

respectfully submits the following, with the statements and tables, as his report to the several inquiries contained in the said resolution :

Statement A is an aggregate recapitulation in a condensed form of the detailed information called for by the first six propositions of the resolution of inquiry. The specific and detailed information in reference to each canal will be found in tables Nos. 1 to 13, inclusive, following consecutively.

Statement B is a balance sheet, showing the net cost or profit to the State of each canal, as deduced from the tables submitted.

These statements and tables were being prepared for the Convention Manual when the call was made upon the Department.

The Auditor submits the following reply to the 7th inquiry of the resolution, which is in these words:

"The amount of outstanding canal debt and when due, and when the same would be paid, assuming as a basis of calculation for the future revenue of the toll receipts the revenue from the same source for the last seven years."

Amount of Debt July 1, 1867.	When due.	Annual interest.	Interest to maturity.
$160 00	July 1, 1837,	No interest.	
10,000 00	After 1860,	do	
247,900 00	October 1, 1868,	$12,395 00	$15,493 75
57,000 00	January 1, 1871,	2,850 00	9,975 00
2,800,000 00	July 1, 1872,	168,000 00	840,000 00
1,000,000 00	January 1, 1873,	60,000 00	330,000 00
2,750,000 00	July 1, 1873,	165,000 00	990,000 00
2,250,000 00	November 1, 1873,	135,000 00	855,000 00
3,000,000 00	January 1, 1874,	150,000 00	975,000 00
2,250,000 00	October 1, 1874,	135,000 00	978,750 00
500,000 00	October 1, 1875,	30,000 00	247,500 00
900,000 00	December 1, 1877,	54,000 00	562,500 00
$15,765,060 00		$912,245 00	
Total interest of debt,			$5,804,218 75
Total principal of debt,			15,765,060 00
Total principal and interest,			$21,569,278 75

In the above statement there is included the sum of $1,700,000 the remainder of the Floating Debt Loan, so called, contracted for canal purposes, under the act, chapter 271 of the Laws of 1859.

The aggregate of the net receipts from tolls or surplus canal revenues, for the seven years ending on the 30th September, 1866, was $20,636,868.26.

This gives an average per year of $2,948,124.03, so that, assuming that the net surplus canal revenues for the next seven years will be as large as the last seven, this debt, principal and interest, can be paid in seven and three-fourths years.

Assume that the whole annual surplus will be,	$2,948,124 03
Deduct from this the annual interest of the whole outstanding canal debt,	912,245 00
Annual remainder to apply on principal,	$2,035,879 03

Multiply this remainder by 7¾ and we have $15,778,062.47.

But these surpluses will not be available to pay this canal debt, until after the extinguishment of the General Fund Debt of 1846, amounting to $5,636,622.22, which by the present Constitution, has a preference in payment to the whole of the above Canal Debt, except $3,257,900, the remainder of the Canal Debt of 1846. The aggregate of the principal of both debts, is $21,401,682.22, and the aggregate of the yearly interest is $1,234,663.35.

On the 30th of September, 1867, the actual and estimated balance in the treasury applicable to the payment of the principal and interest of these debts, after deducting the interest on the Canal Debt, and the contribution of $350,000 to the General Fund Debt Sinking Fund, due the first of October, 1867, will be $2,755,595.26. If this actual and estimated revenue shall be realized on the 30th of September next, it will not be subject to any deductions for interest due up to that time; and if this actual and estimated balance were then applied to the redemption of the principal of these debts, according to their priority, the results below would be obtained, by applying the seven years' averages.

1857, Sept. 30. Aggregate principal of both debts,	$21,401,682 22
1867, Sept. 30. Apply means on hand,	2,755,595 26
Balance of principal outstanding,	$18,646,086 96

Amount of the seven years average,	$2,948,124 03
Yearly interest on the remainder of principal deducted,	1,112,170 35
Yearly balance applicable to principal,	$1,835,953 68

These figures show that both debts will be wiped out in about ten years, if these averages are maintained, as they probably will be if the canals are not depleted in the future as they have been in the past. The last installment of the Canal Debt is due December 1, 1877, and that of the General Fund Debt, July 1, 1878.

What have the canals cost the treasury of the State?

This short and literal exposition of a portion of the tables will answer this question.

There was contributed from the treasury prior to 1846, in aid of the canals:

From taxes levied prior to 1846,	$496,496 05
From vendue duty,	3,592,039 05
From duty on salt,	2,055,458 06
From steamboat tax,	73,509 99
From sales of land,*	320,518 15
From General Fund for deficiencies,	1,386,498 88
Total,	$7,924,520 18
Reimbursed to the treasury from the canal tolls, prior to Sept. 30, 1846,	2,537,602 73
Balance advanced by treasury, without interest,	$5,386,917 45

The credit to the treasury of $320,518.15 for the receipts from the sales of public land, includes the proceeds of the sales of land donated to the Erie and Champlain canals, and, therefore, to the extent of the means thus derived, nothing was taken from the treasury, nor any means whereby the treasury proper could have been

* The Erie and Champlain canals received donations of 110,036 acres of land west of the Seneca river, to aid in their construction.

benefited. When the Convention, in 1846, adjusted the balances between the canals and the treasury for advances, a perpetual annuity of $200,000 a year was imposed upon the surplus canal revenues equal to an annual income at five per cent on $4,000,000 invested; a charge was made upon the canals to pay the General Fund debt and other collateral liabilities which now aggregate $5,636,622.22, and imposed an annual payment upon the canals of $350,000 to cover the accruing interest on this debt, which is $27,581.65 a year in excess of the actual interest paid by the treasury, and this statement may be given.

Paid to the treasury since 1846, on the $200,000 for the support of government, ...	$2,151,113 40
Paid to the treasury since 1846, in excess of the actual interest on the General Fund debt during that period,	551,633 00
Advanced outside of the interest on General Fund Debt,	$2,702,746 40

The adjustment and award made by the Convention in 1846, was supposed to be a finality, and the legislative and fiscal departments of the State are bound to consider the question closed under the present fundamental law. The resolutions of inquiry, which the Auditor has endeavored to answer as fully and elaborately as the means at hand and urgency of the occasion will allow, go far behind that finding and award in 1846, and call for information that in its natural characteristics will give a partial and one-sided view of the subject, and hence this volunteer addition. The State has not paid or advanced a dollar since 1846 to the canals or their debt, which they will not repay with interest according to the terms of the contract on which the advances were made. The periods for the final liquidation of the General Fund debt are rapidly approaching and will soon be consummated; the final payments of the Canal Debt will soon be made without any resort to the State for aid; and the advances made since 1846 will be refunded with interest, and the State will have the canals free of charge or cost, as a commission for advances repaid, and a compensation for indorsements.

The canals are indebted to the treasury $14,396,767.97 for taxes levied and received for canal purposes since 1846, besides the interest, which must be refunded out of the canal revenues after the payment of certain preferred claims.

Respectfully submitted,
N. S. BENTON, *Auditor.*

TABLE NO. 1

Erie and Champlain Canals.

YEAR.	INCOME.				DISBURSEMENTS.							
					FOR CONSTRUCTION.		FOR MAINTENANCE.					
	(1)	(2)	(3)	(4)	(1)	(2)	(3)	(4)	(5)	(6)	(7)	(8)
	Tolls proper.	Legal interest on tolls proper.	Tolls after deducting tolls on contributions from the lateral canals.	Legal interest on tolls after deduct'g tolls on contributions from the lateral canals.	Cost of construction.	Legal interest on cost of construction.	Contractors for repairs.	Superintendents for repairs.	Collectors, inspectors, &c.	Weighmasters.	Tot. payments, including cost of construction and enlargement.	Legal interest on total payments, including cost of construction, &c
1817,	....	....	....	....	$200,000 00	$686,000 00	....	....	....	....	$200,000 00	$668,000 00
1818,	....	....	....	....	466,900 00	1,568,784 00	....	....	....	....	466,900 00	1,568,784 00
1819,	....	....	....	....	587,467 09	1,932,766 73	....	....	....	....	587,467 09	1,932,766 72
1820,	....	....	....	....	668,900 00	2,153,858 00	....	....	....	....	668,900 00	2,153,858 00
1821,	$6,930 00	$2,200 00	$2,200 00	$6,930 00	1,120,500 00	3,529,575 00	....	....	....	....	1,120,500 00	3,529,575 00
1822,	137,019 10	44,486 72	44,486 72	137,019 10	1,955,012 23	6,021,437 67	....	....	....	....	1,955,012 23	6,021,437 68
1823,	361,164 12	119,988 08	119,988 08	361,164 12	1,784,102 61	5,370,148 86	....	....	....	....	1,784,102 61	5,370,148 85
1824,	850,602 50	289,320 58	289,320 58	850,602 51	1,275,543 82	3,750,098 83	....	....	....	....	1,275,543 82	3,750,098 83
1825,	1,496,257 11	521,343 94	521,343 94	1,496,257 11	990,537 84	2,842,843 60	....	....	....	....	990,537 84	2,842,843 60
1826,	2,356,724 36	841,687 27	841,687 27	2,356,724 36	403,255 91	1,129,116 55	....	$124,652 51	....	....	527,908 42	1,478,143 57
1827,	2,404,072 40	880,978 90	880,978 90	2,405,072 40	153,551 67	419,196 06	....	284,654 16	$26,636 61	$450 00	465,292 44	1,270,248 36
1828,	2,204,991 78	828,944 25	828,244 43	2,203,130 18	92,310 92	245,547 05	....	215,809 25	27,042 33	4,052 87	339,215 37	902,312 90
1829,	2,071,361 33	799,753 41	787,710 42	2,040,169 99	48,698 21	126,128 36	....	234,504 21	26,111 47	5,116 63	314,430 52	814,375 04
1830,	2,567,428 67	1,018,820 90	988,442 31	2,490,874 62	18,255 81	46,004 64	....	211,044 19	22,327 28	4,377 88	256,005 16	645,133 00
1831,	1,786,961 67	729,372 11	692,762 32	1,697,267 68	11,377 68	27,875 32	....	156,553 66	22,973 86	2,023 50	192,928 70	472,675 31
1832,	2,578,983 04	1,083,606 32	1,049,578 17	2,497,996 04	32,890 81	78,280 13	....	333,786 05	22,987 29	4,430 59	394,094 74	937,945 48
1833,	3,117,342 16	1,349,498 77	1,306,869 97	3,018,869 63	35,264 66	81,461 36	....	330,759 44	25,052 14	4,602 25	395,678 49	914,017 31
1834,	3,010,015 14	1,343,756 76	1,272,706 51	2,850,862 57	15,006 17	33,613 82	....	423,517 10	25,162 42	4,511 25	468,196 94	1,048,761 14
1835,	3,007,123 35	1,431,854 08	1,342,189 91	2,912,652 10	52,109 05	113,076 64	....	403,473 90	25,764 64	4,781 30	486,128 89	1,054,899 69
1836,	3,237,829 88	1,541,823 75	1,445,906 35	3,036,403 34	66,259 82	139,145 62	....	300,391 32	26,030 90	4,211 20	396,893 24	833,475 80
1837,	2,586,436 32	1,274,106 81	1,209,145 61	2,454,565 59	694,103 10	1,409,029 29	....	361,714 70	29,912 18	5,671 71	1,091,401 69	2,215,545 43
1838,	2,747,341 50	1,401,704 75	1,310,609 81	2,568,795 23	1,244,398 49	2,439,021 04	....	365,661 95	24,335 97	6,350 32	1,640,746 73	3,215,863 59
1839,	3,033,928 67	1,578,798 24	1,491,065 31	2,818,113 44	2,330,664 11	4,404,955 17	....	299,599 53	38,814 32	6,067 85	2,675,145 81	5,056,025 58
1840,	2,800,798 55	1,538,900 30	1,438,565 13	2,618,188 54	3,287,636 70	5,983,498 79	....	296,913 67	39,740 88	5,719 28	3,630,010 53	6,606,619 16
1841,	3,313,872 70	1,893,641 54	1,751,143 43	3,064,501 00	2,569,327 23	4,496,322 65	....	273,433 22	38,293 30	5,290 22	2,886,343 97	5,051,101 95
1842,	2,868,248 73	1,707,290 91	1,605,574 69	2,697,365 48	1,622,692 72	2,726,123 77	....	303,654 96	37,148 35	5,152 55	1,968,648 58	3,307,329 61
1843,	3,001,954 25	1,864,567 86	1,707,117 75	2,748,459 58	575,548 97	926,633 84	....	294,941 49	38,655 48	4,506 84	908,052 78	1,461,964 98
1844,	3,481,660 55	2,260,818 54	2,009,568 40	3,094,735 34	482,305 64	742,750 70	....	353,688 77	32,372 45	4,724 21	873,091 07	1,344,560 25
1845,	3,257,643 94	2,216,084 31	1,903,687 66	2,798,420 86	259,086 44	380,857 07	....	408,024 59	32,891 53	4,985 60	704,968 16	1,036,322 59
1846,	3,664,256 62	2,617,326 16	2,323,984 53	3,253,578 34	102,029 69	142,841 57	....	368,626 45	33,558 13	4,795 93	509,010 20	712,614 28

1847,	4,336,175 70	4,280,283 23	2,864,660 65	3,809,998 66	83,876 49	111,575 73	....	377,750 22	34,786 68	5,066 65	501,480 04	666,968 45
1848,	3,637,234 10	2,886,693 73	2,519,796 25	3,174,943 28	665,267 02	838,236 45	....	515,687 65	39,930 72	5,885 71	1,226,881 10	1,545,807 19
1849,	3,645,985 39	3,063,853 27	2,682,016 39	3,191,599 50	1,009,909 28	1,201,792 04	....	401,862 55	39,153 72	6,178 80	1,457,104 35	1,733,954 17
1850,	3,424,605 40	3,057,683 39	2,631,020 89	2,946,743 40	1,375,300 98	1,540,337 10	....	429,014 55	35,912 99	6,081 93	1,846,310 45	2,067,867 70
1851,	3,476,033 16	3,310,507 77	2,924,063 52	3,070,266 70	1,026,242 73	1,077,554 87	....	485,158 75	51,162 53	7,412 50	1,569,976 51	1,648,475 33
1852,	2,858,368 02	2,916,702 06	2,534,456 75	2,483,767 62	972,704 92	953,250 82	....	555,594 75	45,928 01	7,076 93	1,581,304 61	1,549,678 52
1853,	2,665,779 85	2,929,428 41	2,439,742 60	2,220,165 77	605,269 10	550,794 88	....	566,833 08	47,830 36	7,468 11	1,227,400 65	1,116,934 59
1854,	2,315,334 99	2,756,351 18	2,423,397 63	2,035,654 01	646,939 43	543,429 12	....	705,307 31	50,422 49	7,873 16	1,410,542 39	1,184,855 61
1855,	1,877,209 43	2,437,934 33	2,040,493 89	1,571,180 30	2,250,282 72	1,732,717 69	$16,873 23	540,707 79	54,113 05	8,093 29	2,870,070 08	2,209,953 96
1856,	1,750,348 59	2,500,497 98	2,029,359 59	1,420,551 71	3,361,764 30	2,353,235 01	53,498 54	387,217 91	55,715 16	7,796 73	3,865,992 64	2,706,194 85
1857,	1,456,859 04	2,312,474 66	1,983,582 23	1,249,656 80	2,416,258 51	1,522,242 86	65,979 25	408,853 91	55,222 28	7,779 10	2,954,093 05	1,861,078 62
1858,	1,055,018 95	1,883,962 41	1,577,469 15	883,382 72	1,491,786 68	835,400 54	66,981 61	369,173 98	59,149 44	8,096 78	1,995,188 49	1,117,305 55
1859,	810,921 74	1,654,942 32	1,316,708 79	645,187 31	540,127 31	264,662 38	80,797 10	357,261 37	46,836 13	6,295 93	1,031,317 84	505,345 74
1860,	911,868 54	2,171,115 57	1,564,098 46	656,921 35	2,445,910 67	1,027,282 48	113,978 42	128,798 07	64,805 75	9,867 67	2,763,360 58	1,160,611 44
1861,	1,096,052 76	3,131,579 31	2,574,023 32	900,908 16	768,792 57	269,077 40	141,819 94	68,752 43	45,099 75	8,111 30	1,032,575 99	361,401 60
1862,	1,271,111 39	4,539,683 55	3,886,262 05	1,088,153 38	863,565 97	241,798 47	153,101 18	76,103 27	42,687 95	8,430 85	1,143,889 22	320,288 98
1863,	1,000,876 28	4,766,077 54	4,165,884 49	874,835 74	355,871 38	74,732 99	197,588 02	99,997 35	42,365 26	9,164 07	704,986 08	148,047 08
1864,	566,104 64	4,043,604 53	3,589,141 69	502,479 84	738,961 09	103,454 55	244,567 10	257,968 69	43,645 77	9,256 88	1,294,399 53	181,215 93
1865,	232,199 99	3,317,142 72	2,771,039 11	193,972 74	626,733 28	43,871 33	495,389 06	360,771 89	49,120 97	9,705 70	1,541,720 90	107,920 46
1866,	....	3,995,548 42	3,375,073 22	....	626,932 37	....	396,302 54	290,035 46	54,558 25	11,306 35	1,379,134 97	....
	$100,339,037 90	$92,116,741 67	$81,057,168 87	$91,399,088 14	$46,018,234 19	$69,232,418 84	$2,026,875 99	$13,728,256 10	$1,548,718 79	$248,770 42	$63,570,855 49	$90,429,363 47

ERIE AND CHAMPLAIN CANALS.

(*See Table No.* 1.)

RESULT I.

CREDIT—INCOME.

From tolls proper,		$92,116,741 67	
Interest thereon,		100,339,037 90	
Total income and interest,			$192,455,779 57

DEBIT—EXPENDITURES.

For construction,	$46,018,234 19		
Interest thereon,	69,232,418 84	$115,250,653 03	
For maintenance,	$17,552,621 30		
Interest thereon,	21,196,944 63	38,749,565 93	
Total expenditures and interest,			154,000,218 96
Profit and interest,			$38,455,560 61

RESULT II.

CREDIT—INCOME.

From tolls proper,	$92,116,741 67	
Interest thereon,	100,339,037 90	
Total income and interest,		$192,455,779 57
Less tolls on contributions from lateral canals,.	$11,059,572 80	
Interest thereon,	8,939,949 76	
Total contributions from the laterals and interest,		19,999,522 56
Net income and interest,		$172,456,257 01

DEBIT—EXPENDITURES.

For construction,	$46,018,234 19		
Interest thereon,	69,232,418 84	$115,250,653 03	
For maintenance,	$17,552,621 30		
Interest thereon,	21,196,944 63	38,749,565 93	
Total expenditures and interest,			154,000,218 96
Net profit and interest,			*$18,456,038 05

* In the above result all the tolls contributed by the lateral canals have been restored to the contributing canals, as will appear in the following tables, but the lateral canals have been charged nothing for their proportion of repairs and maintenance of the Erie and Champlain canals, excepting the memorandum at the bottom of each table showing the proportion chargeable to each.

Brought forward,..		$18,456,038 05
Add to this balance the proportion of repairs and maintenance of the Erie and Champlain canals chargeable to the lateral canals, viz:		
Oswego canal, ...	$2,826,648 19	
Cayuga and Seneca canal,....................	579,994 50	
Chemung canal, ...	654,879 47	
Crooked Lake canal,.........................	201,092 20	
Chenango canal, ...	51,856 93	
Black River canal, ...	53,855 47	
Genesee Valley canal,.......................	283,961 20	
		4,652,287 96
Balance of profit and interest,.....		$23,108,326 01

TABLE

Oswego

YEARS.	INCOME.			
	(1)	(2)	(3)	(4)
	Tolls proper.	Tolls contributed to and heretofore credited Erie and Champlain Canals.	Total of tolls proper and contributions.	Legal interest on tolls proper and contributions.
1826,	....	....	....	....
1827,	....	....	....	....
1828,	$2,057 82	$699 85	$2,757 67	$7,335 40
1829,	9,071 93	367 51	9,439 44	24,448 15
1830,	12,430 01	....	12,430 01	31,323 62
1831,	11,465 20	4,805 90	16,271 10	39,864 20
1832,	16,610 65	3,175 55	19,786 20	47,091 16
1833,	22,965 26	....	22,965 26	53,049 75
1834,	22,174 13	20,246 09	42,420 22	95,021 29
1835,	26,267 09	35,989 77	62,256 86	135,097 39
1836,	29,359 93	41,238 11	70,598 04	148,255 88
1837,	24,556 97	18,900 60	43,457 57	88,218 87
1838,	22,961 40	35,923 85	58,885 25	115,415 09
1839,	32,593 80	39,204 68	71,798 48	135,699 13
1840,	29,166 71	35,968 37	65,135 08	118,545 85
1841,	34,630 03	51,605 15	86,235 18	150,911 57
1842,	35,878 82	35,963 70	71,842 52	120,695 43
1843,	31,914 21	63,305 91	95,220 12	153,304 39
1844,	50,013 24	108,753 36	158,766 60	244,500 56
1845,	53,831 17	111,876 25	165,707 42	243,589 91
1846,	60,101 35	128,315 93	188,417 28	263,784 19
1847,	70,839 01	190,161 54	261,000 55	347,130 73
1848,	71,564 58	184,307 60	255,872 18	322,398 95
1849,	86,139 66	224,665 31	310,804 97	369,857 91
1850,	94,524 17	243,590 91	338,115 08	378,688 89
1851,	104,366 58	232,322 30	336,688 88	353,523 32
1852,	82,951 22	237,310 92	320,262 14	313,856 90
1853,	88,839 97	301,962 61	390,802 58	355,630 35
1854,	81,266 00	151,273 51	232,539 51	195,333 19
1855,	64,954 15	234,123 03	299,077 18	230,289 43
1856,	96,136 22	336,379 98	432,516 20	302,761 34
1857,	105,141 39	204,452 79	309,594 18	195,044 33
1858,	83,939 46	173,361 59	257,301 05	144,088 59
1859,	69,348 37	198,234 69	267,583 06	131,115 70
1860,	109,840 03	455,410 02	565,250 05	237,405 02
1861,	131,458 38	452,795 02	584,253 40	204,488 69
1862,	153,006 82	496,703 51	649,710 33	181,918 89
1863,	143,273 75	450,793 05	594,066 80	124,754 03
1864,	142,561 87	321,655 78	464,217 65	64,990 47
1865,	112,063 86	432,047 82	544,111 68	38,087 82
1866,	143,364 27	461,708 04	605,072 31	....
	$2,563,629 48	$6,719,600 60	$9,283,230 08	$6,707,516 38

RESULT.

CREDIT.

By tolls proper,	$2,563,629 48	
By tolls on tonnage contributed to the Erie Canal,	6,719,600 60	
Total income from 1827 to 1866,		$9,283,230 08
Interest on income from 1827 to 1866,		6,707,516 38
Total credit, with interest,		$15,990,746 46

NO 2.

Canal.

DISBURSEMENTS.						
FOR CONSTRUCTION.		FOR MAINTENANCE.				
(1)	(2)	(3)	(4)	(5)	(6)	(7)
Cost of construction.	Legal interest on cost of construction.	Contractors, for repairs.	Superintendents, for repairs.	Collectors, inspectors, &c.	Total payments, including cost of construction.	Legal interest on total payments, including cost of construction.
$237,015 57	$663,643 60	....	....	....	$237,015 57	$663,643 59
175,221 00	478,353 33	....	....	....	175,221 00	439,353 33
83,774 46	222,840 06	....	$8,418 00	....	92,192 46	245,241 94
43,319 99	112,198 80	....	13,186 40	$942 94	57,449 33	137,693 76
3,310 00	8,341 20	....	12,972 51	1,837 25	18,119 76	45,662 79
....	....	....	8,860 48	1,866 77	10,727 25	26,281 76
....	....	....	12,507 99	1,974 39	14,482 38	34,468 06
....	....	....	11,236 72	2,015 03	13,251 75	30,611 54
....	....	....	12,522 48	2,008 51	14,530 99	32,549 41
....	....	....	12,747 26	2,044 97	14,792 23	32,099 13
....	....	....	51,064 14	2,147 44	53,211 58	111,744 31
165 00	334 95	....	54,625 00	2,616 81	57,406 81	116,535 82
1,156 21	2,265 76	....	53,997 56	2,003 13	57,156 90	112,027 52
....	....	....	24,624 60	3,086 62	27,711 22	52,374 20
....	....	....	36,198 40	2,988 44	39,186 84	71,320 04
....	....	....	26,241 95	2,992 96	29,234 91	51,161 09
....	....	....	30,189 57	3,138 64	33,328 21	55,991 39
....	....	....	22,741 60	2,766 86	25,508 46	41,068 62
....	....	....	27,410 68	2,774 31	30,184 99	46,484 88
....	....	....	46,531 82	3,123 21	49,655 03	72,992 89
....	....	....	54,273 11	3,263 75	57,536 86	80,551 60
....	....	....	39,439 41	3,228 30	42,667 71	56,748 05
....	....	....	74,093 10	3,690 67	77,783 77	98,007 55
4,939 70	5,878 60	....	33,470 43	3,855 83	42,265 96	50,296 49
82,507 60	92,408 96	....	29,631 44	3,598 45	115,737 49	129,625 98
60,546 29	63,573 30	....	30,913 20	4,775 91	96,235 40	101,047 17
75,652 45	74,138 96	....	40,972 84	4,468 08	121,093 37	118,671 50
166,726 53	151,721 57	....	39,322 17	4,748 09	210,796 79	191,825 08
308,087 93	258,793 92	....	67,247 64	5,734 16	381,069 73	320,098 57
327,307 14	252,026 89	....	64,635 15	5,708 23	397,650 52	306,190 90
257,828 62	180,480 30	....	59,529 15	6,010 86	323,368 63	226,358 04
214,921 60	135,400 86	....	83,267 97	6,231 47	304,421 04	191,785 25
181,564 60	101,676 40	....	97,565 51	6,668 65	285,798 76	160,047 30
161,053 67	78,916 46	$5,741 08	44,427 25	5,114 67	216,336 67	106,004 96
421,088 67	176,857 38	14,456 55	5,264 93	7,585 87	448,396 02	188,326 32
140,281 93	49,098 70	23,192 76	3,776 53	5,666 25	172,917 47	60,521 11
130,960 61	36,669 08	19,186 96	10,535 49	5,229 85	165,912 91	46,455 61
65,293 12	13,711 53	27,875 71	1,899 18	5,080 09	100,148 10	21,031 10
36,703 92	5,138 56	23,685 80	5,761 16	5,945 10	72,095 98	10,093 43
136,265 89	9,569 28	33,526 93	209,759 45	6,695 61	386,247 88	27,037 35
175,256 74	....	42,259 24	9,956 19	7,199 76	234,671 93	....
$3,490,949 24	$3,174,037 95	$189,925 03	$1,471,818 46	$150,827 93	$5,303,520 66	$4,910,029 43

DEBIT.

To cost of construction, ...	$3,490,949 24		
Interest thereon, ...	3,174,037 95		
		$6,664,987 19	
To cost of maintenance, ...	$1,812,571 42		
Interest thereon, ...	1,735,991 48		
		3,548,562 90	
			$10,213,550 09
			$5,777,196 37
To proportion of cost of repairs and maintenance of Erie and Champlain Canals from 1828 to 1866, ...			2,826,648 19
Net profit, ...			$2,950,548 18

These statements are appended, by request, to Table No. 2, showing the operations of the Oswego Canal.

STATEMENT of property which has passed at Oswego through the Welland Canal, to and from tide water, and also the increase of tolls which would have been produced had all such property passed through the whole line of the Erie Canal for the year named below.

YEAR.	PROPERTY WHICH PASSED THROUGH THE WELLAND CANAL TO WESTERN STATES FROM TIDE WATER.		PROPERTY WHICH PASSED THROUGH THE WELLAND CANAL FROM WESTERN STATES TO TIDE WATER.		INCREASE OF TOLLS PRODUCED IF ALL SUCH PROPERTY HAD PASSED THROUGH THE WHOLE LINE OF THE ERIE CANAL.		
	Tons.	Tolls.	Tons.	Tolls.	From tide water.	To tide water.	Total.
1852,...	75,026	$75,296	186,719	$208,136	$55,841	$154,359	$210,200
1853,...	98,066	95,323	238,790	328,822	70,694	243,903	314,597
1854,...	59,998	56,064	145,985	141,631	41,578	105,027	146,605
1855,...	69,817	66,388	225,080	235,670	49,235	174,825	224,060
1856,...	67,177	79,464	282,533	301,180	58,932	223,363	282,295
1857,...	68,776	112,242	154,338	157,424	81,430	114,210	195,640
1858,...	45,397	37,043	194,468	158,685	26,875	115,125	142,000
1859,...	60,212	24,566	190,593	155,523	17,822	112,831	130,653
1860,...	57,089	46,584	453,103	369,732	33,796	268,236	302,032
1861,...	30,031	24,505	358,536	365,706	17,778	265,316	283,094
1862,...	48,966	39,956	341,188	382,812	28,987	277,727	306,714
1863,...	67,291	54,909	261,692	293,618	39,836	213,017	252,853
1864,...	67,341	41,212	114,081	127,998	29,899	92,861	122,760
1865,...	45,255	27,696	130,473	146,390	20,093	106,204	126,297
1866,...	70,945	43,418	142,222	159,573	31,499	115,788	147,287
	931,387	$824,666	3,419,801	$3,532,900	$604,295	$2,582,792	$3,187,087

In making this statement, it was assumed that all the property which passed through the Welland Canal from Western States to Oswego, came to tide water; and that all the property going from Oswego through the Welland Canal to Western States (except the salt manufactured at the salt works) went from tide water.

There are no returns in the department previous to 1852, from which the property going to, and coming from other States, through the Welland Canal, can be arrived at.

STATEMENT of the salt which passed at Oswego through the Welland Canal, the tolls on the same from Syracuse to Oswego, and also the increase of tolls that would have been produced had such salt passed through the Erie Canal, from Syracuse to Buffalo, for the years named below.

YEARS.	Tons of salt which passed through the Welland Canal to Western States.	Tolls on same on Oswego Canal, from Syracuse to Oswego.	Tolls on same on Erie Canal, from Syracuse to Buffalo.	Increase of tolls produced, if all such salt had passed through Erie Canal to Buffalo.
1852,	43,420	$3,299	$12,852	$9,553
1853,	48,090	3,654	14,234	10,580
1854,	71,575	5,439	21,186	15,747
1855,	62,947	4,783	18,632	13,849
1856,	82,316	6,256	24,365	18,109
1857,	57,409	4,363	16,993	12,630
1858,	77,541	5,893	22,952	17,059
1859,	60,657	4,609	17,954	13,345
1860,	55,651	4,269	16,472	12,203
1861,	60,702	2,306	8,983	6,677
1862,	82,488	6,269	24,416	18,147
1863,	69,812	5,305	20,664	15,359
1864,	50,885	5,800	22,592	16,792
1865,	40,084	4,637	18,663	14,026
1866,	44,315	5,051	19,675	14,624
	907,892	$71,933	$280,633	$208,700

STATEMENT showing the total tons of merchandise going to, and the total tons of all property coming from other States by way of Buffalo and Oswego, for the years named below.

YEAR.	BY WAY OF BUFFALO.		BY WAY OF OSWEGO,		Total merchandise going to other States by way of Buffalo and Oswego.	Total property coming from other States by way of Buffalo and Oswego.	Total merchandise going to and property coming from other States.
	Merchandise going to other States.	Property coming from other States.	Merchandise going to other States.	Property coming from other States.			
1852,...	143,787	770,874	76,013	381,104	219,800	1,151,978	1,371,778
1853,..	163,192	718,493	98,560	495,197	261,752	1,213,690	1,475,442
1854,...	167,550	758,755	64,329	334,511	231,879	1,093,266	1,325,145
1855,...	145,530	752,334	74,936	382,755	220,466	1,135,089	1,355,555
1856,...	114,696	698,774	68,817	513,776	183,513	1,212,550	1,396,063
1857,...	74,733	640,916	43,393	378,196	118,126	1,019,112	1,137,238
1858,...	47,350	790,252	29,540	481,322	76,890	1,271,574	1,348,464
1859,...	72,767	632,017	26,109	403,700	98,876	1,035,717	1,134,593
1860,...	72,030	1,195,466	47,652	700,860	119,682	1,896,326	2,016,008
1861,...	35,278	1,597,893	17,184	559,790	52,462	2,157,683	2,210,145
1862,...	52,945	2,001,669	18,094	592,739	71,039	2,594,408	2,665,447
1863,...	64,124	1,727,082	29,971	448,422	94,095	2,175,504	2,269,599
1864,...	57,338	1,469,808	27,485	435,284	84,823	1,905,092	1,989,915
1865,...	59,175	1,365,776	13,366	536,071	72,541	1,901,847	1,974,388
1866,...	68,375	1,619,272	20,894	509,332	89,269	2,128,604	2,217,873
	1,338,870	16,739,381	656,343	7,153,059	1,995,213	23,892,440	25,887,653

TABLE

Cayuga and

YEARS.	INCOME.			
	(1)	(2)	(3)	(4)
	Tolls proper.	Tolls contributed to and heretofore credited Erie and Champlain Canals.	Total of tolls proper and contributions.	Legal interest on tolls proper and contributions.
1826,	$2,280 75	....	$2,820 75	$7,898 10
1827,	155 19	....	155 19	423 67
1828,	....	....	....	....
1829,	8,370 24	$11,675 48	20,045 72	51,918 41
1830,	13,087 51	30,378 59	43,466 10	109,534 57
1831,	8,859 48	31,803 89	40,663 37	99,625 26
1832,	12,375 77	30,852 60	43,228 37	102,883 52
1833,	15,591 50	42,628 80	58,220 30	134,488 89
1834,	18,053 14	41,451 57	59,504 71	133,290 55
1835,	20,192 61	28,682 84	48,875 45	106,059 73
1836,	19,914 53	29,405 01	49,319 54	103,571 03
1837,	16,648 77	13,146 98	29,795 75	60,485 37
1838,	17,488 82	18,846 17	36,334 99	71,216 60
1839,	19,354 67	18,196 69	37,551 36	70,979 63
1840,	17,787 29	28,949 56	46,736 85	85,061 07
1841,	22,445 46	29,786 96	52,232 42	91,406 74
1842,	17,992 67	19,830 67	37,823 34	63,543 21
1843,	17,938 40	22,548 22	40,486 62	65,183 46
1844,	23,054 19	55,825 82	78,880 01	121,475 20
1845,	28,881 48	40,493 70	69,375 18	101,981 51
1846,	29,395 23	43,263 53	72,658 76	101,722 26
1847,	26,908 78	56,712 97	83,621 75	111,216 93
1848,	28,470 86	52,023 56	80,494 42	101,422 97
1849,	27,735 44	41,013 82	68,749 26	81,811 62
1850,	27,589 59	40,368 51	67,958 10	76,113 07
1851,	26,258 40	29,849 34	56,107 74	58,913 13
1852,	22,524 38	30,546 66	53,071 04	52,009 62
1853,	25,169 84	40,102 05	65,271 89	59,397 42
1854,	24,808 90	37,901 60	62,710 50	52,676 82
1855,	21,915 81	37,596 86	59,512 67	45,824 76
1856,	20,919 78	30,557 15	51,476 93	36,033 85
1857,	19,457 35	31,438 87	50,896 22	32,064 62
1858,	14,400 67	34,121 36	48,522 03	27,172 34
1859,	17,449 54	33,401 14	50,850 68	24,916 83
1860,	20,089 09	39,625 25	59,714 34	25,080 02
1861,	18,778 32	31,601 92	50,380 24	17,633 08
1862,	21,395 82	39,588 13	60,983 95	17,075 51
1863,	25,243 93	39,205 12	64,449 05	13,534 30
1864,	28,040 29	56,644 16	84,684 45	11,855 82
1865,	23,802 22	71,062 62	94,864 84	6,640 54
1866,	34,151 25	67,654 19	101,805 44	....
	$805,517 96	$1,378,782 36	$2,184,300 32	$2,534,142 03

RESULT.

CREDIT.

By tolls proper,	$805,517 96	
By tolls on tonnage contributed to the Erie Canal,	1,378,782 36	
Total income, &c.,		$2.184,300 32
Interest on tolls proper and contributions,		2,534,142 03
Total credits with interest,		$4,718,442 35

NO 3.

Seneca Canal.

DISBURSEMENTS.						
FOR CONSTRUCTION.		FOR MAINTENANCE.				
(1)	(2)	(3)	(4)	(5)	(6)	(7)
Cost of construction.	Legal interest on cost of construction.	Contractors, for repairs.	Superintendents, for repairs.	Collectors, inspectors, &c.	Total payments, including cost of construction.	Legal interest on total payments, including cost of construction.
$42,190 30	$118,132 00	....	....	$255 83	$42,446 13	$118,849 64
65,068 75	177,638 37	....	....	....	65,068 75	177,638 37
90,918 54	241,844 54	....	....	....	90,918 54	241,844 54
20,783 50	53,830 56	....	$8,038 94	....	28,822 44	74,650 11
6,885 55	17,352 72	....	5,833 96	826 50	13,546 01	34,135 94
....	....	....	3,301 39	822 00	4,123 39	10,102 30
100 00	238 00	....	4,132 85	799 17	5,032 02	11,976 20
....	....	....	9,338 71	807 91	10,146 62	23,438 69
90 00	201 60	....	8,926 17	948 73	9,964 90	22,321 37
....	....	....	10,275 83	1,412 96	11,688 79	25,364 67
....	....	....	26,301 78	1,422 95	27,724 73	58,221 93
....	....	....	30,471 56	1,459 73	31,931 29	64,820 51
....	....	....	19,898 53	1,166 16	21,064 69	41,286 79
....	....	....	23,594 36	1,712 01	25,306 37	47,829 03
....	....	....	22,656 16	1,541 09	24,197 25	44,038 99
2,055 41	3,596 25	....	16,330 33	1,509 56	19,895 30	34,816 77
10,819 24	18,175 92	....	14,708 75	1,524 10	27,052 09	45,447 51
....	....	....	10,953 48	1,454 16	12,407 64	19,976 30
4 52	7 70	....	14,127 13	1,337 65	15,469 30	23,822 72
....	....	....	13,853 68	1,496 66	15,350 34	22,564 99
....	....	....	12,947 02	1,567 50	14,514 52	20,320 32
756 40	1,005 48	....	14,099 37	1,526 51	16,382 28	21,788 43
....	....	....	13,048 47	1,390 87	14,439 34	18,193 56
51,932 60	61,800 27	....	11,923 64	1,280 00	65,136 24	77,512 12
70,219 79	78,646 40	....	10,780 52	1,175 55	82,175 86	92,036 96
7,038 48	7,389 90	....	20,894 51	1,547 81	29,480 80	30,954 84
2,096 00	2,054 08	....	27,387 80	1,452 58	31,936 38	31,297 65
14,223 35	12,942 93	....	14,502 06	1,530 29	30,255 70	27,532 68
64,246 84	53,967 48	....	16,834 52	1,903 49	82,984 85	69,707 27
117,821 09	90,722 17	....	10,557 72	2,170 76	130,549 57	100,523 16
168,797 78	118,158 60	....	10,082 85	2,558 28	181,438 91	127,007 23
136,589 28	86,051 07	....	12,688 50	3,034 62	152,312 40	95,956 81
124,207 79	69,556 48	....	30,872 03	3,111 29	158,191 11	88,587 02
36,840 22	18,051 60	$1,113 25	5,278 55	2,397 46	45,629 48	22,358 44
135,590 78	56,948 22	3,360 43	131 24	2,644 40	141,726 85	59,525 27
84,308 31	29,507 80	2,473 08	17,010 38	2,307 26	106,099 03	37,134 66
93,564 74	26,198 20	4,258 70	14.799 98	1,734 80	114,358 22	32,020 30
44,293 70	9,301 74	8,457 48	3,159 49	1,373 21	57,283 88	12,029 61
39,029,63	5,464 20	10,527 92	4,069 54	1,384 39	55,011 48	7,701 60
64,334 92	4,503 45	19,591 65	373 03	1,581 04	85,880 64	6,011 64
25,735 08	....	14,029 44	2,097 49	1,786 67	43,648 68	....
$1,520,542 59	$1,363,287 73	$63,811 95	$496,282 32	$59,955 95	$2,140,592 81	$2,121,346 94

DEBIT.

To cost of construction, ...	$1,520,542 59		
To interest thereon,..............................	1,363,287 73		
		$2,883,830 32	
To cost of maintenance,............................	$620,050 22		
To interest thereon,..............................	758,059 21		
		1,378,109 43	
			$4,261,939 75
Balance, profit,..			$456,502 60
To proportion of cost of repairs and maintenance of Erie and Champlain Canals, from 1826 to 1866,..			$579,994 50
Net cost,..			$123,491 90

TABLE

Chemung

YEARS.	INCOME.			
	(1)	(2)	(3)	(4)
	Tolls proper.	Tolls contributed to and heretofore credited Erie and Champlain Canal.	Total of tolls proper and contributions.	Legal interest on tolls proper and contributions.
1830,	....	....	....	....
1831,	....	....	....	....
1832,	....	....	....	....
1833,	....	....	....	....
1834,	$2,398 39	$8,685 95	$11,084 34	$24,828 92
1835,	4,153 07	15,364 71	19,517 78	42,353 58
1836,	5,078 37	12,375 63	17,454 00	36,653 40
1837,	4,342 99	12,093 67	16,436 66	33,366 42
1838,	4,478 01	15,005 00	19,483 01	38,186 70
1839,	4,767 62	16,539 63	21,307 25	40,270 70
1840,	5,011 50	14,262 50	19,274 00	35,078 68
1841,	7,158 18	33,133 94	40,292 12	70,511 21
1842,	7,206 28	25,104 97	32,311 25	54,282 90
1843,	9,188 51	44,527 71	53,716 22	86,483 11
1844,	12,950 92	39,183 69	52,134 61	80,287 30
1845,	20,281 70	93,409 37	113,691 07	167,125 87
1846,	15,862 99	56,385 69	72,248 68	101,148 15
1847,	13,677 28	69,674 96	83,352 24	110,858 48
1848,	16,821 58	59,211 68	76,033 26	95,801 91
1849,	16,048 96	50,120 58	66,169 54	78,741 75
1850,	16,276 54	73,711 10	89,987 64	100,786 16
1851,	15,986 04	66,303 79	82,289 83	86,404 32
1852,	15,683 31	61,146 39	76,829 70	75,293 11
1853,	20,810 23	81,822 80	102,633 03	93,396 06
1854,	19,635 35	91,251 47	110,886 82	93,144 93
1855,	19,771 91	80,403 36	100,175 27	77,134 96
1856,	17,111 13	62,975 51	80,086 64	56,060 65
1857,	17,101 71	55,555 87	72,657 58	45,774 28
1858,	13,347 95	51,716 31	65,064 26	36,436 99
1859,	16,868 66	55,445 57	72,314 23	35,433 97
1860,	18,579 46	52,036 90	70,616 36	29,658 87
1861,	15,319 04	39,630 03	54,949 07	19,232 17
1862,	19,901 96	56,123 21	76,025 17	21,287 05
1863,	21,628 77	56,963 24	78,592 01	16,504 32
1864,	23,406 86	43,316 93	66,723 79	9,341 33
1865,	16,745 91	21,395 50	38,141 41	2,669 90
1866,	18,173 04	41,923 68	60,096 72	....
	$455,774 22	$1,556,801 34	$2,012,575 56	$1,894,538 15

RESULT.

DEBIT.

To cost of construction,....................................	$1,273,261 86		
To interest thereon,....................................	1,635,704 70		
		$2,908,966 56	
To cost of maintenance,....................................	$1,139,770 30		
To interest thereon,....................................	970,699 26		
		2,110,469 56	
Total disbursements and interest,....................................			$5,019,436 12

NO. 4.

Canal.

DISBURSEMENTS.						
FOR CONSTRUCTION.		FOR MAINTENANCE.				
(1)	(2)	(3)	(4)	(5)	(6)	(7)
Cost of construction.	Legal interest on cost of construction.	Contractors, for repairs.	Superintendents, for repairs.	Collectors, inspectors, &c.	Total payments, including cost of construction.	Legal interest on total payments, including cost of construction.
$69,190 00	$174,358 80	....	....	....	$69,190 00	$174,358 80
148,291 57	363,315 40	....	....	....	148,291 57	363,314 34
75,410 47	179,475 80	....	....	....	75,410 47	179,476 92
47,793 38	110,401 83	....	$26,448 53	....	74,241 91	171,498 81
2,258 91	5,060 16	....	23,703 48	696 48	26,658 87	59,715 87
9 08	19 53	....	11,175 89	1,036 75	12,221 72	26,521 13
....	....	....	9,623 16	1,037 88	10,661 04	22,388 18
3,558 79	7,224 77	....	15,193 82	1,091 13	19,843 74	40,282 50
1,859 91	3,645 60	....	12,106 16	992 97	14,959 04	29,279 72
....	....	....	14,315 71	1,187 94	15,503 65	29,301 90
68 50	125 58	....	11,969 24	1,268 33	13,306 07	24,217 05
100,056 81	175,099 75	....	23,175 22	1,201 54	124,433 57	217,758 75
185,987 49	312,458 16	....	33,451 59	1,076 23	220,515 31	370,465 72
25,417 46	40,921 37	....	14,486 27	1,159 40	41,063 13	66,111 64
3,467 07	5,339 18	....	12,172 23	1,085 80	16,725 10	25,756 65
9 90	14 70	....	17,280 27	1,239 50	18,529 67	27,238 61
1,646 00	2,304 40	....	14,689 55	1,455 00	17,790 55	24,906 77
4,360 86	5,800 13	....	15,485 39	1,561 15	21,407 40	28,471 84
328 66	414 54	....	27,080 33	2,030 00	29,438 99	37,091 33
19,876 96	23,653 63	....	23,897 06	2,136 00	45,910 02	54,632 92
53,768 39	60,220 16	....	28,885 79	1,896 21	84,550 39	94,696 44
11,044 92	11,597 25	....	42,330 76	2,566 35	55,942 03	58,739 13
2,144 06	2,101 12	....	32,952 17	2,198 36	37,294 59	36,548 70
12,665 24	11,525 15	....	23,883 28	2,214 84	38,763 36	35,274 66
3,047 11	2,559 48	....	33,099 05	2,187 62	38,333 78	32,200 38
6,971 63	5,368 44	....	23,094 86	2,252 97	32,319 46	24,886 14
3,223 28	2,256 10	$11,964 48	4,652 49	2,403 11	22,243 36	15,570 35
29,988 16	18,892 44	9,543 45	66,101 23	2,435 05	108,067 89	67,982 77
28,345 22	15,873 20	....	161,702 33	2,604 82	192,652 37	107,885 33
39,026 44	19,122 74	4,660 46	18,786 02	2,195 01	64,667 93	31,687 29
69,787 13	29,310 54	12,031 48	316 67	3,264 81	85,400 09	35,868 04
20,828 36	7,289 80	18,788 48	6,510 67	2,628 39	48,755 90	17,064 57
81,911 75	22,935 36	17,649 07	7,628 96	2,294 62	109,484 40	30,655 63
34,356 39	7,214 76	19,287 83	53,324 59	2,256 50	109,225 31	22,937 32
48,290 86	6,760 74	23,601 19	12,859 91	2,392 74	87,144 70	12,200 25
43,486 76	3,044 09	71,490 25	16,713 24	2,845 55	134,535 80	9,417 51
94,784 34	....	31,357 24	18,218 19	3,189 21	147,548 98	....
$1,273,261 86	$1,635,704 70	$220,373 93	$857,314 11	$62,082 26	$2,413,032 16	$2,606,403 96

CREDIT.

By tolls proper,...	$455,774 22		
By tolls on tonnage contributed to the Erie Canal,..	1,556,801 34		
Total income, &c.,,..		$2,012,575 56	
Interest on tolls proper and contributions,......................		1,894,538 15	
Total credits, with interest,...			$3,907,113 71
To balance,...			$1,112,322 41
To proportion of cost of repairs and maintenance of Erie and Champlain Canals from 1830 to 1866,..			654,879 47
Net cost,..			$1,767,201 88

TABLE

Crooked Lake

YEARS.	INCOME.			
	(1)	(2)	(3)	(4)
	Tolls proper.	Tolls contributed to and heretofore credited Erie and Champlain Canals.	Total of tolls proper and contributions.	Legal interest on tolls proper and contributions.
1831,	....	....	....	....
1832,	....	....	....	....
1833,	....	....	....	....
1834,	$1,007 60	$666 64	$1,674 24	$3,750 29
1835,	1,803 76	9,626 85	11,430 61	24,804 42
1836,	1,953 90	12,898 65	14,852 55	31,190 35
1837,	1,547 61	13,091 51	14,639 12	29,717 41
1838,	1,566 06	15,047 31	16,613 37	32,562 20
1839,	1,893 90	13,339 42	15,233 32	28,790 97
1840,	1,613 16	18,561 84	20,175 00	36,718 50
1841,	2,023 46	17,139 58	19,163 04	33,535 32
1842,	1,216 73	11,534 20	12,750 93	21,421 56
1843,	1,341 60	11,181 79	12,523 39	20,162 65
1844,	1,367 21	19,224 97	20.592 18	31,689 95
1845,	1,662 84	27,493 31	29,156 15	42,859 54
1846,	1,846 37	26,986 96	28,833 33	40.366 66
1847,	1,774 55	24,490 26	26,264 81	34,932 19
1848,	1,858 04	22,872 64	24,730 68	31,160 65
1849,	1,819 17	26,340 84	28,160 01	33,510 41
1850,	1,796 17	25,983 27	27,779 44	31,112 97
1851,	1,714 34	19,305 85	21,020 19	22,071 19
1852,	1,246 02	23,314 02	24,560 04	24,068 83
1853,	1,656 75	22,145 64	23,802 39	21,660 17
1854,	1,303 69	11,926 46	13,230 15	11,113 32
1855,	837 48	16,182 35	17,019 83	13,105 26
1856,	1,154 48	16,041 69	17,196 17	12,037 31
1857,	879 26	7,186 64	8,065 90	5,081 51
1858,	520 82	8,527 11	9,047 93	5,066 84
1859,	715 06	6,338 97	7,054 03	3,456 47
1860,	683 34	8,64(96	9,324 30	3,916 20
1861,	699 94	6,982 94	7,682 88	2,689 40
1862,	712 70	11,227 85	11,940 55	3,343 35
1863,	746 40	5,572 54	6,318 94	1,326 97
1864,	585 88	3,613 62	4,199 50	587 93
1865,	290 65	5,740 44	6,031 09	422 17
1866,	534 96	8,815 52	9,350 48	....
	$42,373 90	$478,042 64	$520,416 54	$638,232 96

RESULT.

DEBIT.

To cost of construction,	$333,287 27		
To interest thereon,	535,896 06		
		$869,183 33	
To cost of maintenance,	$258,282 78		
To interest thereon,	236,180 06		
		$494,462 84	
Total disbursements and interest,			$1,363,646 17

NO. 5.

Canal.

DISBURSEMENTS.						
FOR CONSTRUCTION.		FOR MAINTENANCE.				
(1)	(2)	(3)	(4)	(5)	(6)	(7)
Cost of construction.	Legal interest on cost of construction.	Contractors, for repairs.	Superintendents, for repairs.	Collectors, inspectors, &c.	Total payments, including cost of construction.	Legal interest on total payments, including cost of construction.
$11,350 00	$27,807 50	....	....	....	$11,350 00	$27,807 50
62,906 46	149,716 28	....	....	....	62,906 46	149,717 37
52,461 30	121,184 91	....	....	....	52,461 30	124,485 60
13,293 82	29,778 56	....	$2,437 67	....	15,731 49	35,238 54
1 70	4 34	....	3,694 66	$350 75	4,047 11	8,782 23
255 90	537 60	....	5,063 82	425 25	5,744 97	12,064 44
402 31	816 06	....	5,743 71	725 13	6,871 15	13,948 44
....	....	....	5,060 07	543 54	5,603 61	10,983 07
....	....	....	2,778 31	885 11	3,663 42	6,833 87
....	....	....	4,559 23	873 65	5,432 88	9,887 84
2 00	3 50	....	9,463 07	987 85	10,452 92	18,292 61
....	....	....	8,016 66	918 13	8,934 79	15,010 45
....	....	....	3,674 16	880 78	4,554 94	7,333 45
....	....	....	3,905 84	842 06	4,747 90	7,321 77
9 00	13 23	....	4,844 67	857 28	5,710 95	8,495 10
26,358 42	36,901 20	....	5,384 00	875 73	32,618 15	45,665 41
46,630 76	62,019 23	....	6,065 89	875 00	53,571 65	71,250 29
57,493 78	72,442 44	....	8,558 88	881 87	66,934 53	84,337 51
2,163 61	2,573 97	....	10,208 40	863 42	13,235 43	15,750 16
10,131 25	11,346 72	....	4,983 72	777 04	15,892 01	17,799 05
6,429 28	6,750 45	....	6,118 94	954 80	13,503 02	14,178 17
1,750 92	1,715 98	....	7,975 12	925 42	10,651 46	10,338 43
....	....	....	5,350 00	958 50	6,308 50	5,740 74
1,719 65	1,444 80	....	5,122 08	922 04	7,763 77	6,521 57
2,565 20	1,975 05	....	5,320 39	888 45	8,774 04	6,756 01
780 00	546 00	$3,204 08	694 16	888 02	5,566 26	3,896 38
7,340 70	4,624 83	4,447 37	199 98	703 86	12,691 91	7,995 90
584 20	327 04	9,803 46	....	542 25	10,929 91	6,120 75
147 78	72 52	4,849 53	....	440 09	5,437 40	2,664 49
467 24	196 14	5,033 63	125 00	670 34	6,296 21	2,644 41
573 10	200 55	6,017 13	....	493 98	7,084 21	2,479 47
284 90	79 80	4,692 38	2,468 94	635 69	8,081 91	2,262 93
2,306 66	484 47	5,141 76	....	555 56	8,003 98	1,680 84
13,446 85	1,882 58	19,995 78	....	579 27	34,021 90	4,763 07
6,432 68	450 31	36,200 58	....	627 53	43,260 79	3,028 26
4,997 80	....	6,770 69	273 00	687 63	12,729 12	....
$333,287 27	$535,896 06	$106,156 39	$128,090 37	$24,036 02	$591,570 05	$772,076 12

CREDIT.

By tolls proper,................................	$42,373 90		
By tolls on tonnage contributed to the Erie Canal,......	478,042 64		
Total income from 1834 to 1866,....................................		$520,416 54	
Interest thereon,..		638,232 96	
			$1,158,649 50
			$204,996 67
To proportion of cost of repairs and maintenance of Erie and Champlain from 1834 to 1866,....................................			201,092 20
Net cost,..			$406,088 87

TABLE

Chenango

YEARS.	INCOME.			
	(1)	(2)	(3)	(4)
	Tolls proper.	Tolls contributed to and hertofore credited Erie and Champlain Canals.	Total of tolls proper and contributions.	Legal interest on tolls proper and contributions.
1833,	....	....	....	....
1834,	....	....	....	....
1835,	....	....	....	....
1836,	....	....	....	....
1837,	$4,081 62	$7,728 44	$11,810 06	$23,974 42
1838,	16,751 12	6,272 61	23,023 73	45,126 51
1839,	18,050 33	452 51	18,502 84	34,970 37
1840,	14,023 32	2,592 90	16,616 22	30,241 52
1841,	16,893 02	6,249 83	23,142 85	17,357 14
1842,	15,330 57	1,593 72	16,924 29	28,332 81
1843,	14,668 94	5,578 31	20,247 25	33,598 07
1844,	20,983 05	9,167 32	30,150 37	46,431 57
1845,	23,920 66	13,176 49	37,097 15	54,532 81
1846,	25,578 76	8,209 78	33,788 54	47,303 96
1847,	25,620 01	13,890 42	39,510 43	52,548 87
1848,	28,091 66	10,035 01	38,126 67	48,639 60
1849,	28,028 98	....	28,028 98	30,354 48
1850,	20,343 65	4,283 50	24,627 15	27,582 41
1851,	19,732 35	2,289 96	22,022 31	23,123 43
1852,	16,891 62	2,092 11	18,983 73	18,604 06
1853,	18,107 89	4,331 29	22,439 18	20,419 65
1854,	19,496 15	1,997 39	21,493 54	18,054 57
1855,	20,302 08	1,529 16	21,831 24	16,810 05
1856,	18,634 62	3,174 27	21,808 89	15,266 12
1857,	22,969 47	....	22,969 47	14,470 77
1858,	15,305 64	1,609 38	16,915 02	9,472 41
1859,	17,801 72	2,085 91	19,887 63	9,744 94
1860,	22,214 37	3,087 07	25,301 44	10,626 60
1861,	23,397 24	3,074 52	26,471 76	9,265 12
1862,	22,155 94	2,578 54	24,734 48	6,925 65
1863,	24,354 87	4,169 94	28,524 81	5,990 21
1864,	30,034 43	....	30,034 43	4,204 82
1865,	21,710 98	....	21,710 98	1,519 76
1866,	28,534 53	2,026 02	30,560 55	....
	$614,009 59	$123,276 40	$737,285 99	$708,492 70

RESULT.

DEBIT.

To cost of construction,	$2,782,124 19		
Interest thereon,	5,119,376 29		
		$7,901,500 48	
To cost of maintenance,	$970,169 49		
Interest thereon,	745,683 48		
		1,715,852 97	
Total disbursements and interest,			$9,617,353 45

NO. 6.

Canal.

DISBURSEMENTS.						
FOR CONSTRUCTION.		FOR MAINTENANCE.				
(1)	(2)	(3)	(4)	(5)	(6)	(7)
Cost of construction.	Legal interest on cost of construction.	Contractors, for repairs.	Superintendents, for repairs.	Collectors, inspectors, &c.	Total payments, including cost of construction.	Legal interest on total payments, including cost of construction.
$9,222 65	$21,305 13	....	....	....	$9,222 65	$21,304 32
211,013 44	472,669 12	....	....	....	211,013 44	472,680 11
651,782 45	1,414,366 94	....	....	....	651,782 45	1,414,367 92
911,035 10	1,913,173 50	....	....	....	911,035 10	1,913,173 71
480,807 02	976,038 21	....	$18,663 62	....	499,470 64	1,013,825 40
65,759 17	128,887 64	....	20,270 95	$1,074 85	87,104 97	170,725 74
47,458 98	89,697 51	....	16,990 64	1,576 00	66,025 62	124,788 42
12,232 90	22,264 06	....	14,775 24	1,559 66	28,567 80	51,993 40
5,349 47	9,360 75	....	16,638 05	1,931 42	23,918 94	41,858 15
5,075 33	8,526 00	....	18,467 28	1,821 00	25,363 61	42,610 86
668 05	1,075 48	....	15,917 35	1,395 40	17,980 80	28,949 09
3,942 72	6,072 22	....	15,700 51	1,233 02	20,876 25	32,149 43
153 95	226 38	....	18,283 33	1,198 91	19,636 19	28,865 20
152 47	212 80	....	17,827 13	1,332 00	19,311 60	27,036 24
2,704 28	3,596 32	....	18,404 54	1,226 00	22,334 82	29,605 31
119 06	149 94	....	20,471 02	1,418 49	22,008 57	27,730 80
817 88	973 42	....	27,772 21	1,442 12	30,032 21	35,738 33
5,051 91	5,658 24	....	25,071 12	1,237 68	31,360 71	35,124 00
1,064 75	1,118 25	....	31,110 32	1,426 08	33,601 15	35,281 20
6,112 00	5,989 76	....	34,706 26	1,339 94	42,158 20	41,315 04
....	....	....	37,752 37	1,400 79	39,153 16	35,629 38
....	....	....	49,476 20	1,403 37	50,879 57	42,738 84
3,095 35	2,383 15	....	44,250 04	1,557 00	48,902 39	37,654 84
1,589 35	1,112 30	$11,234 30	10,301 24	1,723 86	24,848 75	17,394 13
160 00	100 80	25,806 50	2,276 18	1,923 39	30,166 07	19,004 62
616 21	344 96	20,700 00	23,785 09	1,981 10	47,082 40	26,366 14
1,933 72	947 66	22,611 54	3,450 19	1,383 66	29,379 11	14,395 76
11,757 84	4,938 36	25,175 90	1,893 95	1,761 57	40,589 26	17,047 49
39,097 72	13,684 30	21,431 65	1,210 98	1,744 35	63,484 70	22,219 65
12,577 91	3,521 84	27,823 68	1,215 98	1,860 74	43,478 31	12,173 92
9,357 43	1,964 97	30,266 31	1,620 78	1,904 36	43,148 88	9,061 26
38,410 12	5,377 40	37,647 49	3,210 97	2,107 10	81,375 68	11,392 60
51,983 95	3,638 88	96,443 14	4,039 74	2,654 17	155,121 00	10,858 47
191,021 01	....	75,635 87	12,333 31	2,888 49	281,878 68	....
$2,782,124 19	$5,119,376 29	$394,776 38	$527,886 59	$47,506 52	$3,752,293 68	$5,865,059 77

CREDIT.

By tolls proper,..	$614,009 59		
By tolls on tonnage contributed to Erie Canal,..........	123,276 40		
		$737,285 99	
Interest thereon,..		708,492 70	
Total income and interest,..			1,445,778 69
			$8,171,574 76
To proportion of cost of repairs and maintenance of Erie Canal from 1833 to 1866, .			51,856 93
Net cost, ...			$8,223,431 69

TABLE

Black River

YEARS.	INCOME. (1) Tolls proper.	(2) Tolls contributed and heretofore credited Erie and Champlain Canals.	(3) Total of tolls proper and contributions.	(4) Legal interest on tolls proper and contributions.
1837,	....	....	....	....
1838,	....	....	....	....
1839,	....	....	....	....
1840,	....	....	....	....
1841,	....	....	....	....
1842,	....	....	....	....
1843,	....	....	....	....
1844,	....	....	....	....
1845,	....	....	....	....
1846,	....	....	....	....
1847,	....	....	....	....
1848,	....	....	....	....
1849,	....	....	....	....
1850,	$1,115 73	$1,514 16	$2,629 89	$2,945 47
1851,	3,834 73	2,139 60	5,974 33	6,273 04
1852,	4,166 05	3,626 67	7,792 72	7,636 86
1853,	5,546 32	4,700 45	10,246 77	9,324 56
1854,	5,843 42	7,499 53	13,342 95	11,208 07
1855,	6,808 05	7,640 32	14,448 37	11,125 24
1856,	5,594 10	5,101 64	10,695 74	7,487 01
1857,	6,575 22	6,014 46	12,589 68	7,931 49
1858,	4,998 48	5,572 01	10,570 49	5,919 47
1859,	5,963 02	7,671 08	13,634 10	6,680 70
1860,	6,330 71	8,780 05	15,110 76	6,346 51
1861,	6,112 73	8,139 17	14,251 90	4,988 16
1862,	8,647 82	9,729 22	18,377 04	5,155 57
1863,	10,172 66	12,248 49	22,421 15	4,708 44
1864,	10,078 30	12,466 74	22,545 04	3,156 30
1865,	10,985 87	9,533 74	20,519 61	1,436 37
1866,	11,802 81	15,649 67	27,452 48	....
	$114,576 02	$128,027 00	$242,603 02	$102,323 26

RESULT.

DEBIT.

To cost of construction,	$3,224,779 55		
To interest thereon,	4,454,243 92		
		$7,679,023 47	
To cost of maintenance,	$445,011 36		
To interest thereon,	270,291 78		
		715,303 14	
Total disbursement and interest,		....	$8,394,326 61

NO. 7.

Canal.

DISBURSEMENTS.						
FOR CONSTRUCTION.		FOR MAINTENANCE.				
(1)	(2)	(3)	(4)	(5)	(6)	(7)
Cost of construction.	Legal interest on cost of construction.	Contractors, for repairs.	Superintendents, for repairs.	Collectors, inspectors, &c.	Total payments, including cost of construction.	Legal interest on total payments, including cost of construction.
$5,255 55	$10,669 68	....	....	....	$5,255 55	$10,668 77
97,735 21	191,560 60	....	....	....	97,735 21	191,561 01
513,154 39	969,861 06	....	....	....	513,154 39	969,861 80
537,794 74	978,786 90	....	....	....	537,794 74	978,789 03
335,973 06	587,952 75	....	....	....	335,973 06	587,952 85
234,824 34	394,504 32	....	....	....	234,824 34	442,504 89
24,928 61	40,135 69	....	....	....	24,928 61	40,135 06
14,528 33	22,373 12	....	....	....	14,528 33	22,373 63
39,147 14	57,546 09	....	....	....	39,147 14	57,546 30
12,852 14	17,992 80	....	....	....	12,852 14	17,993 00
12,326 24	16,393 58	....	....	....	12,326 24	16,393 90
108,522 95	136,738 98	....	....	....	108,522 95	136,738 93
233,373 97	277,715 06	....	....	....	233,373 97	277,715 02
151,492 03	169,671 04	....	$10,014 52	....	161,506 55	180,887 34
95,590 17	100,369 50	....	25,753 83	$317 43	121,661 43	127,744 50
118,356 30	115,988 88	....	29,404 55	529 95	148,290 80	145,324 98
31,957 28	29,080 87	....	24,443 88	525 97	56,927 13	51,803 69
33,026 36	27,741 84	....	30,500 35	554 15	64,080 86	53,827 92
105,539 77	81,265 80	....	35,671 38	752 97	141,964 12	109,312 37
93,437 29	65,405 90	$6,165 28	10,855 81	764 34	111,222 72	77,855 90
61,664 72	38,848 95	12,601 25	1,613 45	783 67	76,663 09	48,297 75
41,297 38	23,126 32	15,406 88	3,062 48	824 40	60,591 14	33,931 04
16,023 62	7,851 76	23,539 65	1,843 98	627 86	42,035 11	20,597 20
101,030 62	42,433 02	21,834 91	366 66	862 67	124,094 86	52,119 84
103,593 31	36,257 55	17,261 63	6,173 28	667 13	127,695 35	41,693 37
33,870 86	9,483 88	18,802,06	2,183 53	640 85	55,497 30	15,539 24
10,053 54	2,111 34	15,582 89	3,491 19	574 76	29,702 38	6,237 50
1,860 84	260 54	15,802 17	6,142 25	503 16	24,308 42	3,483 18
30,229 68	2,116 10	40,227 08	9,582 68	613 25	80,652 69	5,645 69
25,339 11	....	32,697 74	13,745 68	697 76	72,480 29	....
$3,224,779 55	$4,454,243 92	$219,921 54	$214,849 50	$10,240 32	$3,669,790 91	$4,724,535 70

CREDIT.

By tolls proper,..	$114,576 02		
By tolls on tonnage contributed to Erie Canal,........	128,027 00		
Total income, ...		$242,603 02	
Interest thereon, ...		102,323 26	
Total income and interest,..			$344,926 28
Balance,..			$8,049,400 33
To proportion of cost of repairs and maintenance of Erie Canal, from 1837 to 1866,.....			53,855 47
Net cost, ...			$8,103,255 80

TABLE

Genesee Valley

YEARS.	INCOME.			
	(1)	(2)	(3)	(4)
	Tolls proper.	Tolls contributed to and heretofore credited Erie and Champlain Canals.	Total of tolls proper and contributions.	Legal interest on tolls proper and contributions.
1837,........................	....	....	....	....
1838,........................	....	....	....	....
1839,........................	....	....	....	....
1840,........................	....	....	....	....
1841,........................	$12,275 44	$4,582 65	$16,858 09	$29,501 66
1842,........................	12,075 97	7,688 96	19,764 93	33,205 04
1843,........................	13,734 52	10,308 17	24,042 69	38,708 73
1844,........................	18,586 52	19,094 98	37,681 50	58,029 51
1845,........................	20,484 17	25,937 53	46,421 70	68,239 90
1846,........................	24,182 60	30,179 74	54,362 34	76,107 28
1847,........................	25,055 20	40,692 43	65,747 63	87,444 35
1848,........................	26,012 50	38,446 99	64,459 49	81,218 95
1849,........................	25,234 04	39,696 33	64,930 37	77,267 14
1850,........................	28,821 98	37,211 05	66,033 03	73,956 99
1851,........................	25,451 36	34,233 41	59,684 77	62,669 01
1852,........................	25,064 39	24,208 54	49,272 93	47,287 47
1853,........................	30,183 73	34,620 97	64,804 70	57,972 28
1854,........................	30,662 08	31,103 59	61,765 67	51,883 08
1855,........................	28,390 12	19,965 36	48,355 48	37,233 72
1856,........................	23,365 84	16,908 15	40,273 99	28,191 79
1857,........................	25,966 70	24,243 80	50,210 50	31,632 62
1858,........................	25,651 07	31,585 50	57,236 57	32,052 48
1859,........................	28,163 93	35,056 17	63,220 10	30,977 85
1860,........................	30,801 74	39,436 86	70,238 60	29,500 21
1861,........................	29,189 60	15,332 39	44,521 99	15,582 70
1862,........................	28,697 27	37,471 04	66,168 31	18,527 02
1863,........................	32,747 98	31,240 67	63,988 65	13,437 62
1864,........................	27,562 66	16,765 61	44,328 27	6,205 95
1865,........................	15,785 16	6,333 49	22,118 65	1,548 30
1866,........................	17,724 01	22,698 08	40,422 09	....
	$631,870 58	$675,042 46	$1,306,913 04	$1,088,381 65

RESULT.

DEBIT.

To cost of construction,...........................	$5,827,813 72		
Interest thereon, ...	7,969,085 39		
		$13,796,899 11	
To cost of maintenance,.....	$1,405,342 66		
Interest thereon, ...	1,211,081 19		
		2,616,423 85	
Total disbursements and interest,..			$16,413,322 96

NO. 8.

Canal.

DISBURSEMENTS.						
FOR CONSTRUCTION.		FOR MAINTENANCE.				
(1)	(2)	(3)	(4)	(5)	(6)	(7)
Cost of construction.	Legal interest on cost of construction.	Contractors, for repairs.	Superintendents, for repairs.	Collectors, inspectors, &c.	Total payments, including cost of construction.	Legal interest on total payments, including cost of construction.
$22,371 86	$45,415 16	....	....	....	$22,371 86	$45,424 87
229,161 20	449,155 56	....	....	....	229,161 20	449,155 95
764,182 61	1,444,305 87	....	....	....	764,182 61	1,444,305 13
1,151,653 97	2,096,010 28	....	$2,176 00	....	1,153,829 97	2,099,970 54
612,760 50	1,072,331 75	....	12,750 91	$924 73	626,436 14	1,096,263 24
520,409 56	420,687 12	....	18,062 75	1,308 56	539,780 87	906,831 86
170,667 75	274,775 48	....	13,669 85	1,591 78	185,929 38	299,346 30
202,106 67	311,244 78	....	15,719 96	1,540 55	219,367 18	337,825 45
35,311 25	51,907 17	....	15,776 49	1,381 00	52,468 74	77,129 04
39,328 58	55,060 60	....	17,614 20	1,464 00	58,406 78	81,769 49
10,441 67	13,887 86	....	15,782 32	1,506 01	27,730 00	36,880 90
33,035 89	41,625 36	....	26,987 41	1,545 55	61,568 85	77,576 75
184,768 71	219,875 11	....	17,244 51	1,546 75	203,559 97	242,236 36
375,164 73	420,184 80	....	17,350 00	1,387 15	393,901 88	442,170 10
229,380 52	240,850 05	....	34,478 74	2,221 85	266,081 11	279,385 16
208,930 94	204,752 38	....	73,290 05	3,092 61	285,313 60	279,607 32
182,546 38	166,116 86	....	59,291 41	2,801 88	244,639 67	222,622 09
98,939 79	83,109 60	....	44,759 69	3,123 34	146,822 82	123,331 16
123,680 58	95,234 37	....	51,417 00	2,877 76	177,975 34	137,041 01
123,820 60	86,674 70	$9,845 43	22,192 85	3,367 25	159,226 13	111,458 29
69,879 20	44,024 40	19,666 87	41,032 14	3,891 52	134,469 73	84,715 92
74,256 35	41,583 36	33,468 81	49,136 90	4,634 71	161,496 77	90,438 19
59,856 73	29,329 93	16,380 98	33,372 43	3,691 25	113,301 39	55,517 68
78,949 86	33,159 00	29,197 68	12,261 70	4,488 08	124,897 32	52,456 87
15,164 32	5,307 40	27,169 05	1,707 64	2,982 93	47,023 94	16,458 37
46,413 77	12,995 92	48,279 94	16,261 06	2,609 70	113,564 47	31,798 05
16,989 48	3,567 90	47,418 02	3,413 06	2,664 77	70,485 33	14,801 91
17,702 09	2,478 28	120,567 73	18,499 68	2,762 76	159,532 26	22,334 51
49,062 48	3,434 34	154,798 82	97,346 75	3,278 73	304,486 78	21,314 07
80,875 68	....	85,869 57	14,822 51	3,576 53	185,144 29	....
$5,827,813 72	$7,969,085 39	$592,662 90	$746,418 01	$66,261 75	$7,233,156 38	$9,180,166 58

CREDIT.

By tolls proper, ...	$631,870 58		
By tolls on tonnage contributed to the Erie Canal, .	675,042 46		
		$1,306,913 04	
By interest on tolls proper and contributions, ...		1,088,381 65	
Total income and interest, ...			$2,395,294 69
Balance, loss, ...			$14,018,028 27
To proportion of cost of repairs and maintenance of the Erie and Champlain Canal, from 1837 to 1866, ...			283,961 20
Net cost, ...			$14,301,989 47

TABLE

Oneida Lake

YEARS.	INCOME. (1) Tolls proper.	(2) Tolls contributed to and heretofore credited Erie and Champlain Canals.	(3) Total of tolls proper and contributions.	(4) Legal interest on tolls proper and contributions.
1841,	$294 58	....	$294 58	$515 51
1842,	471 85	....	471 85	696 70
1843,	475 04	....	475 04	765 45
1844,	683 67	....	683 67	1,052 84
1845,	678 66	....	678 66	997 63
1846,	604 41	....	604 41	846 17
1847,	487 49	....	487 49	648 36
1848,	671 89	....	671 89	846 58
1849,	794 67	....	794 67	945 65
1850,	2,513 19	....	2,513 19	2,815 09
1851,	6,178 57	....	6,178 57	6,487 49
1852,	7,795 05	....	7,795 05	7,639 14
1853,	10,282 18	....	10,282 18	9,356 78
1854,	9,802 11	....	9,802 11	8,233 83
1855,	7,340 81	....	7,340 81	5,652 42
1856,	8,639 04	....	8,639 04	6,047 32
1857,	4,849 34	....	4,849 34	3,055 08
1858,	1,235 32	....	1,235 32	691 77
1859,	701 41	....	701 41	343 69
1860,	290 33	....	290 33	121 93
1861,	218 86	....	218 86	76 60
1862,	121 83	....	121 83	34 11
1863,	45 21	....	45 21	9 49
1864,	5 00	....	5 00	70
1865,	....	....	....	....
1866,	....	....	....	....
	$65,180 51	....	$65,180 51	$57,880 33

RESULT.

DEBIT.

To cost of construction,	$64,837 68		
To interest thereon,	89,452 58		
		$154,290 26	
To cost of maintenance,	$123,234 92		
To interest thereon,	117,989 42		
		241,224 34	
Total disbursements,			$395,514 60

NO. 9.

Canal.

DISBURSEMENTS.						
FOR CONSTRUCTION.		FOR MAINTENANCE.				
(1)	(2)	(3)	(4)	(5)	(6)	(7)
Cost of construction.	Legal interest on cost of construction.	Contractors, for repairs.	Superintendents, for repairs.	Collectors, inspectors, &c.	Total payments, including cost of construction.	Legal interest on total payments, including cost of construction.
$50,000 00	$87,500 00	....	$2,332 81	$115 50	$52,448 31	$91,784 52
....	....	....	5,554 15	275 11	5,829 26	9,793 15
....	....	....	2,234 25	254 35	2,488 60	4,006 64
....	....	....	1,619 86	350 00	1,969 86	3,033 58
....	....	....	1,406 45	250 00	1,656 45	2,434 98
....	....	....	18,149 50	250 10	18,399 60	25,759 44
....	....	....	6,130 02	233 25	6,363 27	8,843 14
....	....	....	1,866 05	250 01	2,116 06	2,666 23
....	....	....	1,992 58	249 98	2,242 56	2,668 64
15 88	17 92	....	4,719 29	528 88	5,264 05	5,895 73
....	....	....	3,590 16	725 46	4,315 62	4,531 40
....	....	....	5,403 08	649 07	6,052 15	5,931 10
....	....	....	5,761 92	822 13	6,584 05	5,991 48
....	....	....	11,802 83	986 32	12,789 15	10,742 88
....	....	....	6,235 63	1,057 01	7,292 64	5,615 33
....	....	$2,481 71	107 91	1,018 69	3,608 31	2,525 81
20 86	13 23	3,919 00	....	863 39	4,803 25	3,026 04
....	....	4,103 94	....	762 62	4,866 56	2,725 27
1,150 00	563 50	3,975 00	....	600 87	5,725 87	2,805 67
210 75	88 62	4,058 67	....	937 88	5,207 30	2,187 06
1,064 15	372 40	2,841 61	400 00	755 51	5,061 27	1,771 44
....	....	2,375 01	100 00	329 15	2,804 16	785 16
772 44	162 12	2,375 01	....	....	3,147 45	660 96
2,534 64	354 90	2,543 23	....	....	5,077 87	710 90
5,426 71	379 89	2,365 50	....	....	7,792 21	545 45
3,642 25	....	524 47	....	....	4,166 72	....
$64,837 68	$89,452 58	$31,563 15	$79,406 49	12,265 28	$188,072 60	$207,442 00

CREDIT.

By tolls proper,	$65,180 51	
By interest thereon,	57,880 33	
Total income and interest,		123,060 84
Net cost,		$272,453 76

TABLE

Baldwinsville

YEARS.	INCOME. (1) Tolls proper.	(2) Tolls contributed to and heretofore credited Erie and Champlain Canals.	(3) Total tolls proper and contributions.	(4) Legal interest on tolls proper and contributions.
1852,	....	....	....	....
1853,	$472 06	....	$472 06	$429 57
1854,	429 86	....	429 86	361 08
1855,	76 01	....	76 01	58 52
1856,	73 02	....	73 02	51 11
1857,	32 81	....	32 81	20 67
1858,	14 13	....	14 13	7 91
1859,	26 03	....	26 03	12 75
1860,	23 17	....	23 17	9 73
1861,	22 57	....	22 57	7 89
1862,	31 83	....	31 83	8 91
1863,	39 17	....	39 17	8 22
1864,	20 82	....	20 82	2 91
1865,	....	....	....	....
1866,	....	....	....	....
	$1,261 48	....	$1,261 48	$979 27

RESULT.

DEBIT.

To cost of construction,	$23,556 14		
To interest thereon,	16,077 32		
		$39,633 46	
To cost of maintenance,	$25,035 26		
To interest thereon,	7,674 62		
		32,709 88	
Total disbursements and interest,			$72,343 34

NO. 10.

Canal.

DISBURSEMENTS.						
FOR CONSTRUCTION.		FOR MAINTENANCE.				
(1)	(2)	(3)	(4)	(5)	(6)	(7)
Cost of construction.	Legal interest on cost of construction.	Contractors, for repairs.	Superintendents, for repairs.	Collectors, inspectors, &c.	Total payments, including cost of construction.	Legal interest on total payments, including cost of construction.
$2,125 00	$2,082 50	....	....	....	$2,125 00	$2,082 50
....	....	....	....	$159 46	159 46	145 10
12,885 00	10,823 40	....	$2,372 29	432 79	15,690 08	13,179 66
200 00	154 00	....	2,372 66	375 00	2,947 66	2,269 69
....	....	....	422 46	377 58	800 04	560 02
885 13	557 55	....	455 43	178 59	1,519 15	957 06
2,615 00	1,464 40	....	2,381 61	....	4,996 62	2,798 10
....	....	....	413 30	....	413 30	202 51
....	....	....	....	....	....	....
....	....	....	1,069 60	....	1,069 60	374 36
....	....	....	174 67	....	174 67	48 90
4,529 14	951 09	....	72 33	....	4,601 47	966 30
316 87	44 38	....	631 80	....	948 67	132 81
....	....	....	499 00	....	499 00	34 93
....	....	....	12,646 68	....	12,646 68	....
$23,556 14	$16,077 32	....	$23,511 84	$1,523 42	$48,591 40	$23,751 94

CREDIT.

By tolls proper, ...	$1,261 48	
By interest thereon, ...	979 27	
		2,240 75
Net cost, ...		$70,102 59

TABLE

Oneida River

YEARS.	INCOME.			
	(1)	(2)	(3)	(4)
	Tolls proper.	Tolls contributed to and heretofore credited Erie and Champlain Canal.	Total of tolls proper and contributions.	Legal interest on tolls proper and contributions.
1839,	....	....	....	....
1840,	....	....	....	....
1841,	....	....	....	....
1842,	....	....	....	....
1843,	....	....	....	....
1844,	....	....	....	....
1845,	....	....	....	....
1846,	....	....	....	....
1847,	$118 22	....	$118 22	$157 23
1848,	200 50	....	200 50	252 63
1849,	230 71	....	230 71	274 54
1850,	5,555 63	....	5,555 63	6,222 30
1851,	18,409 56	....	18,409 56	19,330 03
1852,	24,540 54	....	24,540 54	24,049 72
1853,	31,275 36	....	31,275 36	28,460 57
1854,	31,992 92	....	31,992 92	24,874 05
1855,	24,004 94	....	24,004 94	18,483 80
1856,	29,035 78	....	29,035 78	20,324 74
1857,	15,758 42	....	15,758 42	9,927 80
1858,	3,725 19	....	3,725 19	2,086 10
1859,	2,044 64	....	2,044 64	1,001 87
1860,	1,015 98	....	1,015 98	426 71
1861,	919 63	....	919 63	321 87
1862,	2,311 06	....	2,311 06	647 09
1863,	4,399 07	....	4,399 07	923 80
1864,	3,572 36	....	3,572 36	500 13
1865,	2,489 87	....	2,489 87	174 29
1866,	2,688 53	....	2,688 53	....
	$204,288 91	....	$204,288 91	$158,439 27

RESULT.

CREDIT.

By tolls proper,	$204,288 91	
By interest thereon, 1847 to 1866,	158,439 27	
Total income and interest,		$362,728 18

NO. 11.

Improvement.

DISBURSEMENTS.						
FOR CONSTRUCTION.		FOR MAINTENANCE.				
(1)	(2)	(3)	(4)	(5)	(6)	(7)
Cost of construction.	Legal interest on cost of construction.	Contractors, for repairs.	Superintendents, for repairs.	Collectors, inspectors, &c.	Total payments, including cost of construction.	Legal interest on total payments, including cost of construction.
....	....	....	....	....	....	....
$16,128 94	$29,354 67	....	....	....	$16,128 94	$29,354 67
21,690 05	37,957 58	....	....	....	21,690 05	37,957 58
19,308 13	32,437 65	....	....	....	19,308 13	32,437 65
....	....	....	....	....	....	....
6,094 98	9,386 26	....	....	....	6,094 98	9,386 26
....	....	....	....	....	....	....
....	....	....	....	....	....	....
1,179 87	1,569 22	....	....	....	1,179 87	1,569 22
....	....	....	....	....	....	....
6,080 00	7,235 20	....	....	....	6,080 00	7,235 20
8,727 37	9,774 24	....	$394 67	....	9,122 04	10,216 68
6,913 07	7,258 65	....	2,249 61	....	9,162 68	9,620 81
....	....	....	1,765 37	....	1,765 37	1,730 06
....	....	....	1,707 40	....	1,707 40	1,553 73
....	....	....	2,876 47	....	2,876 47	2,416 23
1,443 75	1,111 88	....	4,518 79	....	5,962 54	4,591 15
....	....	....	2,481 73	....	2,481 73	1,737 21
4,228 42	2,663 64	....	3,590 51	....	7,818 93	4,925 92
....	....	....	2,797 27	....	2,797 27	1,566 47
....	....	....	1,078 83	....	1,078 83	528 62
182 67	76 72	....	....	....	182 67	76 72
15,054 30	5,269 40	....	....	....	15,054 30	5,269 40
928 00	259 84	....	447 76	....	1,375 76	385 21
....	....	....	....	....	....	....
10,141 92	1,419 86	....	....	....	10,141 92	1,419 86
4,623 32	323 61	....	1,097 09	....	5,720 41	400 42
24,269 23	....	....	....	....	24,269 23	....
$146,994 02	$146,098 42	....	$25,005 50	....	$171,999 52	$164,379 07

DEBIT.

To cost of construction, ...	$146,994 02		
To interest thereon, ...	146,098 42		
		$293,092 44	
To cost of maintenance, ...	$25,005 50		
To interest thereon, ...	18,280 65		
		43,286 15	
Total disbursements and interest, ...			336,378 59
Net profit, ...			$26,349 59

NOTE.—The ordinary repairs of this improvement, for some years past, have been included in the contract for repairs of section 2, Oswego Canal.

TABLE

Seneca River

YEARS.	INCOME.			
	(1)	(2)	(3)	(4)
	Tolls proper.	Tolls contributed to and heretofore credited Erie and Champlain Canals.	Total of tolls proper and contributions.	Legal interest on tolls proper and contributions.
1848,	$423 60	....	$422 60	$532 47
1849,	379 65	....	379 65	451 78
1850,	230 45	....	230 45	258 10
1851,	314 22	....	314 22	329 93
1852,	161 45	....	161 45	158 22
1853,	145 62	....	145 62	132 51
1854,	212 15	....	212 15	178 20
1855,	242 56	....	242 56	186 77
1856,	250 51	....	250 51	175 85
1857,	210 23	....	210 23	128 44
1858,	99 69	....	99 69	55 82
1859,	163 82	....	163 82	80 27
1860,	144 05	....	144 05	60 50
1861,	190 38	....	190 38	66 63
1862,	374 55	....	374 55	104 87
1863,	480 57	....	480 57	100 91
1864,	468 17	....	468 17	65 54
1865,	344 36	....	344 36	24 10
1866,	416 66	....	416 66	....
	$5,251 69	....	$5,251 69	$3,090 41

RESULT.

CREDIT.

By tolls proper,	$5,251 69	
By interest thereon,	3,091 41	
Total income and interest,		$8,343 10

NO. 12.

Towing Path.

DISBURSEMENTS.						
FOR CONSTRUCTION.		FOR MAINTENANCE.				
(1)	(2)	(3)	(4)	(5)	(6)	(7)
Cost of construction.	Legal interest on cost of construction.	Contractors, for repairs.	Superintendents, for repairs.	Collectors, inspectors, &c.	Total payments, including cost of construction.	Legal interest on total payments, including cost of construction.
$456 50	$479 85	....	$19 54	....	$476 04	$499 84
1,031 83	72 23	....	....	....	1,031 83	72 23
$1,488 33	$552 08	....	$19 54	....	$1,507 87	$572 07

DEBIT.

To cost of improvement,	$1,488 33		
To interest thereon,	552 08		
		$2,040 41	
To cost of maintenance,	$19 54		
To interest thereon,	19 99		
		39 53	
			$2,079 94
Net profit,			$6,263 16

NOTE.—No account has been kept of the original cost of this improvement, and the repairs thereof have been of late years included in the contract for repairs of section No. Oswego canal.

TABLE

Cayuga

YEARS.	INCOME.			
	(1)	(2)	(3)	(4)
	Tolls proper.	Tolls contributed to and heretofore credited Erie and Champlain Canals.	Total of tolls proper and contributions.	Legal interest on tolls proper and contributions.
1849,	$121 50	....	$121 50	$144 58
1850,	205 96	....	205 96	230 67
1851,	190 41	....	190 41	199 93
1852,	230 14	....	230 14	225 53
1853,	271 78	....	271 78	247 31
1854,	311 16	....	311 16	261 37
1855,	327 86	....	327 86	252 45
1856,	328 13	....	328 13	229 69
1857,	387 82	....	387 82	244 32
1858,	190 18	....	190 18	106 50
1859,	173 95	....	173 95	85 23
1860,	173 44	....	173 44	72 84
1861,	147 97	....	147 97	51 78
1862,	241 94	....	241 94	67 74
1863,	386 40	....	386 40	81 14
1864,	351 85	....	351 85	49 25
1865,	270 03	....	270 03	18 90
1866,	286 44	....	286 44	....
	$4,596 96	....	$4,596 96	$2,569 23

RESULT.

CREDIT.

By tolls proper,	$4,596 96	
By interest thereon,	2,569 23	
Total income and interest,		$7,166 19

NO. 13.

Inlet.

DISBURSEMENTS.						
FOR IMPROVEMENT.		FOR MAINTENANCE.				
(1)	(2)	(3)	(4)	(5)	(6)	(7)
Cost of improvement.	Legal interest on cost of improvement.	Contractors, for repairs.	Superintendents, for repairs.	Collectors, inspectors, &c.	Total payments, including cost of construction.	Legal interest on total payments, including cost of construction.
....	....	....	....	....	....	....
....	....	....	....	....	....	....
....	....	....	....	....	....	....
....	....	....	....	....	....	....
$17 63	$14 81	....	....	....	$17 63	$14 81
....	....	....	....	....	....	....
....	....	....	....	....	....	....
....	....	....	....	....	....	....
....	....	....	....	....	....	....
....	....	....	....	....	....	....
....	....	....	....	....	....	....
....	....	....	....	....	....	....
1,800 00	378 00	....	....	....	1,800 00	378 00
220 00	30 80	....	....	....	220 00	30 80
....	....	....	....	....	....	....
930 53	....	....	....	....	930 53	....
$2,968 16	$423 61	....	....	....	$2,968 16	$423 61

DEBIT.

To cost of improvements,........	$2,968 16	
To interest thereon,........	423 61	
		$3,391 77
		$3,774 42

NOTE.—The original cost of this improvement, and a portion of the repairs, have been paid by the General Fund. Of late years the ordinary repairs thereof have been included in the contract for repairs of the Cayuga and Seneca Canal.

STATEMENT A.

This is an aggregate recapitulation, in a condensed form, of the detailed information called for by the six first inquiries of the resolution. The specific and detailed information in reference to each canal will be found in tables Nos. 1 to 13, inclusive, following consecutively.

CANALS.	Cost of construction, enlargement, extension, and improvement.	Interest on cost of construction, &c.	Cost of repairs, maintenance, and collection.	Interest on cost of maintenance, &c.
Erie and Champlain,	$46,018,234 19	$69,232,418 84	$17,552,621 30	$21,196,944 63
Oswego,	3,490,949 24	3,174,037 95	1,812,571 42	1,735,991 48
Cayuga and Seneca,	1,520,542 59	1,363,287 73	620,050 22	758,059 21
Chemung,	1,273,261 86	1,635,704 70	1,139,770 30	970,699 26
Crooked Lake,	333,287 27	535,896 06	258,282 78	236,180 06
Chenango,	2,782,124 19	5,119,376 29	970,169 49	745,683 48
Black River,	3,224,779 55	4,454,243 92	445,011 36	270,291 78
Genesee Valley,	5,827,813 72	7,969,085 39	1,405,342 66	1,211,081 19
Oneida Lake,	64,837 68	89,452 58	123,234 92	117,989 42
Baldwinsville,	23,556 14	16,077 32	25,035 26	7,674 62
Oneida River improvement,	146,994 02	146,098 42	25,005 50	18,280 65
Seneca River towing path,	1,488 33	552 08	19 54	19 99
Cayuga Inlet,	2,968 16	423 61	....	....
	$64,710,836 94	$93,736,654 89	$24,377,114 75	$27,268,895 77

CANALS.	Aggregate cost of each canal, including cost of maintenance and legal interest on cost of construction.	Aggregate cost of each canal, including cost of maintenance and legal interest on cost of construction and maintenance.	Aggregate receipts or income from each canal, with interest thereon.	Revenues contributed to the Erie and Champlain Canals, by the lateral canals.
Erie and Champlain,	$132,803,274 33	$154,000,218 96	$192,455,779 57	....
Oswego,	8,477,558 61	10,213,550 09	4,415,957 01	$6,719,600 60
Cayuga and Seneca,	3,503,880 54	4,261,939 75	1,740,049 42	378,782 36
Chemung,	4,048,736 86	5,019,436 12	884,816 98	1,556,801 34
Crooked Lake,	1,127,466 11	1,363,646 17	94,340 87	478,042 64
Chenango,	8,871,669 97	9,617,353 45	1,204,040 85	123,276 40
Black River,	8,124,034 83	8,394,326 61	162,900 89	128,027 00
Genesee Valley,	15,202,241 77	16,413,322 96	1,158,085 43	675,042 46
Oneida Lake,	277,525 18	395,514 60	123,060 84	....
Baldwinsville,	64,668 72	72,343 34	2,240 75	....
Oneida River improvement,	318,097 94	336,378 59	362,728 18	....
Seneca River towing path,	2,059 95	2,079 94	8,348 10	....
Cayuga Inlet,	3,391 77	3,391 77	7,166 19	....
	$182,824,606 58	$210,093,502 35	$202,619,510 08	$11,059,572 80

STATEMENT B.

BALANCE SHEET showing the net cost or profit to the State of each Canal, as deduced from the foregoing tables.

CANALS.	COST.	PROFIT.	COST.	PROFIT.
	Crediting each lateral canal with its tolls proper, and charging it with its cost of construction, maintenance and repairs, charging and crediting interest at seven per cent.		Crediting each lateral canal with its tolls proper and tolls on its contribution to the Erie and Champlain Canals, and charging it with its own cost of construction, maintenance and repairs; also with its proper proportion of the cost of maintenance of the the Erie and Champlain Canals, charging and crediting interest at seven per cent.	
Erie and Champlain, ...	....	$38,455,560 61	....	$23,108,326 01
Oswego,.................	$5,797,593 08	....	....	2,950,548 18
Cayuga and Seneca, ...	2,521,890 33	....	$123,491 90	....
Chemung,...............	4,134,619 14	....	1,767,201 88	....
Crooked Lake, ...	1,269,305 30	....	406,088 87	....
Chenango,...............	8,413,312 60	....	8,223,431 69	....
Black River,.............	8,231,425 72	....	8,103,255 80	....
Genesee Valley,.........	15,255,237 53	....	14,301,989 47	....
Oneida Lake,............	272,453 76	....	272,453 76	....
Baldwinsville,...........	70,102 59	....	70,102 59	....
Oneida river improvem't,	....	26,349 59	....	26,349 59
Seneca river towing path,	....	6,263 16	....	6,265 16
Cayuga inlet,............	....	3,774 42	....	3,774 42
	$45,965,940 05	$38,491,947 78	$33,268,015 96	$26,095,263 36
Present cost to the State of the entire canal system, ...		*7,473,992 27		†7,172,752 60
		$45,965,940 05		$33,268,015 96

* To September 30, 1866.
† Crediting the lateral canals with tolls received to December 31, 1866.

NOTE.—The apparent discrepancy of $301,239.67 in the above balance sheet is accounted for from the fact that the result in one case is obtained from the accounts for *fiscal years*, the entire period closing with September 30, 1866, while the result obtained in the other covers the entire period (with the exception of the account of the Erie and Champlain Canals), ending with *December* 31, 1866—the discrepancy being the amount of revenue or tolls received from the lateral canals from October 1 to December 31, 1866, and the difference in interest.

In ascertaining the amount of tolls contributed by the lateral canals to the Erie, it was necessary (in order to report during the sitting of the Convention) to obtain the result from each year of navigation, instead of for each fiscal year; and this plan favors the lateral canals to the extent of three months' receipts of tolls, without the charge of maintenance and repairs for the corresponding period. If there had been time to ascertain the contributions by fiscal years, the apparent aggregate cost to the State of *all the canals* would have been alike in both results; there would simply have been a difference in the distribution of the cost.

STATE OF NEW YORK.

No. 24.

IN CONVENTION

July 12, 1867.

REPORT

OF COMPTROLLER RELATIVE TO INTEREST, &c., DUE COMMON SCHOOL FUND.

STATE OF NEW YORK.

COMPTROLLER'S OFFICE,
ALBANY, *July 12th*, 1867.

To Hon. WILLIAM A. WHEELER, *President of the Constitutional Convention:*

SIR: The Comptroller, in answer to the following resolution of the Convention, passed June 26th, viz:

"*Resolved*, That the Comptroller be requested to report to this Convention the amount of accrued interest remaining unpaid belonging to the Common School Fund arising from money loaned; also upon bonds for land sold, and the cause why annual interest is not paid; also, if in his judgment any of the bonds or money loaned, or bonds for land sold are insecurely invested; if so, what amount, and that the amounts of each be reported separately;" respectfully submits the following

32

REPORT.

1. The accrued interest on bonds for loans belonging to the Common School Fund remaining unpaid on the 30th of September, 1866, amounted to the sum of $23,713.20.

2. The accrued interest on bonds for lands belonging to the Common School Fund remaining unpaid on the 30th of September, 1866, amounted to the sum of $164,543.51.

The statement here given shows an apparent balance of over due interest of $188,256.71, corresponding with the amount stated in the Manual prepared for the use of the Convention. The following items should, however, be deducted in order to ascertain the actual balance:

1. Antwerp Liberal Literary Institute,	$1,312	50
2. J. W. Bonesteel,	23,188	30
3. Geo. Everson,	3,188	62
4. Edmund Knower,	7,034	38
5. J. B. Taylor & O. W. Brennan,	43,221	93
6. Jonathan K. Wing,	151	54
	$78,097	27

Reducing the aggregate amount of interest due October 1, 1866, to $110,159.44.

In the cases Nos. 2, 4 and 6, the interest has been erroneously computed to October 1, 1866, on balances of deficiencies brought down against insolvent mortgages on sale of premises on foreclosure of the mortgages by the Attorney General.

Acts for relief have been passed by the Legislature in the case of Nos. 1 and 3.

The account of J. B. Taylor and O. W. Brennan, No. 5, is rent on lease of certain premises known as the West Washington market, in New York. The premises included in this lease were sold to the city of New York, in pursuance of chapter 516, Laws of 1860, but the account was not formally closed on the records of this department.

3. It would not be possible to explain with certainty, why the interest on the securities is not in all cases paid when due. It may be stated, however, that under existing provisions of law (see Revised Statutes, 5th edition, volume 1, page 548, section 53), the Commissioners of the Land Office have no power to direct suits to be commenced on obligations where the interest is in arrears, until after the expiration of a year from the date when such interest becomes due. This regulation undoubtedly encourages negligence and indifference in complying with the conditions of the contract, as no steps, it would appear, can be taken to enforce payment until after default for the period mentioned.

By a resolution of the Commissioners of the Land Office all obligations have been put in suit on which the stipulated payments of principal and interest had been in arrears for the period of one year previous to the close of the last fiscal year.

4. In answer to the question included in the resolution of the Convention, whether in the judgment of the Comptroller the moneys represented by these securities are securely invested, the Comptroller is of the opinion that the bonds for loans are good and reliable for the amounts now due on them. With respect to the bonds for lands no intelligent opinion could be given without a more particular acquaintance with the value and location of the lands than is possessed by this Department.

In this connection the Comptroller respectfully refers to the suggestion made in his last annual report to the Legislature with reference to the investment of the capital of the United States Deposit Fund, and recommends that by a constitutional provision the capital of all the funds devoted to the cause of education be required to be invested in the stocks of this State, or of the United States, as soon and as far as it can be judiciously and properly done. This form of security is preferable from its simplicity and safety, and it has the additional recommendation, that it would enable the State to dispense with a large number of officers, and obviate the difficulties which are inseparable from a divided responsibility in the management of large moneyed interests.

Very respectfully yours,

THO. HILLHOUSE, *Comptroller.*

STATE OF NEW YORK.

No. 25.

IN CONVENTION

July 12, 1867.

RESOLUTION

Offered by Mr. Brooks.

Resolved, That in the judgment of this Convention the Legislature of this State should not pass laws, local or special in their character, for any of the following objects, viz:

"Regulating the jurisdiction and duties of justices of the peace and of constables; for the punishment of crimes and misdemeanors; regulating the practice in courts of justice; providing for changing the venue in civil and criminal cases; granting divorces, changing the names of persons.

"For laying out, opening and working on highways, and for the election or appointment of supervisors.

"Locating roads, town plots, streets, alleys and public squares.

"Summoning and empannelling grand and petit juries, and providing for their compensation.

"Regulating county and township business.

"Regulating the election of county and township officers and their compensation.

"For the assessment and collection of taxes for State, county, township or road purposes.

"Providing for supporting common schools and for the preservation of school funds.

"In relation to fees or salaries.

"In relation to interest on money.

"For opening and conducting elections of state, county or township officers, and designating the places of voting.

"Providing for the sale of real estate belonging to minors or other persons laboring under legal disabilities, by executors, administrators, guardians or trustees.

"In all the cases enumerated in the preceding sections, and in all other cases where a general law can be made applicable, all laws shall be general and of uniform operation throughout the State."

STATE OF NEW YORK.

No. 26.

IN CONVENTION

July 12, 1867.

MEMORIAL

FROM DR. FRANCIS LIEBER RELATIVE TO VERDICTS OF JURORS.

NEW YORK, *June 26th*, 1867.

DEAR SIR: Observing in the papers that you have proposed in the Convention to abolish the unanimity of jurors as a requisite for a verdict in civil cases, I beg leave to address to you a few remarks on a subject which has occupied my mind for many years, and which I consider of vital importance to our whole administration of justice. Long ago I gave (in my Civil Liberty and Self-Government) some of the reasons which induced me to disagree with those jurists and statesmen who consider unanimity a necessary, and even a sacred element of our honored jury-trial. Further observation and study have not only confirmed me in my opinion, but have greatly strengthened my conviction that the unanimity principle ought to be given up, if the jury trial is to remain in harmony with the altered circumstances which result from the progress and general change of things.

The present Constitution of our State permits litigants to waive the jury, in civil cases, if they freely agree to do so. This would indicate that the adoption of verdicts by a majority of the jurors, in civil cases, would not meet with insuperable difficulty ; but it seems to me even more important and more consonant with sound reasoning to abandon the unanimity principle in penal cases.

At the beginning of my "Reflections," a copy of which has been laid before each member of the Convention, I stated the different causes of the failure of justice, in the present time. I ought to have added the non-agreement of jurors. It would be a useful piece of information, and an important addition to the statistics of the times, if the Convention would ascertain, through our able State statistician, the percentage of failures of trials resulting from the non-agreement of jurors in civil, in criminal, and especially in capital cases. This failure of agreement has begun to show itself in England likewise, since the coarse means of forcing the jury to agree, by hunger, cold and darkness, has been given up.

In Scotland, no unanimity of the jury is required in penal trials; nor in France, Italy, Germany, nor in any country whatever except England and the United States; and in the English Law it has come to be gradually established in the course of legal changes, and by no means according to a principle, clearly established from the beginning. The unanimity principle has led to strange results. Not only were formerly jurors forced by physical means to agree, in a moral and intellectual point of view, but in old times it happened that a verdict was taken from eleven jurors, if they agreed, and "the refractory juror" was committed to prison! (Guide to English Juries, 1682. I take the quotation from Forsyth, History of Trial by Jury, 1852)

Under Henry II it was established that twelve jurors should agree in order to determine a question, but the "afforcement" of the jury meant that as long as twelve jurors did not agree, others were added to the panel, until twelve out of this number, no matter how large, should agree one way or the other. This was changed occasionally. Under Edward III it was "decided" that the verdict of less than twelve was a nullity. At present a verdict of less than twelve is sometimes taken by consent of both parties.

At first the jurors were the judges themselves, but in the course of time the jury, as judges of the fact, separated from the bench, as judges of the law, in the gradual development of our *accusatorial* trial as contradistinguished to the *inquisitorial trial.* The English trial by jury is one of the great acquisitions in the development of our race, but everything belonging to it as it exists at present, is not perfect; nor does the trial by jury form the only exception to the rule that all institutions need must change or be modified in the course of time, if they are intended to last and outlive centuries.

The French rule, and I believe the Italian also, is in penal as well as civil cases, that if seven jurors are against five, the judge or judges retire, and if the bench decides with the five against the seven, the verdict is on the side of the five. If eight jurors agree against four, it is a verdict, in capital as well as in common criminal cases. There is no civil jury in France.

This seems to me artificial and not in harmony with our conception of the judge, who stands between the parties, especially so when the State, the Crown, or the People, is one of the two parties; nor in harmony with the important idea (although we Americans have given it up in many cases) that the judges of the fact and those of the law must be distinctly separated.

On the other hand what is unanimity worth when it is enforced; or when the jury is "out" any length of time? which proves that the formal unanimity, the outward agreement is a merely *accommodative* unanimity, if I may make a word. Such a verdict is not an intrinsically truthful one; the unanimity is a real "afforcement," or artificial. Again, the unanimity principle puts it in the power of any refractory juror, possibly sympathizing more with crime than with society and right, to defeat the ends of justice by "holding out." Every one remembers cases of the plainest and of well-proved atrocity, going unpunished because of one or two jurors resisting the others, either from positively wicked motives or some mawkish reasons, which ought to have prevented them from going into the jury-box altogether.

I ask then, why not adopt this rule: *Each jury shall consist of twelve jurors, the agreement of two-thirds of whom shall be sufficient for a verdict, in all cases, both civil and penal, except in capital cases, when three-fourths must agree to make a verdict valid. But the foreman, in rendering the verdict, shall state how many jurors have agreed.*

I have never heard or seen in print any objection to the passage above alluded to, in which I have suggested the abandoning of unanimity, than this, that people, the criminal included, would not be satisfied with a verdict, if they knew that some jurors did not agree. As to the criminal, let us leave him alone. I can assure all persons who have investigated this subject less than I have that there are very few convicts satisfied with their verdict. The worst ones will acknowledge that they have committed crimes indeed, but never the one for which they are sentenced, or will insist upon the falsehood of a great deal of the testimony on which they are convicted.

The objection to the non-unanimity is not founded on any psychologic ground. How much stronger is not the fact that all of us have to abide by the decision of the majority in the most delicate cases, when supreme Courts decide constitutional questions, and we do not only know that there has been no unanimity in the court, but we actually receive the *opinions* of the minority, and their whole arguments, which always seem the better ones to many, sometimes to a large majority of the people! Ought we to abolish then the publication of the fact that a majority of the judges only and not the totality of them agreed with the decision? By no means. Daniel Webster once said in my presence that the study of the "Protests" in the House of Lords (having been published in a separate volume) was to him the most instructive reading on constitutional law and history. May we not say something similar concerning many opinions of the minority of our supreme benches?

In legislation, in politics, in general (except, indeed, in diplomacy) the unanimity principle savors of barbarism, or indicates at least a want of development. The United States of the Netherlands could pass no law of importance, except by the unanimous consent of the States General. A single voice in the ancient Polish Diet could veto a measure. Does not perhaps something of this sort apply to our jury unanimity?

Whether it be so or not, I for one, am convinced that we ought to adopt the other rule in order to give to our verdicts the character of perfect truthfulness, and to prevent the frequent failures of finding a verdict at all.

I am, with great regard, Dear Sir, your obed't,

FRANCIS LIEBER.

STATE OF NEW YORK.

No. 27.

IN CONVENTION

July 15, 1867.

REPORT

OF COMMISSIONERS OF LAND OFFICE RELATIVE TO SALT RESERVATION.

To Hon. WILLIAM A. WHEELER, *President of the State Convention:*

In compliance with the resolution of the Convention, passed June 27, 1867, making inquiries of the Commissioners of the Land Office in regard to the salt reservations of this State, the said Commissioners submit the following report:

STATEMENT

OF THE QUANTITY OF LAND ORIGINALLY SET APART BY THE STATE, AND OF THE QUANTITY OF LAND NOW OWNED BY THE STATE AND DEVOTED TO THE MANUFACTURE OF SALT, ALSO THE TOWNS AND COUNTIES WHERE THE SAME ARE LOCATED.

The following lands in the Onondaga Salt Springs Reservation, are to be reseserved by the Constitution (1823) for the manufacture of salt, to wit:

The ground to the extent of two hundred feet in breadth, along the northeasterly side of the Oswego canal, from marsh lot No. 22, at Greenpoint, to the reclaimed lot No. 15, near the village of Liverpool, together with the present manufacturing lots at Liverpool; also, farm lots Nos. 117, 118, 119, 120, 121, 104, 107, 108; also blocks Nos. 1, 2, 3, 4, 5, 6 and 7, at the village of Salina, together with the ground bounded northerly and northeasterly by the old channel of the Mud creek and the Oswego canal, southeasterly by blocks Nos. 1, 2 and 3, and southwesterly by marsh lot No. 25; also, the ground comprehended by the following blocks along the westerly side of the Oswego canal, to wit:

Nos. 44, 45, 65, 66, 77, 92, 93, 97, 98 of the village of Salina, and blocks Nos. 1, 5 and 11 of the village of Syracuse; also, the ground to the extent of 200 feet in breadth along the Oswego canal, from the Walton tract, in the village of Syracuse, to Center street, in the village of Salina; also, the ground to the extent of 200 feet in breadth along the Erie canal, from the first lock west of Syracuse to the natural basin in the village of Geddes; also, farm lots Nos. 54, 55, 56, 332, and No. 40 of the reclaimed lots, together with the old salt manufacturing lots, and block No. 6 in the village of Geddes.

Also, the ground located under the act relative to the manufacturing of coarse salt.

By article 7, section 7 of the present Constitution, adopted in 1846, the Legislature shall never sell or dispose of the Salt Springs belonging to this State. The land contiguous thereto, and which may be necessary and convenient for the use of the Salt Springs, may be sold by authority of law and under the direction of the Commissioners of the Land Office, for the purpose of investing the moneys arising therefrom in other lands alike convenient; but, by such sale and purchase, the aggregate quantity of these lands shall not be diminished.

Salt lands reserved, ...	550	acres.
Purchased or exchanged since 1848,..............	543.12	"
	1093.12	"
Lands sold since 1848, ...	127.25	"
	965.87	
Reclaimed by the lowering of Onondaga lake, ...	209	"
Total,...............................	1174.87	"

These lands are located in the city of Syracuse, and the towns of Geddes and Salina, in Onondaga county.

We do not know the present value of the salt lands belonging to the State, and have no means of making an estimate of the approximate value thereof.

A portion of the inquiries contained in the resolution was referred to the Hon. Geo. Geddes, Superintendent of the Onondaga Salt Springs, and the following is the reply received from that gentleman, which reply we beg leave to make part of this report:

OFFICE OF THE SUPERINTENDENT OF
ONONDAGA SALT SPRINGS,
SYRACUSE, *July* 6, 1867.

HON. ERASTUS CLARK, *Deputy Secretary of State and Clerk of Commissioners of the Land Office:*

SIR—I respectfully reply to the questions referred to me as follows:

1st. "The cost and present value of the salt wells, structures and improvements thereto made and owned by the State."

Fifteen salt wells now in use, cost and present value, as near as can be ascertained, $3,000 each,	$45,000
6 rotary pumps, $250 each,	1,500
1 pump house and machinery at Geddes,	15,000
1 pump house and machinery, 3d ward, Syracuse,	30,000
1 pump house and machinery, 1st ward, Syracuse,	35,000
Old pump house at Syracuse worn out, probably cost $15,000.	
3 high reservoirs, one in 3d ward, one in 1st ward, Syracuse, and one at Geddes, $5,000 each,	15,000
8 reservoirs, at Geddes, 1st ward, Syracuse, and at Liverpool, $2,500 each,	20,000
1 earth reservoir at Syracuse, 3d ward,	20,000
40 miles, as estimated, of log conduits, now worth about 55 cents per lineal foot,	116,160
1 dressed stone office, in 3d ward, Syracuse,	7,500
1 brick office in 1st ward, Syracuse, (one-half of it used as Canal Collector's office.)	4,000
1 brick office at Liverpool,	800
1 brick office at Geddes,	800
1 barrel stand at 1st ward, $350, one at Liverpool, $250,	600
1 barrel stand at Geddes,	350
	$311,710

2d. "The probable value of the salines connected therewith."

I know of no way of determining the value of the salines. The State owns the water and delivers it to various individuals and companies to be made into salt, receiving from these parties such sum as has been determined by law. This sum, since 1846, has been one cent a bushel of 56 pounds. Under the policy of the State, large sums of private capital have been invested in the manufacture of salt, which capital is of little or no value except for making salt; and if the water should fail the whole of it would be sunk, less the value of the kettles for old iron, and the value of timber that might be saved. On the other side, it may be said that, unless the water was made into salt, by parties other than agents of the State, it would be worth nothing. Any one familiar with the business of making salt, knows that it could not be carried on directly by the State without loss.

The value of the salines, must then be considered as that sum that the State may justly demand of the manufacturers for the salt water delivered to them.

The local market for our salt is small, and to compete with salt outside this local market, it is necessary to reduce the cost of the salt to the lowest point. Not only the price of the water, but its strength enters into the cost of salt. To raise the price of the water, or to produce salt beyond the capacity of the wells to furnish *strong* water, is to increase the cost of salt, and thus lessen the quantity that can be produced and sold at a profit to the manufacturer.

3d. "The whole quantity of land reclaimed by lowering the outlet of Onondaga lake, showing the number of acres which inured to the State; also, to individuals by name."

There has been no land reclaimed by lowering the outlet of Onondaga lake within many years. Before the Oswego canal was made, the water in Onondaga lake was lower than it is now, or all the information that I have been able to obtain leads to a false conclusion. The dam across the Oswego river at Phœnix, is but a few inches lower than low water in Onondaga lake, and has the effect to hold the water up in that lake until the freshets have subsided in the river. It was not until the first day of June that the freshets in the river had sufficiently subsided to enable us to get the pumps at the salt wells, on the marsh at the head of the lake, in operation. and then only by constructing a coffer dam around the engine house in three feet of water,—and now a large proportion of the low lands around the lake is flooded. There can be no reclaiming of lands around Onondaga lake while Phœnix dam remains as it is.

4th. "The names of parties now holding grants and leases from the State, for the use of lands for the manufacture of solar salt."

The records necessary to answer this question are to be found in the keeping of the Commissioners of the Land Office, as all the grants of land for making *solar* salt are made by that commission, and there is no official records of them in this office. But the Salt Company of Onondaga has a map showing most of these grants, and by application to the grantees, I have so far supplied such information as could not be otherwise obtained, that I submit the following schedule in the belief that it is substantially correct. I give the number of acres granted to each, of State lands, though not called for in the question:

Western Coarse Salt Company,	60.15 acres.
James M. Gere,	9.45 "
Draper & Porter,	7.37 "
J. A. Robinson & Co.,	14.26 "
Turk's Island Company,	20.00 "
Geddes Coarse Salt Company,	46.83 "
W. & D. Kirkpatrick,	15.00 "
S. C. Brewster,	10.00 "
J. F. Paige,	10.00 "
Union Coarse Salt Company,	99.12 "
Cape Cod Coarse Salt Company,	30.50 "
John White & Co.,	19.40 "
L. Stevens & Co.,	24.00 "
Onondaga Solar Salt Company,	31.00 "
Syracuse Solar Salt Company,	28.85 "
C. Franchot & Co.,	3.54 "
Salt Springs Solar Salt Company,	25.00 "
Salina Solar Salt Company,	40.00 "
Heacock & Berry,	18.82 "
Salina Coarse and Fine Salt Company,	36.00 "
Thomas Gale,	38.00 "
Soule & Doyle,	21.50 "
D. S. Earll,	23.00 "
Thomas Gale,	57.00 "
Highland Coarse Salt Company,	38.75 "
Liverpool Coarse Salt Company,	22.79 "
R. N. & N. S. Gere,	4.55 "
Total acres.	754.88

Trusting that the foregoing answers may be of service to the Commissioners of the Land Office,

I am respectfully, your obd't serv't,

GEO. GEDDES,

Superintendent of Onondaga Salt Springs.

ONONDAGA SALT SPRINGS.

YEARS.	Expenditures.			Receipts.
	Ordinary expenses and improvements.	North side cut canal Onondaga lake improvement.	Total.	Current Revenue.
1846..	$18,917 78	....	$18,917 78	$75,507 34
1847..	30,547 95	....	30,547 95	32,398 64
1848..	25,520 21	....	25,520 21	43,347 67
1849..	29,754 05	....	29,754 05	51,598 98
1850..	*29,027 00	....	29,027 00	44,364 03
1851..	30,000 00	....	30,000 00	45,458 58
1852..	33,911 53	$1,000 00	34,911 53	47,928 17
1853..	24,826 70	....	24,826 70	52,159 85
1854..	25,250 00	....	25,250 00	54,987 88
1855..	51,000 00	....	51,000 00	57,777 90
1856..	43,000 00	....	43,000 00	60,975 82
1857..	52,000 00	14,000 00	66,000 00	53,476 91
1858..	59,000 00	2,300 00	61,300 00	58,138 18
1859..	44,000 00	12,000 00	56,000 00	69,026 54
1860..	†43,916 00	7,500 00	51,416 00	65,875 51
1861..	48,500 00	15,000 00	63,500 00	66,299 57
1862..	39,000 00	4,074 44	43,074 44	87,418 98
1863..	32,000 00	....	32,000 00	76,090 75
1864..	50,000 00	....	50,000 00	88,125 31
1865..	48,000 00	....	48,000 00	62,765 64
1866..	‡49,184 00	....	49,184 00	70,411 66
	$807,355 22	$55,874 44	$863,229 66	$1,264,133 91

* Includes $777—award under chapter 330, Laws of 1849.
† Includes $600—on account of Montezuma Salt Springs.
‡ Includes $7,000—for work, &c., prior to March 1, 1865.

Statement of the lands sold, and moneys expended in the purchase of other lands, expenses, &c., in the Onondaga Salt Springs Reservation, since the adoption of the present Constitution in 1846, *viz:*

Date of sale.	Description.	No of acres.	Sold for.
Feb. 20, 1849	Out lots containing 49 acres, also six blocks at Liverpool, five blocks at Salina, four blocks at Syracuse. Parts of farm lots 153, 301 and 324, together with three pieces or gores on which the Oswego Railroad is located; quantities in all cases not given, done pursuant to Act, chap. 346, Laws of 1848	49	$25,136 00
June 13, 1850	Mill Pond Improvement in Syracuse, per chap. 12, Laws of 1849.	6	14,770 00
April 10, 1852	Lands lying south of Erie canal, and east of West street in Syracuse, per chap. 270, Laws of 1851, granted to occupants	7	7,600 00
May 19, 1853	Lands lying north of Church street and west of Salina street in Syracuse, per chap. 283, Laws of 1851	10	36,246 00
Feb. 1854	Add sale to Syracuse and Utica Railroad Co., Nov. 26, 1850, sub. 5 of farm lot 253	2.92	2,000 00
	Also sale to Oswego and Syracuse Railroad, of June, 1848	4.93	739 50
June 12, 1855	Sale of lots in 5th Ward in Syracuse, lying west of Wyoming st.	10	38,023 00
Dec. 16, 1856	Sale of lots on Genesee street, west of Plum street in Syracuse, part sold	25	28,525 00
July 12, 1867	Additional sales since 1856 to present time	12.40	12,129 24
		127.25	$165,168 74

Onondaga Salt Springs Reservation, sold pursuant to act, chapter 346, *Laws of* 1848. *Vendue at Syracuse, Feb.* 20, 1849.

Block.	Lot.	Value of improvemen s.	Valuation of soil.	Name of purchaser.	Consideration.	Amount paid.
				LIVERPOOL.		
46	....	$500 00	$165 00	Calvin Pierson,	$165 00	$41 25
47	1	200 00	40 00	Justin Corbin,	41 00	10 25
do	2	200 00	75 00	Francis Alvord,	100 00	25 00
48	1	200 00	90 00	Marcus Lyon,	90 00	22 50
do	2	200 00	45 00	Henrietta Adams,	45 00	12 00
do	3	275 00	140 00	Joseph Jacquith,	140 00	40 00
do	4	225 00	100 00	John Matthews,	100 00	25 00
do	5	200 00	100 00	James Cronkhite,	100 00	25 00
do	6	225 00	60 00	James Knapp,	160 00	15 00
do	7	350 00	135 00	Harriet M. Rexford,	135 00	33 75
49	2	325 00	130 00	Reserved,		
do	3	200 00	70 00	James Keith,	70 00	17 50
do	4	200 00	70 00	John G. Boyden,	70 00	70 00
do	5	250 00	70 00	Peter O'Neil,	70 00	17 50
do	6	200 00	70 00	Joseph Jacquith,	70 00	20 00
do	7	250 00	86 00	Isaac Sharp, Wm. D. Scoville & Ed. Cally,	86 00	21 50
do	8	200 00	30 00	Isaac Sharp and Wm. D. Scoville,	30 00	7 50
do	9	500 00	108 00	Joseph Jacquith,	108 00	108 00
do	10	1,200 00	100 00	Justus Corbin,	100 00	25 00
do	11	1,200 00	100 00	Zenas Corbin,	100 00	25 00

	do	12	275 00	80 00	William P. Wentworth,	80 00	20 00
	50	....	300 00	200 00	John Matthews,	200 00	50 00
					SALINA.		
	59	2	....	400 00	William Barnes,	605 00	151 25
	123	1 ac.	....	100 00	Marcellus Farmer,	395 00	98 75
Part of..	7	....	....	66 00	Hiram F. Harroun,	175 00	43 75
					DRY DOCK LOCK IN SALINA.		
Cont'ing	$\frac{59}{100}$ ac.	....	200 00	400 00	Edward Chapman,	400 00	100 00
					PART OF PASTURE LOT IN VILLAGE OF SALINA, SURVEYED BY GEDDES IN 1807.		
		14	200 00	75 00	Asahel Dolbear,	75 00	20 00
	A	1	....	100 00	Thomas G. Alvord,	345 00	86 25
	do	2	....	100 00	do	365 00	91 25
	B	4 $\frac{11}{100}$ ac.	....	411 00	do	680 00	170 00
					SYRACUSE.		
	D	1	....	175 00	Grove Lawrence,	205 00	51 25
	do	2	....	175 00	do	205 00	51 25
	do	3	....	175 00	E. W. Leavenworth and Freeborn G. Jewett	200 00	50 00
	do	4	....	175 00	do do do	195 00	48 75
	do	5	....	175 00	do do do	200 00	50 00
	do	6	....	175 00	do do do	200 00	50 00
	do	7	....	175 00	John Ewen,	210 00	52 50
	do	8	....	200 00	Thomas Spencer,	335 00	83 75
	do	9	....	120 00	Grove Lawrence,	245 00	61 25
	do	10	....	110 00	do	310 00	52 50
	do	11	....	125 00	Jacob Amos,	180 00	45 00
	do	12	....	130 00	do	150 00	37 50

Onondaga Salt Springs Reservation. Vendue of Feb. 20, 1849—*Continued.*

Block.	Lot.	Value of improvements.	Valuation of soil.	Name of purchaser.	Consideration.	Amount paid.
D	13	....	$125 00	E. W. Leavenworth and Freeborn G. Jewett	$150 00	$37 50
do	14	....	125 00	do do do	150 00	37 50
do	15	....	120 00	John Ewen...........................	150 00	37 50
do	16	....	150 00	do	235 00	58 75
do	17	....	200 00	Horatio G. Mattison	240 00	60 00
do	18	....	200 00	Silas F. Smith,.........................	230 00	57 50
do	19	....	200 00	Peter Keenan..........................	250 00	62 50
do	20	....	200 00	Horatio G. Mattison	255 00	63 75
do	21	$300 00	200 00	Abner Bates and Robert M. Pelton	200 00	50 00
do	22	300 00	225 00	do do do	222 00	56 25
E	1	300 00	800 00	Abner Bates..........................	800 00	200 00
do	2	200 00	200 00	do	200 00	50 00
do	3	....	200 00	Abner Bates and Robert M. Pelton......	275 00	68 75
do	4	....	200 00	do do do	305 00	76 25
do	5	....	225 00	do do do	315 00	78 75
I	1	400 00	250 00	Alexander McKinstry.................	250 00	62 50
	2	....	400 00	Charles Manahan......................	1,000 00	250 00
				Lands lying between Salina street and the Onondaga creek in the city of Syracuse, over which the waste waters from the weigh-lock are conducted, &c., called and known as the Red mill. The State reserving the right and privilege to use said waters.		
	3 ac.	....	2,100 00	John Townsend & Aug. James, Oc. 9, 1850	2,100 00	525 00
J	2	200 00	680 00	Sidney Stanton, June 24, 1853	680 00	170 00
do	3	....	....	Reserved.		

	do	4	200 00	50 00	James McBride	50 00	50 00
					PART OF SALT LOT, CALLED THE PETER WALES LOT IN SYRACUSE.		
	8	8	200 00	150 00	Lucinda Wales	150 00	37 50
					ONONDAGA SALT SPRINGS RESERVATION.		
Farm lots	253	Sub. 1	2,000 00	5,200 00	Syracuse and Utica Railroad	5,200 00	1,300 00
do	do	2	500 00	800 00	Syr. Salt Co., by J. Townsend, Feb. 19, 1849	800 00	200 00
do	do	3	....	450 00	James G. Tracy	800 00	200 00
do	do	4	1,000 00	510 00	Syracuse and Utica Railroad Company	510 00	127 50
do	301	1	....	200 00	Thomas George	400 00	100 00
do	do	2	....	150 00	do	215 00	53 75
do	do	3	....	75 00	do	205 00	51 25
Part of..	324	25 ac.	....	....	Exclusive of road, 50 ft. wide being excepted		
				125 00	Harvey Baldwin	126 00	31 50
Part of..	344	$1\frac{42}{100}$ ac.	....	100 00	do	161 00	40 25
					OSWEGO AND SYRACUSE RAILROAD COMPANY.		
1st Piece	....	$2\frac{8}{10}$ ac.	....	....	Exclusive of $2\frac{1}{8}$ acres on Farm lots 265, 289		
2d Piece	....	$5\frac{96}{100}$ ac.	....	....	99 feet wide, reserving the land on which Geddes' reservoir stands, & 10 ft. round it	974 00	243 50
					Total amount of sale,	$25,136 00	
					Add sale to Syr. & Utica R. R. Nov. 26, '50.		
Farm lot	253 sub. 1	$2\frac{93}{100}$ ac.	....	....	....	$2,000 00	
Also ...	do	$4\frac{93}{100}$ ac.	....	....	Sold to Oswego & Syr. Railroad, June, 1848	739 50	
						$2,739 50	

Mill Pond Improvement. Vendue at Syracuse, June 13, 1850.

Block.	Lot.	Valuation.	Name of purchaser.	Consideration.	Am't paid.
105	8	$315 00	Samuel L. McCullock,	$405 00	$101 00
do	9	400 00	Albert A. Hudson, for Origen Vandenburgh,	610 00	153 00
do	10	380 00	Arthur Pattison,	535 00	134 00
do	11	300 00	Joel H. Whitlock,	405 00	101 00
do	12	160 00	Steuben Rexford,	300 00	75 00
do	13	90 00	Geo. L. Maynard,	250 00	63 00
do	14	60 00	James G. Tracey,	155 00	40 00
do	15	60 00	James Davis,	165 00	41 00
do	16	60 00	do	180 00	45 00
do	17	90 00	John F. Wyman,	225 00	56 00
do	18	180 00	do	355 00	89 00
do	19	270 00	Wm. B. Kirk,	460 00	115 00
do	20	400 00	do	600 00	150 00
do	21	500 00	John F. Wyman,	680 00	170 00
118	10	190 00	John J. Hopper,	250 00	62 00
do	11	225 00	Arthur Pattison,	300 00	75 00
do	12	315 00	John F. Wyman,	400 00	100 00
do	13	410 00	Harvey Baldwin,	555 00	138 00
do	14	225 00	do	400 00	100 00
do	15	400 00	George F. Comstock,	500 00	125 00
do	16	400 00	Alfred H. Hovey,	525 00	131 00
do	17	400 00	Henry A. Dillaye,	530 00	133 00

do	18	700 00	John F. Wyman,	765 00	191 00
do	19	570 00	George Barnes and Dudley P. Phelps,	650 00	163 00
do	20	450 00	John F. Wyman,	550 00	138 00
do	21	270 00	do	400 00	100 00
do	22	410 00	do	780 00	195 00
do	23	125 00	Harvey Baldwin,	250 00	62 00
do	24	225 00	Alfred H. Hovey,	265 00	66 00
do	25	225 00	Lucius M. Hollister,	290 00	73 00
do	26	225 00	John J. Hopper,	305 00	76 00
do	27	450 00	do	750 00	187 00
do	28	270 00	John F. Wyman,	360 00	90 00
do	29	225 00	do	315 00	79 00
do	30	225 00	do	305 00	76 00
		$10,200 00	Total amount of sale,	$14,770 00	

The lands lying north of Church street, and west of Salina street, in the city of Syracuse, appraised by Charles Pope, W. Sheldon and George Stevens, May 4, 1853. *Vendue, May* 19, 1853.

Block.	Lot.	Valuation.	Name of purchaser.	Consideration.	Am't paid.
J	1	$5,000 00	George Everson,	$5,300 00	1,325 00
do	17	1,000 00	Grove Lawrence,	1,125 00	285 00
do	18	800 00	George H. Booth, Chas. Manahan, Chas. McGurk, Patrick McGurk, Jno. Dolphin and Christ'r Casey,	1,525 00	381 00
77	11	800 00	James R. Lawrence,	850 00	213 00
do	12	300 00	Frederick Horner, Jr.,	300 00	75 00
do	13	315 00	William Harrop,	330 00	82 00
do	14 A	330 00	Jefferson Phillips for Jacob Amos,	375 00	94 00
do	14 B	350 00	John Newell,	400 00	100 00
do	15	375 00	Dennis McCarthy,	400 00	100 00
do	16	450 00	Richard Raynor,	605 00	152 00
76		25 00	(Small triangle E, of lot A.) Alexander McKinstry,	131 00	32 75
do	Lot A	25 00	James B. Rae,	125 00	35 00
do	do B	50 00	Daniel O'Reiley (resold 1853),	50 00	
do	do 2	300 00	(East of lot B.) Ira Northrop,	300 00	75 00
8	1	800 00	Elisha F. Wallace,	890 00	223 00
do	2	600 00	George F. Grinnell,	610 00	152 00
do	3	600 00	Allen Munroe and John W. Barker,	630 00	157 00
do	4	750 00	do do do	850 00	213 00
do	5	550 00	Michael Dolphin (resold 1853),	675 00	199 00
do	6	650 00	William D. Burrill,	725 00	185 00
do	7	650 00	John F. Voshall,	725 00	182 00
do	8	650 00	John L. Newcomb,	810 00	210 00

do	9	800 00	Josiah B. Butler,	1,105 00	277 00
P B	1	800 00	Samuel P. Gen, George F. Comstock and James Noxon,	905 00	226 00
do	2	700 00	William M. Brewster,	765 00	200 00
do	3	700 00	Chester Hair for Lewis Sporry,	780 00	195 00
do	4	700 00	do do	805 00	202 00
do	5	900 00	John A. Green, Jr.,	1,100 00	275 00
do	6	900 00	Hugh Rogers,	1,130 00	283 00
do	7	800 00	do	890 00	223 00
do	8	850 00	John M. Jaycox,	920 00	230 00
do	9	900 00	Barnard Slocum,	1,190 00	300 00
do	10	1,050 00	James R. Lawrence,	1,600 00	400 00
I	4	500 00	Alexander McKinstry and Willett Hinman,	700 00	175 00
do	5	400 00	John Dolphin,	575 00	144 00
do	6	425 00	do	610 00	152 00
do	7	450 00	do	640 00	160 00
do	8	600 00	Patrick McGurk,	800 00	200 00
2	1	400 00	Edward Farley,	455 00	113 75
do	2	500 00	Alfred Smith and William Jordan,	520 00	130 00
17	1	600 00	George Everson,	615 00	154 00
do	2	500 00	Charles Tallman,	505 00	130 00
do	3	500 00	Dennis Driscoll, Jr.,	555 00	150 00
do	4	500 00	William Strong,	550 00	138 00
do	5	500 00	Jefferson Phillips,	550 00	138 00
E	6	30 00	Edward Farley,	250 00	62 50
		$30,375 00	Total amount of sale,	$36,246 00	

Lands Lying south of Erie canal and east of West street, in city of Syracuse. Sale pursuant to ch. 270, 1851. *April* 10, 1852.

Block.	Lot.	Valuation.	Name of purchaser.	Consideration.	Am't paid.
161 D.	1	$410 00	Henry A. Dillaye,	$410 00	$102 50
do	2	410 00	George F. Comstock for Allen Munroe,	410 00	102 50
do	3	325 00	Harvey Baldwin,	325 00	81 25
do	4	310 00	John F. Wyman for H. Baldwin,	310 00	77 50
do	5	300 00	H. Baldwin for J. F. Wyman,	300 00	75 00
do	6	275 00	John F. Wyman,	275 00	68 75
do	7	125 00	do	125 00	31 25
do	8	425 00	do	425 00	106 25
do	9	400 00	Alfred H. Hovey,	400 00	100 00
do	10	375 00	do	375 00	93 75
do	11	375 00	John F. Wyman,	375 00	93 75
do	12	300 00	do	300 00	75 00
do	13	225 00	Samuel A. Seager,	225 00	56 25
do	14	150 00	Origen Vandenburgh,	150 00	40 00
192 A.	6	125 00	Joel H. Whitlock,	125 00	31 25
do	7	250 00	Arthur Pattison,	250 00	62 50
do	8	125 00	John F. Wyman,	125 00	31 25
192 B.	1	375 00	do	375 00	93 75
do	2	375 00	do	375 00	93 75
do	3	275 00	do	275 00	68 75
do	4	125 00	Arthur Pattison,	125 00	31 25
do	5	325 00	John F. Wyman,	325 00	81 25
do	6	315 00	do	315 00	78 75

do	7	310 00	John F. Wyman,	310 00	77 50
do	8	225 00	Dudley P. Phelps and George Barnes,	225 00	56 25
do	9	250 00	H. Baldwin,	250 00	62 50
do	10	120 00	Henry A. Dillaye,	120 00	30 00
		$7,600 00	Total amount of sale,	$7,600 00	

Blocks and lots in the 5th Ward, city of Syracuse. Bounded on the east by West street and on the west by Wyoming street, sold per ch. 136, *Laws of* 1854. *Vendue at Syracuse, June* 12, 1855.

Block.	Lot.	Valuation.	Name of purchaser.	Consideration.	Am't paid.
241	1	$5,000 00	Cornelius Shirley, Amos P. Granger, and Dan'l O. Salmon,	$7,000 00	$1750 00
do	2	650 00	The City of Syracuse,	650 00	162 50
do	3	500 00	Charles Tallman,	500 00	125 00
do	4	500 00	Charles Tallman and Joseph P. Dunlap,	550 00	137 50
do	5	650 00	Joseph P. Dunlap,	750 00	187 50
do	6	500 00	Charles Tallman,	500 00	125 00
do	7	650 00	George B. Walter,	700 00	175 00
do	8	650 00	William F. Gere,	705 00	176 25
do	9	600 00	do	610 00	152 50
do	10	600 00	Charles Tallman and George B. Walter,	650 00	162 50
do	11	1,000 00	Daniel O. Salmon for Amos P. Granger,	1,280 00	320 00
242	1	600 00	George B. Walter,	620 00	155 00
do	2	450 00	do	500 00	125 00
do	3	450 00	do	500 00	125 00
do	4	500 00	do	600 00	150 00
do	5	500 00	John A. Clarke and Henry Horton,	580 00	145 00
do	6	500 00	George B. Walter,	580 00	145 00
do	7	650 00	Henry A. Dillaye for Dwight Salmon,	850 00	212 50

do	8	650 00	George B. Walter,	795 00	198 75
do	9	600 00	James Burke,	700 00	175 00
do	10	650 00	Charles R. West for James Morgan,	800 00	200 00
do	11	450 00	Theodore F. Andrews,	495 00	123 75
do	12	450 00	Peter Burns,	490 00	122 50
do	13	500 00	George B. Walter,	545 00	136 25
do	14	450 00	Thomas Blanchfield,	490 00	122 50
do	15	450 00	Theodore F. Andrews,	560 00	140 00
do	16	450 00	Daniel P. Wood and Nathan F. Graves,	560 00	140 00
do	17	600 00	Theodore F. Andrews,	825 00	206 25
do	18	750 00	Marcus Cone,	905 00	226 25
243	1	500 00	John A. Clarke and Henry Horton,	535 00	133 75
do	2	400 00	Dennis Driscoll, Jr.,	450 00	112 50
do	3	400 00	Marcus Cone,	410 00	102 50
do	4	450 00	Michael Mahan,	470 00	117 50
do	5	450 00	Thomas Blanchfield,	480 00	120 00
do	6	650 00	Theodore F. Andrews,	800 00	200 00
do	7	600 00	George H. Waggoner and Peter Waggoner,	800 00	200 00
do	8	550 00	Dorastus Spencer for G. H. and P. Waggoner,	770 00	192 50
do	9	500 00	Henry Gifford for Sidney B. Gifford,	700 00	175 00
do	10	400 00	Daniel P. Wood and Nathan F. Graves,	415 00	103 75
do	11	400 00	Peter Burns,	430 00	107 50
do	12	450 00	Daniel P. Wood and Nathan F. Graves,	515 00	128 75
do	13	450 00	do do	470 00	117 50
do	14	450 00	George H. Waggoner and Peter Waggoner,	495 00	123 75
do	15	500 00	Joseph P. Dunlap, Cha's Tallman and Geo. B. Walter,	700 00	175 00
do	16	650 00	Geo. B. Walter, Cha's Tallman and Joseph P. Dunlap,	780 00	195 00
184	3	500 00	do do	525 00	131 25
do	4	450 00	George B. Walter and Joseph P. Dunlap,	480 00	120 00

Blocks and Lots in Syracuse. Vendue of June 12, 1855.—*Continued.*

Blocks.	Lot.	Valuation.	Name of purchaser.	Consideration.	Am't paid.
184	5	$350 00	John A. Clarke and Henry Horton,	$400 00	$100 00
do	6	350 00	Dennis Driscoll, Jr., for John A. Clarke and Henry Horton,	450 00	112 50
do	7	700 00	George B. Walter,	815 00	203 75
do	8	600 00	Titus J. Fenn,	720 00	180 00
33	3 B	50 00	Albina Woolson and Gardner Woolson,	123 00	30 75
		$31,750 60	Total amount of sale,	$38,023 00	

Lots on Genesee street, west of Plum street, in city of Syracuse. Vendue, December 27, 1855.

Block.	Lot.	Valuation.	Name of purchaser.	Consideration.	Am't paid.
423	17	$750 00	Onondaga Coarse Salt Co. (per Henry D. Hatch, agent),	$825 00	$206 25
do	18	1,350 00	Michael Otis,	1,350 00	337 50
do	19	1,550 00	George F. Comstock, Dec. 16, 1856,	1,550 00	387 50
do	20	1,650 00	do do	1,650 00	412 50
do	21	1,750 00	do do	1,750 00	437 50
do	22	2,400 00	do do	2,400 00	600 00
64	16	2,450 00	Joseph Savage, do	2,450 00	612 50
do	17	1,850 00	do	1,850 00	462 50
do	19	2,050 00	V. Rensselaer Richmond,	2,050 00	512 50
do	20	2,150 00	Samuel C. Brewster,	2,150 00	537 50
do	21	2,250 00	Alanson Thorp,	2,250 00	562 50
do	22	3,500 00	Alfred A. Howlett,	3,500 00	875 00
67	6	2,250 00	Robert Gen, May 20, 1856,	2,250 00	562 50
do	7	2,500 00	George N. Kennedy, March 25, 1856,	2,500 00	625 00
		$28,450 00	Total amount of sale,	$28,525 00	

Salt lands sold since December, 1856, to present time. Original sales.

	Lot.	Block.	Valuation.	Name of purchaser.	Consideration.	Am't paid.
				SYRACUSE.		
E. part	18	64	$823 87	Mary C. Barker, May 2, 1866,	$823 87	$823 87
	1	67	1,500 00	W. Brown Smith, Oct. 3, 1863,	1,500 00	375 00
	2	do	1,200 00	Alonzo Wright, Sept. 16, 1863,	1,200 00	300 00
E. part	3	do	687 37	Edward Townsend, May 2, 1866,	687 37	171 84
	4	do	1,270 00	do do do 7, 1860,	1,200 00	300 00
	5	do	1,400 00	H. Lazier, Nov. 2, 1861,	1,400 00	350 00
	4	424	900 00	Calvin S. Totman, April 26, 1860,	900 00	225 00
	5	do	1,000 00	James Johnson, do 28, do	1,000 00	250 00
	6	do	1,000 00	Jerome J. Munger, do do do	1,000 00	250 00
	7	do	1,200 00	Aaron N. Thayer, do 4, do	1,200 00	300 00
				VILLAGE OF GEDDES.		
	3 A	of 33	150 00	Thomas G. White, Sept. 7, 1861,	188 00	47 00
				ONONDAGA SALT SPRINGS FARM LOTS.		
S.½ 120	12 4/10	acr's	623 70	Thomas Gale and John S. Hawley, June 10, 1866,	900 00	225 00
					$11,999 24	

			Also add sale in Syracuse of reserved lots subsequently sold to		
2	49	130 00	John Paddock, per chap. 246, Laws of 1848,...........	130 00	32 50
			Total,..	$12,129 24	

Reclaimed lots in the Onondaga Salt Springs Reservation. Sold at Vendue, 8 July, 1828.

Lot.	Acres.	Per acre.	Per lot.	Purchasers.	Consideration.	Paid.
1	8.8	$10 00	$88 00	Henry Seymour, 8 July, 1828,	$210 00	$52 50
2	7.2	2 50	18 00	Samuel R. Matthews,	45 00	45 00
3	21.8	2 00	43 60	Lyman Bacon,	105 00	26 00
4	7.7	State.	....	Liverpool New Spring.		
5	9.8	State.	....	do		
6	5.6	State.	....	Omit.		
7	5.6	State.	....	do		
8	5.7	75	4 27	Benjamin F. Williams,	25 00	6 25
9	7	75	5 25	Thomas McCarty,	21 00	5 00
10	7	75	5 25	James Johnson,	12 00	3 00
11	11.5	75	8 62	do	30 00	7 50
12	10.8	1 00	10 80	Stephen W. Baldwin,	36 00	9 00
13	10.9	1 00	10 90	James Johnson,	35 00	8 75
14	41.2	....	....	Liverpool Salt Works.		
15	13	50	6 50	Stephen W. Baldwin,	25 00	6 25
16	14.4	50	7 20	do	15 00	3 75
17	12.8	1 00	12 80	State.		
18	14	1 00	14 00	do		
19	12.2	1 00	12 20	do		
20	4.2	2 00	8 40	do		
21	8	2 00	16 00	do		
22	7.3	1 00	7 30	do		
23	5.9	75	4 42	do		
24	6.4	75	4 80	do		

25	6.5	75	4 87	do		
26	6.5	75	4 87	do		
27	8	75	6 00	do		
28	6.1	75	4 57	do		
29	9.8	75	7 35	do		
30	4.8	50	2 40	do		
31	9.6	1 00	9 60	Stephen W. Baldwin, ...	22 00	5 50
32	9.2	1 00	9 20	do	31 00	7 75
33	10.8	1 00	10 80	do	21 00	5 25
34	10	1 00	10 00	do	21 00	5 25
35	5.2	75	3 90	State.		
36	8.4	50	4 20	Stephen W. Baldwin, ...	10 00	2 50
37	6.4	50	3 20	do	10 00	2 50
38	7.2	50	3 60	do	16 00	4 00
39	7	50	3 50	State.		
40	13.6	State	....	New well at Geddes. *Reserved.*		
41	18.6	1 00	18 60	State.		
42	19	1 00	19 00	do		
43	19.8	1 00	19 80	do		
44	25.6	1 00	25 60	Warren Grear, 8 July, 1828, ...	76 00	19 00
45	42	1 00	42 00	do do	57 00	14 25
46	16.2	1 00	16 20	Stephen W. Baldwin, ...	51 00	12 75
47	8.6	9 00	77 40	Benjamin F. Williams, 28 July, 1829, ...	120 00	30 00
48	2.6	12 00	31 20	Ashbel Kellogg, 8 July, 1828, ...	71 00	17 75
	446.3				$1,065 00	

Two hundred and nine acres remaining State property.

Statement of moneys paid for lands on the reservations since 1846, and for damages; also statement of lands exchanged.

		Acres.	Damages. Expenses.	Other land.
1849.				
Mar. 17,..	Syracuse Salt Co. vats, ...	....	$3,000 00	....
Oct. 1,..	City of Syracuse, mill pond improvement, ...	....	4,000 00	....
Dec. 17,..	Purchase of lands Messrs. Clark & Alvord, ...	40	....	$4,800 00
do 24,..	do of Robert Gere for lot No. 45, ...	$22\frac{56}{100}$	....	1,692 00
do 28,..	do of H. White for lots 39, 43, 44, and part 40, ...	$114\frac{94}{100}$	....	9,195 20
do 26,..	do of N. & C. Merrick for lot 46, ...	21.40	....	1,605 00
1850.				
June 28,..	Purchase of Thomas Davis, part of farm lot 340, ...	9	....	1,080 00
1851.				
	Syracuse Salt Co., damages, ...	....	1,287 00	....
1852.				
Feb. 9,..	Syracuse Salt Co., damages, ...	....	3,000 00	....
April 15,..	Syracuse Salt Co., damages, ...	....	2,600 00	....
June 12,..	Syracuse salt vats, ...	....	13,158 00	....
1853.				
	Purchase of lands of J. & S. Jaquiths for part of marsh lots 1, 2, 3 and 4, ...	22.49	....	2,279 50
1855.				
June 15,..	Syracuse Salt Company, ...	....	16,256 00	....
Mar. 15,..	Norton & Stevens for marsh lots 37 and 38, ...	15	....	9,132 00
May 23,..	M. E. Lynch for marsh lots 12 and 13, ...	15	....	4,000 00
May 23,..	L. G. Avery for marsh lot No. 8, ...	10	....	2,000 00
May 23,..	Lorenzo Beckes for marsh lot No. 6, ...	15	....	3,000 00

Date	Description			
May 23,..	B. A. Avery for reclaimed lot No. 42, and 15 acres marsh lots No. 2 and 4,	38	....	5,829 00
Sept. 10,..	Harvey Baldwin, farm lot 290 and part 291, and sub. 1 and 2 of farm lot No. 324,	17	....	2,817 67
Dec. 19,..	Onondaga Salt Company, 7 acres, pasture lots 4 and 5 and part of farm lot No. 327,	25	....	7,500 00
do do ..	Salt Springs Solar Coarse Salt Company, marsh lot Nos. 32, 33 & 41; reclaimed lot No. 48 and pasture lots 1 and 2,	25	....	7,500 00
do do ..	George Sanford and Byron Rice marsh No. 10,	4	....	1,075 00
Dec. 19,..	Wm. Brown Smith, farm lots 316 and 317,	31	....	6,500 00
Sept. 15,..	B. F. Green, for surveys,	....	120 50	....
July 24,..	W. Raynor and others, appraisem't of land on West st., Syracuse,	....	100 00	....
Nov. 26,..	Also on Genesee street,	....	75 00	....
Nov. 27,..	Syracuse Salt Co., removing salt vats, and damages to covers,	....	13,184 00	....
	Sales June 12 and Dec. 25, advertising and expenses,	....	125 41	....
Nov. 23,..	T. D. Barton, increased compensation for abatement of nuisance at Syracuse,	....	1,200 00	....
Nov. 22,..	J. Hughes, for placing stone monuments at Syracuse,	....	27 00	....
Dec. 22,..	B. F. Green, for surveys of same,	....	58 00	....
Dec. 22,..	Due treasury on obligors bonds for the original purchase of secs. 1 and 2 of farm lot No. 324, assigned by H. Baldwin to the State, in Sept., 1855. Int. May 1, 1856,	....	225 42	....
	Do on farm lot No. 290.,	....	410 34	....
	Due H. Baldwin on his sale in Sept., 1855,	....	63 51	....
1856.				
Feb. 12,..	B. F. Green, for surveys,	....	22 00	....
June, ..	Expenses Commissioners of land office,	....	85 00	....
Dec. 16,..	Sale of lots on Genesee street, advertising,	....	33 00	....
Dec. 16,..	Expenses of sale,	....	14 00	....

Statement of moneys paid for lands on the reservations, &c.—Continued.

		Acres.	Damages. Expenses.	Other land.
1856.				
Mar. 20,..	G. F. Comstock and B. D. Noxon, farm lots 318, 319, 320, 321 and part of lot No. 295,	60	....	$14,500 00
June 10,..	Western Coarse Salt Company, two pieces of land,	22.50	....	2,500 00
June 10,..	W. and D. Kirkpatrick, part of farm lots No. 47 and 50,	15	....	1,500 00
June 10,..	W. Winton and H. Stewart, part of farm lots No. 291, 292 and 293,	18.40	....	4,500 00
1858.				
May 10,..	Onondaga Coarse Salt Co., for removing 695 covers at $37,	....	$25,715 00	
	Expenses Commissioners Land Office, appraisements, surveys and advertising in years 1850, '51, '52 and '53,	....	933 47	
		541.59	$85,692 65	$93,005 37
				85,692 65
	Total,	....	....	$178,698 02

LANDS EXCHANGED.

1865.		Bought.	Sold.
Aug. 30.	Exchanged Marsh Lot No. 2, containing 15 acres; also reclaimed Lot No. 47; also all that part of Block 11, in Salina, lying between said lots, containing together 25 acres, with Thomas Gale, for Farm Lot No. 114, Containing same number of acres (25), ...	25	25
Sept.	Exchanged Farm Lot 104, containing 16½ acres adjoining the canal, with the Liverpool Coarse Salt Company, for same number acres of Farm Lot 108 (16½), ...	16½	16½
Sept.	Exchanged so much of Basin Square as lies north of a line running from Mechanics street at right angles, and to the canal and distant 12 rods from Wolf Street, with Simeon Stevens, for an equal quantity of land lying at corner of Park and Exchange street, in 1st ward, city of Spracuse, on Block No. 1. Number of acres not given.		
	Amount, ...	41½	41½

Making total expenditures, ... $941,927 65

Making total revenues and receipts, .. $1,429,402 65

All of which is respectfully submitted.

STEWART L. WOODFORD,

Lieut.-Gov. and Chairman of
Commissioners of the Land Office.

ERASTUS CLARK,
Clerk of the Commissioners of the Land Office.

STATE OF NEW YORK.

No. 28.

IN CONVENTION

July 15, 1867.

REPORT

OF AUDITOR OF CANAL DEPARTMENT AS TO EXTRA COMPENSATION TO CONTRACTORS.

STATE OF NEW YORK.

CANAL DEPARTMENT,
ALBANY, *July 16th*, 1867.

HON. WILLIAM A. WHEELER, *President of the Constitutional Convention.*

SIR: I herewith transmit to the Convention a report in response to the resolution of the 9th instant, calling for the amounts paid to contractors as extra compensation, paid to them within the periods named in the said resolution.

I am, with great respect,

Your ob't servant,

N. S. BENTON,

Auditor.

STATE OF NEW YORK.

CANAL DEPARTMENT,
ALBANY, *July 16th*, 1867.

To the Convention:

The Auditor of the Canal Department in answer to the following resolution of the Convention, viz.:

STATE OF NEW YORK.

CONSTITUTIONAL CONVENTION,
ALBANY, *July*, 9, 1867.

On motion of Mr. Lee:

Resolved, That the Auditor of the Canal Department be respectfully requested to report to this Convention at his earliest convenience, the number and amounts of awards paid by him or his predecessors in office, from 1846 to 1866, inclusive, as extra compensation to contractors for labor and materials furnished the State, by what authority said awards were made, to whom and when they were paid. By order,

LUTHER CALDWELL,
Secretary.

Respectfully submits the following

REPORT:

That the Statement A hereto annexed gives the awards paid at this Department by the undersigned and his predecessors in office from 1846 to 1866 inclusive, as extra compensation to contractors for labor and materials furnished to the State, amounting in the aggregate to $1,293,679.75.

These awards embrace only such as have been made by the canal Board and Contracting Board under the authority of various acts of the Legislature referred to in the statement. Where no such special acts are referred to in the statement, then the awards were made by the Canal Board under the provisions of sections 76, 77 and 78 of article 4, title 9, chapter 9, part 1, of the Revised Statutes, which sections were repealed by the act chapter 348 Laws of 1849, in respect to all contracts entered into after April 11, 1849, but leaving these in force as to all contracts entered into prior to that date.

These awards were not in any instance paid at the Department until after the expiration of sixty days from the period when the awards were made, and not then in all cases.

Respectfully submitted,

N. S. BENTON,

Auditor.

STATEMENT A.

Date.	Names of Contractors.	By what authority awards made.	Amount.
1850, Dec. 26,	Silas Ball,	Canal Board,	$2,309 00
1852, July 6,	Barhydt & Van Vorst,	379, Laws of 1862,	369 30
1850, Apr. 10,	Bigham, Stewart & Co.,	182, Laws of 1850,	11,486 86
1854, Apr. 14,	Bogardus & Bell,	Chap. 60, Laws of 1852,	7,848 33
1856, June 27,	Brady & Hartnet,	Chap. 200, Laws of 1856,	1,506 24
1852, May 14,	Brady & Fitzsimmons,	401, Laws of 1852,	1,038 51
1849, Apr. 9,	Brayton & Cheesbro,	Canal Board,	5,690 35
1851, Jan. 24,	Britton & Baldwin,	do	8,400 00
1851, June 23,	Carmichael, Brayton & Co.,	do	3,500 00
1847, Dec. 25,	Joseph G. Case,	do	1,698 60
1849, Apr. 9,	do do	do	997 99
1847, May 11,	Caswell, Shippy & Co.,	do	521 15
1847, Mar. 17,	Chambers, Adams & Chambers,	do	149 66
1849, Feb. 15,	Clark & Wheeler,	Chap. 299, Laws of 1846,	676 50
1849, Mar. 20,	Cole, Calkins & Richardson,	Chap. 336, Laws of 1848,	668 89
1851, Mar. 12,	Andrew E. Cromwell,	Canal Board,	100 00
1847, June 2,	John Ellis,	Chap. 215, Laws of 1847,	669 40
1846, Apr. 21,	Elwood & Rasback,	Canal Board,	20 27
1851, June 17,	do do	do	884 00
1852, Mar. 18,	do do	do	1,110 87
1847, Mar. 30,	James Farquharson,	do	5,253 48
1846, Apr. 20,	Farquharson & Pierce,	do	734 87
1850, Feb. 21,	H. C. Filmore,	do	92 00
1850, Jan. 29,	Samuel Farwell,	Act April 12, 1842,	316 40

1847, Dec. 8,	Fitzsimmons & Brady,	Chap. 247, Laws of 1847,	4,761 59
1848, Feb. 19,	Francis & Hopkins,	Canal Board,	4,155 66
1852, May 14,	Frazee & Foster,	do	475 00
1851, June 23,	do do	do	1,572 00
1847, May 11,	M. & George Freligh,	do	661 91
1854, Feb. 18,	Geere & Steeves,	196, Laws of 1852,	1,936 07
1849, Dec. 29,	Gilbert & Sprague,	Chap. 204, Laws of 1845,	2,750 00
1848, July 28,	Granger & Todd,	Chap. 353, Laws of 1848,	5,658 00
1851, Apr. 8,	do do	Canal Board,	2,621 00
1847, Dec. 29,	Haight, Blood & Cady,	do	769 36
1849, Nov. 17,	E. Perkins Hayes,	Chap. 384, Laws of 1849,	2,551 85
1850, Dec. 20,	Dean S. Howard,	Canal Board,	3,253 68
1852, Mar. 11,	do do	Chap. 485, Laws of 1851,	11,137 28
1849, Feb. 21,	John B. Ives,	Canal Board,	5,201 54
1849, Mar. 29,	do do	do	529 81
1846, Aug. 21,	Isaac Jackson,	299, Laws of 1846,	2,626 88
1850, Mar. 25,	Johnson & Anderson,	Canal Board,	300 00
1850, Dec. 28,	Kelsey, Vrooman & Tapper,	do	868 31
1853, Oct. 22,	Woodman Kimball,	do	744 00
1846, Mar. 13,	Knapp & Shaw,	do	132 45
1851, June 23,	A. Y. Lansing,	do	3,761 00
1851, Mar, 12,	William Logan & Co.,	do	300 00
1848, July 20,	Marener & Sherman,	do	1,236 69
1850, Dec. 2,	John McCoughin, assignee of King, Taylor & Higgins,	do	6,682 87
1851, Oct. 18,	John McCoughin,	do	4,201 24
1852, May 27,	McDonald, Nichols and others,	do	1,573 70
1846, Aug. 21,	Merriam, Utter, Carr & Wood,	152, Laws of 1846,	2,251 41
1852, May 14,	Maria Miller,	Canal Board,	2,500 00

STATEMENT A—*Continued.*

Date.	Names of Contractors.	By what authority awards made.	Amount.
1855, Dec. 29,	Mitchell & Brown,	458, Laws of 1855,	$4,105 08
1850, Dec. 30,	Zebulon Moore,	148, do 1854,	3,863 57
1852, May 27,	Munger, Sutton & Bames,	234, do 1849,	22,388 12
1853, Dec. 12,	Edward Murray,	Canal Board,	4,037 15
1846, July 3,	Ogden & Durphy,	205, Laws of 1846,	108 00
1853, Nov. 17,	Abijah Osborn,	225, do 1852,	3,063 40
1849, Apr. 19,	do	Canal Board,	2,423 30
1850, Feb. 19,	Daniel Page,	do	601 54
1856, Dec. 30,	Noah Palmer,	193, Laws of 1856,	5,865 35
1856, July 31,	A. & F. J. Patten,	264, Laws of 1854,	3,725 00
1852, Mar. 24,	Pennock & Skinner,	Canal Board,	630 16
1849, Apr. 7,	Phillips & Moore,	170, Laws of 1849,	8,009 00
1850, Apr. 20,	do	do	16,889 87
1852, Apr. 2,	Jerome B. Ransom,	Act 2d April, 1850,	5,646 22
1849, Apr. 4,	Riddle, Cook, & Magee & Co.,	212, Laws of 1845,	228 14
1851, Nov. 28,	Patrick Rogers,	222, do 1851,	3,135 85
1851, Dec. 12,	do	do 1851,	1,222 45
1854, Feb. 21,	Daniel Rogers,	257, Laws of 1852,	414 01
1852, July 8,	Rogers & Layton,	Canal Board,	8,867 49
1853, Oct. 15,	Hezekiah Sage,	do	6,000 00
1852, Jan. 28,	Sage, Walrath & Dunham,	do	6,112 00
1846, May 15,	Sanford and Eggleston,	153, Laws of 1846,	380 54
1851, June 17,	Schuyler & Gay,	Canal Board,	113 28
1856, July 13,	Sherrill & Doty,	153, Laws of 1856,	8,869 04

1847, May 11,	Shippy, Caswell & Co.,	Canal Board,	2,142 80
1849, Dec. 20,	James D. Shuler,	257, Laws of 1845,	2,162 58
1849, Dec. 20,	do	do	400 00
1852, Mar. 25,	Asa T. Smith,	Canal Board,	464 34
1852, May 26,	John P. Smith,	62, Laws of 1852,	25,443 58
1856, May 14,	John P. Smith & Co.,	do	20,993 31
1856, July 31,	do do	do	4,521 63
1856, July 31,	do do	do	904 32
1853, Oct. 14,	Smith & Norton,	197, Laws of 1852,	4,060 00
1846, Apr. 20,	Spencer, Hubbs & Curtiss,	Canal Board,	194 79
1846, Apr. 20,	do do	do	17 60
1851, June 20,	Wm. Sponenbergh,	do	1,048 00
1854, Feb. 21,	James Stewart,	198, Laws of 1852,	866 65
1851, June 23,	John Stroup,	208, do 1851,	3,615 00
1846, May 15,	Thomas & Worden,	69, do 1846,	2,075 50
1848, Apr. 21,	Thompson & Beebe,	156, do 1846,	4,107 39
1848, July 24,	Thompson & Uttley,	Canal Board,	944 25
1853, Mar. 30,	Tibbits & Forsyth,	Act 24 March, 1853,	5,450 31
1850, Dec. 20,	Tobee, Glatt & Glatt,	Canal Board,	1,097 22
1850, Mar. 5,	Tousley & James,	do	4,454 96
1851, May 12,	Treat & Cromwell,	do	100 00
1850, Dec. 26,	Van Debogart & Marselis,	do	218 76
1847, May 11,	John Van Demark,	do	952 34
1849, Oct. 1,	Van Evera & Burdick,	do	50 00
1848, July 26,	Veeder & Harmon,	396, Laws of 1847,	239 61
1855, Dec. 31,	Vernam & Merrill,	Canal Board,	1,063 00
1847, Jan. 27,	Way & Mack,	do	9,255 87
1855, Mar. 30,	Joseph Wells,	do	165 90
1847, Dec. 10,	Wilbur, Briggs & Richardson,	do	9,872 25

STATEMENT A — *Continued.*

Date.	Names of Contractors.	By what authority awards made.	Amount.
1852, Oct. 7,	Wm. H. Williams,	200, Laws of 1852,	$2,302 78
1853, Oct. 17,	do	do do	750 00
1853, Oct. 18,	do	Act April 10, 1850,	11,257 55
1855, Dec. 28,	do	383, Laws of 1852,	1,514 35
1857, Dec. 4,	James L. Beebe and others,	343, do 1857,	4,460 80
1857, Mar. 5,	Bangs, Kingsley & Co.,	Canal Board,	677 89
1856, June 26,	Platt Burlingame,	do	582 55
1855, Nov. 23,	Theodore D. Barton,	206, Laws of 1855,	7,587 93
1857, Dec. 31,	E. S. Ears & H. Adams,	709, do 1857,	17,117 10
1858, Dec. 18,	Wm. Candee & Co.,	252, Laws of 1858,	3,300 00
1858, Feb. 12,	Hull & Shipman,	460, Laws of 1857 and 335, Laws of 1858,	2,211 00
1858, July 1,	Jacob Richman,	362, Laws of 1858,	1,821 00
1859, Dec. 30,	Wm. Candee & Co.,	252, do 1858,	1,450 00
1859, Dec. 30,	John McIntyre,	402, do 1859,	3,882 99
1861, Dec. 12,	R. H. Bangs & S. Pratt,	275, do 1861,	3,000 00
1861, Nov. 13,	H. Chapman and others,	157, do 1845,	220 00
1860, July 19,	John I. Wiles,	424, do 1859,	1,500 00
1863, Nov. 18,	Brazell and McCann,	394, do 1863,	4,370 00
1862, June 25,	Charles A. Danolds,	164, do 1862,	20,000 00
1863, Nov. 18,	John Fitzpatrick,	419, do 1863,	1,000 00
1863, Nov. 19,	Kingsley & Knapp,	349, do 1863,	436 34
1862, June 25,	Lewis M. Loss,	92, do 1862,	2,500 00
1863, June 25,	George D. Lord,	247, do 1863,	25,000 00

1862, Dec. 12,	M, & J. McCarty,	464, Laws of 1862,	903	00
1863, Nov. 19,	Martin & Luckey,	234, do 1863,	8,442	43
1863, Aug. 27,	Noone & Fitzgerald	331, do 1863,	213	60
1860, Sept. 17,	Jas. Oswald & D.A. Van Valkenburgh,	321, do 1862,	6,034	11
1862, June 25,	Gilbert Peterson,	164, do 1862,	10,000	00
1863, Nov. 18,	Pringle & Claffy,	354, do 1863,	808	30
1863, Nov. 19,	Isaac N. Hart,	384, do 1863,	2,769	38
1863, Dec. 4,	Lewis Selye,	131, do 1863,	11,000	00
1862, Dec. 12,	A. Vernam's administrators,	328, do 1862,	1,026	00
1862, Nov. 7,	Williams, Butts & Williams,	271, do 1861,	2,495	00
1864, July 8,	H. D. Dennison,	299, do 1864,	14,000	00
1864, July 8,	John Ecker,	366, d0 1863,	4,823	13
1864, July 26,	George D. Lord,	215, do 1864,	24,600	00
1864, Sept. 23,	Wm. McArthur,	302, do 1864,	19,266	43
1864, Dec. 1,	O'Connor & Sullivan,	389, do 1864,	1,226	75
1864, July 26,	George H. Peck,	241, do 1864,	4,455	89
1864, Dec. 28,	Jacob Schaub,	348, do 1863,	2,000	00
1864, Dec. 28,	Lewis Selye,	301, do 1864,	4,899	25
1865, Nov. 15,	Brazel & Hurst,	626, do 1865,	455	50
1865, Nov. 15,	Brazel, McCann & Dolphin,	626, do 1865,	3,156	75
1865, June 28,	Philip Corkings,	486, do 1865,	4,861	94
1865, June 28,	H. D. Dennison,	669, do 1865,	13,300	28
1865, Oct. 7,	Holbrook & Sherrill,	489, do 1865,	10,968	84
1865, Feb. 9,	John Hutchenson,	203, do 1864,	759	75
1865, June 29,	Byron M. Hanks,	490, do 1865,	51,973	36
1865, June 28,	Martin Holmes,	261, do 1865,	14,382	88
1865, Feb. 10,	Harley Holmes, assignee, &c.,	Canal Board,	7,148	56
1865, June 7,	Lewis M. Loss,	498, Laws of 1865,	3,590	71
1865, June 6,	Ephraim Owens & Henry Holman,	343, do 1864,	3,345	63

STATEMENT A—*Continued.*

Date.	Names of Contractors.	By what authority awards made.	Amount.
1865, Dec. 14,	George H. Peck,	497, Laws of 1865,	$2,534 48
1865, June 7,	John Ryan,	482, do 1865,	5,400 00
1865, Oct. 17,	James Ray,	324, do 1863, 38, do 1865,	7,500 00
1865, July 29,	Albert G. Sage,	524, do 1865,	12,023 73
1865, Nov. 15,	Schaub & Rhorbacker,	482, do 1864, 471, do 1865,	4,293 91
1866, Nov. 14,	Michael Mory,	779, do 1865,	1,952 26
1866, Dec. 4,	Holbrook & Sherrill,	901, do 1866,	7,718 36
1866, Dec. 5,	Justin Arnold,	626, do 1865,	4,089 76
1866, Dec. 28,	Abram Vernam's heirs,	895, do 1866,	5,820 13
1866, Dec. 28,	Snooks & Beebe,	908, Laws of 1866,	40,821 92
1866, Dec. 28,	Schaub & Rhorbacker,	914, do	6,888 70
1866, Dec. 28,	Sampson C. Ames,	520, do	4,385 34
1866, Dec. 28,	James Bellows,	492, do	22,962 32
1866, Dec. 6,	Lewis Selye, assignee of Byron M. Hanks,	902, Laws of 1866,	15,201 00
			$846,278 15

The following are amounts to Repair Contractors for extra compensation upon contracts, under the Act, chap. 252 *Laws of* 1864.

Spencer Jackson,	Erie, Section	1,	$108,730 00
Lewis Selye,	do	2,	11,793 33
Hosch & Louell,	do	4,	11,076 00
Philip Corkings,	do	5,	4,184 13

Thomas Gale,	Erie, Section 7,	6,671 70	
Charles Nichols,	do 8,	4,446 00	
Charles J. Haydon,	do 9,	13,165 83	
Chester B. Thomas,	do 10,	27,807 00	
Byron M. Hanks,	do 11,	26,775 00	
Edward A. Mills,	do 12,	12,813 75	
Francis Hitchins,	do 13,	9,146 66	
Archibald McArthur,	do 14,	13,440 00	
Archibald McArthur,	Champlain, Section 1,	11,078 40	
Anson Bangs,	do 2,	7,440 00	
Henry D. Dennison,	do 3,	15,375 00	
William Avery,	Oswego, Section 1,	11,812 50	
Charles E. Case,	do 2,	11,404 17	
George M. Case,	Cayuga and Seneca,	15,298 12	
James Bellows,	Chemung,	35,910 00	
H. W. Randall,	Crooked Lake,	5,319 88	
A. Peck & Co.,	Chenango, Section 1,	21,567 90	
John P. Smith,	do 2,	3,848 39	
Josiah Brentnall,	do 3,	11,439 16	
E. H. Edwards,	Black River, Section 1,	11,962 50	
B. F. Maxon,	do do 2,	6,092 91	
Ward & McVickar,	do do 3,	3,008 33	
William McArthur,	Genesee Val., Sect'n 1,	6,777 60	
John Lambert,	do do 2,	10,345 50	
William McArthur,	do do 3,	8,671 82	
			447,401 60
			$1,293,679 75

STATE OF NEW YORK.

No. 29.

IN CONVENTION

July 15, 1867.

PREAMBLE AND RESOLUTIONS.

Offered by Mr. Wales.

Whereas, the President and Vice-President of the United States are elected by a board of electors, the members of which are apportioned among the respective States; and

Whereas, the part of said board of electors apportioned to each State respectively, is elected or appointed by each State in accordance with its own rule or law; and

Whereas, the Senators of the United States are appointed by the Legislature of the respective States; and

Whereas, the members of the House of Representatives of the United States are elected by the voters of single districts, into which the respective States are divided; and

Whereas, the Congress of the United States acts reciprocally upon and for the several States respectively, and upon them all collectively; and

Whereas, the Executive and Legislature of each State are, for certain purposes, agents of the United States, especially in time of war, in raising, clothing, forwarding and paying troops; now, therefore, be it

Resolved, That in the election of the board of electors and of the members of the House of Representatives, and in the election of the Governor and Lieutenant-Governor, and the Legislature of the respective States, a uniform system of suffrage ought to prevail; and be it further

Resolved, That the standing committee on the right of suffrage be instructed to inquire into the expediency of authorizing, by constitutional provision, the Legislature of the State to accept such uniform system of suffrage, when such a system shall have been legally perfected and promulgated by the General Government; and be it further

Resolved, That the Secretary of this Convention be requested to send or cause to be sent, a copy of this preamble and of these resolutions, respectively, to the President of the Senate, and to the Speaker of the House of Representatives of the United States, and to the Executive of each of the respective States of the Union.

STATE OF NEW YORK.

No. 30.

IN CONVENTION

July 17, 1867.

REPORT

OF COMMITTEE ON LEGISLATURE, &c., ON ORGANIZATION OF LEGISLATIVE POWER.

The Committee on the Legislature, its organization and the number, apportionment, election, tenure of office, and compensation of its members have prepared and submit the following article of the Constitution, and ask to be discharged from the further consideration of all propositions which have been referred to them by the Convention:

SECTION 1. The Legislative power of this State shall be vested in a Senate and Assembly. Any elector of the State shall be eligible to the office of Senator or member of Assembly.

§ 2. The Senate shall consist of thirty-three members. The State shall be divided into eight senatorial districts. There shall be four Senators in each district.

The first district shall consist of the city and county of New York, and shall be entitled to one additional Senator.

The second district shall consist of the counties of Suffolk, Queens, Kings, Richmond and Westchester.

The third district shall consist of the counties of Putnam, Rockland, Dutchess, Orange, Ulster, Greene, Columbia and Rensselaer.

The fourth district shall consist of the counties of Albany, Schenectady, Fulton, Hamilton, Saratoga, Washington, Warren, Essex, Clinton, Franklin and St. Lawrence.

The fifth district shall consist of the counties of Jefferson, Lewis, Oneida, Onondaga, Oswego, Herkimer and Montgomery.

The sixth district shall consist of the counties of Otsego, Schoharie, Delaware, Sullivan, Broome, Chenango, Madison, Cortland, Tioga, Tompkins, Chemung and Schuyler.

The seventh district shall consist of the counties of Yates, Seneca, Ontario, Cayuga, Wayne, Monroe, Livingston and Steuben.

The eighth district shall consist of the counties of Orleans, Niagara, Erie, Genesee, Wyoming, Allegany, Cattaraugus and Chautauqua. The whole Senate shall be chosen at the first election held under this Constitution; they shall classify themselves, so that one Senator in each district shall go out of office at the end of each year, and the additional Senator for the first district at the end of the fourth year. After the expiration of their terms under such classification the terms of their office shall be four years.

§ 3. An enumeration of the inhabitants of the State shall be taken, under the direction of the Legislature, in the year one thousand eight hundred and seventy-five, and at the end of every ten years thereafter; and the said districts—except the first district—shall be so altered by the Legislature at the first session after the return of every enumeration, that each district shall contain as near as may be an equal number of inhabitants who are citizens of the State, and shall remain unaltered until the return of another enumeration, and shall consist of contiguous territory. No county shall be divided in the formation of a senate district.

§ 4. The Assembly shall consist of one hundred and thirty-nine members who shall be chosen by counties, and shall be apportioned among the several counties of the State, as nearly as may be, according to the number of inhabitants thereof, who are citizens of the State, and shall hold office for one year. Each county shall be entitled to at least one member, except that the counties of Fulton and Hamilton shall, together, elect, until the population of the county of Hamilton shall, according to the ratio, entitle it to a member. No new county shall be erected unless its population shall entitle it to a member. The first apportionment of members of Assembly shall be made by the Legislature, at its first session after the adoption of this Constitution, upon the enumeration of the inhabitants of this State, who are citizens thereof; made in the year one thousand eight hundred and sixty-five. A like apportionment shall be made by the Legislature at its first session, after every such enumeration. Every apportionment when made, shall remain unaltered until another enumeration shall be made.

§ 5. The members of the Legislature shall receive for their services an annual salary of one thousand dollars, and ten cents for each mile they shall travel in going to and returning from their place of meeting by the most usual route. The speaker of the Assembly shall receive an additional compensation equal to one-half of his salary as a member.

§ 6. No member of the Legislature shall be appointed to any civil office within this State by the Governor, the Governor and Senate, or by the Legislature, during the time for which he shall have been elected, and all such appointments and all votes given for any such member therefor shall be void. Nor shall any person being a member of Congress or holding any judicial or military office under the United States, hold a seat in the Legislature. If any person shall after his election as a member of the Legislature, be elected to Congress or appointed to any office, civil or military, under the government of the United States, his acceptance thereof, shall vacate his seat.

§ 7. The election of Senators and members of Assembly under this Constitution shall be held on the Tuesday succeeding the first Monday of November, unless otherwise directed by law. The first election to be in the year one thousand eignt hundred and sixty-eight. The legislative term shall begin on the first day of January, and the Legislature shall every year assemble on the first Tuesday in January, unless a different day be appointed by law. The Senators and members of Assembly who may be in office on the first day of January, one thousand eight hundred and sixty-eight, shall hold their offices until and including the thirty-first day of December of that year, and no longer.

§ 8. A majority of each House shall constitute a quorum to do business. Each House shall determine the rules of its own proceedings, and be the judge of the election, returns and qualifications of its own members; shall choose its own officers; and the Senate shall choose a temporary president when the Lieutenant-Governor shall not attend as President, or shall act as Governor.

§ 9. Each House shall keep a journal of its proceedings and publish the same, except such parts as may require secrecy. The doors of each House shall be kept open, except when the public walfare shall require secrecy. Neither House shall, without the consent of the other, adjourn for more than two days.

EDWIN A. MERRITT,
Chairman.
ERASTUS COOKE,
RICHARD U. SHERMAN,
CLAUDIUS L. MONELL,
GEORGE BARKER,
NATHANIEL JARVIS, JR.

I concur with this report except as to the number of members of Assembly and their manner of election.

M. H. MERWIN.

STATE OF NEW YORK.

No. 31.

IN CONVENTION

July 17, 1867.

REPORT

OF MINORITY OF COMMITTEE ON LEGISLATURE AS TO ORGANIZATION OF LEGISLATIVE POWER.

The undersigned, one of the members of the committee on the Legislature, its organization, etc., in dissenting from the report of that committee, as to the number of the members of Assembly and their manner of election, presents the following as a substitute for section 4 in that report:

§ 4. The term of office of members of the Assembly shall be one year, and their members shall be ascertained by dividing the aggregate of the population of the State, according to the last and each successive enumeration excluding aliens, by twenty thousand, adding one additional member, in case the fraction over-exceeds five thousand; but such number shall never exceed two hundred and fifty. The members of Assembly shall be apportioned among the several counties of the State, by the Legislature, as nearly as may be, according to the number of their respective inhabitants, excluding aliens, and shall be chosen by single districts. The first apportionment shall be made at the first session of the Legislature after the adoption of this Constitution. The several boards of supervisors in such counties as may be entitled to more than one member, upon such apportionment, shall assemble at such time as may be provided by law, and divide their respective counties into assemby districts, equal to the number of members of Assembly to which such counties are entitled by such apportionment, and shall cause to be filed in the offices of the Secretary of State, and of the clerks of their respective counties, a description of such assembly districts, specifying the number of each district, and the population thereof, according to the last preceding State enumeration, as near as can be ascertained. Each assembly district shall contain, as nearly as may be, an equal number of inhabitants, excluding aliens, and shall consist of convenient and contiguous territory; but no town shall be divided in the formation of such districts.

The Legislature, at its first session after the return of every enumeration, shall ascertain the number of members of Assembly and apportion them among the several counties of the State, in the manner aforesaid, and the Board of Supervisors in such counties as may be entitled, under such re-apportionment to more than one member, shall assemble at such time as shall be provided by law, and divide such counties into assembly districts, in the manner herein directed; and the apportionment and districts so to be made shall remain unaltered until another enumeration shall be taken under the provisions of the preceding section.

Every county shall be entitled to one member of Assembly, except that the counties of Fulton and Hamilton shall elect together, until the population of the county of Hamilton shall, according to the ratio, entitle it to a member. No county shall be erected unless its population shall entitle it to a member.

My reasons for this are briefly as follows:

The Constitution of 1777 provided that the Assembly should consist of not less than 70 members, and might be increased by a definite ratio to 300, as the population increased. The amendments of 1801 fixed the number at 100, with a provision for their increase by a certain ratio to 150. The Constitution of 1821 fixed the number at 128, which has since been unchanged. The population of the State in 1780 was 238,897; in 1800, 588,603; in 1820, 1,302,-812, and is now about 4,000,000.

One of the great fundamental ideas of American polity is that the

Legislature should consist of two bodies, one of which, being more numerous than the other, should primarily represent the people, and the nearer it comes to the people and the more directly it emanates from them, the more in accordance it is with a republican form of government. Such a body stands in the place and stead of the people—it is theoretically and practically a representative body, its members are simply agents. The number of these is, in the first instance arbitrary, but the larger it is the more nearly it represents the people. The number should fairly represent the population and still not be so large as to prevent or interfere with the proper discharge of their legislative duties. As population increased the number should increase up to the limit of availability. If 128 was the right number in 1821, it should be increased now as a matter of right, unless there is some good reason for not doing so. The only objection to it that I know of is, that a larger number will interfere with the proper transaction of business. Is this true in fact? The House of Commons, in Great Britain, is composed of over 600 members. The legislative body of France was composed of 267 members prior to 1863, and since that time, of 383. The House of Deputies, in Prussia, has 350 members; and in Italy, 443. The House of Representatives of the United States has 244 members; and the lower house in Massachusetts, 240; in Connecticut, 237. In all these cases, and others that might be cited, there has been no difficulty in transacting business. It seems to me, therefore, that we can safely provide for an increase of the Assembly, graduated by the increase of population, and if we can do it with safety it is our duty to do it. The public wants and feelings call for it. Many consider that a larger body will be less liable to outride influences, less subject to the temptation of mercenary motives. All shades of opinion or interest will stand a better chance of being represented in a larger body than in a small one. My idea is to lay down or establish a rule or principle which will admit of expansion, so that the Constitution, in that respect, will not need remodeling every decade. A ratio is preferred to a fixed number inasmuch as it will do justice to future increase and follow the precedent of the Constitution of the United States as well as our earlier Constitutions.

The ratio of 1 to 20,000 representative population commends itself by its adaptation to the smaller counties, and it will produce a gradual increase from the present number. This ratio will give now

172 members, and in 1875 about 250, but I think the members should never exceed 250.

Members of Assembly should be elected by single districts as now, because

1. No change has been called for in that respect by the people, or is needed by the necessities of the times. Prior to 1846 the people had elected by counties as now proposed, ever since 1777, and the experience of seventy years had convinced them of the necessity of single districts, in order to obtain a correct and responsible representation. The larger the district and the more that are elected together, the less and more divided is the feeling of responsibility, the less direct is the accountability.

2. The people are more nearly represented, their feelings and views more exactly expressed. Whether laws are local or general, each locality may have its peculiar views, or be peculiarly affected and they have a right to have as direct an expression of their views as possible.

3. Minorities will be better represented. The question of the representation of minorities is an important one, and is attracting universal attention. All will admit its propriety and justice in a representative form of government. It is not a partisan question, inasmuch as the party in the majority this year may be in the minnority next year. But the trouble is to fix on some system that will be practical in its operations, and understood by and acceptable to the people. The ingenious theories of Mr. Hare, are more adapted to the evils of the British system than to our own. His fears of the tyranny of majorities has not much foundation in fact with us. Still it is our duty to afford every facility possible for the proper expression in our Legislative bodies of the views of all our citizens. The proposition that any one receiving a certain number of votes, wherever in the State they may be cast, is intended to accomplish this result. But will it do this? If the people act, spontaneously, that is without concert or agreement, in the selection of their candidates, their number will undoubtedly be large, and but a few of the more known or popular will get the required number of votes. And then, in determining which of those receiving a less number, shall go to fill up the necessary number of the Legislative body, as much

injustice may be done to minorities as would be in any other system. If, to avoid this, a plan of union or co operation, before casting the votes, is determined on, this would lead inevitably to the county or State Convention, which should fix or nominate the candidates for the several localities. This result would not, I imagine, be satisfactory, its evils would overbalance any good that might arise from it.

By the cumulative system, recommended by Mr. Mill, any elector, in case more than one member was to be elected in the district, instead of putting on to his ticket several names, might vote for one man, so that it would count for him as many as there were members to be elected, and thus commutate the vote of his favorite candidate. This, of course, would allow a large minority to choose some of the members, and would, to that extent, be beneficial. Taking into account, however, the habits of our people, it is doubtful whether an innovation of this kind would be advisable, if the end can be approximately reached by any other way. As a matter of fact, minorities, as a whole, have always been fairly represented in the lower House, much more so than in the Senate, resulting entirely from the less size of the districts. Retain the future of single districts together with the privilege to any district of choosing a citizen living in any portion of the State, and I think as much will be accomplished towards representing minorities as would be by any other plan.

4. Another advantage of single districts is that nominations will not be as much under the control of central, political regencies. In every large county, at its political center, there is a party power, that would in a great measure control nominations, if made at one time and place for the whole county. This is not right to the mass of the people, especially in electing the more numerous and popular body that peculiarly represents them. It is no answer to this to say, even if true (which I deny), that better men might or would be usually chosen. The same principle might leave it to a State convention, or to an Albany or New York regency to choose all our officers. The question is, how shall it be arranged so that the mass of the people can express their own views by themselves, and not through any self-appointed guardians or political managers. This is more important in view of the fact that the Senate, by the plan now proposed, is placed farther from the people, and will be a more conservative and independent body. We should not retrograde in

this manner. The intelligence of the people can be safely trusted. If improper nominations are made, the remedy of disregarding them can be more effectually applied and better men be more easily chosen.

All which is respectfully submitted,

M. H. MERWIN.

STATE OF NEW YORK.

No. 32.

IN CONVENTION

July 18, 1867.

REPORT

OF AUDITOR OF CANAL DEPARTMENT RELATIVE TO BREAKS AND COSTS OF REPAIR OF SAME IN ERIE CANAL.

STATE OF NEW YORK:
CANAL DEPARTMENT,
ALBANY, *July* 18, 1867.

HON. WILLIAM A. WHEELER, *President of the Convention:*

SIR—I herewith hand you a report to the Convention from this office, in reply to the resolution of inquiry of the 11th instant, respecting the breaks in the Erie canal within the last ten years.

I am very respectfully, your ob't serv't,

N. S. BENTON,
Auditor.

REPORT.

STATE OF NEW YORK:
CANAL DEPARTMENT,
ALBANY, *July* 11, 1867.

To the Convention:

The Auditor of the Canal Department in reply to the following resolution of the Convention, viz:

STATE OF NEW YORK:
CONSTITUTIONAL CONVENTION,
ALBANY, *July* 17, 1867,

On motion of Mr. Verplanck,

Resolved, That the Auditor of the Canal Department report to this Convention the number of breaks in the Erie Canal within the last ten years; the expense of repairing the same and the length of time that each break interfered with the navigation of the said canal.

By order of the Convention,
LUTHER CALDWELL,
Secretary,

Respectfully submits the following

REPORT:

That the records and accounts of this Department do not enable the Auditor to give in detail all the information called for by the resolution. The number of breaks that may happen in each year are not reported to this Department by the Canal Commissioners, Superintendents of repairs, or repair contractors. The amounts expended upon and paid for breaks on the Canals are reported to the Department at the close of the fiscal year, with the aggregate cost of repairs for the whole year, without specifying any particular break on the section, or the number. The length of time that any particular break interfered with the navigation of the canal, is not reported to this Department by the Canal Commissioners, Engineers, or Superintendents of repairs. This information is not within the official knowledge of the Auditor, and he cannot therefore give it upon any reliable data. The statement hereto annexed and submitted gives the amount expended and paid in each year for the last ten years for the repairs of breaks upon the Erie canal, amounting in the aggregate to five hundred and fourteen thousand, four hundred and fifty-five dollars and forty-six cents. This compilation of costs is made up from the reports of the Superintendents of repairs. The above statement does not embrace sums paid by the repair contractors for the repairs of breaks, covered by the terms of their contracts, but only such moneys as have been paid by the State, outside of the repair contracts.

Respectfully submitted,

N. S. BENTON,
Auditor.

STATEMENT.

Amount expended for repairing breaks on the Erie canal for the last ten years, ending 30th September, 1866:

1857,	$55,258	58
1858,	31,170	86
1859,	24,544	68
1860,	15,368	29
1861,	11,893	33
1862,	22,082	03
1863,	25,611	22
1864,	11,405	77
1865,	150,952	10
1866,	166,168	60
	$514,455	46

Canal Department, examined and certified.

N. S. BENTON
Auditor.

STATE OF NEW YORK.

No. 33.

IN CONVENTION

July 17, 1867.

COMMUNICATION

FROM THE CLERK OF THE SUPERIOR COURT OF THE CITY OF NEW YORK IN ANSWER TO A RESOLUTION OF THE CONVENTION.

To the Constitutional Convention of the State of New York:

GENTLEMEN—In accordance with the resolution received by me, requesting a statement to be furnished your honorable body, of the number of causes upon the calendar and the amount of business done by the Superior Court of the city of New York during the year 1866, I have caused an examination to be made of the records of said court, and respectfully submit the following statement therefrom.

Respectfully, &c.,

JAMES M. SWEENY, *Clerk.*

Dated New York, July 12, 1867.

STATEMENT.

GENERAL TERM, 1866.

January,	Number of cases on calendar, ...	40
do	Number of appeals from judgments and orders argued, ...	13
February,	Number of cases on calendar, ...	39

February,	Number of appeals from judgments and orders argued, ...	24
March,	Number of cases on calendar, ...	30
do	Number of appeals from judgments and orders argued, ...	17
April,	Number of cases on calendar, ...	32
do	Number of appeals from judgments and orders argued, ...	9
May,	Number of cases on calendar, ...	36
do	Number of appeals from judgments and orders argued, ...	16
June,	Number of cases on calendar, ...	34
do	Number of appeals from judgments and orders argued, ...	19
July,	Vacation.	
August,	Vacation.	
September,	Vacation.	
October,	Number of cases on calendar, ...	34
do	Number of appeals from judgments and orders argued, ...	9
November,	Number of cases on calendar, ...	35
do	Number of appeals from judgments and orders argued, ...	25
December,	Number of cases on calendar, ...	31
do	Number of appeals from judgments and orders argued, ...	14

RECAPITULATION.

Number of cases on calendar, ...	311
Number of appeals argued, ...	146

SPECIAL TERM AND CHAMBERS, 1866.

January,	Number of cases on Special Term Calendar, ...	39
do	Number of cases tried at Special Term, ...	11
do	Number of motions heard and decided at Chambers, ...	347
February,	Number of cases on Special Term Calendar, ...	36
do	Number of cases tried at Special Term, ...	6
do	Number of motions heard and decided at Chambers, ...	380

March,	Number of cases on Special Term Calendar,....	36
do	Number of cases tried at Special Term,.........	5
do	Number of motions heard and decided at Chambers,..............................	395
April,	Number of cases on Special Term Calendar,....	37
do	Number of cases tried at Special Term,.........	6
do	Number of motions heard and decided at Chambers,..............................	393
May,	Number of cases on Special Term Calendar,....	49
do	Number of cases tried at Special Term,.........	12
do	Number of motions heard and decided at Chambers,..............................	368
June,	Number of cases on Special Term Calendar,....	44
do	Number of cases tried at Special Term,.........	17
do	Number of motions heard and decided at Chambers,..............................	381
July,	Number of motions heard and decided at Chambers,..............................	323
August,	Number of motions heard and decided at Chambers,..............................	250
September,	Number of motions heard and decided at Chambers,..............................	178
October,	Number of cases on Special Term Calendar,....	53
do	Number of cases tried at Special Term,.........	19
do	Number of motions heard and decided at Chambers,..............................	259
November,	Number of cases on Special Term Calendar,....	49
do	Number of cases tried at Special Term,.........	8
do	Number of motions heard and decided at Chambers,..............................	238
December,	Number of cases on Special Term Calendar,....	49
do	Number of cases tried at Special Term,.........	14
do	Number of motions heard and decided at Chambers,..............................	296

RECAPITULATION.

Number of cases on Calendar,.........................	392
Number of cases tried at Special Term,..................	102
Number of motions heard and decided,..................	3,808

TRIAL TERMS, 1866.

Whole number of cases on Calendar, January 1, 1866,		2,351
January,	Number of cases tried in part I,	20
do	Number of cases tried in part II,	17
do	Number of cases added to calendar,	44
February,	Number of cases tried in part I,	17
do	Number of cases tried in part II,	22
do	Number of cases added to calendar,	33
March,	Number of cases tried in part I,	20
do	Number of cases tried in part II,	34
do	Number of cases added to calendar,	28
April,	Number of cases tried in part I,	18
do	Number of cases tried in part II,	11
do	Number of cases added to calendar,	27
May,	Number of cases tried in part I,	6
do	Number of cases tried in part II,	12
do	Number of cases added to calendar,	57
June,	Number of cases tried in part I,	17
do	Number of cases tried in part II,	12
do	Number of cases added to calendar,	38
July,	Vacation.	
August,	Vacation.	
September,	Vacation.	
October,	Number of cases tried in part I,	22
do	Number of cases tried in part II,	26
do	Number of cases added to calendar,	127
November,	Number of cases tried in part I,	18
do	Number of cases tried in part II,	21
do	Number of cases added to calendar,	54

NATURALIZATION IN 1866.

Declarations of Intention (Germany),	951
Declarations of Intention (Great Britain),	807
	1,758
Naturalizations,	5,507

STATE OF NEW YORK.

No. 34.

IN CONVENTION

July 19, 1867.

REPORT

OF STATE ENGINEER AND SURVEYOR RELATIVE TO COST OF LOCKS ON CHEMUNG CANAL.

OFFICE OF THE STATE ENGINEER AND SURVEYOR,
ALBANY, *July* 19, 1867.

HON. WILLIAM A. WHEELER, *President of the Constitutional Convention:*

SIR: I have the honor to transmit herewith a report in answer to a resolution of the Convention, adopted June 6th, calling for an estimate of the cost of enlarging the locks upon the Chemung canal and feeder.

Very respectfully,

J. P. GOODSELL,
State Engineer and Surveyor.

REPORT.

STATE OF NEW YORK:
OFFICE OF THE STATE ENGINEER AND SURVEYOR,
ALBANY, *July* 19, 1867.

HON. WILLIAM A. WHEELER, *President of the Constitutional Convention:*

SIR: The State Engineer and Surveyor, in reply to the following resolution, passed June 6th, 1867, to wit:

"*Resolved*, That the State Engineer and Surveyor be requested to make an estimate of the cost and expenses of enlarging the locks on the Chemung canal and on the Chemung canal feeder, to the size of the locks on the Erie canal, and to submit such estimate to this Convention at as early a day as practicable; and also furnish a table of the cost of construction, maintenance and repairs of said canal;"

respectfully submits the following

REPORT:

The short time allowed for the preparation of this statement rendered the making of a separate detailed estimate for each lock impracticable; the estimates are therefore prepared for one lock each, of 9, 10 and 10½ feet lift, using these as applicable to all locks of those lifts, and a relative proportion for those of other lifts.

There are upon the canal and feeder 53 locks, one of which has been abandoned.

The estimates are for stone locks, 110 feet long and 18 feet wide in the chamber; the walls to be of rubble masonry laid in hydraulic mortar, with fender posts in the chamber and cut-stone hollow quoins.

The estimated cost for 52 locks is, ...	$1,686,500 00
For engineering and contingencies, 15 per cent, ...	252,975 00
	$1,939,475 00

The detailed statements hereto attached, will more fully explain the manner of preparing the estimates and the prices used in estimating the cost of the work.

There is no data in this department from which can be prepared a correct statement of the "cost of construction, maintenance and repairs of said canal."

Respectfully submitted,

J. P. GOODSELL,

State Engineer and Surveyor.

Estimated cost of enlarging to the size of those upon the Erie canal, each and all of the locks upon the Chemung canal and Chemung Canal feeder; the walls of which are to be of rubble masonry laid in hydraulic mortar with fender posts and hollow quoins of cut stone.

No. of Lock.	Chemung Canal.	Lift of Lock.	Amount.
1.	....	13 feet.	$42,000 00
2.	(Old lock composite), ...	10¼ do	31,000 00
3.	....	10¾ do	33,600 00
4.	....	10½ do	33,400 00
5.	....	10¼ do	32,800 00
6.	....	10¼ do	32,800 00
7.	....	10½ do	33,400 00
8.	....	9½ do	31,000 00
9.	(Old lock composite), ...	10¼ do	31,000 00
10.	....	10¼ do	32,800 00
11.	....	10 do	32,300 00
12.	....	10 do	32,300 00
13.	....	10 do	32,300 00
14.	....	10 do	32,300 00
15.	....	10 do	32,300 00

No. of Lock.	Chemung Canal.	Lift of Lock.		Amount.
16.	....	10	feet.	$32,300 00
17.	....	10	do	32,300 00
18.	....	$10\frac{1}{4}$	do	32,800 00
19.	....	$9\frac{3}{4}$	do	31,900 00
20.	....	10	do	32,300 00
21.	....	10	do	32,300 00
22.	....	$10\frac{1}{4}$	do	32,800 00
23.	....	$9\frac{3}{4}$	do	31,900 00
24.	....	$10\frac{1}{4}$	do	32,800 00
25.	....	$10\frac{1}{4}$	do	32,800 00
26.	....	9	do	30,900 00
27.	....	$10\frac{3}{4}$	do	33,500 00
28.	....	$10\frac{7}{8}$	do	32,800 00
29.	....	$9\frac{3}{4}$	do	31,900 00
30.	....	$10\frac{1}{4}$	do	32,800 00
31.	....	$10\frac{1}{4}$	do	32,800 00
32.	....	10	do	32,300 00
33.	....	10	do	32,300 00
34.	....	10	do	32,300 00
35.	....	10	do	32,300 00
36.	....	10	do	32,300 00
37.	....	10	do	32,300 00
38.	....	10	do	32,300 00
39.	....	10	do	32,300 00
40.	....	10	do	32,300 00
41.	....	$10\frac{1}{2}$	do	33,400 00
42.	....	$9\frac{1}{2}$	do	31,500 00
43.	....	$9\frac{1}{2}$	do	31,500 00
44.	(Summit), ...	$10\frac{1}{4}$	do	32,800 00
45.	do	$9\frac{1}{2}$	do	31,500 00
46.	....	9	do	30,900 00
47.	....	9	do	30,900 00
48.	....	$7\frac{1}{4}$	do	28,800 00
49.	River lock at Elmira, abandoned.			
50.	....	9	do	30,900 00
51.	....	$9\frac{1}{2}$	do	31,500 00

No. of Lock.	Chemung Canal.	Lift of Lock.	Amount.
52.	....	9 feet.	$30,900 00
53.	(Guard lock in Chemung river, at Corning), ...	10 do	37,000 00
			$1,686,500 00
	Add 15 per cent for engineering and contingencies, ..		252,975 00
	Total, ...		$1,939,475 00

Detailed estimate of the cost of enlarging to the size of those upon the Erie canal, one lock upon the Chemung canal and Feeder, of rubble stone masonry, 9 feet lift:

Quantities.	Items.	Price.	Amounts.
	Bailing and draining, ...	$500 00	$500 00
8,000	Cubic yds. excavation of earth, ...	30	2,400 00
100	do do rock, with blasting,	1 50	150 00
100	do do rock without do	1 00	100 00
3,500	do embankment, ...	25	875 00
1,400	do lining, ...	50	700 00
1,400	do puddling, ...	15	210 00
80	do slope wall, ...	2 25	180 00
60	do battered wall in cement, ..	6 00	360 00
1,900	do rubble masonry in lock walls, including coping, ...	9 00	17,100 00
80	Cubic yds. concrete, ...	5 00	400 00
16,000	Feet b. m. white oak, ...	70 00	1,120 00
8,500	do white pine, ...	60 00	510 00
100,000	do hemlock, ...	25 00	2,500 00
3,000	Pounds wrought iron, ...	15	450 00
500	do cast iron, ...	10	50 00
1,000	do spike and nails, ...	12	120 00
60	Lineal feet snubbing posts, ...	50	30 00
7,000	do bearing piles, ...	35	2,450 00
1	Per lock, painting gates, ...	50 00	50 00
1	do sulphur and sand cement, ..	15 00	15 00
1	do removing timber and plank in old lock, ...	200 00	200 00
8	Number. Composite valves, ...	30 00	240 00
	Total, ...		$30,710 00

Detailed estimate of the cost of enlarging to the size of those upon the Erie canal, one lock upon the Chemung canal and Feeder, of rubble stone masonry, 10 *feet lift:*

Quantities.	Items.	Price.	Amounts.
	Bailing and draining, ...	$500 00	$500 00
9,000	Cubic yds. excavation of earth, ...	30	2,700 00
100	do do rock with blasting,	1 50	150 00
100	do do rock without do	1 00	100 00
4,000	do embankment, ...	25	1,000 00
1,500	do lining, ...	50	750 00
1,500	do puddling, ...	15	225 00
80	do slope wall, ...	2 25	180 00
60	do battered wall in cement, .	6 00	360 00
2,000	do rubble masonry in lock walls, including coping,	9 00	18,000 00
80	do concrete, ...	5 00	400 00
17,000	Feet B. M., white oak, ...	70 00	1,190 00
9,000	do do pine, ...	60 00	540 00
100,000	do hemlock, ...	25 00	2,500 00
3,000	Pounds wrought iron, ...	15	450 00
500	do cast iron, ...	10	50 00
1,300	do spike and nails, ...	12	120 00
60	Lineal feet snubbing posts, ...	50	30 00
7,000	do bearing piles, ...	35	2,450 00
1	Per lock, painting gates, ...	50 00	50 00
1	do sulphur and sand cement, .	15 00	15 00
1	do removing timber and plank in old lock, ...	200 00	200 00
8	Number. Composite valves, ...	30 00	240 00
Total,	....		$32,200 00

Detailed estimate of the cost of enlarging to the size of those upon the Erie canal, one lock upon the Chemung canal and Feeder, of rubble stone masonry, 10¼ *feet lift:*

Quantities.	Items.	Price.	Amounts.
	Bailing and draining,...............	$500 00	$500 00
9,500	Cubic yds. excavation of earth,.....	30	2,850 00
100	do do rock with blasting,	1 50	150 00
100	do do rock without do	1 00	100 00
4,500	do embankment,...........	25	1,125 00
1,500	do lining,................	50	750 00
1,600	do puddling,...............	15	240 00
80	do slope wall,..............	2 25	180 00
60	do battered wall in cement,..	6 00	360 00
2,020	do rubble masonry in lock walls, including coping,.	9 00	18,180 00
80	Cubic yds. concrete,...............	5 00	400 00
17,500	Feet B. M. white oak,.............	70 00	1,225 00
9,500	do do pine,...........	60 00	570 00
100,000	do hemlock,..............	25 00	2,500 00
3,000	Pounds wrought iron,..............	15	450 00
500	do cast iron,................	10	50 00
1,000	do spike and nails,............	12	120 00
60	Lineal feet snubbing posts,.........	50	30 00
7,000	do bearing piles,...........	35	2,450 00
1	Per lock, painting gates,...........	50	50 00
1	do sulphur and sand cement,..	15 00	15 00
1	do removing timber and plank in old lock,...........	200 00	200 00
8	Number. Composite valves,.......	30 00	240 00
Total,	....		$32,735 00

STATE OF NEW YORK.

No. 35.

IN CONVENTION

July 17, 1867.

REPORT

OF COMMITTEE ON LEGISLATURE, &c., ON ORGANIZATION OF LEGISLATIVE POWER.

The Committee on the Legislature, its organization and the number, apportionment, election, tenure of office, and compensation of its members have prepared and submit the following article of the Constitution, and ask to be discharged from the further consider ation of all propositions which have been referred to them by the Convention:

SECTION 1. The Legislative power of this State shall be vested in a Senate and Assembly. Any elector of this State shall be eligible to the office of Senator or member of Assembly.

§ 2. The State shall be divided into eight senatorial districts There shall be four Senators in each district.

The first district shall consist of the city and county of New York, and shall be entitled to one additional Senator.

The second district shall consist of the counties of Suffolk, Queens, Kings, Richmond and Westchester.

The third district shall consist of the counties of Putnam, Rockland, Dutchess, Orange, Ulster, Greene, Columbia and Rensselaer.

The fourth district shall consist of the counties of Albany, Schenectady, Fulton, Hamilton, Saratoga, Washington, Warren, Essex, Clinton, Franklin and St. Lawrence.

The fifth district shall consist of the counties of Jefferson, Lewis, Oneida, Onondaga, Oswego, Herkimer and Montgomery.

The sixth district shall consist of the counties of Otsego, Schoharie, Delaware, Sullivan, Broome, Chenango, Madison, Cortland, Tioga, Tompkins, Chemung and Schuyler.

The seventh district shall consist of the counties of Yates, Seneca, Ontario, Cayuga, Wayne, Monroe, Livingston and Steuben.

The eighth district shall consist of the counties of Orleans, Niagara, Erie, Genesee, Wyoming, Allegany, Cattaraugus and Chautauqua. The whole Senate shall be chosen at the first election held under this Constitution; they shall classify themselves, so that one Senator in each district shall go out of office at the end of each year, and the additional Senator for the first district at the end of the fourth year. After the expiration of their terms under such classification the terms of their office shall be four years.

§ 3. An enumeration of the inhabitants of the State shall be taken, under the direction of the Legislature, in the year one thousand eight hundred and seventy-five, and at the end of every ten years thereafter; and the said district—except the first district—shall be so altered by the Legislature at the first session after the return of every enumeration, that each district shall contain as near as may be an equal number of inhabitants who are citizens of the State, and shall remain unaltered until the return of another enumeration, and shall consist of contiguous territory. "And the first district shall be entitled to such additional Senators as its citizen population shall, in proportion to that of the entire State, entitle it." No county shall be divided in the formation of a Senate district.

§ 4. The Assembly shall consist of one hundred and thirty-nine members who shall be chosen by counties, and shall be apportioned among the several counties of the State, as nearly as may be, according to the number of inhabitants thereof, who are citizens of the State, and shall hold office for one year. Each county shall be entitled to at least one member, except that the counties of Fulton and Hamilton shall, together, elect, until the population of the county of Hamilton shall, according to the ratio, entitle it to a member. No new county shall be erected unless its population shall entitle it to a member. The first apportionment of members of Assembly shall be made by the Legislature, at its first session after the adoption of this Constitution, upon the enumeration of the inhabitants of this State, who are citizens thereof, made in the year one thousand eight hundred and sixty-five. A like apportionment shall be made by the Legislature at its first session, after every such enumeration. Every apportionment when made, shall remain unaltered until another enumeration shall be made.

§ 5. The members of the Legislature shall receive for their services an annual salary of one thousand dollars, and ten cents for each mile they shall travel in going to and returning from their place of meeting by the most usual route. The speaker of the Assembly shall receive an additional compensation equal to one-half of his salary as a member.

§ 6. No member of the Legislature shall be appointed to any civil office within this State by the Governor, the Governor and Senate, or by the Legislature during the time for which he shall have been elected, and all such appointments and all votes given for any such member therefor shall be void. Nor shall any person being a member of Congress or holding any judicial or military office under the United States, hold a seat in the Legislature. If any person shall after his election as a member of the Legislature, be elected to Congress or appointed to any office, civil or military, under the government of the United States, his acceptance thereof, shall vacate his seat.

§ 7. The elections of Senators and members of Assemby under this Constitution shall be held on the Tuesday succeeding the first Monday in November, unless otherwise directed by law. The first election to be in the year one thousand eight hundred and sixty-eight. The legislative term shall begin on the first day of January, and the Legislature shall every year assemble on the first Tuesday in January, unless a different day be appointed by law. The Senators and members of Assembly who may be in office on the first day of January, one thousand eight hundred and sixty-eight, shall hold their offices until and including the thirty-first day of December of that year, and no longer.

§ 8. A majority of each House shall constitute a quorum to do business. Each House shall determine the rules of its own proceedings, and be the judge of the election, returns and qualifications of its own members; shall choose its own officers; and the Senate shall choose a temporary president when the Lieutenant-Governor shall not attend as President, or shall act as Governor.

§ 9. Each House shall keep a journal of its proceedings and publish the same, except such parts as may require secrecy.

The doors of each House shall be kept open, except when the public welfare shall require secrecy. Neither House shall, without the consent of the other, adjourn for more than two days.

EDWIN A. MERRITT,
Chairman,
ERASTUS COOKE,
RICHARD U. SHERMAN,
CLAUDIUS L. MONELL,
GEORGE BARKER,
NATHANIEL JARVIS, JR.

I concur with this report except as to the number of members of Assembly and their manner of election.

M. H. MERWIN.

STATE OF NEW YORK.

No. 36.

IN CONVENTION

July 19, 1867.

REPORT

OF AUDITOR OF CANAL DEPARTMENT RELATIVE TO COST, &c., OF CHAMPLAIN CANAL.

STATE OF NEW YORK:

CANAL DEPARTMENT, ALBANY, *July* 19, 1867.

Hon. WILLIAM A. WHEELER, *President of the Convention:*

SIR: I herewith transmit to the Convention the reply of the Auditor to the resolution of the 26th of June last, relating to the cost, tolls, maintenance and tonnage of the Champlain canal.

I am, very respectfully yours,

N. S. BENTON,

Auditor.

REPORT.

CANAL DEPARTMENT,
ALBANY, *July* 19*th*, 1867.

To the Convention:

The Auditor of the Canal Department, in compliance with the following resolution of the Convention, to wit:

STATE OF NEW YORK:

IN CONSTITUTIONAL CONVENTION,
ALBANY, N. Y., *June* 26, 1867.

On motion of Mr. Beckwith,

Resolved, That the Auditor of the Canal Department be and he is hereby requested to furnish to this Convention the following information:

1. The original cost of the Champlain canal.

2. The cost of any and all enlargements, repairs and improvements thereof.

3. The tolls received in each fiscal year.

4. The cost of collection, superintendence and repairs thereof.

5. The tons shipped on the Champlain canal each year during that time, stating the same separately from those of the Erie canal so far as practicable.

By order,

LUTHER CALDWELL,

Secretary.

Respectfully submits the following report on the subject matters contained in the said resolution:

The accounts of the original cost of construction of the Erie and Champlain canals, from their commencement to their completion, were kept together as one work, and can only be separated by a particular and critical examination of the yearly accounts of expenditures rendered by the Canal Commissioners, and of payments made by the Comptroller up to 1826.

That examination has heretofore been made on several occasions, and has now been repeated, and the results given in the statement annexed.

There are not any reports or statements in this department showing the number of tons of freight carried on this canal from its completion in 1826 to 1838, and the amount of tonnage carried during that period can only be estimated by the amount of tolls received in each year from 1826 to 1837 inclusive, compared with the twelve succeeding years. Upon this data the whole number of tons carried on this canal from 1826 to 1866 inclusive, would not materially vary from 19,000,000 tons.

The statement annexed shows the following results:

1. The cost of construction, ...	$1,257,604 26
2. The cost of any and all enlargements and improvements other than ordinary repairs, from 1826 to 1866 inclusive, ...	895,147 34
Total original cost and improvements, ...	$2,152,751 60
3. The tolls received in each fiscal year from 1826 to 1866 inclusive, the aggregate of which is, ..	$4,593,908 07
4. The cost of collection, superintendence and ordinary repairs of each year during the same period, the aggregate of which is, ...	3,039,092 58
Excess of tolls over superintendence and repairs,	$1,554,815 49
5. The tonnage carried on the canal each year, the aggregate of which from 1838 to 1866 inclusive is, ...	15,461,195 tons
Estimated number of tons from 1826 to 1837 inclusive, ...	3,538,805 tons
Total tonnage ascertained and estimated, ...	19,000,000 tons

Showing these striking facts: that the tonnage of 1866 has increased over that of 1838, 271 per cent, while the tolls of 1866 only show an increase of 73 per cent over those of 1838. The cost of repairs in 1866 was $67,179.36 less than in 1838.

Respectfully submitted,

N. S. BENTON,

Auditor.

STATEMENT

Showing the original cost of the Champlain canal, the cost of any and all enlargements and improvements thereof, the tolls received in each fiscal year, the cost of collection, superintendence and repairs, and the tons shipped in each year, from 1838 *to* 1866, *inclusive. Original cost of Champlain canal,* $1,257,604.26.

	Cost of all enlargements and improvements.	Tolls received in each fiscal year.	Cost of collection, superintendence and repairs.	TONS SHIPPED ON THE CHAMPLAIN CANAL.		
				At offices on Champlain canal.	At offices on Erie canal.	Total Champlain canal.
1826,	$137,503 00	$74,191 19	$6,376 87	....	....	....
1827,	13,000 00	83,341 02	47,015 41	....	....	....
1828,	20,490 44	107,757 08	57,147 86	....	....	....
1829,	19,869 50	87,171 03	50,228 16	....	....	....
1830,	2,129 87	89,053 78	39,389 29	....	....	....
1831,*	....	102,896 23	30,660 71	....	....	....
1832,	....	110,191 95	52,999 04	....	....	....
1833,	....	132,572 12	70,841 13	....	....	....
1834,	....	115,211 90	99,666 22	....	....	....
1835,	....	116,131 10	49,959 07	....	....	....
1836,	....	115,425 24	67,044 24	....	....	....
1837,	....	94,726 31	119,729 90	....	....	....
1838,	....	104,125 15	144,152 71	266,553	12,033	278,586
1839,	....	113,753 69	120,455 88	263,552	14,468	278,020
1840,	....	102,427 74	90,512 09	245,229	12,946	258,175
1841,†	....	63,535 43	80,497 12	276,418	15,935	292,353
1842,	....	100,934 34	143,850 41	230,844	10,395	241,239
1843,	....	103,307 37	59,900 37	262,212	13,152	275,364

1844,	....	115,763 21	61,113 62	269,546	14,644	284,190
1845,	....	118,296 86	73,858 63	266,922	17,241	284,163
1846,	....	114,169 50	58,795 23	280,480	19,444	299,924
1847,	....	103,058 79	51,649 28	313,124	22,498	335,622
1848,	....	120,753 21	72,791 54	293,889	32,893	326,782
1849,	....	118,190 30	61,672 28	321,345	36,060	357,405
1850,	....	128,761 67	66,688 28	460,219	31,778	491,997
1851,	....	130,386 34	73,952 93	513,793	31,675	545,468
1852,	....	113,659 78	108,851 10	531,001	30,284	561,285
1853,	....	124,143 05	84,399 29	608,354	32,825	641,179
1854,	....	106,683 04	95,434 24	602,913	22,792	625,705
1855,	....	100,635 41	110,670 07	537,108	19,560	556,668
1856,	....	111,014 60	55,025 24	611,610	23,714	635,324
1857,	....	117,410 07	82,117 73	547,236	83,906	631,142
1858,	80,260 14	90,486 10	85,337 29	608,918	61,868	670,786
1859,	8,724 61	103,654 79	77,665 33	751,046	69,627	820,673
1860,	96,930 10	114,128 11	72,827 47	681,157	83,960	765,117
1861,	54,561 13	106,561 00	38,771 89	545,930	53,899	599,829
1862,	67,141 40	101,517 94	63,007 04	647,318	47,559	694,877
1863,	57,779 44	126,502 42	69,571 51	878,920	53,655	932,575
1864,	38,815 53	176,386 49	66,730 68	846,790	42,523	889,313
1865,	99,021 84	154,441 57	100,762 08	815,311	37,679	852,990
1866,	196,920 34	180,551 15	76,973 35	1,001,493	32,951	1,034,444
	$895,147 34	$4,593,908 07	$3,039,092 58	14,479,231	981,964	15,461,195

NOTE.—The total tonnage going from tide-water on the Champlain canal, from 1838 to 1856 inclusive, cannot be furnished, but the tons of merchandise, however, for each of said years is given in the 5th column, and the whole tonnage going from tide-water on the Champlain canal for each year from 1857 to 1866, inclusive, is given in the same column.

* Superintendence and collection for this year was for nine months only.

† Tolls this year from 1st January to 30th September.

CANAL DEPARTMENT,
ALBANY, *July* 19, 1867.

Examined and certified.

N. S. BENTON,

Auditor.

STATE OF NEW YORK.

No. 37.

IN CONVENTION

July 22, 1867.

Presented by E. Brooks.

PETITION

OF THE FIRST DIRECTRESS OF THE NURSERY AND CHILD'S HOSPITAL, IN BEHALF OF THE BOARD OF MANAGERS, PRAYING THAT THE STATE CONVENTION, IN REGULATING THE CHARITIES OF THE STATE, WILL CONSIDER THE CLAIMS FOR A FOUNDLING HOSPITAL.

The undersigned, first directress of the Nursery and Child's Hospital, seeing the interest manifested by the State Convention, in regard to the charities of the State, and a seeming purpose to limit and restrict appropriations by the State, for its necessary charities, begs leave to present the following reasons why a *Foundling Hospital* should be established by the State authorities.

The undersigned, with a Board of Managers, has been for the past thirteen years connected with the *Nursery and Child's Hospital* in the city of New York. The result of the experience there obtained, has been not only to diminish infant mortality, but has been the means of *preventing* crime. Many cases of suicide and infanticide have been saved since their extension of charity for the prevention of foundlings. The nursery was originally intended to check the immense mortality among the children of wet nurses. The necessity for a Child's Hospital induced greater and more enlarged efforts. No illegitimate child was then admitted. But the numbers they were forced to refuse, induced a deeper study into the necessities of these most wretched of all infants. The late Isaac Townsend was then one of the Governors of the Alms House, and prosecuted his search after truth at the same time as the undersigned. The results were the same, and his report was published by the Board of Alms House Governors, showing the great need of a Foundling Hospital in New York.

The statistics of foreign Foundling Hospitals have been collected with great care. Although St. Vincent de Paul was not the founder of the first Hospital in France, which was in 1070, he seems to have been the first to influence the public authorities to acknowledge the civil existence of foundlings. This was in the 17th century. By an edict of Louis XIV, dated 1670, the Foundling Hospital was placed on the same footing as the other Hospitals of Paris. "Considering it," he says, "as a Christian duty to care for these children, whose feebleness and misfortune make them worthy of compassion, and, further than this, their preservation is an advantage, because they may be useful in the country's service." In 1788, a Lying-in Asylum was established under the auspices of Marie Antoinette. In a report made to the King in 1837, Mons. de Gasparin considers this as one of the best instruments for the diminution of the number of abandoned children. Monsieur Dupin also bears testimony to its utility, and says: "When a child has lived a year, and its mother has enjoyed its first smile, there is no danger that she will abandon it." The London Foundling Hospital was founded in 1739, by Thomas Coram, and is now recognized as one of the best and most useful of England's charities. Governor Townsend, after alluding to the English system of education of foundlings, adds: "Should New York decide to provide for and foster the helpless outcasts, who, but for such kindness might have augmented the list of her felons, and have required the outlay of the erection of prisons, she will be guided by no narrow considerations, knowing that in proportion as she furnishes the comparatively meanest and most despicable of her children with the light of intellectual and moral truth, she furnishes good subjects for the government, the material of an effective army or marine, men destined to carry down her nascent glory and greatness to the latest generation."

A select committee of the Board of Councilmen was appointed in New York in 1858, to examine and report on the expediency of establishing a Foundling Hospital. After giving the subject careful attention, and having conferred with eminent physicians (who, from the opportunities of observation of the evils arising from the *want* of a Foundling Hospital, were well calculated to afford information and counsel), reported that "the records of our coroners' inquests, and our criminal courts, show to what an extent the crime of infanticide is practiced; that the evil should, therefore, be met face to face by the law-making and law-keeping classes, for it intrudes everywhere, and will no longer be named in whispers, or elbowed or frowned out of sight; it is as open and patent as drunkenness or pauperism, and should challenge the serious attention of all who have the general good at heart. They report that in one week, out of 503 deaths, no less than 107, or the enormous proportion of 35 per cent, were under one year of age, 54 being returned as still or premature births. If this startling proportion gets into the bills of mortality, who will dare even to guess at the hundreds and thousands of cases occurring every year, which are known only to the woman and her physician; occurring, not only in squalid haunts of poverty, but among the so-called better classes, where exposure would be infamy?" "In Paris, where the well-endowed Foundling Hospital exists, infanticide occurs very rarely, and the vile occupation of the abortionist, so often practiced with impunity here, is almost unknown. When vice rears its Hydra head, not only in the side streets, but in the Fifth Avenue in New York, with its palace walls, raised from proceeds of infants' deaths (and perhaps of many adults), is it not time for legislators to secure some prevention to these crimes?" In speaking of the evil now suggested, an officer in the police department writes: "These evils are so widely spread and deeply rooted as to appal the heart of every philanthropist and Christian who has given the subject the least attention. For the year ending October 31, 1864, the number of foundlings received by police was 211; for the year 1865, 234; 1866, 241.

The present Hospital for Foundlings has been in existence less than two years, yet its results are extremely encouraging. Strict discrimination is used on the admission of children. This was found necessary in England, to prevent the evils arising from the too great facilities of the Paris or Dublin method. "The mother must produce evidence of having borne a good character, until the dark shadow of him who ruined her, fell across her path, and there must be a strong probability that the reception of the child will be the means of rescuing the mother from that course of sin and shame on the brink of which she stands." But the Nursery and Child's Hospital, not only aims to rescue the child, but the mother also, for which purpose a Lying-in Asylum belongs to it, and here are sheltered the young women, many from 14 to 18 years of age, who have been thrust from their parents' houses, on discovery of their condition. What becomes of these, if no door but that leading to further sin or to death, is open to them? The coroner often answers when describing the lifeless forms drawn from the water. Our records, but for their strict privacy, would convince the most skeptical, of the crimes we have prevented. In one case, the father owned his desire to kill his daughter before her infant saw the light, and that he had ordered his son to "put a bullet through the head of her seducer," yet that girl, only 16, was pardoned by her father through our influence, and now leads a virtuous life, safely guarded in her parents' home. But for our Foundling Hospital, this would have been a tripple murder. The Alms House can receive women who have no shame or modesty left which would prevent their seeking refuge in a public charity. These are not the mothers of the waifs and strays of our city. It is those whose dread of discovery is greater than their love of life, and these come from the villages and towns near New York, or in other parts of the State. Out of 195 cases, only 37 belonged to the city itself. In villages where every one is known, infanticide is rare. In the vortex of the city they are unknown, and on pretense of a visit, or an offered situation, they hide themselves till the crime of child murder has further blackened their souls. The Alms House has given its report of numbers received and deaths. It is probably impossible for them to do more than is done to diminish their mortality. They cannot induce women to live in the Alms House to nurse these infants, when, if they have all the nourishment required, they can obtain from 25 to 30 dollars a month in luxurious private families. The Nursery can offer them great advantages, and our success proves how much more can be done by the vigilance of unpaid labor of Christian ladies, devoting time, energy, and means, to this most difficult problem—the saving of infant lives. To offer in an Alms House such a home as we provide would be impolitic, as it would encourage pauperism.

The undersigned believes that the Nursery and Child's Hospital is the first and only Foundling Hospital in the United States. It is not sectarian, as Protestant, Roman Catholic, and Jewish children are received on equal terms.

The undersigned believes,

That it has been the means of saving many lives:

That it has prevented the commission of many crimes:

That we have been far behind every other country in the care of such infants, and thus many valuable lives have been lost to our State:

That the immense number of children now left at our doors, and in our docks, sewers and open lots, call piteously for legislative action:

And that the Nursery and Child's Hospital is better prepared than any known institution, to administer through its lady managers aid and comfort to the helpless infant, and the unfortunate mother.

They are prepared to support many children even now, but the number who, for want of room, must die if refused, induces a strong desire on the part of the undersigned, in the name of the managers, to apply to your honorable body to provide, that the Legislature shall not be restricted in making appropriations for foundlings, and that they may be considered the children of the State, as they are in England, France, Russia, Italy, Austria, Sweden, Ireland and South America, Spain and Portugal.

MARY A. DU BOIS,

First Directress of the Nursery and Child's Hospital, in behalf of the Board of Managers.

STATE OF NEW YORK.

No. 38.

IN CONVENTION

July 23, 1867.

RESOLUTION

Offered by Mr. Sherman.

Resolved, That the following article be adopted as a part of a proposed constitution, to be submitted to the people pursuant to chapter 194 of the Laws of 1867.

ARTICLE

SECTION 1. Exclusive authority is given to Boards of Supervisors to legislate in their respective counties on the following specified subjects:

1. The location, erection, purchase and reparation of bridges, except over navigable streams.

2. The location and purchase of town and county buildings and lands, and the construction, care and preservation of such buildings.

3. The creation of separate road districts on public highways.

4. The discontinuance, with the consent of the corporators, or

by lawful abandonment, of plank, turnpike and macadamised roads, and the use and working of them as public highways.

5. The fencing, working and improvement of public highways, laid out in pursuance of the general laws of the State, in cases where the general laws of the State are insufficient to accomplish the object.

6. The laying out, opening, extension, improvement and alteration of lines of streets in cities and incorporated villages in cases where provision may not be made in their charters or by the general laws of the State for that purpose.

7. The consolidation of School districts, the change of boundaries of such districts, the raising and application of the funds consequent thereon, and of funds for the location, erection, and reparation of school houses where exceeding the amount authorized by the general laws of the State, subject otherwise, however, to such general laws; but no action under this subdivision shall be operative until a certificate of approval shall be made by the Superintendent of Public Instruction, and filed in the office of the Secretary of State.

8. The legalization of the acts of town meetings in reference to the raising of moneys authorized by law, and the legalization of the irregular acts of town officers in cases where the county court shall recommend such legalization.

9. The fixing of the salaries of county officers and of the

number, grades and pay of clerks and subordinate employees in county offices, whose compensation may be a county charge.

10. The draining of swamp lands lying exclusively within the county.

11. The borrowing of money for town and county purposes in anticipation of taxation authorized by law.

The Legislature shall provide for the publication, in such form as they shall deem necessary, of all laws passed by Boards of Supervisors, pursuant to the provisions of this article.

§ 2. The concurrent action of the Boards of Supervisors, shall be necessary to authorize the location, purchase, erection or reparation of bridges between such counties.

No. 39.

IN CONVENTION

July 23, 1867.

RESOLUTION

Offered by Mr. Sherman.

Resolved, That the following article be adopted as a part of a proposed Constitution to be submitted to the people, pursuant to chap. 194, of the Laws of 1867:

SECTION 1. The Legislature shall provide by general laws for the following specified objects, and they shall not be made in any case, the subjects of special legislation:

1. The creation of corporations, except for municipal purposes.

2. The adjustment of all pecuniary claims against the State.

3. The laying out and opening of public and private roads, except in cities and incorporated villages.

4. The regulation of the fees of State, county and town officers, in cases where the payment of fees for official services may be deemed proper.

INDEX.

NOTE.—For more convenient reference, the provisions of the Constitution, as agreed upon by the Convention, are alphabetically arranged according to subjects, under the head "Constitution as Adopted."

A.

No. Doc.		Page.
38.	Abandoned plank and turnpike roads, to vest power over in boards of supervisors, ...	2
115.	Abbey, D. C., statement of lands sold to,............	30
	Abel, Alanson, D., statement of lands sold to,........	248
	Abel, Alvin, jr., statement of lands sold to,..........	46
	Abel, James, statement of lands sold to,............	176
	Abel, L. & O., statement of lands sold to,...........	47
	Abel, O., jr., statement of lands sold to,.... 369, 378,	379
	Abell & Gliddon, statement of lands sold to,.........	373
	Abell & Williams, statement of lands sold to,........	379
	Abrams, Daniel, statement of lands sold to,..........	109
	Abrams & Young, statement of lands sold to,........	145
15.	Absent voters, provision for taking votes of, ...	2, 3
55.	Academies, appropriations to, from 1847 to 1866 inclusive, ...	92
116.	revenues to be applied to support of, ...	1
115.	Ackerman, H., statement of lands sold to,...........	349
40.	Ackerly, Nathan, testimony of, relative to letting of canal contracts, 28th December,............	58
	testimony of, relative to contracting board, and letting of canal contracts,.................	659–61
115.	Adams, Gardiner, statement of lands sold to,........	303
	Adams, Simeon, statement of lands sold to,..........	213

No. Doc.		Page.
115.	Adams Wm., statement of lands sold to, ...	126
55.	Addison Academy, appropriations to, ...	8, 11
74.	Adirondack company, report of State Engineer relative to lands sold by, ...	1, 3
97.	report by Commissioners of Land Office of lands granted to or acquired by, ...	1, 12
21.	Adirondack railroad, amount of freight carried during the year 1866:	
	whole number of tons, ...	34
	products of the forest, number of tons, ...	34
	vegetable food, number of tons, ...	34
	manufactures, number of tons, ...	34
	merchandise, number of tons, ...	34
115.	Agard, Jno., statement of lands sold to, ...	250
54.	Aged and Indigent Female Institution, New York, re-report of donations to, ...	6
55.	Agricultural College, appropriations to, ... 5–7,	92
52.	Agricultural drains, to authorize construction of, ...	1
149.	Agricultural leases, provision relative to, ...	5
145.	Albany, communication from authorities of, tendering use of hall for Convention, ...	1, 2
55.	Academy, appropriations to, ...	8–11
8.	Argus, to provide for publishing verbatim reports in, ...	2–4
57.	basin, contract for dredging, ...	53
55.	Dispensary, appropriations to, ...	77–79
8.	Evening Journal, to provide for publishing verbatim reports in, ...	2–4
55.	Eye and Ear Infirmary, appropriations to, ...	77–79
	Female Academy, appropriations to, ...	8–11
	Female Seminary, appropriations to, ...	8–11
	Guardian Society and Home of the Friendless, appropriations to, ...	57–59
	Hospital, appropriations to, ...	72–75
	Juvenile Retreat, appropriations to, ...	62, 63
	Lunatic Asylum, appropriations to, ...	88–90
	Medical College, appropriations to, ...	80–83
137.	National Commercial Bank, offer of, to advance moneys to pay expenses of Convention, ...	7

No. Doc.		Page.
21.	Albany Northern Railroad, amount of freight carried over during the year 1855:	
	whole number of tons,	12
	products of forest, number of tons,	12
	animals, number of tons,	12
	vegetable food, number of tons,	12
	other agricultural products, number of tons,	12
	manufactures, number of tons,	12
	merchandise, number of tons,	12
	other articles, number of tons,	12
	(See "Albany, Vermont & Canada Railroad.")	
55.	Albany Orphan Asylum, appropriations to,	56–59
21.	Albany & Schenectady Railroad, amount of freight carried over each year from 1851 to 1853, inclusive:	
	whole number of tons,	5–8
	products of forest, number of tons,	5–8
	animals, number of tons,	5–8
	vegetable food, number of tons,	5–8
	other agricultural products, number of tons,	5–8
	manufactures, number of tons,	5–8
	merchandise, number of tons,	5–8
	other articles, number of tons,	5–8
55.	St. Vincent's Orphan Asylum, appropriations to,	64–67
21.	Albany & Susquehanna railroad, amount of freight carried over each year from 1864 to 1866, inclusive:	
	whole number of tons,	30–34
	products of the forest, number of tons,	30–34
	animals, number of tons,	30-34
	vegetable food,	30–34
	other agricultural products, number of tons,	30–34
	manufactures, number of tons,	30–34
	merchandise, number of tons,	30–34
	other articles, number of tons,	30–34
	Albany, Vermont & Canada railroad, amount of freight carried over each year from 1856 to 1858, inclusive:	
	whole number of tons,	14–16
	products of the forest, number of tons,	14–16

No. Doc. Page.

21. Albany, Vermont & Canada Railroad—*Continued.*
animals, number of tons, ... 14–16
vegetable food, number of tons, ... 14–16
other agricultural products, number of tons,.... 14–16
manufactures, number of tons,................ 14–16
merchandise, number of tons, ... 14–16
other articles, number of tons,................ 14–16
Albany & West Stockbridge railroad, amount of freight carried over each year from 1851 to 1866, inclusive:
whole number of tons, ... 5–34
products of forest, number of tons,............ 5–34
animals, number of tons, ... 5–34
vegetable food, number of tons, ... 5–34
other agricultural products, number of tons,.... 5–34
manufactures, number of tons,................ 5–34
merchandise, number of tons, ... 5–34
other articles, number of tons,................ 5–34
40. Alberger, Franklin A., testimony of relative to letting of canal contracts, 28th December, ... 821–39
testimony of, relative to combinations by canal contractors,.............................. 841–44
testimony of, relative to contract for repairs of section one, Erie canal, and dredging Albany basin, ... 825–27
refusal of to answer certain questions, ... 839–41
55. Albion Academy, appropriations to, ... 8–11
115. Aldrich & Stewart, statement of lands sold to,........ 90, 91
Aldrich, David, statement of lands sold to, ... 332
Aldrich, Seth, statement of lands sold to, ... 86, 283
Alrich, McDonald & Walton, statement of lands sold to, 90
Alrich, McDonald & Wells, statement of lands sold to,. 90
Alexander, Elisha, statement of lands sold to,........ 95
Alexander, J., statement of lands sold to, ... 205
Alexander, Samuel, statement of lands sold to,....... 95
Alexander, Wm. H., statement of lands sold to,...... 382
55. Alfred Academy, appropriations to, ... 8–11
14. Allegany Indian Reservation, quantity of land on,.... 1
population on, ... 1
agricultural statistics of, ... 4–8

No. Doc.		Page.
1, 12.	Allen, Augustus F., delegate 32d district, Chautauqua county,	3, 1
118.	report of, relative to taxation,	1, 2
115.	Allen, A. F., statement of lands sold to,	381
	Allen, Benjamin & Isaac, statement of lands sold to,.	212
	Allen, B., statement of lands sold to, 361,	368
	Allen, Clark, statement of land sold to,	103
1, 12.	Allen, Cornelius L., delegate 12th district, Washington county,	2, 1
115.	Allen, Doty, statement of lands sold to, 85,	199
	Allen, Hannah, statement of lands sold to,	123
1, 12.	Allen, Norman M., delegate 32d district, Chautauqua county,	3, 1
115.	Allen, Otis, statement of lands sold to, 305, 371, 372, 373, 384, 385,	386
	Allen, Richard L., statement of lands sold to,	38
	Allen, Geo. W., statement of lands sold to,	331
	Allen & Ewards, statement of lands sold to,	305
1, 12.	Alvord, Thos. G., delegate 22d district, Onondaga Co.,	3, 1
159.	testimony of, before committee on salt springs,	
115.	statement of lands sold to, 307, 325, 342,	366
55.	Amenia Seminary, appropriations to,	8, 11
54.	American Female Guardian Society, New York, report of donations to,	8
55.	appropriations to,	56–59
54.	American Seamen's Friends' Society, New York, report of donations to,	9
55.	Ames Academy, appropriations to,	8–11
28.	Ames, Sampson C., extra compensation paid to,	10
115.	Anable, Samuel, statement of lands sold to,	161
	Anderson, A. A., statement of lands sold to,	330
	Anderson, Jno., statement of lands sold to,	368
55.	Andes Collegiate Institute, appropriations to,	11
1, 12.	Andrews, Charles, delegate at large, Onondaga county,	1, 1
115.	Andrews, G. R., statement of lands sold to, 285, 313,	330
	Andrews, Hannibal, statement of lands sold to,	337
	Andrews, Luther, statement of lands sold to, ... 142, 144, 269, 297,	302
	Andrews, Judson, statement of lands sold to,	329
12.	Andrus, Byron, messenger, Monroe,	8

No. Doc. Page.

55. Angelica Academy, appropriations to, ... 10, 11
54. Anglo American Free Church of St. George the Martyr, New York, grant of land to, ... 19
55. Antwerp Liberal Literary Institute, appropriations to, 10, 11
18. Appeals decided and pending in Court of Appeals, .. 3
55. Arcade Academy, appropriations to,............... 11
54. Archbishop of New York, grant of land to, ... 22
1, 12. Archer, Ornon, delegate 25th district, Wayne county, 3, 1
115. Archibald, John, statement of lands sold to,.. 46, 47, 76, 88
233, 277, 301
Archibald, Thomas, statement of lands sold to,...... 142
55. Argyle Academy, appropriations to, ... 8–11
115. Armour, D., statement of lands sold to, ... 205
Armour, P., statement of lands sold to, ... 349
Armour, S. B., statement of lands sold to,.......... 360
Armour, V. M., statement of lands sold to, ... 363
Armsby, Israel, statement of lands sold to, ... 213
12. Armstrong, James, doorkeeper, New York,......... 8
1, 12. Armstrong, Jonathan P., delegate 12th district, Washington county, ... 2, 1
115. Armstrong, Thomas, statement of lands sold to, 243, 244
Armstrong, Wm., statement of lands sold to,........ 321
28. Arnold, Justin, extra compensation paid to,......... 10
115. Arnold, Levi, statement of lands sold to,........... 165
Arnold, Stakely, statement of lands sold to, ... 162
Ash, Barney, statement of lands sold to,............. 258
Aspinwall, Chauncey B., statement of lands sold to,.. 16
Aspinwall & Hurlbuts, statement of lands sold to, ... 17
30. Assembly, number and apportionment of members of, 2, 3
enumeration of inhabitants for subsequent apportionments, ... 3
compensation of speaker,.................. 3
members of, to be elected annually, ... 2, 3
49. amendment of Mr. Greeley relative to organization of, ... 2, 3
to provide for minority representation in,..... 3
districts, amendment of Mr. Greeley relative to apportionment of, ... 2
61. Assessors, election and term of office of, ... 2, 3
removal of,............................. 3

No. Doc. Page.

67. Assistant superintendents of public works, appointment and term of office of, ... 3
removal of, ... 3
86. provisions of minority report relative to, ... 1–6
55. Astoria Institute, appropriations to, ... 8–11
54. Asylum for Idiots, N. Y., report of donations to, ... 14
21. Atlantic & Great Western railroad, amount of freight carried over each year from 1862 to 1866, inclusive:
whole number of tons, ... 26–34
products of the forest, number of tons, ... 26–34
animals, number of tons, ... 26–34
vegetable food, number of tons, ... 26–34
other agricultural products, number of tons, .. 26–34
manufactures, number of tons, ... 26–34
merchandise, number of tons, ... 26–34
other articles, number of tons, ... 26–34
67. Attorney-General to be one of commissioners of canal fund, ... 1
73. to be member of executive council, ... 2
84. election and term of office of, ... 2, 3
compensation and powers and duties of, ... 4
qualifications required for eligibility to office of, 3
135. communication from, relative to alleged fraudulent canal contracts, ... 1–13
137. communication from, relative to payment of expenses of Convention, ... 4–6
115. Atwill, Ammon, statement of lands sold to, ... 286
Atwell, Paul, statement of lands sold to 93
55. Auburn Academy, appropriations to, ... 8–11
Auburn Female Seminary, appropriations to, ... 8–11
23. Auditor of Canal Department, report of relative to cost and revenues of canals, ... 1–39
28. report of, relative to extra compensation paid to canal contractors, ... 1–11
32. report of, relative to number of breaks in Erie canal and the cost of their repair, ... 1–4
36. report of, relative to cost, expense of repairs and amount of tolls and tonnage on Champlain canal, ... 1–8

No. Doc.		Page.
Auditor of Canal Department—*Continued.*
56.	report of, relative to contracts for repairs and improvements of canals,..................	1–148
67.	appointment and term of office of, ...	2
powers and duties of,..........................	1, 2
suspension or removal of,..................	2
report of, relative to statistics of Champlain canal, ...	1–8
120.	and Comptroller, report by, relative to moneys advanced for canals, ...	1–8
55.	Augusta Academy, appropriations to,..............	8–11
Aurora Academy, appropriations to,..............	8–11
115.	Austin, A. O., statement of lands sold to, ...	340
Austin, Elam, statement of lands sold to,...........	363
Austin, Moses, statement of lands sold to,...... 141,	143
Austin, Orrin, statement of lands sold to,...........	340
Austin, Orrin and Amos, statement of lands sold to,.	211
Austin, Sands H., statement of lands sold to, ...	124
Austin, Silas, statement of lands sold to, ...	202
Austin, Vincent, statement of lands sold to,.........	123
Austin, Wait and W. Jr., statement of lands sold to,.	124
Austin, Wm., statement of lands sold to,...........	348
Avery, B. G., statement of lands sold to,...........	324
Averill, Chas. K., statement of lands sold to,... 328,	329
Avery, J. N., statement of lands sold to,.............	381
28.	Avery, William, extra compensation paid to,........	11
21.	Avon, Genesee & Mt. Morris railroad, amount of freight carried over each year from 1860 to 1866, inclusive:
whole number of tons,.................. .	22–34
products of the forest, number of tons,......	22–34
animals, number of tons, ...	22–34
vegetable food, number of tons, ...	22–34
other agricultural products, number of tons, ..	22–34
manufactures, number of tons,..............	22–34
merchandise, number of tons, ...	22–34
other articles, number of tons,..............	22–34
1, 12.	Axtell, Nathan G., delegate 16th district, Clinton county, ...	2, 1
115.	Ayers, John, statement of lands sold to, ...	96

B.

No. Doc. Page.

115. Babcock, Geo. R., statement of lands sold to,........ 351
Babcock, Raymond P., statement of lands sold to,.... 141
Babcock, Russell, statement of lands sold to,........ 189
Bacon, Fred'k, statement of lands sold to,........... 239
Bagg, James L., statement of lands sold to,......... 382
149. Bail, not to be excessive,........................ 3
115. Bailey, B., statement of lands sold to,.............. 308
40. Bailey, Hardin, testimony of, relative to management of Champlain canal, ... 305–07
115. Bailey, David, statement of lands sold to,....... 26, 27, 29
Baker, Abraham, statement of lands sold to,........ 23
1, 12. Baker, Hezekiah, delegate 15th district, Montgomery county,.................................. 2, 1
115. Baker, Isaac V., statement of lands sold to, ... 341, 387
Baker, J., statement of lands sold to,.............. 206
Baker, J. & F. N., statement of lands sold to,....... 206
Baker, Luke, statement of lands sold to,........ 54, 60, 61
Baker, Palmer M., statement of lands sold to,....... 117
Baker, Selah, statement of lands sold to, ... 338
Baker, William, statement of lands sold to,......... 38
Baker, Ziba D., statement of lands sold to,......... 30
Baker & Abbott, statement of lands sold to,......... 361
Baldwin, Harvey, statement of lands sold to,.... 28, 239, 307, 342, 343
Baldwin, Jacob L., statement of lands sold to,....... 319
Baldwin, James, statement of lands sold to,......... 358
Baldwin, Joseph C., statement of lands sold to,...... 56
Baldwin, S. W., statement of lands sold to,......... 21
55. Baldwinsville Academy, appropriations to,.......... 11
23. Baldwinsville canal, income from, and disbursements for,............................. 30, 31, 38
cost of over revenues,.................... 39
55. Ball Seminary, appropriations to,.................. 8–11
28. Ball, Silas, extra compensation paid to,............ 4
1, 12. Ballard, Horatio, delegate 22d district, Cortland county, 3, 1
115. Ballow, William B., statement of lands sold to,...... 307
Bancroft, Joseph, statement of lands sold to,........ 232

No. Doc. Page.

115. Bangle, Joseph, statement of lands sold to, ... 337
28. Bangs, Anson, extra compensation paid to, ... 11
40. Bangs, Eli T., testimony of, relative to letting canal contracts, 28th December, ... 694–701
relative to combinations by canal contractors, 759–63
relative to payment of money to public officers, ... 701–04
relative to transactions between Canal Commissioner Whalen and Auditor Benton, ... 751–58, 763–65, 770–72
refusal to answer certain questions, ... 702–04
115. statement of lands sold to, ... 368
40. Bangs, Myron, testimony of, relative to contract for repairs of section one of Erie Canal, and dredging Albany basin, ... 671, 672
testimony of, relative to letting canal contracts, 28th December, ... 669–71
28. Bangs, Kingsley & Co., extra compensation paid to, .. 8
Bangs & Pratt, extra compensation paid to, ... 8
51. Banking Corporations, to provide for individual liability of stockholders in, 1, (also, Doc. No. 53,) 1, 2
53. bills or notes of, to be registered, ... 1
laws authorizing suspension of specie payments by, prohibited, ... 1
Banking, Currency and Insurance, (see "Currency.")
115. Barber, B. F., statement of land sold to, ... 208, 358
Barber, Ezekiel, statement of lands sold to, ... 136
Barber, Freeman, statement of lands sold to, ... 241
Barber, Hiram, statement of lands sold to, ... 103, 133
Barber, Ralph, statement of lands sold to, ... 85
Barber, Robert, statement of lands sold to, ... 199
Barber, Thomas, statement of lands sold to, ... 336
Barber, Zaccheus, statement of lands sold to, ... 211
Barhydt, T. D., statement of lands sold to, ... 94
28. Barhydt & Van Voorst, extra compensation paid to, .. 4
115. Barker, Andrew, statement of lands sold to, ... 160
Barker, E. A., statement of lands sold to, ... 354
Barker, Gardner T., statement of lands sold to, ... 87
1, 12. Barker, George, delegate 32d district, Chautauque Co., 3, 1

No. Doc. Page.

159. Barker, Jno. W., testimony of, before committee on salt springs, ... 6–10
115. Barker, Orlando, statement of lands to, ... 17
Barker, Uzel M., statement of lands sold to, ... 241, 242
Barley, William, statement of lands sold to, ... 39
1, 12. Barnard, Daniel P., delegate 2d district, Kings Co., .. 1, 1
115. Barnard, F. J., statement of lands sold to, ... 293, 311
Barnes, H. L., statement of lands sold to, ... 356
Barnes, Leman, statement of lands sold to, ... 334
Barnes, Linus B., statement of lands sold to, ... 355
Barnes, Philip, statement of lands sold to, ... 120
Barnes and Buck, statement of lands sold to, ... 356
Barnes and Dent, statement of lands sold to, ... 252
Barnes and Miller, statement of lands sold to, ... 350
Barney, Corse & Thorn, statement of land sold to, ... 118
Barnum, E. K., statement of lands sold to, ... 339
Barnum, Platt, statement of land sold to, ... 100
Barr, James, statement of lands sold to, ... 355
Barrett, Amos, statement of lands sold to, ... 47, 327
Barrett, David, statement of lands sold to, ... 275, 289
Barrett, D. W., statement of lands sold to, ... 332
Bartlett, Charles, statement of lands sold to, ... 79
Bartlett, Christopher, statement of lands sold to, ... 79
Bartlett, E., statement of lands sold to, ... 293
Bartlett, James, statement of lands sold to, ... 87
Bartlett, John, statement of lands sold to, ... 87
Bartlett, O. H., statement of lands sold to, ... 352
1, 12. Barto, Henry D., delegate at large, Tompkins county, 1, 1
115. Bartow, Benjamin, statement of lands sold to, ... 34, 35, 135, 143, 246
28. Barton, Theodore D., extra compensation paid to, ... 8
115. Barstow, E., statement of lands sold to, ... 206
Bascom, Ansel, statement of lands sold to, ... 313
40. Bascom, Oliver, testimony of, relative to management of Champlain canal, ... 320–29
55. Batavia Union School, appropriations to, ... 14, 15
115. Batchelder, Ivory, statement of lands sold to, ... 41
Bates, Ebenezer, statement of lands sold to, ... 88
Bates, Roswell, statement of lands sold to, ... 126
Bates & Twiss, statement of lands sold to, ... 332

No. Doc.		Page.
115.	Battershall, L. A., statement of lands sold to, ...	389
	Baxter, Benjamin, statement of lands sold to, ...	49
	Baxter & Ward, statement of lands sold to, ...	176
	Beach, Artemus, statement of lands sold to, ...	353
	Beach, Benjamin P., statement of lands sold to, ...	105
	Beach, Lyman, statement of lands sold to, ...	211
	Beadlestow, Job, statement of lands sold to, ...	144
1, 12.	Beadle, Tracy, delegate at large, Chemung county, ...	1, 1
	Beals, Oliver B., delegate 20th district, Herkimer Co.,	2, 1
115.	Beardsley, Jehiel, 2d, statement of lands sold to, ...	254
1, 12.	Beckwith, George M., delegate 16th district, Clinton county, ...	2, 2
115.	Becker, Hiram, statement of lands sold to, ...	241
	Beebe, Abijah, statement of lands sold to, ...	245
	Beebe, D. T. statement of lands sold to, ...	337
	Beebe, Eli, Jr., statement of lands sold to, ...	200
28.	Beebee, James L., and others, extra compensation paid to, ...	8
115.	Beebe, L., statement of lands sold to, ...	21
	Beebe, Martin, statement of lands sold to, ...	123
	Beebe, Thomas W., statement of lands sold to, ...	263
	Beebe, William L., statement of lands sold to, ...	15
	Beecher, S., statement of lands sold to, ...	323
	Beekman, J. S., statement of lands sold to, ... 148, 151, 152, 153, 154, 155, 156, 272,	150, 288
	Behan, Matthew, statement of lands sold to, ...	241
40.	Belden, James J., testimony of, relative to manner of letting contracts by contracting board, ...	782–85
	testimony of, relative to management of Champlain canal, ...	792–94
	testimony of, relative to contract for repairs of section one, Erie canal, and dredging Albany basin, ... 617–22,	657
	testimony of, relative to letting canal contracts, 28th December, ...	772–80
	testimony of, relative to his work for repairs of section nine, Erie canal, ...	786–92
	testimony of, relative to Kingsley Brook reservoir and certain locks on Chenango canal, .	794–96
115.	statement of lands sold to, ...	384

No. Doc. | | Page.
115. Belden, Sarah, statement of lands sold to,........... 86
Belknap, Zina, statement of lands sold to, ... 305
1, 12. Bell, James A., delegate 18th district, Jefferson county, 2, 2
115, Bell, John, heirs of, statement of lands sold to,...... 258
Bell, Willard, statement of lands sold to,........... 369
Bellair, Francis, statement of lands sold to, ... 231
55. Belleville Union Academy, appropriations to........ 50, 51
115, Bellor, Joseph, statement of lands sold to, ... 231, 232
28. Bellows, James, extra compensation paid to, ... 10, 11
115. Benedict, F. N., statement of lands sold to, ... 356, 376
Benedict, Lewis, statement of lands sold to, ... 235, 236
Benjamin, Caleb, statement of lands sold to, ... 97
Benjamin, Eli F., statement of lands sold to,........ 14
Benn, James, statement of lands sold to, ... 92
Bennett, Jesse, statement of lands sold to, . 336, 338, 339
Bennett, Oliver, statement of lands sold to, ... 131
Bennett, Phineas, statement of lands sold to,......... 241
Bentley, Richard, statement of lands sold to,........ 271
Bentley S., statement of lands sold to, ... 30
Benton, Alvah, statement of lands sold to,.......... 365
40. Benton, Nathaniel S., testimony of, relative to contract for repairs of section one Erie canal, and dredging Albany basin,.......... 617-22, 657
testimony of, relative to payment of money to public officers, ... 888-92
testimony of, relative to Contracting Board and letting of canal contracts 28th Dec.,...... 617-47
testimony of, relative to letting canal contracts 28th December,.......... 47, 76, 622-47, 902-06
testimony of, relative to award to Charles J. Degraw, ... 647-57, 907-12
95. testimony of, relative to management of canals, 57-66
1, 12, Bergen, Teunis G, delegate 3d district, Kings county,. 2, 2
86, Bergen, Mr., and Mr. Seymour, minority report of, on canals,...................................... 1-6
115. Best, Benjamin, statement of lands sold to, ... 99
55. Bethany Academy, appropriations to,.............. 12-15
115. Betsinger, Lewis, statement of lands sold to, ... 360
Betts, Daniel, statement of lands sold to,............ 141
Bevan, Thomas, statement of lands sold to, ... 92

No. Doc. Page.

115. Bevins, E., statement of lands sold to, ... 375
Bevins, John L., statement of lands sold to, ... 109
Bevins, Solon, statement of lands sold to, ... 354
Bickford, Joshua, statement of lands sold to, ... 242
1, 12. Bickford, Marcus, delegate 18th district, Jefferson Co., 2, 2
115. Bickford & Darling, statement of lands sold to, ... 343
98. Biennial sessions of the Legislature, provision for, ... 3
115. Bierce, Austin, statement of lands sold to, ... 92
Bidwell, Elias, statement of lands sold to, ... 115
28. Bigham, Stewart & Co., extra compensation paid to, .. 4
3. Bill of rights, provision for committee on, ... 1
9. committee on, ... 1
149. report of committee on, ... 1–6
175. article on, as amended and referred to committee on revision, ... 1–7
98. Bills, may originate in either branch of Legislature, .. 5
enacting clause of, ... 5
a majority of each house required for passage of, 5
cannot be revived after final rejection by either house, ... 5
to be signed by presiding officer in presence of members, ... 6
cannot be introduced during last five days of session, ... 5
legislative proceedings in case of veto of, ... 12
43. Bills relating to New York city, report of clerk of last Assembly, of titles of, ... 1–23
115. Bingham, Abial, statement of lands sold to, ... 107, 108
55. Binghamton Academy, appropriations to, ... 12–15
115. Bird, Wm. A., statement of lands sold to, ... 276
Bird & Holley, statement of lands sold to, ... 350 351
Bishop, Basil, statement of lands sold to, ... 79, 177
Bishop & Deming, statement of lands sold to, ... 174
Bissell, Noah, statement of lands sold to, ... 258
Bissell, Oliver, statement of lands sold to, ... 142
Black, Joseph, Jr., statement of lands sold to, ... 207
23. Black River canal, income from and disbursements for, 24, 25, 38
tolls contributed to Erie canal by, ... 25
proportion chargeable to, for repairs and maintenance of Erie and Champlain canals, ... 11, 25

No. Doc. Page.
23. Black River canal—*Continued.*
cost of, over revenues, ... 39
42. report of number of unsettled claims for damages on, ... 4
21. Black River & Utica railroad, amount of freight carried over each year from 1855 to 1860, inclusive:
whole number of tons, ... 12–22
products of the forest, number of tons, ... 12–22
animals, number of tons, ... 12–22
vegetable food, number of tons, ... 12–22
other agricultural products, number of tons,.. 12–22
manufactures, number of tons, ... 12–22
merchandise, number of tons, ... 12–22
other articles, number of tons, ... 12–22
115. Blair, Charles, statement of lands sold to,........... 232
Blair, Joseph, statement of lands sold to, ... 96
Blanchard, Hunneman, statement of lands sold to,... 13
Blass, Hiram, statement of lands sold to, ... 244
115. Bleekman, N. O., statement of lands sold to, ... 357
Bletsoe, John M., statement of lands sold to,........ 52–61
54. Blind Asylum, N. Y., graduates of, report of donations to, ... 14
Blind, Institution for, N. Y., report of donations to,.. 14
55. Blind Institution, New York city, appropriations by State to,.............................. 3–7, 92
54. Blind Mechanics' Institution, N. Y., report of donations to,.................................... 12
Blind of New York city, report of donations for,.... 14
55. Blind, New York State Institution for, appropriation to,.................................. 3–7, 92
115. Bliss, Lyman, statement of lands sold to,........... 340
Blodgett, Phineas, statement of lands sold to,....... 147
Blood, Gardner, statement of lands sold to,......... 147
Bloodgood, L. & S. D. W., statement of lands sold to, 248–9
Bloore, Joshua, statement of lands sold to,.......... 215
21. Blossburgh & Corning railroad, amount of freight carried over each year from 1855 to 1862, inclusive:
whole number of tons,.................... 12–26

No. Doc. Page.

21. Blossburgh & Corning railroad—*Continued.*
products of the forest, number of tons,....... 12-26
merchandise, number of tons,............... 12-26
other articles,........................... 12-26
115. Bly, Warren, statement of land sold to,............ 101
61. Boards of supervisors, powers and duties of,........ 5-7
equalization of representation in,........... 7
president of,............................ 6
28. Bogardus & Bell, extra compensation paid to,....... 4
115. Bolles, William B., statement of lands sold to, 38, 39, 257
Bolton, Daniel, statement of land sold to,........... 101
Bolton, Thos. E., statement of lands sold to,........ 354
55. Bond Street Homœopathic Dispensary, New York,
appropriations to, ... 79
54. report of donations to, ... 9
75. Bonding towns for benefit of corporations, prohibition
of, ... 2, 3
98. in aid of corporations, Legislature prohibited
from authorizing,...................... 7
115. Bonner, James, statement of lands sold to,.......... 360
Bordwell, Consider, statement of lands sold to,...... 117
Boughton, David, statement of lands sold to,........ 288
Boughton, John R., statement of lands sold to,...... 72
Bouton & Frisbie, statement of lands sold to, ... 141
66. Bounty debt, amount of,........................ 2
provision for payment of,.................. 4, 5
sinking fund, provisions for, ... 4, 5
115. Bovee, Abram, statement of lands sold to,.......... 361
Bovee, Fred'k, statement of lands sold to, ... 361
40. Bow, Mary, testimony of, relative to management of
Champlain canal,........................ 557-59
1, 12. Bowen, Levi F., delegate 29th district, Niagara county, 3, 2
115. Bayer, David, statement of lands sold to,........... 360
Boyd, Jno. H., statement of lands sold to,.. 295, 297, 329
Boyd, Jno. I., statement of lands sold to,.. 129, 176, 278
Boyd, Jno. L., statement of lands sold to,........... 348
Boyden, Justus, statement of lands sold to, ... 205
Boynton, N. C., statement of lands sold to, ... 354
Brace, Horace, statement of lands sold to, ... 235
Brace, Lester, statement of lands sold to, ... 320

No. Doc.		Page.
115.	Brackett, C. H., statement of lands sold to, ...	298
	Brackett, Wm. W., statement of lands sold to, ...	298
	Bradley, Geo., statement of lands sold to,...........	371
	Bradley, C. C., statement of lands sold to,..........	383
	Bradley, Geo., statement of lands sold to, ...	330
	Bradley & Underwood, statement of lands sold to, ...	365
	Bradt, Richard, statement of lands sold to,..........	107
28.	Brady & Hartnett, extra compensation of, ...	4
	Brady & Fitzsimmons, extra compensation paid to,...	4
115.	Braidwood & Dugan, statement of lands sold to,.....	243
	Brailey, Geo., statement of lands sold to,....... 250,	251
	Braman, Horace, statement of lands sold to, ...	378
	Bramhall, Edward, statement of lands sold to,.......	100
	Brandreth, statement of lands sold to,..............	194
28.	Brayton & Cheesebro, extra compensation paid to,....	4
	Brazell & Hurst, extra compensation paid to,........	9
	Brazell & McCann, extra compensation paid to,......	8
	Brazell, McCann & Dolphin, extra compensation paid to,	9
115.	Breed, A. S. & R., statement of lands sold to,.......	77
90.	Breed, Joseph, testimony of, relative to improvements of Erie canal,..............................	28–32
115.	Breese, S. S., statement of lands sold to,............	267
	Breese, Samuel, statement of lands sold to, ...	283
	Breese & Seymour, statement of lands sold to,.......	131
28.	Brentnall, Josiah, extra compensation paid to,.......	11
115.	Brewer, Erastus, statement of lands sold to,.........	211
	Brewster, David P., statement of lands sold to, .. 15,	16, 17
	Brewster, Isaac W., statement of lands sold to, ...	342
	Brewster, Thomas, statement of lands sold to, 75, 76,	309
11.	Bribery at elections, to be cause for excluding from suffrage, ...	1
15.	persons convicted of, to be deprived of elective franchise, ...	2
	Bribes received or promised, to deprive of suffrage,..	2
115.	Bridge, Amos, statement of lands sold to, ...	206
	Bridge, Jesse, statement of lands sold to,...........	212
	Bridge, Jonas, statement of lands sold to,...........	212
38.	Bridges, to vest power for erection, &c., of, in boards of supervisors,............................	1

No. Doc. Page.

115. Briggs, Benjamin, statement of lands sold to, 65, 66, 137
Briggs, Eliakim, statement of lands sold to,......... 126
40. Briggs, Ryal C., testimony of, relative to letting of canal contracts, 28th December, ... 106-24
115. Bristol, Daniel, statement of lands sold to,.......... 38
Bristol, William, statement of lands sold to, ... 17
28. Britton & Baldwin, extra compensation paid to,...... 4
55. Brockport Collegiate Institute, appropriations to,..... 12-15
115. Brodhead, Charles C., statement of lands sold to,.... 17, 31
Bronson, Alvin, statement of lands sold to,... 17, 19, 21
55. Brookfield Academy, appropriations to, ... 12-15
Brooklyn, Roman Catholic Orphan Asylum at, appropriations to, ... 60-63
Church Charity Foundation, appropriations to,· 70-71
City Hospital, appropriations to,............ 72-75
Central Dispensary, appropriations to, ... 78-79
Dispensary, appropriations to,.............. 76-79
Homœopathic Dispensary, appropriations to,.. 77-79
Graham Institute, appropriations to,......... 86, 90
Collegiate and Polytechnic Institute, appropriations to,............................ 12-15
Female Academy, appropriations to, ... 12-15
Orphan Asylum, appropriations to,.......... 56-59
Industrial School Association, appropriations to, 58, 59
112. legislative power of, to be vested in a common council, ... 2
aldermen of, their election, classification and term of office, ... 2
officers of board of aldermen, how chosen,... 3
assistant aldermen of, number, election, and term of office of, ... 2
assistant aldermen of, officers of board of, how chosen, ... 3
comptroller of, election and term of office of,.. 3, 4
comptroller of, to appoint subordinate officers,. 3
comptroller of, removal of,................ 3, 4
veto power of mayor of,................... 3
receiver of taxes, election and term of office of,. 3, 4
receiver of taxes, to appoint his subordinates, 3
receiver of taxes, removal of, ... 3, 4

No. Doc. Page.
115. Brooks, Horace, statement of lands sold to,......... 145
1, 12. Brooks, Elijah P., delegate 27th district, Chemung county,.................................... 3, 2
1, 12. Brooks, Erastus, delegate 1st district, Richmond county,.............................. 1, 2
25. resolution of, relative to local or special legislation,................................. 1, 2
119. amendment proposed by, to section 1 of article on finance,............................ 1
1, 12. Brooks, James, delegate 7th district, New York county 2, 2
115. Brooks, Naomi, statement of lands sold to,.......... 137
Broughton, Samuel, statement of lands sold to,...... 283
1, 12. Brown, Edward A., delegate 18th district, Lewis county, 22
115. Brown, E. J., statement of lands sold to,............ 380
Brown, Geo. W., statement of lands sold to, ... 238
Brown, Jabez, statement of lands sold to,........... 340
Brown, J. C., statement of lands sold to,............ 234
40. Brown, Jeremiah, testimony of, relative to management of Champlain canal,................. 351, 352
115. Brown, John, statement of lands sold to,........ 97, 335
Brown, Joseph, statement of lands sold to, ... 231
Brown, Nathan, statement of lands sold to,......... 96
Brown, Oliver, statement of lands sold to, ... 208
Brown, Robert, statement of lands sold to,.......... 336
Brown, Thomas, statement of lands sold to,......... 64
Brown, William, statement of lands sold to, ... 47
1, 12. Brown, William C., delegate 17th district, St. Lawrence county,................................ 2, 2
115. Brown and Carpenter, statement of lands sold to,.... 208
Brown & Spier, statement of lands sold to, 108, 109, 111, 112
40. Bruce, Benjamin F., testimony of relative to letting canal contracts, 28th December, ... 797–806
testimony of, relative to repairs of section 9, Erie canal,.......................... 806–11
testimony of, relative to manner of letting contracts by contracting board, ... 811, 812
testimony of, relative to contract for repairs of section one, Erie canal and dredging Albany basin, ... 800–802

No. Doc. Page.

40. Bruce, Benjamin F., refusal of, to answer certain questions, ... 812, 813
115. Bruce, Joseph, statement of lands sold to, ... 49, 74, 134
Bryant, Oliver, statement of lands sold to, ... 361
Buck, Hiram, statement of lands sold to, 289, 295, 297, 299
326, 327, 343, 352, 353, 354, 355, 377
Buck, Samuel, statement of lands sold to, ... 262
Buck & Knox, statement of lands sold to, ... 343
40. Buckley, Patrick, testimony of, relative to management of Champlain Canal, ... 546–50
115. Bucklin, Isaac B., statement of lands to, ... 161
Buckman, John S., statement of lands sold to, ... 44
Buell, Jesse, statement of lands sold to, ... 266
Buell & Hoggart, statement of lands sold to, ... 359
55. Buffalo Central School, appropriations to, ... 14, 15
City Dispensary, appropriations to, ... 77–79
Providence Lunatic Asylum, appropriations to, 90
Female Academy, appropriations to, ... 13–15
23. merchandise from other States entering Erie canal at, ... 15
55. Orphan Asylum, appropriations to, ... 56–59
St. John's Orphan's Home, appropriations to.. 59
Le Couteulx Deaf and Dumb Asylum, appropriations to, ... 63
St. Joseph's Male Orphan Asylum, appropriations to, ... 65–67
St. Vincent's Female Orphan Asylum, appropriations to, ... 64–67
St. Vincent's Infant Asylum, appropriations to, 65–67
St. Mary's Orphan Asylum, appropriations to, 66, 67
Church Charity Foundation, appropriations to, 71
General Hospital, appropriations to, ... 74–75
Hospital, Sisters of Charity, appropriations to, 72–75
St. Mary's Lying-in Hospital, appropriations to, 73–75
107. Superior Court, provisions relative to, ... 8, 9
21. Buffalo, Corning and New York railroad, amount of freight carried over, each year from 1852 to 1856, inclusive:
whole number of tons, ... 6–14

No. Doc. Page.

21. Buffalo, Corning and New York railroad—*Continued.*

product of the forest, number of tons,....... 6–14
animals, number of tons, ... 6–14
vegetable food, number of tons, ... 6–14
other agricultural products, number of tons,.. 6–14
manufactures, number of tons, ... 6–14
merchandise, number of tons,.............. 6–14
other articles, number of tons,.............. 6–14

Buffalo & New York City railroad, amount of freight carried over, each year from 1853 to 1855, inclusive:

whole number of tons, ... 8–12
products of the forest, number of tons,....... 8–12
animals, number of tons, ... 8–12
vegetable food, number of tons,............. 8–12
other agricultural products, number of tons,.. 8–12
manufactures, number of tons,.............. 8–12
merchandise, number of tons, ... 8–12
other artitcles, number of tons, ... 8–12

Buffalo, New York & Erie railroad, amount of freight carried over, each year from 1858 to 1865, inclusive:

whole number of tons,.................... 18–32
products of the forest, number of tons, ... 18–32
animals, number of tons, ... 18–32
vegetable food, number of tons, ... 18–32
other agricultural products, number of tons,.. 18–32
manufactures, number of tons, ... 18–32
merchandise, number of tons,.............. 18–32
other articles, number of tons,............. 18–32

Buffalo & Niagara Falls railroad, amount of freight carried over, each year from 1851 to 1853, inclusive:

whole number of tons,.................... 5–8
products of the forest, number of tons, ... 5–8
animals, number of tons, ... 5–8
vegetable food, number of tons, ... 5–8
other agricultural products, number ot tons,.. 5–8
manufactures, number of tons, ... 5–8

No. Doc. Page.

21. Buffalo and Niagara Falls railroad—*Continued.*
merchandise, number of tons, ... 5–8
other articles, number of tons,............... 5–8
Buffalo & Rochester railroad, amount of freight carried over, each year from 1851 to 1853, inclusive:
whole number of tons,.................... 5–8
products of the forest, number of tons,...... 5–8
animals, number of tons,.................. 5–3
vegetable food, number of tons, ... 5–8
other agricultural products, number of tons,.. 5–8
manufactures, number of tons, ... 5–8
merchandise, number of tons, ... 5–8
other articles, number of tons,.............. 5–8
Buffalo & State Line railroad, amount of freight carried over, each year from 1852 to 1866, inclusive:
whole number of tons, ... 6–34, 39
products of the forest, number of tons, ... 6–34, 39
animals, number of tons,................ 6–34, 39
vegetable food, number of tons,.......... 6–34, 39
other agricultural products, number of tons, 6–34, 39
manufactures, number of tons, ... 6–34, 39
merchandise, number of tons,............ 6–34, 39
other articles, number of tons, ... 6–34, 39

115. Bull, Absalom, statement of lands sold to,.......... 320
Bull, Edward, statement of lands sold to, ... 164

12. Bull, George W., reporter, Erie,.................. 9

115. Bull, Harvey, statement of lands sold to,........... 142

40. Bullard, Daniel A., testimony of, relative to management of Champlain canal, ... 613–17

115. Bulger, Patrick, statement of lands sold to, ... 205
Bunner, Rudolph, statement of lands sold to, ... 14
Burbank, Daniel, statement of lands sold to, ... 111
Burckle, C. J., statement of lands sold to,... 18, 338, 339
Burdick, A., statement of lands sold to,............ 295
Burge, Calvin, statement of lands sold to, ... 250
Burgess, Martin, statement of lands sold to,......... 117

98. Burial grounds, may be exempted from taxation, ... 10

28. Burlingame, Platt, extra compensation paid to, ... 8

115. Burlison, Wm., statement of lands sold to, ... 209
Burnham, Cyrus, statement of lands sold to, ... 91

No. Doc.		Page.
115.	Burnham, Eleazer, statement of lands sold to,... 237,	242
1, 12.	Burrill, John E., delegate 4th district, New York Co.,	2, 2
115.	Burrington, Jno., statement of lands sold to, ...	242
40.	Burrows, Orlando F., testimony of, relative to management of Champlain canal, ...	343–51
115.	Burt, Benjamin, statement of lands sold to, ...	17
	Burt, James, statement of lands sold to,............	144
	Burton, Jesse, P., statement of lands sold to,........	86
	Burton, Wm., statement of lands sold to,...........	132
	Burwell, Isaac, statement of lands sold to,..........	163
	Burwell, Jno., statement of lands sold to,...........	322
	Buryea, David, statement of land sold to, ...	362
	Bush, Charles, statement of lands sold to, ...	231
	Bush, David, statement of lands sold to,............	231
	Bushnell, James, statement of lands sold to, ...	49
	Bushnell, Zina, statement of lands sold to,..........	305
3.	Business of Convention, report by committee of sixteen of plan for,............................	1, 2
115.	Butler, B., statement of lands sold to,.............	376
	Butler, Charles, statement of lands sold to, ...	304
95.	Butler, Richard T., testimony of, relative to management of canals, ...	82, 83
115.	Buyce, Jno., statement of lands sold to, ...	189
	Buys, James A., statement of lands sold to, ...	146
	Byrne, Elizabeth, statement of lands sold to,........	206
	Byrne, John & Samuel, statement of lands sold to,...	93

C.

No. Doc.		Page.
115.	Cady, Daniel, statement of land sold to, ... 99, 149,	273
	Cady, Heman, statement of lands sold to,.. 199, 254,	255
	Cady, John W., statement of lands sold to,.........	108
	Cady & Bloore, statement of lands sold to,..........	253
	Cadwell, Elias, statement of lands sold to,...... 302,	312
	Caldwell, Absalom, statement of lands sold to,......	112
12.	Caldwell, Luther, Secretary, Chemung,..............	8
115.	Caldwell, Samuel, statement of lands sold to,........	113
	Caldwell & Harris, statement of lands sold to,.......	286
12.	Calkins, Hiram, reporter, New York,...............	9
115,	Calkins, W. E., statement of lands sold to,..... 327,	329

No. Doc.		Page.
115.	Calkins, Norman, statement of lands sold to,........	47
	Caulkin, Caleb, statement of lands sold to,..........	288
	Call, Joel, statement of lands sold to,..............	238
	Call, Joseph, statement of lands sold to,.. 52, 53, 57, 61, 164, 166, 168, 222, 233, 234,	58, 267
55.	Cambridge Washington Academy, appropriations to,.	12–15
115.	Cameron, James, statement of lands sold to,.... 331,	332
	Camp, Thomas S., statement of lands sold to, ...	211
	Campbell, R. A., statement of lands sold to, ...	311
	Campbell, Sylvanus, statement of lands sold to, ...	123
55.	Canajoharie Academy, appropriations to,...........	12–15
3.	Canals, provision for committee on,................	2
9.	committee on,............................	3
40.	report of testimony taken by committee to investigate management of,................	928
95.	additional testimony relative to management of,	1–86
42.	report of number of unsettled claims for damages on, ...	4
56.	minority report on, relative to lateral canals,..	1
62.	minority report relative to superintendents of public works,.........................	1–7
10.	report of Commissioners of Canal Fund relative to cost, income, &c., of,..............	1–4
57.	contracts for repairs of, report of Auditor relative to,................................	1–148
	names of present contractors and terms of contracts for repairs of,.....................	5
	notices to contractors for repairs of,... 12–27, 34–46 55–71,	79–148
	western division, notices for proposals for repairs of,....................... 12, 38,	59, 83
	middle division, notice for proposals for repairs of, ... 16, 57, 81, 111, 119,	137
	eastern division, notices for proposals for repairs of.......... 16, 35, 44, 55, 79, 119,	127
64.	number of tons of wheat and flour reaching the Hudson river by, each year from 1852 to 1866, inclusive,......................	14
	number of tons transported on, each year, from 1853 to 1866, inclusive, ...	15, 16

No. Doc.		Page.
	Canals — *Continued.*	
64.	number of lockages to and from Hudson river each year, from 1847 to 1866, inclusive,....	16
	lockage capacity of,......................	16, 17
23.	cost and revenues of, report of auditor relative to,	1–39
	amount contributed, prior to 1846, for construction of, ...	6
	lands donated to, for construction of, ...	6
	contributions to treasury from, ...	7
	taxes levied since 1846, for, ...	7
87.	report of majority of committee on,.........	1–27
	tonnage and value of, carried on each year, from 1837 to 1866, inclusive,............	14
	plan for enlargement of, and cost thereof,.....	18–25
66, 67.	sale or lease of, prohibited,.................	6, 8
67.	article reported by committee on, ...	1–8
	provisions for enlargement and improvement of,	6, 7
85.	minority report of Mr. Champlain on, ...	1–3
86.	minority report of Messrs. Seymour and Bergen on, ...	1–6
61.	subordinate officers and employees on, how appointed,............................	4
98.	Legislature prohibited from authorizing sale or lease of,............................	8, 9
120.	payments from general fund on account of,....	4–8
134.	article on, as amended in committee of the whole, ...	1–5
153.	article on, as amended and referred to committee on revision,........................	1–4
42.	Canal Appraisers, report of, relative to unsettled claims before board of, ...	1–4
67.	provision for abolishing office of,...........	4
	Canal Board, provision for abrogation of, ...	4
164.	report by, of capacity of Erie canal locks to pass boats eastward, ...	1–74
67.	Canal bridges, provision and restrictions relative to,..	4
	Canal Commissioners, provision for abolishing office of,	4
89.	report of, relative to number of breaks in Erie canal, ...	1–7

No. Doc.		Page.
28.	Canal Contractors, report of Auditor relative to extra compensation paid to,	1–11
135.	Canal contracts, communication from Attornel-General relative to,	1–13
42.	Canal damages, report of Canal Appraisers relative to unsettled claims for,	1–4
67.	provisions and restrictions relative to,	4, 5
23.	Canal debt, amount of,	5
	annual interest on,	5
66.	Canal debt of 1846, so called,	1
	under amendment of 1854,	1
	floating,	1
	sinking fund, advances to by taxation since 1846,	2
120.	Canal fund, contributions from to general fund, from 1841 to 1866, inclusive,	2, 3
28.	Canal repairs, report of Auditor relative to extra compensation paid for,	10, 11
66.	Canal revenues, disposition to be made of,	2–4
69.	Canal stock debt, statement of and provisions for paying,	5–8
23.	Canal tolls, net amount of for 7 years,	5
67.	by whom fixed and regulated,	1
55.	Canandaigua Academy, appropriations to,	12–15
21.	Canandaigua & Elmira railroad, amount of freight carried over, each year from 1852 to 1856, inclusive, and the year 1858:	
	whole number of tons,	6–14
	products of the forest, number of tons,	6–14
	animals, number of tons,	6–14
	vegetable food, number of tons,	6–14
	other agricultural products, number of tons,	6–14
	manufactures, number of tons,	6–14
	merchandise, number of tons,	6–14
	other articles, number of tons,	6–14
	Canandaigua & Niagara Falls railroad, amount of freight carried over, during each of the years 1853, 1855 and 1856:	
	whole number of tons,	8–14
	products of the forest, number of tons,	8–14

No. Doc. Page.
21. Canandaigua & Niagara Falls railroad—*Continued.*
animals, number of tons, ... 8–14
vegetable food, number of tons, ... 8–14
other agricultural products, number of tons, .. 8–14
manufactures, number of tons, ... 8–14
merchandise, number of tons, ... 8–14
other articles, number of tons, ... 8–14
55. Canandaigua St. Mary's Orphan Asylum, appropriations to, ... 65–67
40. Candee, Horace, testimony of relative to Snook and Beebe award, ... 765–70
28. Candee, William & Co., extra compensation paid to, .. 8
55. Canton Academy, appropriations to, ... 12–15
115. Card, Daniel, statement of lands sold to, ... 23
Carmichael, Daniel, statement of lands sold to, ... 111
28. Carmichael, Brayton & Co., extra compensation paid to, 4
115. Carnicrosse, Isaac, statement of lands sold to, ... 242
Carnrike, John G., statement of lands sold to, ... 108
1, 12. Carpenter, B. Platt, delegate 11th district, Dutchess county 2, 2
115. Carpenter, Joseph, statement of lands sold to, ... 98
Carrington, Elisha, statement of lands sold to, ... 14, 23
Carrington, F. T., statement of lands sold to, .. 15, 17, 18, 21
40. Carrington, Levi, testimony of, relative to management of Champlain canal, ... 421–27
115. Carrington & Pardee, statement of lands sold to, 30, 338, 339
Carter, Charles, statement of lands sold to, ... 20, 21
Carter, John, statement of lands sold to, ... 34, 209, 321
Carter, Joseph, statement of lands sold to, ... 335
Carver, Austin, statement of lands sold to, ... 207
55. Cary Collegiate Seminary, appropriations to, ... 12–15
115. Carey, James, statement of lands sold to, ... 12
Cary, Jno., statement of lands sold to, ... 202
40. Cary, Owen, testimony of, relative to management of Champlain canal, ... 576, 577
Case, Charles E., testimony of, relative to letting of canal contracts, 28th December, ... 191–214
28. extra compensation paid to, ... 11
Case, George M., extra compensation paid to, ... 11
115. Case, Hosea, statement of lands sold to, ... 341

No. Doc. Page.
40. Case, John, testimony of, relative to management of Champlain canal,.......................... 563-65
115. Case, Jonathan, statement of lands sold to, 21, 22, 235, 237
28. Case, Joseph G., extra compensation paid to,........ 4
1, 12. Case, Lester M., delegate 21st district, Madison county, 2, 2
40. Case, William N., testimony of, relative to Kingsley Brook reservoir and certain locks on Chenango canal,......................... 704-08
testimony of, relative to points taken in declaring bids informal, ... 708-10
115. Case & Hinman, statement of lands sold to,......... 209
1, 12. Cassidy, William, delegate 13th district, Albany Co.,.. 2, 2
28. Caswell, Shippy & Co, extra compensation paid to,... 4
115. Catlin, S., statement of lands sold to,.......... 175, 176
14. Cattaraugus Indians, number of, ... 2
quantity of land on reservation, ... 2
agricultural statistics of,.................. 4-8
12. Caypless, Edgar, messenger, Albany, ... 8
55. Cayuga Academy, appropriations to,............... 12-15
Cayuga Lake Academy, appropriations to,.......... 14, 15
14. Cayuga Indians, relative to, ... 2
23. Cayuga inlet, income from and disbursements for, 36, 37, 38
revenues of, over cost,..................... 39
55. Cayuga Orphan Asylum, appropriations to, ... 57-59
23. Cayuga and Seneca canal, income from and disbursements for,............................ 16, 17
tolls contributed by, to Erie canal, ... 16, 38
proportion chargeable to, for repairs and maintenance of Erie and Champlain canals,..... 11, 17
cost of, over revenues,.................... 39
42. report of unsettled claims for damages on,.... 4
57. notice for proposals for repairs of, ... 59, 83, 100, 103, 106
21. Cayuga & Susquehanna railroad, amount of freight carried over each year from 1851 to 1866, inclusive:
whole number of tons,.................... 5-34
products of the forest, number of tons, ... 5-34
animals, number of tons, ... 5-34
vegetable food, number of tons, ... 5-34

No. Doc. Page.

21. Cayuga & Susquehanna railroad—*Continued.*
other agricultural products, number of tons, .. 5–34
manufactures, number of tons, ... 5–34
merchandise, number of tons, ... 5–34
other articles, number of tons, ... 5–34

55. Central Homœopathic Dispensary, New York, appropriations to, ... 79

28. Chambers, Adams & Chambers, extra compensation paid to, ... 4

1, 12. Champlain, Marshall B., delegate at large, Allegany county, ... 1, 2

85. minority report of, on canals, ... 1–4

55. Champlain Academy, appropriations to, ... 12–15

36. Champlain canal, report of Auditor relative to cost, expense of maintenance, and amount of tolls and tonnage of, ... 1–8
original cost of, ... 4, 6, 7
tolls received from, from 1826 to 1866, inclusive, ... 4, 6, 7
cost of collection, superintendence and ordinary repairs of, ... 4, 6, 7
tonnage carried on, from 1838 to 1866, inclusive, ... 4, 6, 7
excess of tolls on, over superintendence and repairs, ... 4
estimated tonnage carried on, from 1826 to 1837, inclusive, ... 4

42. report of number of unsettled claims for damages on, ... 4

69. report of Auditor relative to statistics of, ... 1–8
original cost of, and interest thereon, ... 4, 6, 7, 8
cost of enlargements and improvements, and interest thereon, ... 4, 6, 7, 8
cost of collection, superintendence and repairs, and interest thereon, ... 4, 6, 7, 8
income of, and interest thereon, ... 4, 6, 7, 8
excess of expenditures on, over income of, ... 4, 8

22. Chancery fund, held by Court of Appeals, ... 6–8, 19–23

115. Chapman, Chas., statement of lands sold to, ... 249
Chapman, G. S., statement of lands sold to, ... 313

No: Doc. Page.
28. Chapman, H., and others, extra compensation paid to, 8
115. Chapman, S., statement of lands sold to,............ 364
Chapman, Stephen R., statement of lands sold to, 282, 285
Chappel & Hart, statement of lands sold to,......... 205
4. Charities, public and private, to provide for committee on, ... 2
9. Charities and charitable institutions, committee on,... 5
106. article reported by committee on, ... 1–4
explanatory report by committee on, ... 4–11
board of commissioners of, provisions for,.... 1, 2
endowment of, provisions relative to, ... 2, 3
conditions requisite for State aid to, ... 3
powers and duties of board of commissioners of, 2, 3
provisions for investment of funds donated to, 3, 4
105. minority report of Mr. Livingston relative to, 1, 2
101. Charitable institutions, dissent of minority of committee, against prohibition of donations to,.... 1
98. appropriations to by State prohibited, ... 6
54. Charitable institutions in the city of New York, report of Comptroller relative to donations to,.......... 1–23
55. Charitable and Educational institutions, report by Comptroller of appropriations to,............... 1–92
115. Chase, Edwin R., statement of lands sold to,........ 64, 65
Chase, Henry, statement of lands sold to,.... 85, 199 268
Chase, R. C. R., statement of lands sold to, ... 352
90. Chase, Sylvanus G., testimony of, relative to improvements of Erie canal, ... 6–12
115. Cheeseman & Brewer, statement of lands sold to, ... 94
34. Chemung canal, report of State Engineer relative to cost of enlarging locks on,............... 1–8
detailed estimate of cost of enlarging locks on, 4–8
42. report of number of unsettled claims for damages on,.......................... 4
23. income from and disbursements for,... 18, 19, 38
tolls contributed to Erie canal,.............. 19
proportion chargeable to, for repairs and maintenance of Erie and Champlain canals,..... 11, 19
cost of, over revenues, ... 39
57. notice for proposals for repairs of,. 57, 81, 99, 102
105

No. Doc.		Page.
23.	Chenango canal, income from and disbursements for,.	22, 23
		38
	tolls contributed by, to Erie canal, ...	23
	proportion chargeable to, for repairs and maintenance of Erie and Champlain canals,.....	11, 23
	cost of, over revenues,.....................	39
42.	extension, unsettled claims for damages on,...	4
57.	notice for proposals for repairs of,.. 110, 135,	142
70.	report of State Engineer, relative to state of work on extension of, and cost of completing the same, ...	1–6
	estimated cost of extension at contract prices,.	3–6
	amount expended on extension of, ...	3–6
	amount required to complete extension of,....	3–6
	amount appropriated for extension of,........	6
115.	Cheney, A. N., statement of lands sold to,..........	74
	Cheney & Arms, statement of lands sold to,.........	73, 74
115.	Cheritree, Anna E., statement of lands sold to, 71, 96, 217, 224, 225, 226, 288, 302, 310, 312, 328, 331, 332,	100, 344
1, 12.	Cheritree, Andrew J., delegate 16th district, Warren county, ...	2, 2
55.	Cherry Valley Academy, appropriations to,.........	12, 15
1, 12.	Chesebro, Henry O., delegate at large, Ontario county,	1, 2
55.	Chester Academy, appropriations to,...............	12, 15
54.	Childrens' Aid Society, N. Y., report of donations to,	7
115.	Childs, Theodore P., statement of lands sold to, ...	348
1, 12.	Church, Sanford E., delegate at large, Orleans county,	1, 2
54.	Church of the Redeemer, Yorkville, grant of land to,	23
98.	Churches may be exempted from taxation,..........	10
55.	Cincinnatus Academy, appropriations to, ...	14, 15
107.	Circuit Courts, provision for, ...	7
3.	Cities, provision for committees on,................	2
9.	committee on,...........................	3
112.	article reported by committee on, ...	1–6
109.	minority report of Mr. Murphy on,.........	1–3
114.	minority report of Mr. Francis, relative to,...	1–7
138.	article reported by minority of committee on,.	1–7
	explanatory report of minority of committee on,	7–13
173.	article on, as amended and referred to committee on revision, ...	1–3

No. Doc.		Page.
101.	Cities, argument against government of, by commissions,	2–11
112.	legislative power of, how vested,	2
	heads of departments of, to be appointed by mayors,	4
	local judicial officers of, their election and term of office,	4, 5
	commissions for government of, to be abolished,	5
	general laws to be enacted for incorporation of,	5
	time for elections in,	5
	laws for government of, to be codified,	6
	taxation for city purposes to be determined by the authorities thereof,	6
	mayors of, their election and term of office,	1
	to be ineligible for reëlection at succeeding election,	1
	to hold no other office,	1
	how removable,	2
107.	judicial officers of, provision relative to,	11
126.	Citizens' Association, communication from, relative to Metropolitan commissions,	1–26
4.	Claims, to provide for committee on,	2
39.	against the State, to require general laws for adjustment of,	1
115.	Clapp, E. W., statement of lands sold to,	139
	Clapp, Otis, statement of lands sold to, . 87, 132, 139,	147 267
55.	Clarence Academy, appropriations to, ... 14,	15
115.	Clark, Charles, statement of lands sold to,	117
	Clark, David, statement of lands sold to,	320
	Clarke, Edwin W., statement of lands sold to, ... 26,	27
1, 12.	Clarke, Freeman, delegate 28th district, Monroe county,	3, 2
4.	resolution of, for amendment of preamble,	3
64.	minority report of, relative to finance,	9–21
	financial article reported by,	1–8
102.	communication from, relative to his report on finance,	1, 2
115.	Clarke, H. E., statement of lands sold to,	368
	Clark, Henry W., statement of lands sold to,	237

No. Doc. Page.

88. Clark, James, testimony of, relative to capacity of Erie canal locks, ... 7–11
40. Clark, James C., testimony of, relative to management of Champlain canal, ... 536, 537, 538
115. Clark, James W., statement of lands sold to, ... 359
Clark, Jehiel, statement of lands sold to, ... 15
Clark, Joseph, statement of lands sold to, ... 232
Clark, Jaline, statement of lands sold to, ... 138
Clark, Orville, statement of lands sold to, ... 331–33, 344
Clark, Solomon, statement of lands sold to, ... 113
Clark, Sylvester, statement of lands sold to, ... 272, 300
28. Clark & Wheeler, extra compensation paid to, ... 4
55. Clarkson Academy, appropriations to, ... 12–15
115. Clary, Joseph, statement of lands sold to, ... 36, 145, 276
Clary & Allen, statement of lands sold to, ... 37
55. Claverack Academy and Hudson River Institute, appropriations to, ... 12–15
115. Claxton, George, statement of lands sold to, ... 293
43. Clerk of last Assembly, report by, of titles of bills relating to New York city, ... 1–23
45. report by, of titles of bills relating to corporations, introduced at last session of Assembly, 1–48
18. Clerk of Court of Appeals, report of, relative to number of cases in, ... 1, 3
22. report of, relative to trust fund in charge of, .. 1–24
107. provision relative to appointment and removal of, ... 3
to keep his office at the seat of government, .. 12
compensation of to be fixed by law, ... 12
115. Cleveland, H. H., statement of lands sold to, ... 361
55. Clifton St. Mary's Orphan Asylum, appropriations to, 65–67
115. Cline, George, statement of lands sold to, ... 232
Cline, M. & G., statement of lands sold to 232
55. Clinton Academy, appropriations to, ... 16–19
Grammar School, appropriations to, ... 16–19
Liberal Institute, appropriations to, ... 16–19
1, 12. Clinton, Geo. W., delegate 31st district, Erie county, . 3, 2
116. Clinton, Mr., dissent of, from report on education, ... 4
55. Clover Street Seminary, Rochester, appropriations to, 16–19

No. Doc. Page.

20. Coal transportation on Genesee Valley canal, prospective increase of, ... 2–4
Coal companies, arrangements of, for shipping coal on Genesee Valley canal, ... 3
115. Coates, Sarah H., statement of lands sold to, ... 383
Cobb, Sanford, statement of lands sold to, ... 73
Cochran, James, statement of lands sold to, 14, 16, 20, 21, 31
1, 12. Cochran, Robert, delegate 9th district, Westchester Co., 2, 2
115. Coddington, J. M., statement of lands sold to, ... 240
Cody & Leavenworth, statement of lands sold to, ... 304
1, 12. Colahan, Stephen I., delegate 3d district, Kings Co., .. 2, 2
4. ..... resolution of, for committee on education, ... 1
115. Cole, Daniel W., statement of lands sold to, .. 14, 15, 22, 26
Cole, Delos W., statement of lands sold to, ... 360
Cole, Elisha, statement of lands sold to, ... 211
Cole, Jno. B., statement of lands sold to, ... 274
Cole, Welcome, statement of lands sold to, ... 244
28. Cole, Caulkins & Richardson, extra compensation paid to, ... 4
40. Coleman, Edward, testimony of, relative to management of Champlain canal, ... 289–98
115. Collar, Joshua, statement of lands sold to, ... 250
61. Collector, election and term of office of, ... 2, 3
removal of, ... 3
47. College land scrip, donated by United States, report of Commissioners of Land Office, relative to, .. 1–24
act of 1866, relative to, ... 9, 10
failure of People's College to comply with act of 1863, relative to, ... 3
proposition of Ezra Cornell, relative to, ... 5–7
agreements for purchase of by Ezra Cornell, .. 8–18
amount of, delivered to Mr. Cornell, ... 23
116. College land scrip fund, capital to be paid into treasury, 1
revenues of, to be applied to support of Cornell University, ... 2
investment of, ... 2
55. Colleges, universities &c., appropriations to, from 1847 to 1866, inclusive, ... 92
115. Collins, Jno., statement of lands sold to. 241
Collins, Jeremiah, statement of lands sold to, ... 232

No. Doc. Page.

54. Colored Home, N. Y., report of donations to, ... 12
55. Colored children's schools, appropriations to, ... 85, 90
54. Colored Orphans' Asylum, N. Y., report of donations to, 6
grant of land to, ... 23
115. Colver, Nathaniel, statement of lands sold to, ... 126
101. Commissions for government of cities, argument of minority of committee against, ... 2-11
107. Commissioners of Appeals, provisions relative to, ... 3, 4
provision for new, appointment of, ... 4
10. Commissioners of Canal Fund, report of relative to cost, income, &c., of canals, ... 1-4
67. composition of board of, ... 1
powers and duties of, ... 1, 2
61. Commissioners of highways (see "highway commissioners").
27. Commissioners of Land Office, report of, relative to salt reservations, ... 1-31
47. report of, relative to sale of lands donated by the United States, ... 1-24
97. report by, of lands granted to certain railroads, 1-12
115. report by, of unsold lands belonging to school fund, ... 5-9
report by, of school lands sold by State Engineer and Surveyor, ... 11, 392
54. Commissioners of Public Charities and Correction, N. Y., report of donations to be disbursed by, ... 16
13. Commissioners of Taxes and Assessments, New York city, report of, relative to number of tax payers in, 1, 2
77. Commissioners of Taxes and Assessments, report of relative to value of property belonging to religious denominations in city of New York, exempt from taxation, ... 1
9, 17. Committees, list of and members of, ... 1-6
9. Committees, standing, list of:
on canals, ... 3
on charities, ... 5
on cities, ... 3
on contingent expenses, ... 6
on corporations, ... 4
on counties, towns and villages, ... 3

No. Doc.		Page.
9.	Committees, standing, list of—*Continued.*	
	on currency, banking and insurance, ...	4
	on education, ...	5
	on engrossment and enrollment, ...	6
	on finance, ...	3
	on future amendments,....................	5
	on Governor & Lieutenant-Governor,........	2
	on Indians,................................	5
	on industrial interests, ...	5
	on judiciary, ...	2
	on Legislature, its organization, &c.,.........	1
	on Legislature, its powers and duties,........	1
	on militia,................................	4
	on pardoning power,......................	4
	on preamble and bill of rights,.............	1
	on printing, ...	6
	on privileges and elections, ...	5
	on salt springs, ...	5
	on State officers, ...	2
	on State prisons, ...	4
	on suffrage,...............................	2
	on town and county officers, ...	2
3.	Committee of sixteen, report by, of plan of business of Convention,............................	1, 2
71.	Common schools, report of Superintendent of Public Instruction relative to statistics of, ...	1–8
98.	Legislature required to provide for free instruction in, ...	9
116.	instruction in, to be free, ...	3
23.	Common school fund, report of Comptroller relative to,	1–3
	unpaid interest on loans from,..............	2
	unpaid interest on lands belonging to, ...	2
116.	capital of, to be paid into the treasury,.......	1
	disposition of revenues of, ...	1
	investment of, ...	2
76.	Commutations of sentences, power of Governor relative to, ...	4
5.	Comptroller, communication from, on behalf of commissioners of canal fund, ...	1

No. Doc.		Page.
24.	Comptroller, report of, relative to common school fund,	1–3
55.	report by, of appropriations to charitable and educational institutions from 1847 to 1867, inclusive,	1–92
67.	to be one of the commissioners of canal fund,.	1
72.	report of, relative to stocks deposited to secure payment of taxes on lands donated to Upper Hudson and Wilderness railroad,	1
84.	election and term of office of,	2, 3
	compensation and powers and duties of,	4
116.	to be member of State board of education,	3
120.	and Auditor, report by, relative to moneys advanced for canals,	1–8
137.	communication from, relative to payment of expenses of convention,	1–7
54.	Comptroller of city of New York, report of, relative to donations to charitable institutions,	1–23
115.	Comstock, Asa, statement of lands sold to,	93
	Comstock, Eliza, statement of lands sold to,	365
1, 12.	Comstock, George F., delegate at large, Onondaga Co.,	1, 2
158.	minority report of, relative to salt springs,	1–16
12.	Comstock, Nathan, reporter, New York,	9
115.	Comstock, Peter, statement of lands sold to, 117, 375,	391
	Comstock, Sebastian, statement of lands sold to,. 265,	271
	Comstock, Zachariah, statement of lands sold to,	115
1, 12.	Conger, Abraham B., delegate 9th district, Rockland county,	2, 3
116.	dissent of, from report on education,	4
115.	Conine, David J., statement of land sold to,.... 107,	108
149.	Conscience, liberty of, secured,	2

183. Constitution as adopted:

	Art.	Sec.
Abandoned turnpike, plank or macadamized roads may be used as highways,	7	3
Academies, literature fund to be applied to support of,	9	1
Actions or suits, not to be affected,	1	17
by or against corporations,	10	3
Adjournment, final, of the Legislature to be at 12 o'clock at noon,	3	15

No. Doc.		Art.	Sec.
183.	Constitution as adopted—*Continued.*		
	Adjournment, neither house to adjourn without consent of the other, ...	3	9
	Agricultural lands, leases extending over twenty years to be void, ...	1	14
	Alienation of lands, restraints upon, to be void,...	1	15
	Amendments, to bills may be made in either house, ...	3	11
	to the Constitution (see Constitution).		
	Appeals, Court of (see Court of Appeals).		
	Apportionment, of members of Assembly, ...	3	4
	not to be altered until new enumeration,....	3	4
	of Senate districts,......................	3	2
	Appropriation bills, no moneys to be paid out of State treasury except in pursuance of,.	8	7
	payments in pursuance of, to be made within two years, ...	8	7
	to be passed by two-third vote, ...	8	8
	laws authorizing, what to specify,.........	8	7
	Assembly, has power of impeachment, ...	6	1
	Secretary of State to call to order, ...	3	8
	to preside over, until election of speaker,	3	8
	to consist of 139 members,...............	3	4
	to choose its own officers,................	3	8
	members of, all electors eligible, ...	3	1
	acceptance of office under U. S. government, to vacate seat,............	3	6
	compensation of, ...	3	5
	each county (except Fulton and Hamil-Hamilton) entitled to at least one,....	3	4
	election of, to be held in November,....	3	7
	first election, when held,.............	3	7
	majority of, necessary to pass bills,....	3	13
	may not be appointed to civil office in State,.........................	3	6
	no new county to be made unless its population entitle it to one,.........	3	4
	not to be questioned elsewhere for words used in debate, ...	3	10

No. Doc.	Art.	Sec.
183. Constitution as adopted—*Continued.*		
Assembly, members of, to be apportioned upon enumerations of inhabitants,	3	4
to hold office for one year,	3	4
quorum, majority to constitute,	3	8
shall determine rules of its own proceedings,	3	8
speaker to have additional compensation,	3	5
to judge of the election, returns and qualifications of its members,	3	8
to keep and publish journal of proceedings,	3	9
(See Legislature.)		
Attempt to bribe declared a felony,	13	2
punishment of,	13	2
(See Bribery.)		
Attorneys, district (see District Attorney).		
Attorney-General, a commissioner of the canal fund,	5	4
costs or allowances recovered by, to be paid into treasury,	5	3
election and term of office of,	5	1
not to receive any fees to his own use,	5	3
salary of, to be established by law,	5	3
Ayes and noes, to be taken in legislature on motions to amend constitution,	14	3
on bills appropriating money,	8	8
on bills creating debt,	8	11
on bills returned by governor, with objections,	4	10
on final passage of bills,	3	13
on questions of removal of judicial officers,	6	11
to be entered on journal,	4	10
in boards of supervisors, votes when to be taken by,	7	3
Banking associations, in cases of insolvency of, bill holders to have preference,	10	4
individual liability of stockholders,	10	5
suspension of specie payment by, not to be sanctioned,	10	4
notes or bills to be registered,	10	4
security for redemption of,	10	4

No. Doc.		Art.	Sec.
183.	Constitution as adopted—*Continued.*		
	Bail, excessive, not to be required,	1	5
	Ballot, election to be by, except for certain town officers,	2	5
	Betting at elections, penalty for,	2	2
	Bills, laws to be passed by,	3	12
	local or private, not to be passed unless notice has been given,	3	24
	enacting clause,	3	12
	assent of majority of both branches of the Legislature necessary to passage of,	3	13
	appropriating money or property, to be passed by a two-third vote,	8	8
	ayes and noes upon final passage of, to be entered on journal,	3	13
	question upon final passage, when to be taken,	3	13
	passed by one house, may be amended in the other,	3	11
	to be presented to Governor,	4	10
	to be returned by Governor within ten days,	4	10
	reconsideration of, after veto by Governor,	4	10
	vote on, to be taken by ayes and noes,	4	10
	effect of adjournment before expiration of ten days,	4	10
	creating debt, proceedings in case of,	8	11
	may originate in either house,	3	11
	special, for certain purposes, may not be passed,	3	25
	Boards of Supervisors (see Supervisors).		
	Borrowing money, cities and villages to be restricted in,	7	8
	State may borrow money for deficit in sinking fund,	8	9
	not exceeding $1,000,000,	8	9
	to be repaid within two years,	8	9
	to repel invasion,	8	10
	assent of the people necessary,	8	11
	Bounty debt, Comptroller may renew,	8	16
	Legislature may appropriate unappropriated funds of State to payment of,	8	16

No. Doc.		Art.	Sec.
183.	Constitution as adopted—*Continued.*		
	Bounty debt, in case of appropriation, sinking fund to be reduced,	8	16
	new stock may be issued for,	8	16
	rate of interest on, not to exceed seven per cent,	8	16
	principal and interest to be secured by tax,	8	16
	proceeds of new stock, how applied,	8	16
	rate at which new stock may be issued,	8	16
	to be paid within eighteen years,	8	16
	Bribe, persons offering, penalty,	13	2
	person charged with receiving, offering or promising, may testify in his own behalf,	13	3
	Bribery, at elections,	2	2
	Legislature may pass laws disfranchising persons guilty of,	2	2
	declared a felony,	13	1
	district attorney failing to prosecute for, to be removed from office,	13	4
	expenses of investigation and prosecution, how paid,	13	4
	Bridges, over canals,	5	6
	supervisors to regulate and have charge of,	7	3
	between two counties,	7	3
	Brooklyn, city court,	6	12
	judges, how chosen,	6	13
	compensation,	6	14
	expenses, how defrayed,	6	14
	official term of,	6	13
	to appoint chief judge,	6	12
	term of office of chief judge,	6	12
	vacancies in office of, how filled,	6	12
	Buffalo, Superior Court of city of,	6	12
	judges composing,	6	12
	compensation of,	6	14
	how chosen,	6	13
	term of office of,	6	12
	term of office of,	6	13
	to appoint chief judge from their number,	6	12

No. Doc.		Art.	Sec.
183.	Constitution as adopted—*Continued.*		
	Buffalo, Superior Court of city of, term of office of chief judge,	6	12
	vacancies, how filled,	6	12
	Canals, bids for materials or work on, informalities in,	5	7
	claims for damages to be made within two years,	5	6
	not to be leased, sold or disposed of,	8	6
	revenues, how applied,	8	4
	debt,	8	1
	revenue set apart for payment of interest and principal,	8	2
	deficiency, if any, to be supplied by taxation,	8	2
	not to be anticipated or pledged,	8	4
	tax providing sinking fund to pay, to be suspended,	8	2
	surplus, how applied,	8	4
	tolls on, not to be reduced except, &c.,	5	4
	to remain under management of State,	8	6
	Canal Appraiser, office abolished,	5	10
	Canal board, office abolished,	5	10
	Canal claims (see Court of Claims).		
	Canal Commissioner, office abolished,	5	10
	Census, Legislature to provide for taking, in 1875,	3	3
	to arrange Senate districts the following session,	3	3
	to arrange Assembly districts the following session,	3	4
	Change of name, by special laws, prohibited,	3	25
	Cities, general laws to be passed for government of,	7	6
	lands under water within boundaries of,	7	7
	mayor to be chosen,	7	4
	powers and duties of,	7	4
	members of common council to hold no other office in,	7	5
	officers of, how chosen,	7	5
	not to hold seat in Legislature,	7	5
	to be restricted in their powers,	7	8

No. Doc.		Art.	Sec.
183.	Constitution as adopted—*Continued.*		
	Cities, wharves, piers or slips in, ...	7	7
	Citizen, need not testify against himself in criminal cases, ...	1	6
	not to answer for crime, except on indictment, &c., ...	1	6
	not to be disfranchised without due process of law, ...	1	1
	not to be twice put in jeopardy for same offense, ...	1	6
	right to petition government not to be abridged, ...	1	10
	to be secure against unreasonable searches and seizures, ...	1	9
	Claims of State, against incorporated companies, to be enforced, ...	8	5
	Clerks in county offices, duty of supervisors relative to, ...	7	3
	Clerks of counties, election of, ...	7	1
	to be clerk of Supreme Court, ...	6	20
	Clerk of Court of Appeals, compensation, ...	6	20
	to be paid out of public treasury, ...	6	20
	to keep his office at seat of government, ...	6	20
	College land scrip fund, revenues to be applied to Cornell University, ...	9	1
	to be preserved inviolate, ...	9	1
	Colonial acts, the law of this State, ...	1	16
	Commissioners of Appeals, causes undetermined by, how disposed of, ...	5	5
	decisions to be certified to, ...	5	5
	five to be appointed, ...	5	4
	four to constitute a quorum, ...	5	4
	commission to continue no longer than three years, ...	5	5
	reporter of Court of Appeals to act for, ...	5	5
	when to enter upon duties, ...	6	24
	vacancies to be filled by Governor, ...	5	5
	appointments to fill, when to expire, ..	5	5
	Commissioners of Canal Fund, duties of, ...	5	4
	of whom to consist, ...	5	4

No. Doc.		Art.	Sec.
183.	Constitution as adopted—*Continued.*		
	Common council, restrictions of, relative to compensation of officers,	7	8
	Common law, part of the law of this State,	1	16
	Common school fund, capital to remain inviolate,	9	1
	part of revenue of United States deposit fund to be added to,	9	1
	revenues, how applied,	9	1
	Common schools, free instruction in, of all persons between the ages of seven and twenty years,	9	2
	revenues of common school fund to be applied to support of,	9	1
	Compensation, common council and supervisors restricted,	7	8
	for private property taken for public use,	1	7
	of members of legislature,	3	5
	deduction to be made for non-attendance,	3	5
	not to be increased or diminished during term of service,	3	17
	of Governor to be determined by legislature,	4	4
	of judges of court of claims,	5	8
	of judges of Court of Appeals and justices of Supreme Court,	6	14
	of county judges,	6	15
	of justices of city court,	6	14
	of Lieutenant-Governor,	4	9
	of public officer, agent or contractor, except that of judicial officer, may not be increased or diminished during term,	3	17
	of solicitor of claims,	5	9
	of speaker of Assembly,	3	5
	Comptroller, bonds, stocks and securities issued by State to be signed by,	8	14
	election and term of office of,	5	1
	may renew any or all the bounty debt,	8	16
	money not to be drawn from treasury without warrant from,	8	14
	salary of, to be established by law,	5	3

No. Doc.		Art.	Sec.
183.	Constitution as adopted—*Continued.*		
	Comptroller, salary of, not to be increased or diminished during term of office, ...	5	3
	to be a commissioner of the canal fund,....	5	4
	Conscience, liberty of, not to excuse acts of licentiousness, &c.,.........................	1	3
	persons exempt from military duty,.......	12	2
	Constitution (see Manner of Submission).		
	and amendments must be ratified by people,	14	4
	when to take effect,.....................	14	5
	amendments to, proceedings in legislature,..	14	3
	to be submitted to the people,........	14	3
	to be published for three months previous to general election, ...	14	3
	convention to revise, question to be submitted in 1888, ...	14	4
	legislature to provide for election of delegates to,......................	14	4
	Cornell endowment fund, capital to remain inviolate, ...	9	1
	revenue, how applied,..................	9	1
	Cornell University, certain revenues to be applied to, ...	9	1
	Coroners, election and tenure of office of,.......	7	1
	may be removed by Governor, after hearing defense,..........................	7	1
	Corporate rights or charters, not to be affected,..	1	17
	Corporations, banking, liability of stockholders,.	10	5
	dues from, to State, how secured,.........	10	2
	funds of State not to be invested in,.......	8	17
	to be formed under general laws,.........	10	1
	may sue and be sued by corporate name,..	10	3
	term, defined,.........................	10	3
	railroads, owning parallel or competing line, Legislature may not authorize consolidation of, ...	10	1
	Corruption, official, person charged with, may testify in his own behalf, ...	10	3
	declared a felony, ...	13	1

No. Doc.		Art.	Sec.
183.	Constitution as adopted—*Continued.*		
	Corruption, official, district attorney to prosecute,	13	4
	penalty for neglect,	13	4
	Counsel, party accused entitled to,	1	6
	County, not to be divided in forming Senate districts, except, &c.,	3	3
	each to have at least one member of Assembly, except Fulton and Hamilton,	3	4
	new, not to be made, unless population entitle it to member of Assembly,	3	4
	not to be responsible for acts of sheriff,	7	1
	officers, how elected or appointed,	7	1, 2
	powers and duties of supervisors,	7	3
	buildings, power of supervisors relative to,	7	3
	County clerks, election of,	7	1
	powers and duties of,	6	20
	to be clerks of supreme court,	6	20
	County courts, powers and jurisdiction,	6	15
	County judge, election or appointment of, question to be submitted,	6	17
	and surrogate, Legislature may provide for election of persons to perform duties of,	6	16
	may not receive to his own use, any fees or perquisites of office,	7	21
	may not practice as attorney or act as referee,	7	21
	salary of,	6	15
	tenure of office of present incumbent,	6	15
	to hold county court and act as surrogate,	6	15
	with two justices of the peace, to hold courts of sessions,	6	15
	restriction as to age,	6	13
	County officers, may be removed by Governor for cause,	7	1
	not already provided for, how chosen,	7	2
	County Treasurers, election of, and term of office,	7	1
	Governor may remove for cause,	7	1
	Court of Appeals, attendants, court may appoint and remove,	6	2
	causes in, January 1, 1869, how disposed of,	6	4

No. Doc.		Art.	Sec.
183.	Constitution as adopted—*Continued.*		
	Court of Appeals, causes in present, to be vested in court hereby established, ..	6	4
	certain, to be heard and determined by a commission, ...	6	4
	clerk, court to have power to appoint, ...	6	2
	reporter may be appointed by, ...	6	2
	commission, of whom to be composed, ...	6	4
	four to constitute a quorum, ...	6	4
	reporter of, ...	6	5
	vacancies in office of, how filled, ...	6	5
	concurrence of four judges necessary to decision, ...	6	2
	judges, how and when chosen, ...	6	2
	compensation of, ...	6	14
	not to be increased or diminished during term of office, ...	6	14
	how removed, ...	6	11
	may not practice as attorney, or act as referee, ...	6	21
	not to hold other offices of public trust,	6	10
	restriction as to age, ...	6	13
	vacancies in office of, how filled, ...	6	3
	when to enter upon duties, ...	6	24
	judgments of certain courts of record in cities may be removed directly to, for review, ...	6	22
	of whom composed, ...	6	2
	powers and jurisdiction of, not to be suspended by reason of non-appointment, &c.,	6	3
	quorum in, ...	6	2
	Court of Claims, to be established, ...	5	8
	of whom to be composed, ...	5	8
	proceedings in, ...	5	8
	claims against state to be adjudicated in, ...	5	8
	decisions of, may be reviewed on the law, on appeal to court of appeals, ...	5	8
	duties of judges where claim amounts to five hundred dollars or more, ...	5	8

No. Doc.		Art.	Sec.
183.	Constitution as adopted—*Continued.*		
	Court of claims, judges, how appointed,	5	8
	jurisdiction exclusive,	5	8
	solicitor of claims to take charge of interests of state in,	5	9
	term of office and compensation of judges,	5	8
	Court of impeachment (see Impeachment).		
	Court of oyer and terminer, justice of Supreme Court may preside in,	6	7
	Court, supreme (see Supreme Court).		
	Courts, inferior local, may be established by legislature,	6	19
	Courts of record in cities, judgments of, may be removed to court of appeals for review,	6	22
	Courts of sessions, by whom held,	6	15
	Courts of special sessions, jurisdiction,	6	26
	Credit of the State, not to be loaned,	8	8
	Crime, infamous, person guilty of, may be deprived of voting,	2	2
	no one to be tried for, except on presentment, &c.,	1	6
	Debate, legislative, freedom of, secured,	3	10
	Debt, canal, specified,	8	1
	provided for by revenues,	8	2
	deficiencies in revenues, to be supplied by taxation,	8	2
	tax authorizing sinking fund to pay floating, suspended after October 1, 1868,	8	2
	State may contract, for special object to be named in law authorizing,	8	11
	law authorizing, to be approved by the people,	8	11
	not to be submitted within three months,	8	11
	to provide for a tax to pay interest on,	8	11
	form of question on final passage,	8	11
	question on final passage, to be taken by ayes and noes,	8	11

No. Doc.		Art.	Sec.
183.	Constitution as adopted—*Continued.*		
	Debt, law authorizing payment of State, may be repealed,	8	11
	not to be voted for at election where amendments to Constitution are proposed,	8	11
	principal to be paid within 18 years,	8	11
	tax for, irrepealable,	8	11
	State may temporarily contract, to meet casual deficits or failure in revenues,	8	9
	not to exceed $1,000,000,	8	9
	money borrowed, how applied,	8	9
	to be paid within two years,	8	9
	to repel invasion or suppress insurrection,	8	10
	money borrowed, how applied,	8	10
	Debts, obligation or, not to be impaired,	1	17
	Decisions, judicial, to be published,	6	23
	publication to be free,	6	23
	of courts of record in cities, may be removed into Court of Appeals for review,	6	22
	District Attorney, election of,	7	1
	Governor may remove for cause,	7	1
	salary of, to be determined by supervisors,	7	3
	term of office,	7	1
	to prosecute for bribery or corruption,	13	4
	failure to prosecute, penalty,	13	4
	Divorce, not to be granted except by judgment of court of competent jurisdiction,	1	20
	Drains and ditches for agricultural purposes, general laws may be passed allowing,	1	7
	Duration of office, when not fixed by law,	3	20
	Elections, betting on result of, penalty for,	2	2
	bribery at, how punished,	2	2
	qualifications of voters at,	2	1
	to be by ballot,	2	5
	who may vote at,	2	2
	Electors, absent from home in military service of U. S. in time of war, Legislature to prescribe manner of taking vote of,	2	3

No. Doc.		Art.	Sec.
183.	Constitution as adopted—*Continued.*		
	Electors, all eligible to office of Senator and member of Assembly, ...	3	1
	colored (see "Manner of Submission").		
	guilty of bribery, may be deprived of right of voting, ...	2	2
	Legislature may enact laws disfranchising persons guilty of bribery, &c., ...	2	2
	may not vote unless registered, ...	2	4
	qualifications of, ...	2	1
	residence defined, ...	2	3
	Engineer (see State Engineer and Surveyor).		
	Enumeration of inhabitants, Assembly districts to be arranged after return of, ...	3	4
	Senate districts to be arranged after return of,	3	3
	when taken, ...	3	3
	Escheated lands, ...	1	11
	Executive power, vested in Governor, ...	4	1
	Extra compensation to public officers, contractors, &c., not to be allowed, ...	3	17
	Fees, Attorney-General may not receive, to his own use, ...	5	3
	costs or allowances recovered by, to be paid into the treasury, ...	5	3
	Comptroller may not receive, to his own use,	5	3
	judicial officer, except justices of the peace, not to receive to his own use, ...	5	3
	Secretary of State, not to receive, to his own use, ...	5	3
	Treasurer, not to receive, to his own use, ...	6	20
	Feudal tenures, abolished, ...	1	12
	Fines, excessive, not to be imposed, and quarter sales to be void, ...	1	15
	Fish, right to take, in international waters of State secured, ...	1	19
	Freedom of speech and of the press, secured, ...	1	8
	of debate in legislature, ...	3	10
	religious, ...	1	3
	not to excuse acts of licentiousness, ...	1	3

No. Doc.		Art.	Sec.
183.	Constitution as adopted—*Continued.*		
	Free instruction provided for all between the ages of seven and twenty, ...	9	2
	Funds of State, common school, literature, United States deposit, college land scrip, and Cornell University, capital to remain inviolate, ...	9	1
	not to be invested in stock of corporations, .	8	17
	revenues, how applied, ...	9	1
	no money to be paid from the State without appropriation by law, ...	8	14
	Gauging, office for, not to be created, ...	3	22
	General laws, corporations may be formed under,	10	1
	cities and villages may be incorporated under, ...	7	6
	may be passed for constructing drains and ditches for agricultural purposes across lands of others, ...	1	7
	Governor, to be resident of State for 5 years preceding election, ...	4	2
	not less than 35 years of age, ...	4	2
	bills to be presented to, for approval, ...	4	10
	executive power vested in, and term of office,	4	1
	compensation to be fixed by legislature, ...	4	4
	commander-in-chief of army and navy, ...	4	4
	impeachment of, ...	4	5
	in case of a tie, legislature to elect, ...	4	3
	may convene the senate or legislature, ...	4	6
	may grant pardons, reprieves, &c., ...	4	7
	may remove certain county officers for cause, after opportunity to be heard in defense, .	7	1
	may suspend Treasurer, ...	5	2
	not to appoint members of legislature to office, ...	3	6
	to communicate to legislature by message, ..	4	4
	to communicate to legislature cases of reprieve, &c., ...	4	7
	to nominate Superintendent of Public Works, ...	5	5
	to sign bills within ten days if he approve..	4	10

No. Doc.		Art.	Sec.
183.	Constitution as adopted—*Continued.*		
	Governor, if he disapprove bill it shall be returned with objections, ...	4	10
	may remove certain county officers, ...	7	1
	may remove judicial officers with consent of Senate, ...	6	11
	to appoint commissioners of appeals, ...	6	4
	board of managers of prisons, ...	11	1
	solicitor of claims, ...	5	9
	superintendent of public works, ...	5	5
	to see that laws are faithfully executed, ...	4	4
	to suspend execution in cases of treason, ...	4	7
	to report pardons and reprieves, yearly, ...	4	7
	to transact necessary business with officers of government, ...	4	4
	when and how elected, ...	4	3
	when duties of, to devolve on lieutenant-governor, ...	4	5, 8
	when out of State at head of military force,	4	5
	who eligible, ...	4	2
	Grand jury, no person to be tried for capital offense before indictment by, except, &c., ...	1	6
	Grants, certain, with rents reserved, void, ...	1	14
	for agricultural lands hereafter made, not to exceed twenty years, ...	1	14
	from king of Great Britain, ...	1	17
	for constructing street railways, how obtained,	3	25
	Habeas Corpus, writ of, not to be suspended, except, &c., ...	1	4
	Hamilton county, with Fulton, to elect one member of Assembly, ...	3	4
	Highways, abandoned turnpike, plank or macadamized roads, may be used as, ...	7	3
	laying out or discontinuing, to be provided for by general laws, ...	3	25
	erection of, into separate road districts, ...	7	3
	improvement of, by supervisors, ...	7	3
	Impeachment, articles of, preferred against judicial officer, effect of, ...	6	1

No. Doc.		Art.	Sec.
183.	Constitution as adopted—*Continued.*		
	Impeachment, Assembly to have power of,.....	6	1
	concurrence of two-thirds necessary to convict,..............................	6	1
	court for trial of, of whom composed, ...	6	1
	duty of Governor relative to, ...	4	7
	duty of members of court of, ...	6	1
	judgment in cases of conviction, to what to extend,............................	6	1
	members of court to be sworn, ...	6	1
	on trial of Governor, Lieutenant-Governor may not act as member of court,........	6	1
	parties impeached, liable to indictment and punishment according to law, ...	6	1
	Incorporated companies, claims of State against, to be enforced............................	8	5
	Indians, purchase of land from, void,..........	1	18
	Indictment, persons held for capital or infamous crimes not to be tried without, ...	1	6
	persons convicted on impeachment, liable to,	1	6
	Infamous crimes, persons guilty of, may be deprived of right to vote,................	2	2
	not to answer for, unless on presentment by grand jury,..........................	1	6
	Inferior local courts, may be established,.......	6	19
	Inhabitants of State, to be enumerated, ...	3	3
	Inspections, all officers for, abolished, and not to be again created,.........................	3	22
	International waters of State, right of citizens to take fish in, not to be denied,...............	1	19
	Invasion or insurrection, State may contract debts to repel, ...	8	11
	money raised, how applied, ...	8	11
	Jeopardy, no person to be put twice in, for same offense,................................	1	6
	Journals, of each house to be kept and published, except, &c.,.........................	3	9
	yeas and nays to be entered in,...........	3	13
	objections of Governor to be entered on,...	4	10

No. Doc.		Art.	Sec.
183.	Constitution as adopted—*Continued.*		
	Judges of Court of Appeals, of whom composed,	6	2
	how chosen,	6	2
	term of office,	6	2
	first election of,	6	24
	five to form a quorum,	6	2
	concurrence of four necessary to a decision,	6	2
	vacancies, how filled,	6	3
	when Governor may appoint to fill,	6	3
	appointees to fill, term of office,	6	3
	powers and jurisdiction, not suspended in certain cases,	6	3
	shall not sit in review of case decided by him,	6	8
	not to hold any other office of public trust,	6	10
	votes given for, to be void,	6	10
	may be removed by concurrent resolution of both houses of Legislature,	6	11
	removals, cause to be entered on journals,	6	11
	accused to have opportunity of defense,	6	11
	chief judge and associate, manner of appointment of, to be submitted to the people,	6	17
	may not practice as attorney or counsellor in any court of record in this State, or act as referee,	6	21
	when to enter upon their duties,	6	24
	to be member of court of impeachment,	6	1
	not to hold office after seventy years of age,	6	13
	Judges of courts of record, may not practice as attorneys or act as referees,	6	21
	Judicial decisions, free for publication,	6	23
	Judicial officers, except justices of the peace, not to receive fees or perquisites of office,	6	21
	Legislature to direct time and manner of appointment,	6	19
	may not serve after seventy years of age,	6	13
	Jury, in laying out private roads, damages to be ascertained by,	1	7
	in prosecutions for libel, to determine law and fact,	1	8

No. Doc.		Art.	Sec.
183.	Constitution as adopted—*Continued.*		
	Jury, right of trial by, secured; when may be waived,	1	2
	to assess value of property in certain cases,	1	7
	when may consist of less than twelve men,.	1	2
	Justices of the Supreme Court, term of office of present incumbents,	6	6
	how many to reside in each district,	6	6
	number necessary to hold general terms,	6	7
	presiding, to act as such during term of office,	6	7
	may not sit in review of decision made by court of which he was at the time a member,	6	8
	vacancies, how filled,	6	9
	may not hold any other office or public trust,	6	10
	votes for, other than judicial office, void,	6	10
	may be removed by concurrent resolution passed by two-third vote,	6	11
	removals, cause to be entered on journals,	6	11
	question on, how taken,	6	11
	to be chosen by electors of respective judicial districts,	6	13
	official term,	6	13
	not to hold office after seventy years of age,	6	13
	compensation,	6	13
	not to be diminished during term of office,	6	13
	question as to manner of apppointment to be submitted to the people,	6	17
	may not receive to his own use, any fees or perquisites of office,	6	21
	may not practice as attorney or act as referee,	6	21
	may not serve after seventy years of age,	6	13
	to appoint reporter,	6	23
	Justices of peace, and district court justices, election of,	6	18
	election and tenure of office,	6	18
	expiration of term of those in office,	6	25
	may be removed for cause, after opportunity for defense,	6	18
	may receive fees,	6	21

No. Doc.		Art.	Sec.
183.	Constitution as adopted—*Continued.*		
	Justices of peace and district court justices, may hold courts in other counties, ...	6	15
	members of court of sessions, ...	6	15
	compensation as such, ...	6	15
	number and classification regulated, ...	6	18
	to be elected at annual town meetings, ...	6	18
	to hold unexpired terms, ...	6	18
	vacancy, how filled, ...	6	18
	Justices' courts, trials by juries of less than twelve men may be provided for in, ...	1	2
	King of Great Britain, grants of land by, ...	1	17
	Land, adjacent to salt springs, may be sold under direction of commissioners of land office, .	8	18
	aggregate quantity of, adjacent to salt springs, not to be diminished, ...	8	18
	agricultural, leases or grants hereafter made for more than twenty years, void, ...	1	14
	alienation of, restraint upon, to be void, ...	1	15
	purchases of, from Indians, void, ...	1	18
	all, declared to be allodial, ...	1	13
	failure of title, when to escheat to the State,	1	11
	feudal tenures abolished, ...	1	12
	ultimate property in, ...	1	11
	Land office, land adjacent to salt springs may be sold under direction of commissioners of, . ..	8	18
	Law and equity, Supreme court of (see Supreme Court).		
	Laws, and judicial decisions, to be published, publication free for all, ...	6	23
	creating loan, to be submitted to people, ...	8	11
	not to be submitted within three months after passage, nor at any election where amendments to constitution are voted on, ...	8	11
	general, to be passed for certain objects, ...	3	25
	how revived, altered or amended, ...	3	14
	special, may not be passed for certain objects,	3	16
	do do do do	3	25

No. Doc.		Art.	Sec.
183.	Constitution as adopted—*Continued.*		
	Laws, subject to be named in title, ...	3	14
	to be enacted by bill only,...............	3	12
	to embrace but one subject, ...	3	14
	(See Bills.)		
	Laws of limitation, not to revive claims already barred, ...	5	8
	to prevail in favor of State as in favor of individuals, ...	5	8
	when limitation to begin to run, ...	5	8
	Lease or grant of agricultural land, when void, .	1	14
	Legislative power, vested in Senate and Assembly,	3	1
	Legislature, acceptance of office under United States to vacate seat of member,........	3	6
	compensation of members of,.............	3	5
	doors to be kept open, except, &c.,.........	3	9
	duties of, relative to revising Constitution,..	14	3
	each house to determine rules of its own proceedings,........................	3	8
	to keep a journal, ...	3	9
	final adjournment of, to be at the hour of 12, noon, ...	3	15
	election of members of, when held, ...	3	7
	for words used in debate in, members are not to be questioned in any other place, .	3	10
	Governor may call special session of, ...	4	6
	to communicate reprieves, &c., to,.....	4	7
	laws may not be passed at special sessions, except, &c., ...	4	6
	legislative term,........................	3	7
	may authorize judgments, &c., of courts of record in cities removed to Court of Appeals for review, ...	6	22
	may, by two-third vote, change manner of electing militia officers,................	12	5
	may confer upon courts of record powers to perform duties of surrogates,...........	6	27
	may establish inferior local courts, ...	6	19

No. Doc.		Art.	Sec.
183.	Constitution as adopted—*Continued.*		
	Legislature, may not authorize consolidation of railroad corporations owning parallel or competing lines, ...	10	1
	may not grant extra compensation, ...	3	17
	may not pass special laws in certain cases, .	3	25
	member of, may not be appointed to civil office, ...	3	6
	to take oath of office, form of oath, ...	14	1
	may not be twice expelled for same offense, ...	3	9
	member of Congress or United States officer may not hold seat in, ...	3	6
	neither house may adjourn for more than two days without consent of the other, ...	3	9
	no member may be twice expelled for same offense, ...	3	8
	non-attendance, reduction may be made in salary, ...	3	5
	not to sell or dispose of salt springs, ...	8	18
	officers of cities may not hold seats in, ...	7	5
	power of, over quarantine, ...	7	7
	proceedings in, to amend Constitution, ...	14	3
	quorum, in each house, ...	3	8
	restrictions of, to apply to common councils of cities, ...	7	8
	speaker of Assembly, salary of, ...	3	5
	term, when to begin, ...	3	21
	to cause enumeration of inhabitants, ...	3	3
	to choose its own officers, ...	3	8
	to direct as to appointment of judicial officers,	6	19
	to elect Governor in case of tie, ...	4	3
	to enact laws disfranchising persons guilty of bribery, &c., ...	2	2
	to fix compensation of Governor and Lieut.-Governor, ...	4	4, 9
	to judge of the qualification, &c., of its members, ...	3	8
	to pass laws to give effect to article seven, ..	7	5

No. Doc.		Art.	Sec.
183.	Constitution as adopted—*Continued.*		
	Legislature, to provide for a reporter of decisions of Supreme Court, ...	6	23
	to provide for filling vacancies, ...	3	18
	for publication of all statutes, ...	6	25
	for registry of electors, ...	2	4
	for registration of bills circulated as money, ...	10	4
	for reserve officers in the national guard,	12	6
	for taking and canvassing of votes of electors absent in time of war, in service of United States, ...	2	3
	free instruction for all between the ages of seven and twenty-one, ...	9	2
	to require security for redemption of bank bills, ...	10	4
	to submit question of revising Constitution to people in 1888, ...	14	4
	form of ballot submitting, ...	14	4
	vote of majority elected necessary to expel member of either house, ...	3	8
	vote on removal of certain judicial officers, how taken, ...	6	11
	to be entered on journals, ...	6	11
	votes on amendments to Constitution to be entered on journals, ...	14	3
	to be taken by ayes and noes, ...	14	3
	Liability of corporations and stockholders (see Corporations).		
	Libel, truth may be given in evidence, ...	1	8
	law and fact to be determined by jury, ...	1	8
	Liberty of conscience, not to excuse acts of licentiousness, ...	1	3
	Liberty of speech, and of the press, secured, ...	1	8
	Lieutenant-Governor, compensation, ...	4	9
	to receive no other compensation for services performed under Constitution or laws of State, ...	4	9
	to act as Governor in certain cases, ...	4	8

No. Doc.		Art.	Sec.
183.	Constitution as adopted—*Continued.*		
	Lieutenant-Governor, member of court for trial of impeachment,	6	1
	not to sit on trial of Governor,	6	1
	to be president of Senate,	3	8
	must have attained 35th year of his age,	4	2
	to be resident of State for five years preceding election,	4	2
	when acting as Governor, Senate to choose president pro tem.,	3	8
	Life, liberty or property, no one to be deprived of, without due process of law,	1	6
	Literature fund, capital to remain inviolate,	9	1
	revenue, how applied,	9	1
	Loan, deficiency not to extend beyond six years,	8	13
	Local bills, to embrace one subject; subject to be expressed in title,	3	14
	Local judicial officers, in office, expiration of term of office,	6	25
	Legislature may provide for election of two, to perform duties of county judge and surrogate,	6	16
	Lottery tickets, sale of, prohibited,	3	23
	Manner of submission of Constitution (see Resolution, page 43).		
	Majority, of each house necessary to form a quorum,	3	8
	to pass bills,	6	13
	Measures and weights, standards of, may be supplied,	3	22
	Measuring, office for, abolished and not to be again created,	3	22
	Message, Governor to communicate by, to Legislature,	4	4
	to communicate objections to bill within ten days,	4	10
	Militia, able-bodied male citizens, between ages of 18 and 45, to be annually enrolled,	12	1
	active, to be known as the National Guard of the State of New York,	12	2

No. Doc.		Art.	Sec.
183.	Constitution as adopted—*Continued.*		
	Militia, commanders of battalions to appoint their staff officers, ...	12	5
	commissioned officers, how removed, ...	12	4
	term of office of, ...	12	4
	commissions, expiration of, ...	12	3
	general officers, to appoint their staff officers,	12	4
	commissions issued by, expiration of,..	12	4
	Legislature may change manner of election of officers,..................	12	5
	Governor, commander-in-chief of,.........	4	4
	to appoint aids and military secretary,.	12	3
	to appoint chief of staff departments,..	12	3
	major-generals, how appointed...........	12	3
	national guard, Legislature to provide for officers of,......................	12	6
	officers of, may be commissioned by Governor,......................	12	6
	officers of companies, how chosen, ...	12	5
	officers responsible for military property or funds of State to give security,...	12	3
	officers to be commissioned by the Governor, ...	12	4
	to be divided into active and reserved forces, ...	12	2
	when in active service officers to be appointed by Governor,.............	12	5
	who exempt, ...	12	2
	Minors, special laws may not be passed relative to real property of, ...	3	25
	Misdemeanors, jurisdiction of courts of special sessions to offenses of grade of,............	6	26
	Money, not to be paid, when appropriated, unless applied for within two years,...........	8	7
	how drawn from treasury, ...	8	14
	State may raise by loan to meet casual deficits or failure in revenue,..........	8	9
	not to exceed $1,000,000,............	8	9
	how applied,......................	8	9

No. Doc.		Art.	Sec.
183.	Constitution as adopted—*Continued.*		
	Money so raised, to be repaid within two years,.	8	9
	how raised, to repel invasion or suppress insurrection,	8	10
	how applied,	8	10
	Municipal corporations (see Corporations).		
	Names of persons, may not be changed by special law,	3	25
	National Guard (see Militia).		
	New York city, court of common pleas in,	6	12
	judges, compensation of,	6	14
	first election of,	6	24
	how chosen,	6	13
	may hold special terms of Supreme Court,	6	12
	term of office of,	6	13
	vacancies in, how filled,	6	12
	when to enter upon duties,	6	24
	judges of court of common pleas, restriction as to age,	6	13
	expenses, how defrayed,	6	14
	power and jurisdiction of,	6	12
	superior court of city of,	6	12
	chief judge to be appointed,	6	12
	compensation of judges,	6	14
	expenses, how defrayed,	6	14
	judges of, may be detailed and hold special terms of Supreme Court,	6	12
	vacancies in office of, how filled,..	6	12
	term of office of,	6	13
	Oath of office, form of,	14	1
	refusal to take, or swearing falsely, to forfeit office,	14	1
	no other test required,	14	2
	Officers, city and town, how elected or appointed,	7	5
	county, how elected or appointed,	7	1
	removal of, other than judicial,	3	19
	militia, how chosen,	12	5
	major-generals, &c.,	12	3
	oath of,	14	1

No. Doc.		Art.	Sec.
183.	Constitution as adopted—*Continued.*		
	Officers, militia, tenure of office, when not fixed by law or Constitution, ...	3	20
	offices for weighing, inspecting, &c., prohibited, ...	3	2
	not to extend to office for protecting health, &c., ...	3	22
	Official corruption, declared a felony, ...	13	1
	Oyer and Terminer (see Court of).		
	Pardons, reprieves and commutations, Governor may grant, ...	4	7
	to report yearly to Legislature, ...	4	7
	Petition, right of, not to be abridged, ...	1	10
	Plank and macadamized roads, abandoned, may be used as highways, ...	7	3
	Political year, ...	3	21
	President of Senate, Lieutenant-Governor, to have casting vote, ...	4	8
	pro tem., when chosen, ...	3	8
	when to act as Governor, ...	4	8
	Prisons, board of managers to be appointed, ...	11	1
	compensation, ...	11	1
	Governor may remove, for cause, ...	11	3
	Legislature to limit expenses of board, ...	11	1
	powers and duties of, ...	11	1
	salary of secretary, ...	11	1
	term of office of, ...	11	1
	to appoint secretary, ...	11	1
	warden, clerk, physician and chaplain, ...	11	2
	to have charge of State prisons, ...	11	1
	Private roads, may be opened in manner prescribed by law, ...	1	7
	damages to be found by jury, ...	1	7
	Property, for private road, proceedings for taking,	1	7
	no person to be deprived of, without due process of law, ...	1	6
	private claims against State, how paid, ...	3	16
	private, not to be taken for public use, without, &c., ...	1	6

No. Doc.		Art.	Sec.
183.	Constitution as adopted—*Continued.*		
	Property, right of, not affected, ...	1	17
	ultimate, in lands, possessed by the State,..	1	11
	value of private, taken for public use, how ascertained, ...	1	7
	Property qualifications of colored voters (see Manner of Submission).		
	Public or private roads, special laws relative to, may not be passed, ...	3	25
	Public works, see Superintendent of Public Works, ...	5	5
	Punishment, cruel or unusual, not to be inflicted,	1	5
	Qualifications, of members of Legislature, each house to determine, ...	5	5
	of voters, ...	2	1
	Quarter sales, to be void, ...	1	15
	Questions to be submitted to people, election or appointment of judges, justices, &c., ..	6	17
	amendments to Constitution, ...	14	3
	calling Constitutional Convention, ...	14	4
	creating a loan, ...	8	11
	election or appointment of judge of Court of appeals and justice of Supreme Court, ...	6	17
	Quorum, what to constitute in Court of Appeals,	6	2, 4
	in Legislature, ...	3	8
	Railroads, authority to construct, how obtained,.	3	25
	fee of land taken for tracks, when to remain in owners, ...	1	7
	Legislature may not authorize consolidation of corporations owning parallel or competing lines, ...	10	1
	Real property of minors, Legislature not to pass special law authorizing sale, leasing or mortgaging, ...	3	25
	Rebellion or invasion, writ of habeas corpus may be suspended in case of, ...	1	4
	State may borrow money in case of, ...	8	10
	Registry of electors, failure to register forfeits right to vote, ...	2	4

No. Doc.		Art.	Sec.
183.	Constitution as adopted—*Continued.*		
	Registry of electors, mode to be uniform in all cities,	2	4
	to be completed four days before election,	2	4
	Religion, free exercise and enjoyment of, secured,	1	3
	no person incompetent as a witness on account of,	1	3
	not to be construed so as to tolerate acts of licentiousness,	1	3
	citizen may be excused from military service on account of,	12	2
	Removal from office, provision for,	3	19
	Rents and services, certain, saved and protected,	1	12
	Reporter of Court of Appeals, to be appointed by court,	6	2
	of Supreme Court, to be appointed,	6	23
	Reports of decisions, to be published,	6	23
	publication free to all,	6	23
	Reprieves and pardons, may be granted by Governor,	4	7
	mode of applying for, to be adhered to,	4	7
	to be communicated to Legislature yearly,	4	7
	Resolutions, certain, law of the State,	1	16
	Residence of electors, not lost or gained in certain cases,	2	3
	Rights of citizens, not to be deprived of life, liberty or property without due process of law,	1	6
	not to be disfranchised or deprived of any right unless by law,	1	1
	religious freedom secured to all,	1	3
	not to excuse acts of licentiousness,	1	3
	to be secure in their persons, houses and effects against unreasonable seizures and searches,	1	9
	to petition government, or any department thereof,	1	10
	to take fish in international waters bordering State,	1	19

No. Doc.		Art.	Sec.
183.	Constitution as adopted—*Continued.*		
	Rights of citizens, writ of habeas corpus, not to be suspended except in case of invasion or rebellion,	1	4
	Right of suffrage, persons guilty of bribery, infamous crimes, &c., may be excluded from,	2	2
	who entitled to,	2	1
	Road districts, supervisors may erect separate, from portions of public highways,	7	3
	Roads, private, relative to laying out,	1	7
	abandoned, may be used as highways,	7	4
	Rules, each house to determine its own,	3	8
	Salaries of town and county officers, supervisors to regulate,	7	3
	(See Compensation.)		
	Salt springs, aggregate quantity of land not to be diminished,	8	13
	lands adjacent to, may be sold for specific objects,	8	13
	may not be sold or disposed of,	8	13
	Secretary of State, compensation not to be increased or diminished during term,	5	3
	not to receive fees to his own use,	5	3
	election and term of office of,	5	1
	to call Assembly to order,	3	8
	to preside until speaker is elected and qualified,	3	8
	Seizures and searches, citizens secure against unreasonable,	1	9
	warrant not to issue without probable cause supported by oath, or affirmation,	1	9
	Senate, Assembly and, legislative power vested in,	3	1
	districts, State to be divided into thirty-two,	3	2
	enumerated,	3	2
	to be rearranged after each new enumeration,	3	3
	Senators, first elected, when to vacate office,	3	2
	salary of,	3	5
	not to be appointed to any civil office,	3	6

No. Doc.		Art.	Sec.
183.	Constitution as adopted—*Continued.*		
	Senate, members of, accepting office under U. S. government, or as member of Congress, to vacate seat,	3	6
	election of Senators, when held,	3	7
	term of office,	3	7
	majority to constitute a quorum,	3	8
	members of court for trial of impeachments,	6	1
	Lieutenant-Governor to act as president,	4	8
	to have casting vote only,	4	8
	to choose president pro tem. to serve in absence of Lieutenant-Governor,	3	8
	to choose its own officers,	3	8
	to keep and publish journal of proceedings, except, &c.,	3	9
	freedom of debate in,	3	10
	final adjournment to be at the hour of 12, noon,	3	15
	Governor may convene on extraordinary occasions,	4	6
	president, when to act as Governor,	4	8
	appointments to certain offices to be made by Governor and,	6	9
	judicial officers may be removed by, on recommendation of Governor,	6	11
	to judge of the election, returns and qualifications of its members,	3	8
	Senator, all electors to be eligible to office of,	3	1
	term of office,	3	2
	(See Senate.)		
	Sheriffs, counties not responsible for acts of,	7	1
	election and term of office,	7	1
	Governor may remove for cause after opportunity to be heard on written charges,	7	1
	ineligible for three years after term expires,	7	1
	security, renewal may be required,	7	1
	in default of renewal, office deemed vacant,	7	1
	to hold no other office,	7	1

No. Doc.	Art.	Sec.
183. Constitution as adopted—*Continued.*		
Sinking fund, deficiency, loan may be made for,	8	13
loan not to extend beyond six years,......	8	13
Solicitor of claims, duties and compensation of,..	5	9
may be removed by Governor for cause,...	5	9
when office may be abolished,............	5	9
Speaker of Assembly, duty of Secretary of State until election and qualification of,.......	3	8
compensation, ...	3	5
Special acts, may not be passed where object may be attained by general laws, ...	7	6
Special sessions of Legislature, Governor may convene, ...	4	6
laws not to be passed at, except, &c.,......	4	6
Specie payments, no law to be passed authorizing or sanctioning suspension of,............	10	4
Speech, freedom of, and of the press, secured,...	1	8
State, bonds, stocks and securities issued by, to be signed by Comptroller, ...	8	14
canals, to remain under management of,....	8	6
claims against corporations to be enforced,.	8	5
debts contracted by, to specify object,.....	8	11
may temporarily contract debts, ...	8	9
debts temporarily contracted not to exceed one million dollars,...................	8	9
may contract debts to repel invasion,......	8	10
members of, not to be disfranchised or deprived of any of the privileges of citizens, without due process of law, ...	1	1
moneys raised by loans to be faithfully applied,.........................	8	9,10
to be paid within two years after being contracted, ...	8	9
not to invest funds in shares of any corporation, ...	8	17
not to loan its credit to any individual, corporation or association,................	8	8
salt springs to remain property of, ...	8	18
treasury, moneys not to be paid from, except in pursuance of law,.................	8	7

No. Doc.		Art.	Sec.
183.	Constitution as adopted—*Continued.*		
	State prisons (see Prisons).		
	State treasury, no money to be paid except in pursuance of law, ...	8	7
	laws making appropriations, what to specify,	8	7
	questions appropriating moneys from, to be taken by ayes and noes, ...	8	8
	Statutes and legal decisions, Legislature to provide for speedy publication of, ...	6	23
	publication free to all, ...	6	23
	certain, of colonial congress, laws of this State,	1	16
	Street railroads, constructed under general laws,	3	25
	may not be constructed without consent of corporate authorities and owners of property, or of consent of Supreme Court,...	3	25
	Suffrage, right of, ...	2	1
	who may be deprived of, ...	2	2
	for men of color (see Manner of Submission).		
	proofs of, laws to be made for ascertaining,..	2	4
	Superintendent of Public Works, how appointed,	5	5
	four assistants may be appointed, ...	5	5
	to give security for performance of duties,..	5	5
	may be suspended from office,...........	5	5
	in case of vacancy, assistant to perform duties of, ...	5	5
	salary to be determined by law, ...	5	5
	Supervisors, jurisdiction, subject to modification by Legislature, ...	7	3
	boards of, may appoint certain county officers,	7	2
	how elected in each county,..............	7	3
	may borrow money in anticipation of taxes authorized by law,....................	7	3
	duty as to clerks and subordinates in county offices,............................	7	3
	erection of portions of public highways into separate road districts, ...	7	3
	jurisdiction, not to be exercised without authority of majority of all members elected,	7	3
	legalizing informal acts of town meetings in ceatain cases, ...	7	3

No. Doc. Art. Sec.

183. Constitution as adopted—*Continued.*

Supervisors, to regulate public highways, ... 7 3
powers of, ... 7 3
restricted as to salaries of officers, ... 7 8
to purchase real estate and locate, erect and have charge of county buildings, ... 7 3
to regulate pay and grade of clerks in county offices, ... 7 3
to regulate location, repair and erection of bridges, ... 7 3
to regulate salaries of county officers, ... 7 3
jurisdiction, majority of all elected necessary to confer, ... 7 3
vote conferring, to be taken by ayes and noes, ... 7 3
Supreme Court, of whom composed, ... 6 6
presiding justice to preside during term of office, ... 6 7
general terms, of whom composed, ... 6 7
to be held in each judicial district, ... 6 7
jurisdiction in law and equity, ... 6 6
reporter of decisions to be appointed, ... 6 23
decisions to be free for publication to all, ... 6 23
justices, how chosen, ... 6 14
may not practice as attorney or act as referee, ... 6 21
not to hold other office or public trust, . 6 10
number of, to reside in each district, .. 6 6
official term of, ... 6 13
special terms and Circuit Courts may be held by, ... 6 7
vacancies in office of, how filled, ... 6 9
may preside in courts of Oyer and Terminer, ... 6 7
restriction as to age, ... 6 13
when consent to be obtained for constructing street railways, ... 3 25
Surplus revenues of canals, how applied, ... 8 4
not to be anticipated or pledged, ... 8 4

No. Doc.		Art.	Sec.
183.	Constitution as adopted—*Continued.*		
	Surrogate, county judge to act as,	6	15
	courts of record may perform duties of, in certain cases,	6	27
	election of, may be provided for,	6	16
	may be elected in counties where population exceeds 40,000,	6	15
	salary of,	6	15
	election of special, may be provided for,	6	16
	tenure of office of present occupants,	6	25
	term of office,	6	15
	Surrogates' courts, how relieved in certain cases,	6	27
	Tax, law authorizing, to state amount and object to which applied,	8	12
	to be passed by ayes and noes,	8	11
	providing for sinking fund to pay floating canal debt, to be suspended after October 1, 1868,	8	2
	uniform rule of, on real and personal property,	8	15
	Term of office, of Governor and Lieutenant-Governor,	4	1
	Senators,	3	2
	members of Assembly,	3	4
	Secretary of State, Comptroller, Treasurer and Attorney-General,	5	1
	Superintendent of Public Works,	6	5
	Assistant Superintendent of Public Works,	5	5
	judges of court of claims,	5	8
	solicitor of claims,	5	9
	judges of the Court of Appeals,	6	2
	justices of Supreme Court,	6	13
	county officers,	7	1
	Title of bills, to embrace subject,	3	14
	Testimony, in charges of corruption or bribery, accused may give,	13	3
	in equity cases, how taken,	6	8
	no one incompetent on account of religious belief,	5	3

No. Doc.		Art.	Sec.
183.	Constitution as adopted—*Continued.*		
	Town meetings, informal acts of, how legalized,.	7	3
	Town officers, elected or appointed, ...	7	5
	irregular acts of, how legalized,...........	7	3
	Travel of members of the Legislature, allowance for, ...	3	5
	Treason, duty of Governor relative to persons convicted of,............................	4	7
	Treasurer, election and term of office of,........	5	1
	may be suspended from office,............	5	2
	one of the commissioners of the canal fund,.	5	4
	of counties (see County Treasurers).		
	Treasury, money, how drawn from, ...	8	14
	not to be drawn without warrant of comptroller,..............................	8	14
	Trial, by jury, to remain inviolate, ...	1	2
	may be waived by parties in civil cases,	1	2
	in justices's courts, provision may be made for juries of less than twelve men,......	1	2
	no person incompetent as a witness on account of his religious belief, ...	1	3
	party to be confronted with witness against him,..............................	1	6
	right to appear and defend in person and by counsel, ...	1	6
	when not to be had without indictment,....	1	6
	Turnpikes, abandoned, may be used as public highways, ...	7	3
	Two-thirds vote, necessary to pass certain bills,..	8	8
	of all elected necessary to pass bills returned by Governor with objections,.......	4	10
	to remove judge of Court of Appeals or justices of Supreme Court, ...	6	11
	United States deposit fund, capital to remain inviolate, ...	9	1
	revenue, how applied,..................	9	1
	part of revenue to be added to common school fund, ...	9	1
	Vacancies, in elective offices,.................	3	18
	judge of Court of Appeals,..........	6	3
	justice of Supreme Court, ...	6	9

No. Doc.		Art.	Sec.
183.	Constitution as adopted—*Continued.*		
	Vacancies, Legislature to provide for filling, ...	3	18
	term of office of persons elected to fill, ...	6	18
	to be defined by general laws, ...	3	18
	Voters (see Electors).		
	men of color (see Manner of Submission).		
	Veto, of the Governor (see Bills).		
	Warrants, for searches and seizures, when may be issued, ...	1	9
	to describe places and persons, ...	1	9
	Waters, international, bordering on State, right to take fish in, secured, ...	1	19
	Weights and measures, standards may be supplied,	3	22
	Witness, in criminal cases, may not be compelled to testify against himself, ...	1	6
	no person rendered incompetent on account of religious belief, ...	1	3
	not to be unreasonably detained, ...	1	5
	to confront party against whom they testify,	1	6
	Year, political and legislative, ...	3	21
	Yeas and nays (see Ayes and Noes).		

No. Doc.		Page.
180.	Constitution, submission of, to the people, report of select committee on, ...	1–4
66.	Contingent debt of the State, ...	2
	Contingent expenses, provision for committee on, ...	
9.	committee on, ...	6
67.	Contracting board, provision for abrogation of, ...	4
135.	communication to Attorney-General from, relative to alleged fraudulent canal contracts, ..	4–13
137.	Convention, communication from Comptroller relative to payment of expenses of, ...	1–7
	opinion of Attorney-General relative to payment of expenses of, ...	4–6
	proffer of National Commercial Bank to advance moneys for payment of expenses of, ..	7
145.	communication from authorities of Albany city, tendering hall for use of, ...	1, 2

No. Doc.		Page.
152.	Convention, report by Secretary of, concerning condition of business of, ...	1–4
172.	report of Secretary of condition of business of,	1–6
3.	report by select committee of sixteen, of plan of business for, ...	1, 2
115.	Cook, Bates, statement of lands sold to, ...	34
	Cook, Benjamin, statement of lands sold to, ...	256
	Cook, Caspar J., statement of lands sold to,.........	322
	Cook, Eli, Jr., statement of lands sold to, ...	112
1, 12.	Cooke, Erastus, delegate at large, Ulster county, ...	1, 3
111.	plan of, for reorganization of the judiciary,...	1–4
115.	Cook, Joseph, statement of lands sold to,...........	112
	Cook, Joseph B., statement of lands sold to, ...	244
	Cook, Lathrop, statement of lands sold to, ... 34,	331
	Cook, Rebekah, statement of lands sold to, ...	272
	Cook, Solomon, statement of lands sold to, ...	209
	Cook, William, statement of lands sold to, .. 40, 116,	118
	Cook, Zebulon, statement of lands sold to,..........	105
40.	Cool, K. P., testimony of, relative to management of Champlain canal,............................	559–63
115.	Cooley, Robert, statement of lands sold to, ...	26
	Cooley & Bond, statement of lands sold to, ...	18
	Coolidge, Benjamin F., statement of lands sold to, ...	75, 76
	Coolidge, Ira A., statement of lands sold to, ...	76
	Coonley, Benjamin, statement of lands sold to,......	277
	Coope, David, statement of lands sold to,.. 151, 152,	153
	154, 155,	156
	Cooper, John T., statement of lands sold to, ...	248
1, 12.	Corbett, Patrick, delegate, 22d district, Onondaga county, ...	3, 3
28.	Corkings, Philip, extra compensation paid to, ...	8, 10
47.	Cornell, Ezra, proceedings relative to purchase of college land scrip by, ...	5–24
115.	Cornell, Nelson, statement of lands sold to,.........	335
116.	Cornell endowment fund, capital of, to be paid into treasury, ...	1
	investment of, ...	2
	revenues of, to be applied to support of Cornell University,.......................	2

No. Doc.		Page.
47.	Cornell University, donation of proceeds of college land scrip to,	2, 3
	revenues to be applied to support of,	2
1, 12.	Corning, Erastus, delegate, 13th district, Albany Co.,	2, 3
55.	Corning Free Academy, appropriations to,	18, 19
61.	Coroners, election and term of office of,	1
	removal of, by Governor,	2
115.	Cornwell, Elisha, statement of lands sold to,	238
	Cornwell, Wm. D., statement of lands sold to,	123
65.	Corporation Counsel of New York, report of, relative to judgments against the city,	1, 2
3.	Corporations, provisions for committee on,	2
9.	committee on,	4
39.	to require general laws for formation of,	1
46.	report of titles of bills relating to, introduced at last session of Assembly,	1–48
53.	currency, banking and insurance, report of joint committee on,	1–2
	individual liability of stockholders in,	1–2
	to be formed only under general laws,	1
	suspension of specie payments by, forbidden to be sanctioned by law,	2
59.	minority report on,	1–4
92.	article on, as amended and referred to committee on revision,	1–3
98.	term defined as used in constitution,	10, 11
	general laws required for formation of,	10
101.	dissent of minority of committee from prohibition of formation of, except by general laws,	1–2
55.	Cortland Academy, appropriations to,	16–19
	Cortlandville Academy, appropriations to,	16–19
115.	Cotton, Henry S., statement of lands sold to,	240
	Cott, Isaac, Jr., statement of lands sold to,	35
3.	Counties, towns and villages, provision for committee on,	2
9.	committee on,	3
75.	report of committee on,	1–3
	provisions for local taxation by,	3
96.	article reported by committee on, as amended and referred to committee on revision,	1, 2

No. Doc.		Page.
61.	County clerk, election and term of office of, ...	1
	removal of, by the Governor, ...	2
107.	to be clerk of Supreme Court, ...	12
	County Courts, provision for, ...	9, 10
	County judge, election and term of office of, ...	9
	to perform duties of surrogate in counties of certain population, ...	10
61.	County officers, election and term of office of, ...	1
	power of Governor relative to removal of, ...	2
	provisions relative to residence of, ...	4
	penalties for neglect of duty by, ...	4
	vacancies in, how filled, ...	4
38.	salaries of, to be regulated by supervisors, ...	2
98.	County seats, special laws for location or change of, prohibited, ...	14
61.	County supervisor, election and term of office of, ...	1
	removal of, by Governor, ...	2
	powers and duties of, ...	6
38.	County and town buildings, to vest power for location and erection of, in boards of supervisors, ...	1
61.	County treasurer, election and term of office of, ...	1, 3
	removal of, by the Governor, ...	2
18.	Court of Appeals, report relative to causes in, ...	3
22.	report relative to trust funds held by, ...	1–24
	chancery fund held by, ... 6–8,	19–23
	library fund held by, ... 4, 5,	9–19
107.	provisions relative to, ...	2, 3
	judges of, number, election and term of office of,	2, 3
	clerk of, appointment and removal of, ...	3
	reporter of, appointment and removal of, ...	3
	chief justice of, how designated, ...	2, 3
	judges of, prohibited from holding other office,	5
	terms of, provision relative to, ...	7
	removal of judges of, ...	7
	vacancies in office of judges of, ...	6
98.	Court of claims, provisions for organization of, ...	7
	claims in, to be tried without a jury, ...	7
	judges of, their appointment and term of office,	7
	judges of, to view property in certain cases, ...	7
	statute of limitations in, ...	8

No. Doc. Page.

107. Court of common pleas of New York (see "New York").
107. Courts of oyer and terminer, provision for, ... 7
115. Covell, Geo., statement of lands sold to, ... 258
Coveney Robert, statement of lands sold to, ... 351
Cowan, James & Warren, statement of lands sold to,. 12
Cox, Elias, statement of lands sold to, ... 353
55. Coxsackie Academy, appropriations to, ... 16–19
115. Cragin, Geo., statement of lands sold to, ... 360, 361
Cramer, Henry, statement of lands sold to, ... 150
Cramer, Jno. statement of lands sold to, ... 149
Cramer, Wm., statement of lands sold to, ... 362
Crampton, Jonathan, statement of lands sold to, ... 92
Crandall, G., statement of lands sold to, ... 312
Crandall, Timothy, statement of lands sold to, ... 123
Crane, Albert, statement of lands sold to, ... 338
Crane, E. R., statement of lands sold to, ... 361
Crane, Hunter, statement of lands sold to, .. 30, 338, 339
Crane, James, statement of lands sold to, ... 138
Crane, Robert, statement of lands sold to,. 48, 56, 57, 59, 66, 68, 175
Crannell, W. W., statement of lands sold to, ... 248
Crary, John, statement of lands sold to,.. 79, 80, 87, 88, 132, 135, 140
Crary, L. P., statement of lands sold to, ... 36
Crary, Nathaniel, statement of lands sold to, ... 125
Crawford, William, statement of lands sold to, ... 93
Crocker, L. B., statement of lands sold to, ... 19, 22
Crafut, Norman S., statement of lands sold to, ... 147
Crolius, J. M. & J., statement of lands sold to, ... 338
Cromelian, Rowland, statement of lands sold to, ... 38
28. Cromwell, Andrew E., extra compensation paid to, .. 4
23. Crooked Lake canal, income from, and disbursements for, ... 20, 21, 38
tolls contributed by, to Erie canal, ... 21
proportion chargeable to, for repairs and maintenance of Erie and Champlain canals, ... 11, 21
cost of over revenues, ... 39
42. report of number of unsettled claims for damages on, ... 4
57. notice for proposals for repairs of, ... 37, 146

No. Doc. | | Page.
115. Croswell, Edwin, statement of lands sold to,........ 359
Croswell, Jacob, statement of ladds 'sold to, ... 320
Crowl, Lyman, statement of lands sold to,.......... 281
Crowley, Jno., statement of lands sold to, ... 254
Cuddeback, Nathan, statement of lands sold to, ... 244
Culbert, Alex. C., statement of lands sold to, ... 321
Culbert, John, statement of lands sold to,....... 38, 256
Culon, Benjamin, statement of lands sold to,........ 41
Culver Benjamin, statement of lands sold to, ... 200
3. Currency, banking and insurance, provision for committee on,.......................... 2
9. committee on,.......................... 4
51. minority report of committee on, relative to individual liability of stockholders of banking corporations, ... 1
53. Currency, banking, insurance and other corporations, joint report of committees on,................. 1, 2
115. Currier, Joseph, statement of lands sold to,........ 231
Curtice, Alfred P., statement of lands sold to,....... 305
1, 12. Curtis, George William, delegate at large, Richmond county, ... 1, 3
115. Cushman, Joseph P., statement of lands sold to,..... 298

D.

115. Daby, John L., statement of lands sold to,.......... 75
1, 12. Daly, Chas. P., delegate 4th district, New York county, 2, 3
115. Dalrymple, Luther, statement of lands sold to,....... 147
Damon, E. H., statement of lands sold to, ... 319
19. Danforth, Asa, superintendent of salt springs,....... 4
115. Daniels, Gad, statement of lands sold to, ... 239
28. Danolds, Charles A., extra compensation paid to, ... 8
55. Dansville Seminary, appropriations to, ... 18, 19
115. Dart, Wm. A., statement of lands sold to,.......... 159
55. Davenport Institute for Female Orphan Children, appropriations to, ... 59
40. Davis, Emerson E., testimony of, relative to management of Champlain canal, ... 329-43
115. Davis, Thos. F., statement of lands sold to, ... 323

No. Doc. Page.

115. Davis, William, statement of land sold to, ... 16
40. Davidson, John, testimony of, relative to letting canal contracts 28th Dec., ... 166–91
115. Day, Ira T., statement of lands sold to, ... 300
Day, Thomas, statement of lands sold to, ... 37
Day, Wm., statement of lands sold to, ... 350
Dayton, James, statement of lands sold to, ... 373
Dayton, Joel, statement of lands sold to, ... 138
54. Deaf and Dumb Asylum, N. Y., report of donations to, 14
grant of land to, ... 19
55. appropriations by State to, ... 3–7, 92
Deaf and Dumb Institution, appropriations to, ... 16–19
115. Dean, D. W., statement of lands sold to, ... 312
Dean, Jonathan, statement of lands sold to, ... 358
Dean, Thomas, statement of lands sold to, ... 208, 210
8. Debates and proceedings, report of committee relative to publication of, ... 1–4
contract price for printing, ... 1, 2
98. Deeds, informal, special laws for legalization of, prohibited, ... 14
66. Deficiency loans, provision for, ... 6, 7
limitations and restrictions relative to, ... 9
67. plan proposed by canal committee for, ... 8
115. DeGraff, John J., statement of lands sold to, ... 48
95. DeGraw, Charles J., testimony of, relative to management of canals, ... 30–32
40. testimony of, relative to his award for loss of lumber in Chemung river, ... 254–67
115. DeGraw, Jno. J., statement of lands sold to, ... 175
88. Delamater, James, testimony of, relative to capacity of Erie canal locks, ... 11–16
55. Delancey Institute, appropriations to, ... 16–19
115. Delano, A. P., statement of lands sold to, ... 298
55. Delaware Academy, appropriations to, ... 16–19
Literary Institute, appropriations to, ... 16–19
1. Delegates, list of, ... 1
Delegates at large, list of, ... 1
Delegates from senatorial districts, ... 1, 2, 3
12. Demers, Eugene L., doorkeeper, Rensselaer, ... 8
Demers, George W., reporter, Rensselaer, ... 9

No. Doc.		Page.
54.	Demilt Dispensary, N. Y., report of donations to,....	4, 5
25.	appropriations to, ...	77–79
115.	Denmore, C. R., statement of lands sold to, ...	322
28.	Dennison, H. D., extra compensation paid to, ...	9, 11
40.	testimony of, relative to repairs of section 9 of Erie canal, ...	913–18
115.	statement of lands sold to, ... 366,	367
	Denison, Samuel, statement of lands sold to, ...	300
	Densmore, Amos, jr., statement of lands sold to,....	59
	Densmore, Wildes, statement of lands sold to, ...	62
	DePecy, Henry W., statement of lands sold to,......	193
	DeRosia, Lewis, statement of lands sold to, ...	231
	DeRosia, L., jr., statement of lands sold to,.........	231
55.	DeRuyter Institute, appropriations to,...............	16–19
54.	Destitute children, society for, N. Y., report of donations to,..................................	11
115.	DeVeaux, Samuel, statement of lands sold to,... 237,	313
1, 12.	Develin, John E., delegate 8th district, New York Co.,	2, 3
115.	DeVoe, Gilbert, statement of lands sold to,..... 248,	249
12.	DeWigne, Ferdinand, librarian, Schenectady,.......	8
159.	DeWolf, Mr. testimony of, before committee on salt springs, ...	23
115.	Dewey & Base, statement of lands sold to,..........	20
	Dexter, James & Geo., statement of lands sold to, 160,	165
	Dezeng, W. S., statement of lands sold to,..........	230
	Dibble, Owen, statement of lands sold to,..........	48
	Dibble, Tyler, statement of lands sold to,...........	286
	Dibble & Estes, statement of lands sold to, ...	278
	Dick, Jacob E., statement of lands sold to, ...	95
	Dickey, Daniel, statement of lands sold to, ... 206,	207
	Dickey, Joseph, statement of lands sold to,.........	206
	Dickey, S., statement of lands sold to, ...	340
	Dickinson, A. C., statement of lands sold to, ...	27
	Dickenson, Hiram, statement of lands sold to,.......	95
	Dillon, Timothy, statement of lands sold to,........	151
	Dingman, Jacob R., statement of lands sold to,......	113
171.	Disabled soldiers, report of select committee on,.....	1–3
55.	Dispensaries, appropriations to, from 1847 to 1866, inclusive, ...	92

No. Doc. Page.

61. District attorneys, to be appointed by Governor,.... 2
term of office of, ... 2
removal of by Governor,................. 2
98. Divorces, special laws for, prohibited,.............. 14
115. Dixon, Sylvanus, statement of lands sold to,........ 135
Dobbe, Thomas, statement of lands sold to,......... 338
35. Document number, duplicate of, report of committee on organization of Legislature, ... 1-6
8. Documents, contract price for printing,............ 1
40. Dodge, Alanson, testimony of, in regard to work on Chenango canal extension,....... 143-49, 155
testimony of, relative to conduct of Commissioner Bruce, in regard to contracts on Cayuga and Seneca canal,........ 139-44, 152, 153
testimony of, relative to award to Charles J. DeGraw, ... 149-51
testimony of, relative to combinations by canal contractors,........................ 158, 159
testimony of, relative to letting of contracts for section one, Erie canal,.............. 150, 151
115. Dodge, Lyman, statement of lands sold to,......... 134
Dodge, Nathaniel, statement of lands sold to,........ 273
Dodge, Samuel, statement of lands sold to,.......... 161
Dolph, George, statement of lands sold to,.......... 117
Dolph, Norman, statement of lands sold to,......... 117
Doolittle, Luther, statement of lands sold to, ... 68
54. Dorcas Society, N. Y., report of donations to,....... 8
115. Dorrance, Daniel, statement of lands sold to,........ 341
40. Dorn, Henry A., testimony of, relative to work on Chenango canal extension,..................... 155-58
Dorn, Robert C., testimony of, relative to letting canal contracts, 28th December, ... 846-55
testimony of, relative to purchase by him of a boat for the State,..................... 845, 846
testimony of, relative to management of Champlain canal,.......................... 858-61
testimony of, relative to contract for repairs of section one, Erie canal, and dredging Albany basin, ... 851-53

No. Doc. Page.

115. Dorsheimer, P., statement of lands sold to, ... 351
Doubleday, Ammi, statement of lands sold to,..93, 94, 95, 377
Doubleday, Ammi, Jr., statement of lands sold to, 389, 390
Doud, Chauncey, statement of lands sold to, ... 280
Doud, Giles, statement of lands sold to, ... 105
Dougherty, James, statement of lands sold to,....... 265
Dougherty, John, statement of lands sold to, ... 72, 344
389, 390
Douglas, Calvin S., statement of lands sold to, ... 71
Douglas, Leander, statement of lands sold to, ... 71
Douw, Volkert P., statement of lands sold to,.. 70, 99, 235
376, 390, 391
Dow, John, statement of lands sold to,............. 69
Downer, J. L., statement of lands sold to, ... 356
Downing, Roswell, statement of lands sold to, .. 361, 362
Drake, Benjamin, statement of lands sold to,........ 241
Driscoll, D., statement of lands sold to, ... 383, 392

65. Drooy, John C., judgment in favor of, against city of New York,................................ 1

115. Drum, Jacob, statement of lands sold to, ... 275
Drum, Jno. statement of lands sold to,............. 124
Drum & Stevens, statement of lands sold to, ... 124
Duane, James, statement of lands sold to, ... 226, 227
Dubois, S. V., statement of lands sold to,........... 368
Dudley, Asa, statement of lands sold to,............ 138
Dudley, Chas. E., statement of lands sold to, ... 248, 249
281, 283, 293, 294, 295, 298
Dudley, J. K., statement of lands sold to, ... 309
Dudley, L. G., statement of lands sold to, ... 380
Dudley, Sardis, statement of lands sold to, ... 141
Dudley & Olcott, statement of lands sold to, ... 303

1, 12. Duganne, Augustine J. H., delegate at large, New York county,......................... 1, 3

4. resolution of, for committee on industrial interests, ... 2

73. plan of, for executive council, ... 1–3

115. Duncan, Jno. T., statement of lands sold to,......... 328
Duncan, John and Thomas, statement of lands sold to, 102

55. Dundee Academy, appropriations to, ... 17–19

115. Dunham, David, statement of lands sold to, ... 211

No. Doc. Page.

55. Dunkirk St. Mary's Orphan Asylum, appropriations to, 66, 67
115. Dunn, Joel, statement of lands sold to,............. 337
40. Dunn, Peter, testimony of, relative to his proposal for repairs of Genesee Valley canal, ... 214–20
115. Dunn & Vosburgh, statement of lands sold to,....... 200
Dunning & Wayne, statement of lands sold to,.. 111, 113
115. Durand, Charles, statement of lands sold to, ... 79
40. Durkee, Archibald W., testimony of, relative to management of Champlain canal, ... 580–88
115. Durkee, Justus, statement of land sold to, ... 205
Dusenberre, G. & H., statement of lands sold to,..... 322
Dusenbury, George, statement of lands sold to,...... 93
55. Dutchess County Academy, appropriations to,....... 8, 11
1, 12. Dwight, Chas. C., delegate 25th district, Cayuga county, 3, 3
123. Dwight, C. C., minority report of, relative to State prisons, ... 1, 2
115. Dwight, T. C., statement of lands sold to,....... 320, 321
1, 12. Dwight, Theodore W., delegate 19th district, Oneida county, ... 2, 3
4. Dwight, Mr. T. W., resolution of, for committee on charities, ... 2
115. Dwinelle, Benjamin, statement of lands sold to,...... 160
Dyer, B. H., statement of lands sold to, ... 381

E.

19. Earll, N. H., superintendent of salt springs,......... 5
28. Ears & Adams, extra compensation paid to,......... 8
55. East Bloomfield Academy, appropriations to, ... 16–19
54. Eastern Dispensary, N. Y., report of donations to, ... 4, 5
appropriations to, ... 76–79
55. East Genesee Conference Seminary, appropriations to, 19
65. Eastman, Arthur M., judgment in favor of, against city of New York, ... 2
115. Eaton & Perkins, statement of lands sold to, ... 209
28. Ecker, John, extra compensation paid to,........... 9
54. Eclectic Dispensary, N. Y., report of donations to,.... 16
1, 12. Eddy, John, delegate, 20th district, Otsego county, .. 2, 3
115. Eddy, Jno. W., statement of lands sold to, ... 341

No. Doc. Page.

115. Eddy, Seneca, statement of lands sold to, ... 340
115. Edgerton, Albert, statement of lands sold to,........ 146
115. Edson & Beach, statement of lands sold to, ... 208
3. Education, provision for committee on,............. 2
9. committee on, ... 4
116. article reported by committee on, ... 1–3
explanatory report of committee on, ... 3, 4
dissent of certain members from report on, ... 4
superintendent of (see " Superintendent of Public Education ").
State Board of (see State "Board of Education ").
169. article on, as amended and referred to committee on revision, ... 1, 2
55. Educational and charitable institutions, report by Comptroller of appropriations to, ... 1, 92
116. funds to be paid into the treasury, and preserved inviolate, ... 1
revenues from, how to be applied, ... 12
how to be invested,.................. 2
institutions, provisions relative to general or special endowment of, ... 2
4. interests, resolution to provide for committee on,................................... 1
15. qualification for suffrage, relative to, ... 7
28. Edwards, E. H., extra compensation paid to,........ 11
115. Efner, E. D., statement of lands sold to,........... 36, 351
Eglin, Thomas, statement of lands sold to,.......... 149
45. Eight-hour law, petition of New York State Workingmen's Assembly relative to, ... 1–4
115. Eldred, Rufus, statement of lands sold to, ... 364
15. Elections, challenges at,........................ 2
betting on, cause of exclusion from franchise,. 2
to be by ballot except in certain cases, ... 3
Election oath,................................ 2
11. Elective franchise, bribery at elections cause of exclusion from,............................ 2
15. qualifications necessary to,................ 1
term of citizenship and residence necessary for, 1, 2

No. Doc.		Page.
15.	Elective franchise, causes for exclusion from, ...	2
115.	Ellenwood, G. W., statement of lands sold to, ...	363
55.	Ellington Academy, appropriations to, ...	17–19
115.	Ellis, Charles, statement of lands sold to, ...	123
	Ellis, Esquire, statement of lands sold to, ...	112
28.	Ellis, John, extra compensation paid to, ...	4
115.	Ellis & Shaw, statement of lands sold to, ... 239,	240
	Elmendorf, J., statement of lands sold to, ...	22
	Elmer, Orville, statement of lands sold to, ...	258
	Elmore, Martin, statement of lands sold to, ...	109
55.	Elmira Academy, appropriations to, ...	16–19
21.	Elmira, Canandaigua & Niagara Falls railroad, amount of freight carried over, during the year 1857:	
	whole number of tons, ...	16
	products of the forest, number of tons, ...	16
	animals, number of tons, ...	16
	vegetable food, number of tons, ...	16
	other agricultural products, number of tons, ..	16
	manufactures, number of tons, ...	16
	merchandise, number of tons, ...	16
	other articles, number of tons, ...	16
55.	Elmira Ladies' Relief Association, appropriations to, .	75
	Female College, appropriations to, ...	83
	Soldiers' Home, appropriations to, ...	90
21.	Elmira & Williamsport railroad, amount of freight carried over during each of the years, 1861, 1862, 1864, 1865 and 1866:	
	whole number of tons, ...	24–34
	products of the forest, number of tons, ...	24–34
	animals, number of tons, ...	24–34
	vegetable food, ...	24–34
	other agricultural products, number of tons, ..	24–34
	manufactures, number of tons, ...	24–34
	merchandise, number of tons, ...	24–34
	other articles, number of tons, ...	24–34
28.	Elwood & Rasback, extra compensation paid to, ...	4
1, 12.	Ely, Lorenzo D., delegate 28th district, Monroe county,	3, 3
115.	Emerson, Amos, statement of lands sold to, ...	125
	Emmons, Moses, statement of lands sold to, ...	51

No. Doc.		Page.
98.	Enacting clause of bills,	5
116.	Endowment of Literary or Educational Institutions, provisions relative to,	2
1, 12.	Endress, Isaac L., delegate 30th district, Livingston county,	3, 3
3.	Engrossment and enrollment, provision for committee on,	2
9.	committee on,	6
40.	Ensign, J. T., testimony of, relative to management of Champlain canal,	441–43
55.	Erasmus Hall Academy, appropriations to,	16–19
23.	Erie canal, merchandise from other states passed through by way of Buffalo,	15
42.	report of number of unsettled claims for damages on,	4
57.	section No. 5, contract for repairs of,	6–12
	section No. 2, contract for repairs of,	28–34
	section No. 1, contract for repairs of,	47–54
	section No. 11, contract for repairs of,	71–78
64.	number of tons moved on, each year from 1852 to 1866, inclusive,	14, 15
69.	cost of construction and maintenance, and interest thereon,	5
	income of, and interest thereon,	4
	excess of income over expenditures,	5
87.	tonnage of freight from western States carried on each year from 1837 to 1866, inclusive,	13
	tonnage of freight from the State of New York reaching tide water by, each year from 1837 to 1866, inclusive,	13
	total tonnage reaching tide water by, each year from 1837 to 1866, inclusive,	13
	cost of transporting freight on, compared with New York Central Railroad,	16
88.	report of committee relative to capacity of locks on,	1–16
	time required to pass boats through lock east of Syracuse,	2
	number of lockages at Alexander's Lock from 1860 to 1866, inclusive,	4

No. Doc. Page.

88. Erie canal, number of lockages at Lock 49 during the month of November, 1866, ... 15
average cargo of boats on, ... 14–15
89. report of Canal Commissioners relative to breaks in, ... 1–7
number of breaks in, from 1856 to 1866, inclusive, ... 4–7
90. testimony taken by canal committee relative to cost of improvements of, ... 1–60
127. Lock No. 49, report by Commissioner Hayt of test of working capacity of, ... 1–15
164. report of Canal Board relative to capacity of locks on, to pass boats eastward, ... 1–74
tons of freight from western States transported to tide water on, from 1846 to 1866, inclusive, ... 32
32. report of Auditor relative to number of breaks in, ... 1–4
expense of repairing breaks in, from 1857 to 1866, inclusive, ... 4
164. cost of enlarging locks on, ... 12
locks at Fort Plain, test of capacity of, ... 41–74
23. Erie and Champlain canals, income since 1817 from, and disbursements for, ... 8–11, 38
proportion of disbursements chargeable to lateral canals, ... 11
revenues of, over cost, ... 39
164. number of tons delivered at tide water by, each year from 1860 to 1866, inclusive, ... 15
21. Erie railway, amount of freight carried over each year from 1862 to 1866, inclusive:
whole number of tons, ... 26–34, 38
products of the forest, number of tons, ... 26–34, 38
animals, number of tons, ... 26–34, 38
vegetable food, number of tons, ... 26–34, 38
other agricultural products, number of tons, 26–34, 38
manufactures, number of tons, ... 26–34, 38
merchandize, number of tons, ... 26–34, 38
other articles, number of tons, ... 26–34, 38

No. Doc.		Page.
115.	Estes, Joseph, statement of lands sold to, ...	63
	Estes & Walker, statement of lands sold to, ...	146
	Esty, Geo. W., statement of lands sold to, ...	344
55.	Evans Academy, appropriations to, ...	19
115.	Evans, Richard & William, statement of lands sold to,	72
1, 12.	Evarts, William M., delegate at large, New York county, ...	1, 3
115.	Everest, Hiram, statement of lands sold to, .. 79, 87,	143
	Everett, Hovey, statement of lands sold to, ...	147
	Everson & Hagenin, statement of lands sold to, ...	17
	Ewers, Tallmadge, statement of lands sold to, ...	389
73.	Executive council, plan of Mr. Duganne to provide for,	1–3
28.	Extra compensation to canal contractors, report of auditor relative to, ...	1–11
98.	Extra compensation to public officers or employès prohibited, ...	8
54.	Eye and Ear Infirmary, New York, report of donations to, ...	4, 5

F.

No. Doc.		Page.
115.	Fairchild, L., statement of lands sold to, ...	322
	Fairchild & Lyon, statement of lands sold to, ...	386
55.	Fairfield Academy, appropriations to, ...	16–19
115.	Falley, Geo. F., statement of lands sold to, ...	236
55.	Falley Seminary, appropriations to, ...	16–19
115.	Fancher, Hori, statement of lands sold to, ...	144
	Farland, Dudley, statement of lands sold to, ...	264
	Farlin, Dudley, statement of lands sold to, ...	44
55.	Farmers' Hall Academy, appropriations to, ...	20–23
115.	Farnham, Joshua, statement of lands sold to, ...	240
	Farnham, Le Roy, statement of lands sold to, ...	256
1, 12.	Farnum, Edward J., delegate 30th district, Allegany county, ...	3, 3
28.	Farquharson, James, extra compensation paid to, ...	4
	Farquharson & Pierce, extra compensation paid to, ...	4
115.	Farrington, Nelson, statement of lands sold to, ...	379
	Farrington, Wm., statement of lands sold to, ...	211
	Farrington & Raymond, statement of lands sold to, ..	311
28.	Farwell, Samuel, extra compensation paid to, ...	4

No. Doc.		Page.
115.	Faulkner, James, statement of lands sold to, ...	359
	Favill, William, statement of lands sold to, ...	85
	Fay, Jonas, statement of lands sold to, ...	313
55.	Fayetteville Academy, appropriations to, ...	20–23
115.	Feagles, Nathaniel, statement of lands sold to, ...	241
39.	Fees, to require general laws for regulation of, ...	2
115.	Fellows, Joseph, statement of lands sold to, 371, 372,	385
15.	Felons, to be deprived of suffrage, ...	2
115.	Felters, Joshua S., statement of lands sold to,. 58, 621	176
4.	Female suffrage, resolution relative to, ...	1
15.	relative to, ...	6
115.	Fenton, Lossen, statement of lands sold to, ...	45
	Ferguson, Alexander, statement of lands sold to,....	145
	Ferguson, Daniel, statement of lands sold to,........	378
	Ferguson, David, statement of lands sold to,........	376
	Ferguson, Jno., statement of lands sold to, ... 278,	292
	Ferrill, Joel, statement of lands sold to, ...	15
	Ferrill, Jno. A., statement of lands sold to,..... 120,	279
	Ferrill, T. N., statement of lands sold to, ... 121,	289
	Ferrill & Patten, statement of lands sold to,.........	121
	Ferrill & Schuyler, statement of lands sold to,.. 121,	122
1, 12.	Ferry, Elijah E., delegate 20th district, Otsego county,	2, 3
121.	plan for judiciary, presented by,............	1–10
149.	Feudal tenures, provision relative to,...............	4, 5
1, 12.	Field, Ben, delegate 29th district, Orleans county,....	3, 3
4.	resolution of, for committee on claims,.......	2
115.	Files, Geo., statement of lands sold to, ...	240
	Files, Geo. P., statement of lands sold to,...........	247
28.	Filmore, H. C., extra compensation paid to,.........	4
3.	Finance, provision for committee on,...............	2
9.	committee on, ...	3
63.	minority report of Mr. Hatch, relative to,....	1–29
64.	minority report of Mr. Clark, relative to, ...	1, 2
66.	majority report on, ...	9–21
	article on, reported by majority of committee on,	1–9
118.	minority report of Mr. A. F. Allen, on, relative to taxation,......................	1, 2
119.	amendment of section 1 of article on, proposed by Mr. E. Brooks,.....................	1

No. Doc.		Page.
129.	Finance, article on, as amended at time of adjournment, 24th of September, ...	1-8
142.	proposed substitute for section 8, of article on,	1, 2
154.	article on, as amended and referred to committee on revision, ...	1-8
15.	amendment proposed by Mr. Magee, to section 15, of article on, ...	1, 2
73.	Financial audit and assessment, to provide for boards of,	2, 3
	secretary of, to be member of executive council,	2
115.	Finch, D. & J. W., statement of lands sold to, ...	376
	Finch, Isaac, statement of lands sold to, ... 160, 161,	162
	Finch, J., statement of lands sold to, ...	376
	Finch, J. S. & J., statement of lands sold to, ...	157
	Finch, James C., statement of lands sold to, 148, 149,	295 296
	Finch, Joshua, statement of lands sold to, ...	161
	Finch, Martin, statement of lands sold to, ...	287
	Finch, S. & J. C., statement of lands sold to, 148, 149,	150
	Finch, Samuel, statement of lands sold to, ... 156,	157
	Finch, William, statement of lands sold to, 51, 59, 60, 163, 166,	115 282
	Finch & Lamoreaux, statement of lands sold to, ...	59-62
149.	Fines, not to be excessive, ...	3
73.	Fire and insurance, to provide for boards of, ...	2
	secretary of, to be member of executive council,	2
58.	Fish in international waters, report of committee on industrial interests relative to, ...	1, 2
115.	Fish, Aaron G., statement of lands sold to, ...	236
	Fish, E., statement of lands sold to, ...	376
	Fish, Thomas, statement of lands sold to, ...	201
	Fisher, George, statement of lands sold to, ...	23, 26
	Fisher, Samuel B., statement of lands sold to, ...	48
	Fisher & Kent, statement of lands sold to, ...	48
	Fitch, Ebenezer, statement of lands sold to, ...	243
	Fitch & Foster, statement of lands sold to, ...	258
	Fitzhugh, Henry, statement of lands sold to, ...	274
	Fitzpatrick, Henry, statement of lands sold to, ... 25,	27, 30
12.	Fitzpatrick, J. C., reporter, New York, ...	9
28.	Fitzpatrick, John, extra compensation paid to, ...	8

No. Doc. Page.

28. Fitzsimmons & Brady, extra compensation paid to,... 5
54. Five Points Gospel Union Mission, N. Y., report of donations to, ... 10
House of Industry, N. Y., report of donations to, ... 10
appropriations to, ... 58, 59
115. Flanders, Chapin, statement of lands sold to,... 137, 138
Flanders, Moses & David, statement of lands sold to,. 124
Flagg, Elisha, statement of lands sold to,....... 46, 292
Flagg, E. & A., statement of lands sold to, ... 326
Flagg, William, statement of lands sold to,......... 146
1, 12. Flagler, Thomas T., delegate 29th district, Niagara county, ... 3, 3
115. Fleming, Robert, statement of lands sold to,......... 34, 35
Fletcher, F. P., statement of lands sold to, ...357, 365
23. Floating debt loan, amount of,..................... 5
115. Flood, R. A., statement of lands sold to,....... 315, 327
164. Flour and grain, shipments of during the year 1862, from ports on Lake Michigan,............ 33
exports of, during the year 1862, from certain ports,.............................. 34
amount of, sent eastward from lake regions, from 1856 to 1862, inclusive,............. 35–40
21. Flushing railroad, amount of freight carried over, each year from 1854 to 1856, inclusive:
whole number of tons, ... 10–16
115. Flusquin, William, statement of lands sold to, ... 16
Fobes, P. W., statement of lands sold to,........... 324
Forbes & West, statement of lands sold to, ... 166
1, 12. Folger, Charles J., delegate at large, Ontario county, . 1, 3
115. Folsom, John, statement of lands sold to,.. 115, 116, 142
55. Fonda Academy, appropriations to,................ 20–23
115. Fondey, Wm. H., statement of lands sold to,........ 281
Foot, John, statement of lands sold to,............. 107
Forbes, F. W., statement of lands sold to, ... 381
Forbes, Philander, statement of lands sold to,....... 237
Forbes, Fartlett & Bartell, statement of lands sold to,. 166
Ford, John, statement of lands sold to,............. 69
95. Forrest, David P., testimony of, relative to management of canals,.............................. 51, 52

No. Doc. Page.

40. Forrest, David P., testimony of, relative to Peter Dunn's bid for repairs of Genesee Valley canal,.. 876–86

55. Forrest Orphan Institute, appropriations to,......... 59

115. Fort, John, statement of lands sold to,............. 25

Fort & Marvin, statement of lands sold to, ... 118

55. Fort Covington Academy, appropriations to,........ 20–23

Fort Edward Collegiate Institute, appropriations to,.. 23

Fort Plain Seminary and Female Collegiate Institute, appropriations to, ... 21–23

115. Foster, Eleanor, statement of lands sold to,......... 250

Foster, John L., statement of lands sold to,......... 51

Foster, John S., statement of lands sold to, .. 52, 55, 56, 165, 170

Foster & Bennett, statement of lands sold to,........ 258

Foster, Mason & Foster, statement of lands sold to,... 123

Foster & Noyes, statement of lands sold to,......... 12

37. Foundling Hospital, petition of directors of, relative to Foundling Hospital,........................ 1–5

54. Foundling Hospital or Infants' Home, New York, report of donations to,....................... 8

115. Fowler, Chas., statement of lands sold to,...... 312, 330

1, 12. Fowler, Loring, delegate 21st district, Madison county, 2, 3

115. Fowler & Caulkin, statement of lands sold to, .. 288, 311

Fox, A. & N., statement of lands sold to,........... 131

Fox, John F., statement of lands sold to, ... 109

Fox, Wm., statement of lands sold to,.............. 161

Francis, David, statement of lands sold to,.......... 208

Francis, James, statement of lands sold to,.......... 361

1, 12. Francis, John M., delegate 12th district, Rensselaer county,.............................. 2, 3

114. minority report of, relative to organization and government of cities,................... 1–7

28. Francis & Hopkins, extra compensation paid to, ... 5

1, 12. Frank, Augustus, delegate at large, Wyoming county, 1, 3

55. Franklin Academy, Malone, appropriations to, ... 20–23

Plattsburgh, appropriations to, ... 20–23

115. Franklin, Henry L., statement of lands sold to, ... 247

28. Frazee & Foster, extra compensation paid to,........ 5

115. Frazer, Spencer & Brown, statement of lands sold to,. 133

Frazer & Wakefield, statement of lands sold to, ... 142

No. Doc.		Page.
115.	Frazier, Ira G., statement of lands sold to, ...	357
55.	Fredonia Academy, appropriations to, ...	20–23
98.	Free colleges may be exempted from taxation, ...	10
	Free schools, Legislature required to provide for, ...	9
116.	provision relating to, ...	3
55.	Free school of Academy of the Sacred Heart, Manhattanville, appropriations to, ...	59
115.	Freeman, Orris, statement of lands sold to, ...	209
	Freeman, Samuel, statement of lands sold to, ...	358
	Frege, Francis, statement of lands sold to, ...	337
	Frege, Joseph, statement of lands sold to, ...	337
28.	Freligh, M., & George, extra compensation paid to, ...	5
115.	French, Elias, statement of lands sold to, ...	139
	French, Jasper, statement of lands sold to, ...	242
	French, Luman, statement of lands sold to, ...	160
	French, Nathaniel, statement of lands sold to, ...	361
	French, William, statement of lands sold to, ...	361
55.	Friends Academy, appropriations to, ...	22–23
	Friendship Academy, appropriations to, ...	20–23
115.	Frisbie, Joseph, statement of lands sold to, ...	13
	Frost, J. G., statement of lands sold to, ...	311
	Fuller, Chauncey, statement of lands sold to, ...	53
1, 12.	Fuller, Jerome, delegate, 28th district, Monroe Co., ..	3, 3
115.	Fuller, Luman, statement of lands sold to, .. 48, 100,	308
115.	Fuller, R. H., statement of lands sold to, ... 353,	386
1, 12.	Fullerton, Stephen W., delegate, 10th district, Orange county, ...	2, 3
55.	Fulton Academy, appropriations to, ...	20–23
115.	Furman, Henry, statement of lands sold to, ...	239
	Furman, Robert, statement of lands sold to, ...	307
3.	Future amendments of Constitution, provision for committee on, ...	2
9.	committee on, ...	5
108.	report of committee on, ...	1–5
	article reported by committee on, ...	5, 6
166.	article on, as amended and referred to committee on revision, ...	112

No. Doc. Page.

G.

115. Gage, Walter, statement of lands sold to,........... 358
Gage, Wm., statement of lands sold to, ... 212
Gale, Alonzo H., statement of lands sold to, ... 61
Gale, Daniel, statement of lands sold to,............ 309
28. Gale, Thomas, extra compensation paid to,.. 11, 367, 382
383, 384
115. Galusha, Joseph, statement of lands sold to, ... 345
55. Galway Academy, appropriations to,............... 20–23
40. Gandell, James R., testimony of, relative to management of Champlain canal, ... 565–69
115. Gannett, Warren, statement of lands sold to,........ 382
1, 12. Garvin, Samuel B., delegate 4th district, New York county,...................................... 2, 3
115. Gates, Jeremiah, statement of lands sold to, ... 235
Gates, Willis, statement of lands sold to, 80, 265, 278, 379
Gaylord, Henry T., statement of lands sold to, ... 329
40. testimony of, relative to management of Champlain canal,.......................... 290–92
19. Geddes, George, superintendent of salt springs,...... 6
159. testimony of before committee on salt springs, 1, 2, 5
40. Geer, R. Nelson, testimony of relative to letting canal contracts, 28th December, ... 724–40
testimony of, relative to Parker's contract for repairs of section one of Chenango canal,. 724–30
28. Geere & Steves, extra compensation paid to, ... 5
19. Gere, Robert, superintendent of salt springs, ... 5
115. statement of lands sold to,................. 392
120. General Fund, payments from on account of canals,.. 4–8
contributions from canal fund to, ... 2, 3
23. General fund debt, amount of, ... 5, 6
66. statement of,............................ 1
39. General laws, resolution of Mr. Sherman, relative to,. 1, 2
98. for formation of corporations, required, ... 10
91. General orders, list of,.......................... 1, 2
110. list of 3d of September,.................. 1–3
128. list of 24th of September, ... 1–3
55. Genesee College, appropriations to, ... 81–83
Genesee Conference Seminary, appropriations to, ... 22, 23

No. Doc.		Page.

55. Genesee Valley Seminary, appropriations to,........ 22, 23
Genesee Wesleyan Seminary, appropriations to, ... 20–23
Genesee and Wyoming Seminary, appropriations to,. 20–23
20. Genesee Valley canal, memorial of citizens of Pennsylvania in favor of, ... 1–4
projected improvements to connect with,..... 2, 3
coal, iron and lumber to be shipped by,...... 2–4
23. income from and disbursements for,...... 26, 27, 38
tolls contributed by, to Erie canal,.......... 27
proportion chargeable to, for repairs and maintenance of Erie and Champlain canals,..... 11, 27
cost of, over revenues,..................... 39
42. report of number of unsettled claims for damages on,.............................. 4
57. notice for proposals for repairs of,.......... 147
55. Geneseo Academy, appropriations to, ... 20–23
Geneva Classical Union School, appropriations to, ... 21–23
Geneva College, appropriations to,................. 80–83
115. George, Henry, statement of lands sold to,.......... 311
Gerard, Charles, statement of lands sold to, ... 69
54. German-American School, 19th ward, N. Y., report of donations to, ... 15
German Dispensary, New York, report of donations to, 11
55. New York, appropriations to, ... 79
54. German Hospital, New York, grant of land to,...... 22
1, 12. Gerry, Elbridge T., delegate 5th district, New York county, ... 2, 3
115. Gibbs, Russell, statement of lands sold to, ... 46
Gibbons, Alfred, statement of lands sold to, ... 110
Gibson, H., statement of lands sold to,............. 374
Gifford, Asa, statement of lands sold to, ... 258, 259
Gifford, Jonathan, statement of lands sold to,....... 116
Gifford, William, statement of lands sold to, ... 86
Gilbert, E. F., statement of lands to,............... 38
Gilbert, Liberty, statement of lands sold to,......... 72
28. Gilbert & Sprague, extra compensation paid to,...... 5
55. Gilbertsville Academy and Collegiate Institute, appropriations to, ... 20–23
115. Gilchrist, Ira A., statement of lands sold to,......... 313

No. Doc. Page.

40. Gilchrist, James H., testimony of, relative to management of Champlain canal, ... 551–55
115. Gillett, Amos, statement of lands sold to, ... 367
Gillett, Watson, statement of lands sold to, ... 141
Gillmore, J. & M., statement of lands sold to, ... 293, 349
Gilson, Ami, statement of lands sold to, ... 87
Gilson, Joel, statement of lands sold to, ... 143
40. Gilson, Nathan T., testimony of, relative to management of Champlain canal, ... 374–85
115. Glazier, Artemas, statement of lands sold to, ... 240
Gleason, Barnes, statement of lands sold to, ... 124
55. Glens Falls Academy, appropriations to, ... 20–23
12. Glidden, Henry A., assistant secretary, Orleans, ... 8
115. Glover, Ezekiel, statement of lands sold to, ... 124
55. Gloversville Union Seminary, appropriations to, ... 22, 23
115. Godard, Walter, statement of lands sold to, ... 365
Goff, Levi C., statement of lands sold to, ... 47
Goff, Lyman, statement of lands sold to, ... 349, 360, 381
Golden, Matthew, statement of lands sold to, ... 381
Golden, Thomas, statement of lands sold to, ... 353
Goodenow, Timothy, statement of lands sold, ... 88
Goodrich, Guy H., statement of lands sold to, ... 104
1, 12. Goodrich, Milo, delegate 24th district, Tompkins county, ... 3, 3
117. minority report of, on judiciary, ... 1–15
115. Goodrich, Sarah, statement of lands sold to, ... 379
Goodman, O., statement of lands sold to, ... 357
Goodell, Jabez, statement of lands sold to, ... 36, 38
90. Goodsell, James P., testimony of, relative to improvements of Erie canal, ... 41–52
40. Goodsell, J. Platt, testimony of, relative to letting canal contracts 28th Dec., ... 241–43, 861–76
testimony of, relative to points taken in declaring bids informal, ... 866–69
testimony of, relative to contract for repairs of sec. one, Erie canal, and dredging Albany basin, ... 869, 870
12. Goodwin, Nathaniel, janitor, Albany, ... 8
115. Gordon, Lawrence P., statement of lands sold to, ... 54, 55

No. Doc. Page.

115. Gorton, Joshua, statement of lands sold to, ... 101
Goss, Surry, statement of lands sold to, ... 46
Goucher, Sidney, statement of lands sold to, ... 53
Gould, Horace, satement of lands sold to, ... 59, 162
Gould, Jno., statement of lands sold to, ... 276
1, 12. Gould, John Stanton, delegate 11th district, Columbia county, ... 2, 3
55. Gouverneur Wesleyan Seminary, appropriations to, ... 24–27
115. Gove, Elisha, statement of lands sold to, ... 166
Gove, Geo. B. R., statement of lands sold to, ... 127
48. Governor, report by, of list of applications for pardons, from 1849 to 1867, inclusive, ... 1–18
60. election and term of office of, ... 4, 5
qualifications required for, ... 4
to be commander-in-chief, ... 5
compensation of, ... 5
may call special sessions of Legislature or Senate only, ... 5
impeachment of, ... 6
power of, relative to vetoing and signing bills,. 7, 8
may veto parts of bills, ... 7
61. power of, to remove county officers, ... 2
76. power of, to reprieve, pardon, or commute, ... 4, 5
94. to be commander-in-chief of militia, ... 2
3. Governor and Lieutenant-Governor, provision for committee on, ... 2
9. committee on, ... 2
60. report of committee on, ... 1–8
93. article on, as amended and referred to committee on revision, ... 1–5
40. Graham, Nicholas, testimony of, relative to management of Champlain canal, ... 593–97
55. Grammar School of Columbia College, appropriations to, ... 24–27
of Madison University, appropriations to, ... 25–27
of New York Central College, appropriations to, ... 26–27
of University of City of New York, appropriations to, ... 24–27

No. Doc. | | Page.
115. Granger, Barlow, statement of lands sold to,........ 325
Granger, H. F., statement of lands sold to,.......... 310
28. Granger & Todd, extra compensation paid to, ... 5
115. Grant, A. P., statement of lands sold to, ... 18, 33
Grant, Gurdon, statement of lands sold to, ... 310
1, 12. Grant, John, delegate 23d district, Delaware county,.. 3, 3
115. Grant, Joseph, statement of lands sold to, ... 119
Grant, Warren, statement of lands sold to,.......... 323
Grant & Allen, statement of lands sold to,.......... 30
Grant & Randall, statement of lands sold to,........ 33
55. Granville Academy, appropriations to,............. 24-27
1, 12. Graves, Ezra, delegate 20th district, Herkimer county, 2, 4
4. resolution of, relative to female suffrage,..... 1
7. preamble and resolutions of, relative to prohibition or regulation of sale of intoxicating liquors, ... 1, 2
115. Graves, Jacob & Daniel, statement of lands sold to,.. 97
Graves, Morris C., statement of lands sold to,....... 267
Graves & Marsh, statement of lands sold to, ... 146
Gray, James, statement of lands sold to,............ 112
Gray, Michael, statement of lands sold to,.......... 149
Gray, Rebekah, statement of lands sold to, ... 124
Gray, Thos. S., statement of lands sold to, ... 377, 379
Gray, William, statement of lands sold to,.......... 332
Gray, Burhans & Pierce, statement of lands sold to,.. 354
1, 12. Greeley, Horace, delegate at large, Westchester Co.,.. 1, 4
49. amendment of, relative to organization of the Legislature, ... 1-3
115. Gregg, Absalom, statement of lands sold to, ... 206
Gregg, David, statement of lands sold to,........... 361
Gregg, Hannah, statement of lands sold to, ... 205
Gregg, Wm. T., statement of lands sold to,......... 208
Green, Artemus, statement of lands sold to,......... 205
Green, Francis, statement of lands sold to,.......... 212
Green, James, statement of lands sold to, ... 13, 264, 293
Green, Jonathan, statement of lands sold to, ... 206
Green, S. J., statement of lands sold to,........ 367, 383
Green, Wm., statement of lands sold to,............ 120
55. Greenbush and Schodack Academy, appropriations to, 24-27

No. Doc.		Page.
55.	Greenville Academy, appropriations to, ...	24–27
115.	Greenye, Peter, statement of lands sold to, ...	231
	Griffen, Daniel, statement of lands sold to, ...	15
	Griffen, David, statement of lands sold to, ...	16, 21
	Groat, David, statement of lands sold to, ...	244
1, 12.	Gross, Magnus, delegate 6th district, New York Co.,	2, 4
55.	Groton Academy, appropriations to, ...	24–27
115.	Guest, James, statement of lands sold to, ...	92
	Guilfoyle, Jno., statement of lands sold to, ...	383
	Gulick, Hiram G., statement of lands sold to, ...	241
	Gumair, Elias, statement of lands sold to, ...	244
	Gumand, L., statement of lands sold to, ...	345
	Gurney, Abram, statement of lands sold to, ...	147
	Guthrie, Abel, statement of lands sold to, ...	210

H.

No. Doc.		Page.
149.	Habeas corpus, provision relative to, ...	2
115.	Hallock, James, statement of lands sold to, ...	242
1, 12.	Hadley, Sterling G., delegate 26th district, Seneca Co.,	3, 4
115.	Hadley & Dean, statement of lands sold to, ...	304
	Hagaman, Wm., statement of lands sold to, ...	392
	Haggart, James, statement of lands sold to, ...	257
28.	Haight, Blood & Cady, extra compensation paid to, ..	5
1, 12.	Hale, Matthew, delegate 16th district, Essex county,	2, 4
140.	section relative to Supreme Court, proposed by,	1, 2
115.	Hale, R. S., statement of lands sold to, ...	380
55.	Halfmoon Academy, appropriations to, ...	24–27
115.	Hall, Clark, statement of lands sold to, ...	376
	Hall, Elihu, statement of lands sold to, ...	47
	Hall, Elisha, statement of lands sold to, ... 115,	146
	Hall, Isaac, statement of lands sold to, ...	95
	Hall, Joseph, statement of lands sold to, ...	125
	Hall, Monroe, statement of lands sold to, ... 76, 96,	115
	308, 309, 326, 327, 328, 355, 365, 369, 370, 371, 376,	390
	Hall, Samuel H. P., statement of lands sold to, ...	93, 95
	Hallett, Mason, statement of lands sold to, ...	88
	Halsey, Nicol, statement of lands sold to, ...	242
40.	Halsted, Daniel J., testimony of, relative to payment of money to public officers, ... 268–70, 715,	716

No. Doc.		Page.
115.	Halsted, J. & C., statement of lands sold to,.........	85
	Halsted, Platt R., statement of lands sold to,.. 46, 75, 76, 77 79, 80, 137, 176, 265, 268, 270, 297,	326
	Halsted & Myrick, statement of lands sold to,. 47, 175,	176
	Hamlin, Truman, statement of lands sold to, ... 278,	345
	Hammond, Ebenezer, statement of lands sold to, ...	144
	Hammond, J. C., statement of lands sold to, 294, 314,	326
1, 12.	Hammond, John M., delegate 30th district, Allegany county,......................................	3, 4
115.	Hammond, Stephen H., statement of lands sold to, ..	357
	Hammond, N. S., statement of lands sold to, ... 300,	312
	Hamilton, Erastus, statement of lands sold to,.......	109
	Hamilton, Robert, statement of lands sold to, ...	68
	Hamilton, Tilly, statement of lands sold to,.........	210
	Hamilton, Wm., statement of lands sold to, ...	360
55.	Hamilton Academy, appropriations to, ...	24–27
	Hamilton College, appropriations to,...............	80–83
	Hamilton Female Seminary, appropriations to,......	25–27
115.	Hancock, John, statement of lands sold to, ...	104
	Hand, A. C., statement of lands sold to,............	343
	Hand, Samuel P., statement of lands sold to,........	249
1, 12.	Hand, Stephen D., delegate 24th district, ...	3, 4
28.	Hanks, Byron M., extra compensation paid to, ...	9, 11
115.	Hanor, Harvey M., statement of lands sold to, ...	123
65.	Harbeck, Carl, judgment in favor of, against city of New York,..................................	1
1, 12.	Hardenburgh, Jacob, delegate at large, Ulster county,	1, 4
115.	Harmon, E. & E., statement of lands sold to,........	142
	Harmon, Jacob, statement of lands sold to,.........	163
	Harrington, J., statement of lands sold to,..........	206
	Harris, Alfred W., statement of lands sold to, ...	356
	Harris, Charles, statement of lands sold to,. 116, 263,	297 299
40.	Harris, Charles E., testimony of, relative to management of Champlain canal,....................	427–41
1, 12.	Harris, Ira, delegate at large, Albany county, ...	1, 4
115.	Harris, J. & B., statement of lands sold to,..........	276
	Harris, J., Jr., statement of lands sold to,...........	290
	Harris, James, statement of lands sold to,...........	90
	Harris, Joel, statement of lands sold to, ...	335

No. Doc.		Page.
115.	Harris, John J., statement of lands sold to,.. 86, 135, 202, 330,	136, 344
40.	Harris, Joseph H., testimony of, relative to management of Champlain canal,....................	307-13
115.	Harris, Joseph L., statement of lands sold to,........	90
	Harris, Moses, statement of lands sold to, ...	250
	Harris, Wm. B., statement of lands sold to,.........	147
	Harris, Wm. W., statement of lands sold to, ...	116
	Harris, Barnes & Briggs, statement of lands sold to,..	256
	Harris & Mead, statement of lands sold to,..........	345
	Harrison, William S., statement of lands sold to,.....	93
	Hart, Erastus, statement of lands sold to;...........	210
28.	Hart, Isaac N., extra compensation paid to,.........	9
115.	Hart, Orris, statement of lands sold to,.............	33
	Hart, Samuel, statement of lands sold to,...........	236
	Hart, Samuel S., statement of lands sold to, ...	210
	Hart & Bulger, statement of lands sold to,...........	205
	Hartshorn, Jno., statement of lands sold to,.........	296
	Hartson, Thomas, statement of lands sold to,........	78
	Hartwell, Imla, statement of lands sold to,..........	146
	Hartwell & Shattuck, statement of lands sold to,.....	127
55.	Hartwick Seminary, appropriations to, ...	24-27
115.	Hasbrook, B. R., statement of lands sold to, ... 352,	353
	Hasbrouck, Peter, statement of lands sold to,.... 98, 310, 311, 328,	301, 329
	Haskins, Amos, statement of lands sold to, ...	104
12.	Hastings, H. J., reporter, Albany, ...	8
115.	Hatch, Chas., statement of lands sold to,............	283
	Hatch, Charles B., statement of lands sold to,.... 78,	134
	Hatch, H. D., statement of lands sold to,............	384
1, 12.	Hatch, Israel T., delegate 31st district, Erie county, ..	3, 4
63.	financial sections of Constitution proposed by,	22-29
	report of, relative to finance, ...	1-29
103.	amendment of, to his minority report on finance,	1-3
115.	Hatch, Lemuel, statement of lands sold to, ...	97
	Hatch, Moses P., statement of lands sold to,..... 15,	17, 35
40.	Hathaway, Robine, testimony of, relative to boat purchased by Robert C. Dorn for the State,..........	23-28
115.	Hawes, Frederick, statement of lands sold to,.. 79, 80, 135, 174,	88, 176

No. Doc. Page

115. Hawkins, Malcolm N., statement of lands sold to,.... 92
Hawley, A., statement of lands sold to,............ 375
Hayden, A., statement of lands sold to,........ 350, 351
28. Haydon, Charles J., extra compensation paid to,..... 11
Hayes, E. Perkins, extra compensation paid to,...... 5
115. Hayes, Thomas, statement of lands sold to, ... 86
Hayward, David, statement of lands sold to, ... 139
Hayward, Daniel, statement of lands sold to,........ 139
127. Hayt, Hon. S. T., report by, of working capacity of Erie canal locks, ... 1–26
115. Hazard, R. B., statement of lands sold to,.......... 326
Hazard, Robert H., statement of lands sold to, ... 288
Hazard & Fitzgerald, statement of lands sold to,..... 250
Heald, Asa, statement of lands sold to,............ 308
Heald, Noah, statement of lands sold to, ... 78
Heath, Josiah, statement of lands sold to, ... 94
54. Hebrew Benevolent Society, N. Y., report of donations by,.............................. 10
.... grant of land to, ... 21
55. .... appropriations to, ... 59
115. Hedger, Wm., statement of lands sold to,.......... 144
Heimstreet, Chas., statement of lands sold to,....... 275
55. Hempstead Seminary, appropriations to,............ 24–27
115. Hendricks, Amos, statement of lands sold to,....... 112
Hendrick, Polly, statement of lands sold to, ... 295
Henderson, James, statement of lands sold to,....... 250
55. Herkimer Academy, appropriations to,.............. 24–27
115. Herrick, H. A., statement of lands sold to, ... 311
Herrick, William W., statement of lands sold to, 125, 126
Herring, Silas, statement of lands sold to, ... 340
Hersey, Henry, statement of lands sold to, ... 18
Hershey, Joseph, statement of lands sold to,........ 102
Heustice, B. B., statement of lands sold to,......... 352
Hewitt, J., statement of lands sold to,.............. 209
Hewitt, Jonah, statement of lands sold to,.......... 361
Hewitt, Josiah W., statement of land sold to,........ 280
Hickok, James C., statement of lands sold to,....... 264
Higby, Elisha, statement of lands sold to, ... 386
Higby, Seba, statement of lands sold to,............ 250

No. Doc.		Page.
115.	Higginbotham, Sands, statement of lands sold to, 145,	357 359
	Higgins, B., statement of lands sold to, ...	353
38.	Highways, to give supervisors exclusive control of,..	2
98.	special laws relative to, prohibited,..........	14
61.	Highway commissioners, election and term of office of,	2, 3
	removal of,..............................	3
115.	Hill, Isaac, statement of lands sold to, ...	238
	Hill, Thos., statement of lands sold to,.............	281
	Hills, Milo W., statement of lands sold to,..........	282
	Hillibert, Jno., statement of lands sold to,...... 345,	350
	Hilliker, Henry W., statement of lands sold to,.....	254
	Hilliker, Jno., statement of lands sold to, ...	290
	Hillman, Joseph, statement of lands sold to,........	328
	Hinckly, H. & S., statement of lands sold to,... 128,	233
	Hinckley, Squire, statement of lands sold to,. 51, 53,	233
	Hinckley & Call, statement of lands sold to, ...	46
	Hinman, Grove, statement of lands sold to,.... 209,	210
1.	Hiscock, L. Harris, delegate 22d district, Onondaga county, ...	3
1, 12.	Hitchcock, Adolphus F., delegate 12th district, Washington county, ...	2, 4
115.	Hitchcock, Aretus M., statement of lands sold to, 124,	126
	Hitchcock, Ira S., statement of lands sold to,........	245
	Hitchcock, L., statement of lands sold to,....... 20,	323
	Hitchcock, M. E., statement of lands sold to,... 349,	360
	Hitchcock & Emerson, statement of lands sold to,....	126
28.	Hitchins, Francis, extra compensation paid to,.......	11
1, 12.	Hitchman, Wm., delegate 8th district, New York Co.,	2, 4
115.	Hoadley, Elias, statement of lands sold to,..........	40
55.	Hobart Free College, appropriations to, ...	82, 83
	Hobart Hall Academy, appropriations to, ...	24–27
115.	Hodges, Amasa, statement of lands sold to,.........	151
	Hodge, Benjamin, Jr., and William, Jr., statement of lands sold to, ...	38
	Hogar, Jno., statement of lands sold to, ...	341
	Hogan & Slocum, statement of lands sold to,........	20, 21
95.	Holbrook, Amariah, testimony of, relative to management of canals, ...	24–30
28.	Holbrook & Sherrill, extra compensation paid to, ...	9, 10

No. Doc.		Page.
55.	Holley Academy, appropriations to,	24–27
115.	Holley, George W., statement of lands sold to,	230
28.	Holmes, Martin, extra compensation paid to,	9
115.	Holt, Alvah, statement of lands sold to,	177
	Holt, Harvey, statement of lands sold to,	146
	Holt & Mack, statement of lands sold to,	206
28.	Holmes, Harley, assignee, extra compensation paid to,	9
115.	Holmes, Israel, statement of lands sold to,	102
54.	Holy Innocents' School, 37th street, N. Y., report of donations to,	17
	Home for Deaf Mutes, N. Y., report of donations to,	8
55.	Home for Destitute Children of Seamen, Richmond county, appropriations to,	51–59
54.	Home for Discharged Prisoners, New York, report of donations to,	6
55.	Homœopathic Dispensary, 7th street, N. Y., appropriations to,	79
115.	Hooker, Horace, statement of lands sold to,	97
	Hooker, Samuel P., statement of lands sold to,	87
55.	Hoosick Falls Union School, appropriations to,	27
95.	Hopkins, Elisha W., testimony of, relative to management of canals,	67–77
115.	Hoquet, Anthony, statement of lands sold to,	233
	Horan, James, statement of lands sold to,	282
	Horn, Philip, statement of lands sold to,	110
	Horner, John, statement of lands sold to,	92
65.	Hornstein, Henry, judgment in favor of, against city of New York,	2
115.	Horton, R. H., statement of lands sold to,	337
55.	Hospital, appropriations to, from 1847 to 1866 inclusive,	92
54.	Hospital of Sisters of St. Francis, report of donations to,	15
28.	Hosch & Lovell, extra compensation paid to,	10
115.	Hotchkiss, A. V. E., statement of lands sold to,	335
	Hotchkiss, A. V. E. & H. F., statement of lands sold to,	335
	Hotchkiss, Calvin, statement of lands sold to, ... 13, 34, 35, 135, 246,	247
	Hotchkiss, F., statement of lands sold to,	94
	Hott, James S. & Harvey, statement of lands sold to,	48
	Hotchkiss, Joseph, statement of lands sold to,	250

No. Doc.		Page.

115. Hotchkiss, Wm., statement of lands sold to,. 354, 374, 377, 376 391
Houghton, Emery, statement of lands sold to, ... 164
House, Christian, statement of lands sold to, ... 383
House, Jno. A., statement of lands sold to, ... 350, 362
54. House of the Friendless, N. Y., report of donations to, 6
House of the Good Shepherd, New York, report of donations to, ... 12
House of Industry and Home of the Friendless, New York, report of donations to, ... 4, 5
House of Mercy, Bloomingdale, report of donations to, 11
New York, report of donations to, ... 11
55. House of Reception, Mariners' Harbor, Staten Island, appropriations to, ... 90
54. House of Refuge, New York, report of donations to,. 4, 5
1, 12. Houston, William H., delegate 10th district, Orange county, ... 2, 4
115. Hovey, Alfred, statement of lands sold to,.......... 240
28. Howard, Dean S., extra compensation paid to,....... 5
115. Howard, Elisha, statement of lands sold to,......... 337
Howe, Cyrenus, statement of lands sold to,...... 92, 272
Howe, Horace, statement of lands sold to, ... 208
Howe, John, statement of lands sold to,............ 23, 26
Howe & Van Benthuysen, statement of lands sold to, 200
Howland, Humphrey, statement of lands sold to, 239, 242, 240 308
Howland, Joseph, statement of lands sold to,........ 144
Howland, William P., statement of lands sold to,.... 70
Howlett, A. A. statement of lands sold to,.......... 384
Howson, Robert, statement of lands sold to, ... 261
Hoyt, Levi, statement of lands sold to,............. 97
Hubbard, Dexter, statement of lands sold to, ... 359, 360
55. Hubbardsville Academy, appropriations to,......... 24–27
Hudson Academy, appropriations to, ... 24–27
21. Hudson & Berkshire railroad, amount of freight carried over each year during the years 1851 and 1852:
whole number of tons,..................... 5, 6
products of the forest, number of tons, ... 5, 6

No. Doc. Page.

21. Hudson & Berkshire railroad—*Continued.*
animals, number of tons,.................. 5, 6
vegetable food, number of tons, ... 5, 6
other agricultural products, number of tons,.. 5, 6
manufactures, number of tons, ... 5, 6
merchandise, number of tons,.............. 5, 6
other articles, number of tons,............. 5, 6

Hudson & Boston railroad, amount of freight carried over each of the years 1855 to 1866, inclusive, excepting the year 1857:
whole number of tons,..................... 12–34
products of the forest, number of tons, ... 12–34
animals, number of tons, ... 12–34
vegetable food, number of tons, ... 12–34
other agricultural products, number of tons,.. 12–34
manufactures, number of tons, ... 12–34
merchandise, number of tons,.............. 12–34
other articles, number of tons,............. 12–34

55. Hudson Orphan and Relief Association, appropriations to, ... 60–63

21. Hudson River railroad, amount of freight carried over each year from 1851 to 1866, inclusive:
whole number of tons,.................... 5–34, 40
products of the forest, number of tons, ... 5–34, 40
animals, number of tons,................. 5–34, 40
vegetable food, number of tons, ... 5–34, 40
other agricultural products, number of tons, 5–34, 40
manufactures, number of tons,............ 5–34, 40
merchandise, number of tons, ... 5–34, 40
other articles, number of tons,............ 5–34, 40

115. Huff, Jno., statement of lands sold to,............... 162
Huffman, Catherine, statement of lands sold to, ... 300
Hugenin, Abram D., statement of lands sold to,..... 16
Hugenin, D., Jr., statement of lands sold to,........ 31
Hugenin, P. D., statement of lands sold to, ... 23, 31
Hughson, Clement, statement of lands sold to,....... 109
Hulett, A., statement of lands sold to, ... 375
Hull, Alden, statement of lands sold to,............ 47
Hull, J, & A., statement of lands sold to,........... 146
Hull, Jno. Q., statement of lands sold to,........... 202

No. Doc. | | Page.
115. Hull, W. H. H., statement of lands sold to, ... 293
Hull & Estes, statement of lands sold to, ... 327
28. Hull & Shepman, extra compensation paid to, ... 8
115. Humaston, Maria, statement of lands sold to, ... 259
Humes, Elijah, statement of lands sold to, ... 40, 42, 133
Humes, Wm., statement of lands sold to, ... 201
150. Humphrey, Wolcott J., testimony of before committee on official corruption, ... 34–36
55. Hungerford Collegiate Institute, appropriations to, ... 27
115. Hunt, Jno., statement of lands sold to, ... 206
Hunter, James, statement of lands sold to, ... 384
Hunter, Stephen R., statement of lands sold to, ... 145
Hunter & Anable, statement of lands sold to, ... 149
1, 12. Huntington, Benjamin N., delegate 19th district, Oneida county, ... 2, 4
115. Huntington, C. T., statement of lands sold to, .. 363, 364, 377, 381
Huntington, Geo., statement of lands sold to, ... 12
Huntington, J. F., statement of lands sold to, ... 349
Huntington N., statement of lands sold to, ... 207
55. Huntington Union School, appropriations to, ... 27
115. Hupman, John, statement of lands sold to, ... 92
Hutchins, Jno., statement of lands sold to, ... 231
1, 12. Hutchins, Waldo, delegate at large, New York county, 1, 4
115. Hutchins, Willard, statement of lands sold to, ... 231
Hutchinson, Holmes, statement of lands sold to, ... 236
28. Hutchinson, John, extra compensation paid to, ... 9
115. Hutchinson, Jno., statement of lands to, ... 321
Hutton, Thomas L., statement of lands sold to, ... 15
Hyde, Franklin, statement of land sold to, ... 100
95. Hyde, Porter W., testimony of, relative to management of canals, ... 53–56

I.

15. Idiots, to be deprived of suffrage, ... 2
54. Idiot Asylum, N. Y., report of donations to, ... 14
55. appropriations to, ... 4–7, 92
115. Igler, George, statement of lands sold to, ... 49
107. Impeachment, court of, provisions relative to, ... 2

No. Doc.		Page.
4.	Indians, to provide for committee on, ...	2
9.	committee on, ...	5
168.	report of committee on, ...	1, 2
	contracts for purchase of lands from, prohibited,	1
	lands of, may be subdivided and leased, ...	1, 2
	citizenship may be conferred on, ...	2
	lands of, may be taken for public use of, for manufacturing purposes, ...	2
170.	minority report of committee on, ...	1, 2
55.	Indian schools, appropriations for, ...	84–90
14.	tribes and reservations, report of Secretary of State relative to, ...	1–8
	reservations, number of schools on, ...	3
55.	youths, appropriations for support of among farmers, ...	86, 90
51.	Individual liability of stockholders of banking corporations, to provide for, ...	1
	(See also Document No. 53, p.p. 1, 2.)	
4.	Industrial interests, to provide for committee on, ...	2
9.	committee on, ...	5
52.	report of committee on, relative to agricultural drains, ...	1
58.	report of committee on, relative to catching fish in international waters, ...	1, 2
155.	report of committee on, ...	1, 2
54.	Industrial School of Sisters of Charity, New York, report of donations to, ...	12
	Inebriate Reform Society, N. Y., report of donations to, ...	9
107.	Inferior local courts, provisions relative to, ...	10
	removal of judges or justices of, ...	11
54.	Infirmary of New York College of Dentists, report of donations to, ...	16
115.	Ingalls, Caleb, statement of lands sold to, ...	128
	Ingalls, E. F., statement of lands sold to, ...	327
	Ingers, James, jr., statement of lands sold to, ...	381
55.	Ingham Collegiate Institute, appropriations to, ...	25–27
	University, appropriations to, ...	82, 83
	academic department, appropriations to,	30, 31
115.	Ingraham, Abel, statement of lands sold to, ...	209

No. Doc. Page.

115. Ingraham, Martin, statement of lands sold to,....... 201
Ingraham, Nathaniel, statement of lands sold to,.... 42
54. Irish Aid Society, New York, report of donations to, 7
115. Irwin, Alexander, statement of lands sold to,....... 34
98. Inspection laws prohibited,...................... 13
54. Institution of Mercy, N. Y., report of donations to, .. 15
Insurance, banking and currency (see "Currency").
55. Ithaca Academy, appropriations to,............... 28–31
7. Intoxicating liquors, preamble and resolutions relative to,.............................. 1, 2
147. report of committee on,.................... 1
laws to regulate the sale of, to be general and uniform,........................... 1
148. minority report on,...................... 1–5
55. Ithaca Cascadilla Place, appropriations to, ... 90
28. Ives, John B., extra compensation paid to,.......... 5

J.

115. Jackson, Eliza Ann, statement of lands sold to, ... 259
28. Jackson, Isaac, extra compensation paid to,......... 5
Jackson, Spencer, extra compensation paid to,....... 10
95. Jackson, Thomas W., testimony of, relative to management of canals,.......................... 18–21
115. Jacobs, Clark, statement of lands sold to,........... 152
Jacobs, Edwin A., statement of lands sold to,... 150, 153
154, 155, 156
Jacobs, Enoch, statement of lands sold to,.. 148, 149, 150
151, 152, 153, 154, 155, 162
Jacobs, Joseph, statement of lands sold to,.......... 146
Jacobs, Truman, statement of lands sold to, ... 64
James, Jno. W., statement of lands sold to,......... 229
James, Wm., statement of lands sold to,............ 143
55. Jamestown Academy, appropriations to,............ 28–31
115. Jaquays, Samuel N., statement of lands sold to, ... 213
Jaques, B. H., statement of lands sold to,........... 308
Jaqueth, Joseph, statement of lands sold to, ... 324
Jaquez, Jno., statement of lands sold to,............ 162
1, 12. Jarvis, Nathaniel, Jr., delegate 5th district, New York county,.............................. 2, 4

No. Doc. Page.

115. Jaycox, Wm., statement of lands sold to,........... 231

55. Jefferson Academy, appropriations to, ... 28–31

Jefferson County Institute, appropriations to,........ 28–31

Jefferson County Orphan Asylum, appropriations to,. 63

115. Jenks, Charles, statement of lands sold to,.......... 119

Jenkins, H. T., statement of lands sold to,.......... 381

Jenkins, Harriet, statement of lands sold to, ... 392

Jenkins, Jno., statement of lands sold to,........... 249

Jenkins, Joseph R., statement of lands sold to,...... 322

Jenkins, Timothy, statement of lands sold to, ... 364

Jenkins & McDonald, statement of lands sold to, ... 137

Jenkins & Pettibone, statement of lands sold to,..... 313

40. Jenne, Daniel C., testimony of, relative to management of Champlain canal, ... 473–528

115. Jerome, Wm., statement of lands sold to,........... 234

Jesup, B. B., statement of lands sold to,............ 144

Jewell, Henry C., statement of lands sold to,........ 262

Jewell, B. R. & H., statement of lands sold to, ... 271

55. Jews' Hospital, New York, appropriations to, ... 75

115. Job, John, statement of lands sold to,.............. 212

12. Johnson, A. G., reporter, Rensselaer,............... 9

115. Johnson B., statement of lands sold to,............. 375

Johnson, Cyrenus, statement of lands sold to, ... 50

Johnson, Ebenezer, statement of lands sold to,...... 36, 145

Johnson, Elijah, statement of lands sold to,......... 75

Johnson, George, statement of lands sold to, ... 117

Johnson, Jacob, statement of lands sold to, ... 98

Johnson, James, statement of lands sold to, ... 285, 306

Johnson, John, statement of lands sold to,.......... 209

Johnson, Luther H., statement of lands sold to, ... 294

Johnson, Miles, statement of lands sold to, ... 145

Johnson, Mortimer F., statement of lands sold to, 38, 256 257

Johnson, Reuben, statement of lands sold to,........ 48

Johnson, S. B., statement of lands sold to,.......... 360

Johnson, S. R., statement of lands sold to,.......... 233

Johnson, Seth, statement of lands sold to, ... 75

Johnson, Silas, statement of lands sold to,.......... 164

28. Johnson & Anderson, extra compensation paid to,.... 5

115. Johnson & Favel, statement of lands sold to,........ 149

No. Doc.		Page.
55.	Johnstown Academy, appropriations to,	28–31
115.	Jones, Elnathan, statement of lands sold to,	145
	Jones, Ezra, Jr., statement of lands sold to,	69
	Jones, Jno., statement of lands sold to,	353
	Jones, Leonard, statement of lands sold to,	388
	Jones, Luke, statement of lands sold to, ... 175, 291,	327 387
	Jones, Reuben, statement of lands sold to,	75
	Jones, Russell, statement of lands sold to,	286
	Jones, William E., statement of lands sold to,	123
55.	Jonesville Academy, appropriations to,	28–31
	Jordan Academy, appropriations to,	28–31
115.	Jordon, Laurence P., statement of lands sold to,	64, 66
8.	Journal of Convention, contract price for printing,	1
98.	Journal of Legislature, to be kept by each house of,	4
115.	Jourdin, Peter, statement of lands sold to,	162
	Judd & Simons, statement of lands sold to,	265
107.	Judges prohibited from sitting in review of their own decisions,	5
	vacancies in office of, how filled,	6
	question of election or appointment of, to be submitted to the people,	6, 7
	of certain courts prohibited from holding other office,	7
	of the Court of Appeals, election and term of office of,	2
	compensation of,	9
	prohibited from practicing as attorneys except in certain cases,	12
	time of first election of,	12, 13
98.	Judicial decisions, provision relative to publication of,	13
107.	departments, division of the State into,	4
	reorganization of,	11
	districts, provisions relative to,	4
	reorganization of,	11
	ees, provisions relative to,	12
	officers in cities and villages, provision relative to,	11
3.	Judiciary, provision for committee on,	2
9.	committee on,	2

No. Doc.		Page.
107.	Judiciary, article reported by committee on, ...	1–14
French system of, report on, by Mr. Daley, ..	17–25
English system, report on by Mr. T. W. Dwight, ...	26–44
Scotch system of, report Mr. T. W. Dwight,..	45
111.	plan of Mr. Cooke for reorganization of,......	1–4
117.	minority report on, by Mr. Goodrich,... 1–3,	15
article reported by Mr. Goodrich from minority of committee on, ...	3–14
121.	plan of Mr. Ferry for organization of, ...	1–10
160.	article on as amended in committee of the whole,................................	1–15
163.	article on as amended in Convention,........	1–16
165.	article on, as amended and referred to committee to report complete, ...	1–16
115.	Judson, D. C., statement of lands sold to, ...	337
26.	Jurors, memorial of Dr. Francis Lieber, relative to unanimous verdicts by, ...	1–4
149.	Jury trial, provision relative to, ...	2
107.	Justices of Supreme Court, number and residence of,	5
vacancies in office of, how filled,...........	6
removal of,..............................	7
election and term of office of, ...	9
Justices of the peace, provision relative to,..........	11
removal of,............................	11
of sessions, provisions relative to,...........	9, 10
54.	Juvenile Delinquents, Society for Reformation of, N. Y. report of donations to,................	6
54.	grant of lands to,.........................	20
55.	Juvenile Delinquents in New York city, appropriations of the State to Society for Reformation of, 3–7,	92
54.	Juvenile Guardian Society, N. Y., report of donations to, ...	15

K.

115. Kallay, James & Alexander, statement of lands sold to, 49
Kearne & Murray, statement of lands sold to, ... 205
Kee, Archibald, statement of lands sold to,......... 78
Keese, Peter, statement of lands sold to, ... 301

No. Doc. Page.

115. Keese, Richard, statement of lands sold to, ... 301
55. Keeseville Academy, appropriations to, ... 28–31
115. Kelley, Patrick, statement of lands sold to, ... 335
Kellogg, Ashbel, statement of lands sold to,.... 300, 306
Kellogg, Daniel, statement of lands sold to, ... 99
Kellogg & Hale, statement of land sold to,.......... 380
28. Kelsey, Vrooman & Tappen, extra compensation paid to, ... 5
115. Kelsey, William, statement of lands sold to, ... 131
12. Kemper, John H., assistant sergeant-at-arms, Wayne, 8
115. Kennedy, Robert, statement of lands sold to,....... 308
Kent, Ezra, statement of lands sold to,............. 266
Kent, Jno. W., statement of lands sold to,.......... 199
Kenton, N. W., statement of lands sold to, ... 351
Kenyon, C. L., statement of lands sold to,.......... 333
Kenyon, G W., statement of lands sold to,......... 332
Kenyon, Hiram & Son, statement of lands sold to,... 388
Kenyon & Parker, statement of lands sold to,....... 331
1, 12. Kernan, Francis, delegate at large, Oneida county,... 1, 4
115. Kerr, Angus, statement of lands sold to, ... 338
40. Ketcham, James, testimony of, relative to award to Charles J. DeGraw,......................... 283–87
1, 12, Ketcham, Leander S., delegate 25th district, Wayne county,.. 3, 4
115. Ketchum, Zebulon, statement of lands sold to,... 37, 38, 39
136, 256, 257, 320, 321
Kibling, Otis, statement of lands sold to, ... 89
Kidd, James, statement of lands sold to,.. 48, 49, 50, 51, 52
72, 73, 89, 90, 129, 132, 140, 177, 233, 234, 246
Kidder, Maynard, statement of lands sold to, 79, 87, 143
Kiersted & Osborn, statement of lands sold to, 203, 204, 263
Kimball, James, statement of lands sold to, ... 75, 234
Kimball, Nathaniel, statement of lands sold to,...... 313
Kimball, R. B., statement of lands sold to, ... 301
28. Kimball, Woodman, extra compensation paid to,.... 5
115. Kine, William, statement of lands sold to,.......... 37
55. Kinderhook Academy, appropriations to,........... 28–31
115. King, H. F., statement of lands sold to, ... 323
King J. Howard, statement of lands sold to,........ 364

No. Doc.		Page.
115.	King, Jno., statement of lands sold to, ...	155
	King, William, statement of lands sold to, ... 310,	344
28.	King, Taylor & Higgins, extra compensation paid to, (see "McCoughlin, John.")	
55.	Kingsboro' Academy, appropriations to, ...	28–31
115.	Kingman, Lyman, statement of lands sold to, ...	242
95.	Kingsley, Ebenezer, testimony of, relative to management of canala, ...	41–46
28.	Kingsley & Knapp, extra compensation paid to, ...	8
55.	Kingston Academy, appropriations to, ...	28–31
1, 12.	Kinney, Oliver H. P., delegate 24th district, Tioga Co.,	3, 4
115.	Kip, Henry, statement of lands sold to, ...	102
19.	Kirkpatrick, Wm., superintendent of salt springs, ...	4, 5
115.	Klock, Henry J., statement of lands sold to, ...	305
65.	Knapp, G. L., judgment in favor of, against city of New York, ...	2
115.	Knapp, Hiram, statement of lands sold to, ...	49, 50
28.	Knapp & Shaw, extra compensation paid to, ...	5
115.	Knettle, John R., statement of lands sold to, ...	50, 51
	Kniffen, William J., statement of lands sold to, ...	25
40.	Knights, Abraham, testimony of, relative to management of Champlain canal, ...	392–95
115.	Knights, R. M., statement of lands sold to, ...	321
	Knower, Benjamin, statement of lands sold to, .. 124, 265, 284,	285
	Knower, Edmund, statement of lands sold to, ...	18
	Knower & Stevens, statement of lands sold to, ...	18
	Knox, James C., statement of lands sold to, ...	391
	Knox, John, statement of lands sold to, ... 47,	209
	Knox, O. L., statement of lands sold to, ...	343
55.	Knoxville Academy, appropriations to, ...	30, 31
115.	Koplin, Jno., statement of lands sold to, ...	241
	Kruger, Chas., statement of lands sold to, ...	366
1, 12.	Krum, Hobart, delegate 23d district, Schoharie Co., ..	3, 4

L.

115.	Lacy, Wm. H., statement of lands sold to, ...	257
54.	Ladies' Home Mission, Five Points, New York, report of donations to, ...	15

No. Doc.		Page.
54.	Ladies' Home Missionary Society, New York, report of donations to, ...	10
	Ladies' Mission Society, N. Y., report of donations to,	6
	Ladies' Educational Union, N. Y., report of donations to, ...	12
	Ladies' Union Aid Society, N. Y., report of donations to, ...	8
	Ladies' Union Relief Association, N. Y., report of donations to, ...	15
94.	Lake Ontario & Hudson River R. R. Co., report of State Engineer relative to lands sold by, ...	1–3
	report by Commissioners of Land Office of lands granted to, or acquired by, ...	1–12
115.	Lamb, Jno. E., statement of lands sold to, .. 297, 298,	313
	Lamb, Martin, statement of lands sold to, ...	289
28.	Lambert, John, extra compensation paid to, ...	11
115.	Lamoreaux, Andrew, statement of lands sold to, . 58,	175
	Lamoreaux, James, statement of lands sold to, . 51, 52, 53, 55, 59, 60,	62
	Lamoreaux & Finch, statement of lands sold to, ...	61
	Lamport, Jno. T., statement of lands sold to, ...	189
	Lamson, Benjamin P., statement of lands sold to, ...	165
55.	Lancaster Academy, appropriations to, ...	28–31
	Lancaster St. Joseph's Orphan Asylum, appropriations to, ...	65–67
115.	Lanchman, Richard, statement of lands sold to, .. 55, 58, 60, 61, 62, 65,	66
1, 12.	Landon, Judson S., delegate 15th district, Schenectady county, ...	2, 4
115.	Lane, Matthew, statement of lands sold to, ... 288,	289
	Langdon, Amos, statement of lands sold to, ...	92
	Langdon, A. W., statement of lands sold to, ... 356, 358, 365, 369,	374
28.	Lansing, A. Y., extra compensation paid to, ...	5
115.	Lansing, Jacob, statement of lands sold to, ...	281
	Lansing, Jacob J., statement of lands sold to, ...	281
55.	Lansingburgh Academy, appropriations to, ...	28–31
1, 12.	Lapham, Elbridge G., delegate 26th district, Ontario county, ...	3, 4

No. Doc.		Page.
1, 12.	Larremore, Rich. L., delegate 8th district, New York county,	2, 4
116.	dissent of, from report on education,	4
115.	Lasher, John E., statement of lands sold to,	34
56.	Lateral canals, minority report relative to,	1
115.	Latham, Benjamin, statement of lands sold to,	378
1, 12.	Law, George, delegate at large, New York county,	1, 5
98.	Laws, to embrace but one subject, to be expressed in its title,	5
	Legislature required to provide for publication of,	7
	when altered or amended to be reënacted and published at length,	5, 6
1, 12.	Lawrence, Abraham, delegate 27th district, Schuyler county,	3, 5
	Lawrence, Abraham R., Jr., delegate 4th district, New York county,	2, 5
115.	Lawrence, A. R., statement of lands sold to, 357,	358
	Lawrence, Asa, statement of lands sold to,	114
	Lawrence, Charles, statement of lands sold to,	106
	Lawrence, Grove, statement of lands sold to, 305,	366
	Lawrence, James R., statement of lands sold to,	238
1, 12.	Lawrence, Melatiah H., delegate 26th district, Yates county,	3, 5
4.	resolution of, relative to abolition of useless offices,	1
115.	Lawrence, Moses B., statement of lands sold to,	145
	Lawrence, R. M., statement of lands sold to,	251
	Lawrence, Wm., statement of lands sold to,	252
	Lawrence & Battelle, statement of lands sold to,	20
55.	Lawrenceville Academy, appropriations to,	30, 31
115.	Lawyer, John W., statement of lands sold to,	70
54.	Leake & Watts Orphan Asylum, New York, report of donations to,	9
115.	Leander & Westcott, statement of lands sold to,	46
	Leavenworth, E. W. statement of lands sold to,	325
	Leavenworth, William, statement of lands sold to,	135
	Leavenworth & Jewett, statement of lands sold to,	307
55.	Leavenworth Institute, appropriations to,	30, 31

No. Doc.		Page.
115.	Leavins, Joseph B., statement of lands sold to, ...	201
	Lee, Jno. A., statement of lands sold to,....... 264,	357
1, 12.	Lee, M. Lindley, delegate 21st district, Oswego county,	2, 5
115.	Leet, Pelatiah M., statement of lands sold to,........	70
	Leggett, D. W., statement of lands sold to, ...	74
	Leggett, Samuel, statement of lands sold to, ...	230
	Legislature:	
3.	its organization, &c., provision for committee on,	1
9.	committee on,........................	1
30.	report of committee on, ...	1–4
31.	minority report on, ...	1–6
79.	article on, as amended and adopted, ...	1–7
3.	its powers and duties, provision for committee on,.............................	1
98.	report of committee on, ...	1–14
	article reported by committee on, ...	3–14
101.	minority report on, ...	1–11
113.	supplemental report of minority of committee on,......................	1–11
130.	article on, as acted on by committee of the whole, up to 3d of September, ...	1–9
136.	article on, as completed in committee of the whole,........................	1–8
143.	proposed amendment to article on,......	1, 2
167.	article on, as amended and referred to committee on revision,.................	1–7
30.	members of, ineligible to hold certain offices,..	3
	compensation of members of,...............	3
	to hold annual sessions, ...	3
	quorum of,............................	4
	each house of to keep journal, ...	4
	each house of to determine its own rules and be judges of election and qualification of its members, ...	4
	sessions of to be open, except in certain cases,	4
	neither house to adjourn for more than two days, without consent of the other,........	4
60.	Governor may call special sessions of, ...	5
98.	bills not to be introduced in either house during last five days of session,................	5

No. Doc. | Page.

Legislature—*Continued.*

98. bills finally rejected by either branch of, cannot be revived during session, ... 5
bills, enacting clause of, ... 5
laws passed by, to embrace but one subject, to be expressed in its title, ... 5
bills to be signed by presiding officers during sessions, ... 6
final adjournment to be at noon, ... 6
prohibited from appropriating money or property of State to charitable institutions, ... 6
biennial sessions of, provided for, ... 3
special sessions of, to legislate only on subject stated in proclamation, ... 3
members of, ineligible to civil appointments by Governor or Legislature, ... 3
members of Congress or Federal officers ineligible to seat in, ... 4
prohibited from giving or loaning money or property of State to corporations, ... 6, 7
authorizing issue of municipal bonds to corporations, ... 7
auditing or allowing any private claim against the State, ... 7
granting extra compensation to public officers or employés, ... 8
selling or leasing canals or salt springs, .. 8, 9
sanctioning suspension of specie payments, 12, 13
passing inspection laws, ... 13
passing special laws for granting divorces, 14
sale, mortgage, or lease of real estate of minors, ... 14
changing names of persons, ... 14
relative to public or private roads or highways, ... 14
locating or changing county seats, ... 14
legalizing invalid official acts, ... 14
granting power to construct street railroads, ... 14
legalizing invalid deeds or wills, ... 14

No. Doc.		Page.
	Legislature—*Continued.*	
98.	prohibited from passing special laws in any case where provision is made by general law,	14
	required to provide for court of claims, ...	7
	prohibited from exempting property from taxation, ...	10
	to pass general laws for formation of corporations,................................	10
	may provide for local county judges and surrogates, ...	13
	to provide for speedy publication of statute laws, ...	12
	required to provide for free schools,.........	9
	to provide for vacancies in office, ...	9
	to provide for removal of public officers,.....	9, 10
30.	Legislative term, commencement of,................	3
60.	proceedings in case of vetoed bills,..........	7, 8
115.	Lienhart, Peter, statement of lands sold to, ...	383
55.	LeRoy Academic Institute, appropriations to,.......	31
	Female Seminary, appropriations to, ...	28–31
115.	Lester, James, statement of lands sold to,...........	123
	Letchworth, Josiah, statement of lands sold to,......	365
40.	Levien, Douglas A., testimony of, relative to repairs of section 9 of Erie canal, ...	101–06
115.	Lewis, David, statement of lands sold to,....... 48,	108
	Lewis, Epenetus, statement of lands sold to, ...	151
	Lewis, Joseph, statement of lands sold to,..........	260
	Lewis, Nellie, statement of lands sold to,...........	258
	Lewis, Samuel, statement of lands sold to,..........	339
	Lewis, William, statement of lands sold to,.........	65
	Lewis, W. J., statement of lands sold to, ...	64
	Lewis & Taylor, statement of lands sold to,.........	125
55.	Lewiston Academy, appropriations to, ...	28–31
115.	Leynes, Alexander, statement of lands sold to, ...	367
55.	Liberty Normal Institute, appropriations to, ...	28–31
22.	Library fund held by Court of Appeals, ... 4, 5,	9–19
26.	Lieber, Dr. Francis, memorial of, relative to unanimous verdicts of jurors, ...	1–4
115.	Lieber, John, statement of lands sold to,..........	109–113

No. Doc.		Page.
60.	Lieutenant-Governor, election and term of office of,....	4, 5
	qualifications required for,..................	6
	compensation of, ...	6
	to act as Governor in certain cases,..........	6
	to be President of the Senate,...............	6
115.	Lighthall, Nicholas, statement of lands sold to, ...	161
	Lincoln, Allen, statement of lands sold to,..........	126
	Lincoln, Calvin, statement of lands sold to, ...	69
	Lindsey, Francis W., statement of lands sold to,.....	52
116.	Literary institutions, provision for general or special endowment of,.............................	2
	Literature fund, capital of, to be paid into treasury,..	1
	investment of, ...	2
	revenues of, to be applied to support of Academies, ...	1
115.	Little, Wm., statement of lands sold to, ...	124
55.	Little Falls Academy, appropriations to,............	8–11
115.	Littlejohn, Jno., statement of lands sold to, ...	161
90.	Littlejohn, DeWitt C., testimony of, relative to improvements of Erie canal, ...	12–22
115.	Livingston, R. & S., statement of lands sold to,......	252
1, 12.	Livingston, Walter L., delegate 2d district, Kings Co.,	1, 5
105.	minority report of, relative to charities and charitable institutions,..................	1, 2
98.	Local bills, notice of application for, to be published,.	13
107.	Local courts, provision for,......................	10
25.	Local or special legislation, resolution of Mr. E. Brooks relative to, ...	1, 2
40.	Lockey, Benjamin, testimony of, relative to management of Champlain canal,....................	313–20
55.	Lockport Union School, appropriations to,..........	28–31
115.	Lockwood, Luke, statement of lands sold to, ...	301
1, 12.	Loew, Frederick W., delegate 6th district, New York county, ...	2, 5
19.	Logan, Sheldon, superintendent of salt springs,......	4
28.	Logan, William & Co., extra compensation paid to, ..	5
115.	Long, John, statement of lands sold to,............	14
55.	Long Island College Hospital, appropriations to,.....	75

No. Doc. Page.

21. Long Island railroad, amount of freight carried over, each year, from 1851 to 1856, inclusive:
whole number of tons, ... 5–34
products of the forest, number of tons, ... 6–34
animals, number of tons, ... 6–34
vegetable food, number of tons, ... 6–34
other agricultural products, number of tons, .. 6–34
manufactures, number of tons, ... 6–34
merchandise, number of tons, ... 6–34
other articles, number of tons, ... 6–34
115. Loomis, Geo. J., statement of lands sold to, ... 157
Loomis, N. S., statement of lands sold to, ... 305
Loomis, Kirby & West, statement of lands sold to, ... 198
28. Lord, George D., extra compensation paid to, ... 8, 9
40. testimony of, relative to letting canal contracts, 28th December, ... 172–90
28. Loss, Lewis M., extra compensation paid to, ... 8, 9
115. Loucks, Hiram, statement of lands sold to, ... 360
Love, Isaac, statement of lands sold to, ... 242
Love, Levi, statement of lands sold to, ... 351
Loveland, R. A., statement of lands sold to, ... 349
Loverin, Caleb A., statement of lands sold to, ... 166
Loverin, W. H. C., statement of lands sold to, ... 166
Lovett, J. E., statement of lands sold to, ... 283, 285
150. Low, Henry R., testimony of before committee on official corruption, ... 36–38
1, 12. Lowry, Charles, delegate 2d district, Kings county, .. 1, 5
55. Lowville Academy, appropriations to, ... 28–31
40. Ludington, Archibald N., testimony of, relative to award to Charles J. De Graw, ... 243–53
1, 12. Ludington, Clinton V. R., delegate 10th district, Sullivan county, ... 2, 5
55. Lunatic Asylum, Utica, appropriations to, ... 3–7, 92
15. Lunatics, to be deprived of suffrage, ... 2
115. Lush, Samuel S., statement of lands sold to, .. 59, 60, 131
54. Lying-In Asylum, New York, report of donations to, 6
115. Lyman, Chas. G., statement of lands sold to, ... 379
55. Lyons Union School, ... 33–35
115. Lyons, James, statement of lands sold to, ... 235, 236

No. Doc. Page.

M.

55. Macedon Academy, appropriations to, ... 32–35
115. Mack, Bryan, statement of lands sold to,........... 94
Mack, Elisha, statement of lands sold to,........... 178
Mack, Ezra, statement of lands sold to, ... 206
Macy, Chas. B., statement of lands sold to, ... 347
55. Madison University, appropriations to,............. 80–83
54. Magdalen Society, New York, report of donations to, 15
1, 12. Magee, John, delegate at large, Schuyler county, ... 1, 5
161. amendment proposed by, to article on finance, 1, 2
115. Mahan, Jno., statement of lands sold to,............ 339
Main, Jno., statement of lands sold to, ... 374
Main, P. R., statement of lands sold to, ... 340
Mallory, James, statement of lands sold to, ... 164
Manchester, David, statement of lands sold to, ... 212
40. Manchester, William T., testimony of, relative to Kingsley Brook reservoir, and certain locks on Chenango canal,............................... 686–94
115. Mancius, Jacob, statement of lands sold to, ... 134
Mandingo, Zebulon, statement of lands sold to,...... 232
54. Manhattan Dispensary, N. Y., report of donations to, 12
55. appropriations to, ... 79
Manlius Academy, appropriations to, ... 32–35
115. Manly, Chas., statement of lands sold to, ... 256
Mann, Asa, statement of lands sold to,.............. 208
Manning, Patrick, statement of lands sold to, ... 289
Marble, Horace, statement of lands sold to, ... 161
28. Marenes & Sherman, extra compensation paid to, ... 5
55. Marion Collegiate Institute, appropriations to, ... 34, 35
Marine Hospital, Staten Island, appropriations to,.... 72–75
54. Mariners' Industrial Society, New York, report of donations to,.............................. 8
115. Markham, Nathan B., statement of lands sold to, 115, 353
Markham, Walter, statement of lands sold to, ... 211
19. Marks, Enoch, superintendent of salt springs,....... 5
115. Marsh, Elisha, statement of lands sold to,...... 270, 327
Marsh, L. W., statement of lands sold to,........... 384
Marshall, Chederlaomer, statement of lands sold to,.. 53, 66
Marshall & Putnam, statement of lands sold to, ... 63

No. Doc.		Page.
55.	Marshall Infirmary, Troy, appropriations to, ...	74, 75
	Marshall Seminary of Easton, appropriations to,.....	35
12.	Martin, C. B., reporter, Orange,..................	9
115.	Martin, Edward G., statement of lands sold to, ...	352
40.	Martin, Elisha A., testimony of, relative to management of Champlain canal, ...	366–74
115.	Martin, J. B. & K., statement of lands sold to, ...	117
	Martin, Reuben, statement of lands sold to, ... 124,	125
	Martin, Sewell, statement of lands sold to,..........	89
28.	Martin & Lucky, extra compensation paid to, ...	9
95.	Martindale, John H., testimony of, relative to management of canals, ...	47–50
115.	Marvin, James M., statement of lands sold to,.......	290
	Marvin, Nathan, statement of lands sold to, ...	211
95.	Marvin, Selden E., testimony of, relative to management of canals, ...	50, 51
115.	Marvin, Thos. J., statement of lands sold to,.... 298,	315
1, 12.	Masten, Joseph G., delegate at large, Erie county,....	1, 5
115.	Mather, Heman, statement of lands sold to, ...	354
	Matteson, H., statement of lands sold to, ...	330
	Matteson, H. G., statement of lands sold to,.........	382
	Matthews, Alinus, statement of lands sold to, ...	110
	Matthews, Jno., statement of lands sold to, ...	342
	Matthews, Sylvester, statement of lands sold to, ...	36
1, 12.	Mattice, Manly B., delegate 14th district, Greene Co.,.	2, 5
28.	Maxon, B. F., extra compensation paid to,..........	11
115.	May, Elam, statement of lands sold to,.............	209
	May, Chester, statement of lands sold to, ...	121
	May, J. W., statement of lands sold to,.............	22, 31
	Maynard, Elisha A., statement of lands sold to,... 39,	257
	Maynard, J. W., statement of lands sold to,.........	238
	Maynard, William S., statement of lands sold to, ...	21, 25 26, 30
55.	Mayville Academy, appropriations to, ...	32–35
90.	McAlpine, William J., testimony of, relative to improvements of Erie canal,......................	22–28
28.	McArthur, Archibald, extra compensation paid to,...	11
	McArthur, William, extra compensation paid to, ...	9, 11
115.	McCarty, William, statement of lands sold to,.......	21

No. Doc.		Page.
28.	McCarty, M. & J., extra compensation paid to, ...	9
115.	McChesney, Leonard, statement of lands sold to,.....	329
	McClenethan, Wm., Jr., statement of lands sold to, 163,	164
	McCollum, Joel, statement of lands sold to,.........	246
28.	McCoughin, John, assignee of King, Taylor & Higgins, extra compensation paid to,..............	5
	extra compensation paid to,................	5
115.	McCue, Jno. B., statement of lands sold to, ...	125
	McDermott, Jno., statement of lands sold to, ...	256
	McDole, Jesse, statement of lands sold to,...........	208
1, 12.	McDonald, Angus, delegate 26th district, Ontario Co.,	3, 5
4.	resolution of, relative to distribution of verbatim reports,...........................	3
139.	section relative to taxation proposed by, ...	1, 2
162.	minority report of, relative to salt springs, ...	1–39
12.	McDonald, John T., messenger, Albany, ...	8
115.	McDonald, William, statement of lands sold to,...... 116, 128, 214, 228, 229, 234,	79, 84, 301
	McDonald & Finch, statement of lands sold to,.......	334
	McDonald & Jenkins, statement of lands sold to,. 216,	219, 234
	McDonald & Myrick, statement of lands sold to,.. 88,	277
28.	McDonald, Nichols and others, extra compensation paid to,..................................	5
115.	McDowell, Jno., statement of lands sold to, ...	162
40.	McEchron, William, testimony of, relative to management of Champlain canal,.....................	533–36
115.	McElwaine, Geo., statement of lands sold to, ...	124
	McElwane, Jno., statement of lands sold to,..........	124
	McFarlane & Carswell, statement of lands sold to, ...	112
	McGarry, Daniel, statement of lands sold to, ...	212
	McGraw, Harvey, statement of lands sold to,.........	241
95.	McGourkey, William, testimony of, relative to management of canals,................................	56, 57
115.	McHenry, Abram, statement of lands sold to, ...	147
	McIntyre, Archibald, statement of lands sold to, ...	97
28.	McIntyre, John, extra compensation paid to,........	8
40.	McIntyre, John E., testimony of, relative to management of Champlain canal, ...	453–62

No. Doc. Page.

115. McIntyre, Major, statement of lands sold to,........ 241
McIntyre & McMartin, statement of lands sold to,... 67
McKenzie, H. & L. W., statement of lands sold to,.. 352
378
McKernan, Thomas, statement of lands sold to,..... 271
McKeenan, Thomas, statement of lands sold to,..... 93
McKinstry, Alex., statement of lands sold to,........ 366
McLaughlin, James, statement of lands sold to,...... 113
McLean, Jno., statement of lands sold to,............ 327
McLeod, Duncan, statement of lands sold to,........ 102
McLeod, James A., statement of lands sold to,...... 165
McLeod, Thomas, statement of lands sold to,....... 115
McMahon, Thomas, statement of lands sold to,...... 94
12. McManus, William, doorkeeper, Rensselaer,........ 8
115. McMartin, Duncan, Jr., statement of lands sold to,... 98
McMartin, Malcolm, statement of lands sold to,...... 132
McMillan, Jno. H., statement of lands sold to,....... 373
McMillan, Hugh, statement of lands sold to,........ 256
McMurdy, Robert, statement of lands sold to,....... 366
McMurdy, R. S., statement of lands sold to,........ 378
McNamara, Hugh, statement of lands sold to,.. 305, 306
307, 322, 323, 324
McNamara & Marshall, statement of lands sold to,... 323
McNair & Matthew, statement of lands sold to,..... 14, 23
McNaughton, Muirhead & Baldwin, statement of lands sold to,.................................. 104
McPhail, J. B., statement of lands sold to,......... 93
40. McPhail, Thomas, testimony of relative to management of Champlain canal,.................... 588-93
115. McPherson, Jno., statement of lands sold to,........ 212
40. Mead, Jacob A., testimony of, relative to transactions on Chenango canal extension and Genesee Valley canal,........................ 124-33
testimony of, relative to Peter Dunn's proposal for repairs of Genesee Valley canal, 139
115. Mead, Shadrach, statement of lands sold to,......... 250
Mead, Wm., statement of lands sold to,............ 344
Meadon, Maria, statement of lands sold to,.......... 305
54. Mechanics' Institute, New York, report of donations to, 8
55. Mechanicsville Academy, appropriations to,........ 35

No. Doc. | | Page.

176. Medicine, practice of, see "State Medical Board."
55. Medina Academy, appropriations to,............... 32–35
115. Meeker, Uriah D., statement of lands sold to,... 126, 297
Melett, Jno., statement of lands sold to,............ 231
Mellen, James, statement of lands sold to, ... 139
Mearl, John, statement of lands sold to,............ 111
Mears, Henry, statement of lands sold to, ... 109
55. Mendon Academy, appropriations to, ... 32–35
115. Menzie, Robert, statement of lands sold to, ... 361
Merenes, James, statement of lands sold to,......... 107
Merriam, Aaron B., statement of lands sold to,...... 14
28. Merriam, Utter, Carr & Wood, extra compensation paid to,................................ 5
115. Merrill, Dyer, statement of lands sold to,........... 165
Merrill, Elam, statement of lands sold to, ... 302, 303
Merrill, Laura, statement of lands sold to, ... 17
Merrill, Milo, statement of lands sold to, ... 64, 65
1, 12. Merrill, Wm. H., delegate 30th district, Wyoming Co., 3, 5
Merritt, Edwin A., delegate 17th district, St. Lawrence county,.................................. 2, 5
115. Merwin, Isaac, statement of lands sold to, ... 209
1, 12. Merwin, Milton H., delegate 18th district, Jefferson county,.................................. 2, 5
115. Mesick, Jacob, statement of lands sold to, ... 144
Metcalf, D., statement of lands sold to,............. 22
126. Metropolitan commissions, communication from Citizens' Association, relative to,.................. 1–26
132. Metropolitan Board of Excise, report of, relative to licenses granted and revoked, complaints, &c., ... 1, 2
144. Metropolitan Fire Department, report by commissioners relative to statistics of, ... 1–6
133. Metropolitan Police, report relative to statistics of force of,................................ 1–9
68. report of board of, of expenses of force detailed as attendants on courts in city of New York, 1–5
55. Mexico Academy, appropriations to,.............. 32–35
115. Mickler & Yost, statement of lands sold to, ... 160
55. Middlebury Academy, appropriations to, ... 32–35
115. Miles, Mary, statement of lands sold to,............ 15, 17

No. Doc.		Page.
3.	Militia, provision for committee on, ...	2
9.	committee on, ...	4
94.	report of committee on, ...	1–5
	annual enrollment of, provided for, ...	1
	to be divided into active and reserved force, ..	1
	Governor to be commander-in-chief of, ...	2
	number of reserves in 1866, ...	5
100.	article reported by committee on, as amended and referred to committee on revision, ...	1–4
115.	Milk, Elkanah B., statement of lands sold to, ...	123
	Millard, Harlow, statement of lands sold to, ...	307
	Miller, Chas. & Manoah, statement of lands sold to, ..	131
	Miller, Henry, statement of lands sold to, ...	241
40.	Miller, Jared F., testimony of, relative to management of Champlain canal, ...	528–31
115.	Miller, M., statement of lands sold to, ... 352,	380
	Miller, Manoah, statement of lands sold to, ... 47,	136
28.	Miller, Maria, extra compensation paid to, ...	5
115.	Miller, Oscar, statement of lands sold to, ...	391
	Miller, Philip, statement of lands sold to, ...	301
	Miller, Pliny, statement of lands sold to, ...	161
1, 12.	Miller, Samuel F., delegate 23d district, Delaware Co.,	3, 5
115.	Miller, Timothy J., statement of lands sold to, ...	109
	Miller, Wm. T., statement of lands sold to, ...	136
	Miller & Cooper, statement of lands sold to, ...	326
	Milne, Alexander, statement of lands sold to, ...	355
28.	Mills, Edward A., extra compensation paid to, ...	11
115.	Mills, Frederick C., statement of lands sold to, ... 14,	20, 21
40.	Mills, Myron H., testimony of, relative to Peter Dunn's proposal for repairs of Genesee Valley canal, 220–26,	231
55.	Millville Academy, appropriations to, ...	32–35
12.	Mines, J. F., reporter, Westchester, ...	9
49.	Minority representation in Senate, to provide for, ...	1, 2
	in Assembly, to provide for, ...	3
98.	Minors, real estate of, special laws for lease or sale of, prohibited, ...	14
95.	Mirick, Ira, testimony of, relative to management of canals, ...	37–41
57.	Miscellaneous appropriations to charitable institutions from 1847 to 1866, inclusive, ...	92

No. Doc.		Page.
115.	Mitchell, Gabriel, statement of lands sold to, ...	231
	Mitchell, Roswell, statement of lands sold to, ...	231
28.	Mitchell & Brown, extra compensation paid to, ...	6
1, 12.	Monell, Claudius L., delegate 8th district, New York county, ...	2, 5
115.	Monroe & Baker, statement of lands sold to, ...	382
55.	Monroe Academy, appropriations to, ...	32–35
115.	Montague, Wm., statement of lands sold to, ...	337
	Montgomery, D., statement of lands sold to, ...	31
55.	Montgomery Academy, appropriations to, ...	32–35
	Monticello Academy, appropriations to, ...	33–35
115.	Moody, Jacob S., statement of lands sold to, ...	52
	Moone, James, statement of lands sold to, ...	205
	Mooney, Thos., statement of lands sold to, ...	369
	Moore, Amasa C., statement of lands sold to, ...	252
	Moore, Isaac, statement of lands sold to, ...	349
28.	Moore, Zebulon, extra compensation paid to, ...	6
115.	Mooers, Benjamin, statement of lands sold to, ...	252
	Moot, Jno., statement of lands sold to, ... 359,	360
	Moot, Wm. H., statement of lands sold to, ...	359
55.	Moravia Institute, appropriations to, ...	32–35
1, 12.	More, Ezekiel P., delegate 14th district, Greene county,	2, 5
115.	Morehouse, Andrew K., statement of lands sold to, .. 138, 146, 148–52, 155, 183–89, 251, 260, 261, 271, 311, 313,	113 280 314
	Morey, Chas., statement of lands sold to, ...	262
28.	Morey, Michael, extra compensation paid to, ...	10
115.	Morgan, James, statement of lands sold to, ... 385,	389
	Morgan, Moses P., statement of lands sold to, ...	49
	Morgan, Parker, statement of lands sold to, ...	287
	Morgan, T. S., statement of lands sold to, ... 16, 17, 28, 31 34, 35, 138, 143, 246,	247
	Morgan & Bronson, statement of lands sold to, ... 14,	20–25 27–32
	Morgan & Lapham, statement of lands sold to, ...	385–87
55.	Moriah Academy, appropriations to, ...	35
115.	Morris, Aaron, statement of lands sold to, ...	361
	Morris, Ira, statement of lands sold to, ...	360
	Morris, Jno., statement of lands sold to, ...	362

No. Doc.		Page.
115.	Morris, L. N. & W. R., statement of lands sold to, ... 176, 177,	175 268
1, 12.	Morris, Wm. H., delegate 9th district, Putnam county,	2, 5
115.	Morrison, John, statement of lands sold to, ...	119–121
	Morrison, Norman, statement of lands sold to,.. 120,	121
	Morrow, Michael, statement of lands sold to,........	205
	Morse, Jedediah, statement of lands sold to, ...	101
	Morse, Ralsey, statement of lands sold to, ...	233
	Morse, Nathan, statement of lands sold to,...........	164
	Moseley, John, statement of lands sold to,..........	56, 57
	Mosher, John, statement of lands sold to,...........	244
	Mosher, Wm. H., statement of lands sold to,........	358
	Mosier, Seneca, statement of lands sold to,..... 116,	117
	Moseley, Fanny, statement of lands sold to,.........	125
	Mott & Freeman, statement of lands sold to, ...	139
55.	Mount Pleasant Academy, appropriations to,........	32–35
	Mount Morris Union Free School, appropriations to,	34, 35
115.	Moyer, Duncan, statement of lands sold to,.........	286
	Moyer, Jno., statement of lands sold to,.............	360
	Moyers, S. C., statement of lands sold to,...........	111
	Mulford, Thomas, statement of lands sold to, ...	147
	Mullen, James, statement of lands sold to, ...	68
	Mullett, Chilion, statement of lands sold to,.........	99
	Mumford, William W., statement of lands sold to, 99,	288
40.	Munger, Geo. G., testimony of, relative to Parker's contract for repairs of section one of Chenango canal,..................................	718–24
115.	Munger, Eliel, statement of lands sold to, ...	206
28.	Munger, Sutton & Barnes, extra compensation paid to,	6
115.	Munroe, Allen, statement of lands sold to, ... 367,	383
55.	Munro Collegiate Institute, appropriations to, ...	32–35
28.	Murray, Edward, extra compensation paid to,.......	6
115.	Murray, John, statement of lands sold to,...........	135
	Murphy, Allen, statement of lands sold to, ...	261
	Murphy, Benjamin, statement of lands sold to,......	296
40.	Murphy, Elijah W., testimony of, relative to management of Champlain canal, ...	611–13
1, 12.	Murphy, Henry C., delegate at large, Kings county,..	1, 5
109.	minority report of, relative to government of cities, ...	1–3

No. Doc. | | Page.
115. Mussey, Thaddeus, statement of lands sold to,.. 208, 211
Myer, Nicholas D., statement of lands sold to,....... 95
Myrick, Barnabas, statement of lands sold to, 46, 175, 277
Myrick, Luther, statement of lands sold to,.......... 210

N.

98. Names of persons, special laws for change of, prohibited, 14
55. Naples Academy, appropriation to,................ 35
94. National guard, provision for organization of, ... 1, 2
reserve officers of, provided for, ... 3, 4
officers of, how to be appointed, ... 2, 3
number of, to be fixed by law,.............. 1
number of in 1866,...................... 5
115. Nash, Aaron, statement of lands sold to,............ 208
Nash, Jno., statement of lands sold to, ... 363
Nash, Pliny, statement of lands sold to,............ 64
Nash, Samuel, statement of lands sold to, ... 211
Nash, Timothy S., statement of lands sold to,....... 57, 65, 370, 380
Neal, Miles, statement of lands sold to, ... 143
15. Negro suffrage, reasons for, ... 4
16. relative to, and separate submission of,....... 3, 4
115. Nellis, B., statement of lands sold to, ... 322
Nelson, Elisha, statement of lands sold to,.......... 363
1, 12. Nelson, Homer A., delegate at large, Dutchess county, 1, 5
115. Nelson, Robert, statement of lands sold to,.......... 232
Nelson, Wm., statement of lands sold to,........... 323
55. Newark Union Free School, appropriations to, ... 35
New Berlin Academy, appropriations to, ... 32–35
Newburgh Academy, appropriations to, ... 36–39
Newburgh Home of the Friendless, appropriations to, 59
115. Newbury, John, statement of lands sold to,......... 48
Newell, Horace, statement of lands sold to, ... 69
Newell, Pollaus A., statement of lands sold to,...... 51, 53
Newell, Wm., statement of lands sold to,........... 311
Newkirk, James, statement of lands sold to, ... 205
55. New Paltz Academy, appropriations to,............ 36–39
54. News Boys' Lodging House, New York, report of donations to,................................ 9

No. Doc. Page.

115. Newton, Abram S., statement of lands sold to, ... 68
Newton, Jno. M., statement of lands sold to, ... 248
Newton, Samuel, statement of lands sold to, ... 135
Newton, Wm., statement of lands sold to, ... 270, 278
55. New York Blind Mechanics' Association, appropriations to, ... 90
112. New York board of supervisors, to be abolished, ... 5
55. New York Central Academy, appropriations to, ... 39
21. New York Central Railroad, amount of freight carried over each year from 1853 to 1866, inclusive:
whole number of tons, ... 8–34, 37
products of the forest, number of tons, ... 8–34, 37
animals, number of tons, ... 8–34, 37
vegetable food, number of tons, ... 8–34, 37
other agricultural products, number of tons, 8–34, 37
manufactures, number of tons, ... 8–34, 37
merchandise, number of tons, ... 8–34, 37
other articles, number of tons, ... 8–34, 37
55. New York Church of the Immaculate Conception, appropriations to, ... 90
New York Conference Seminary, appropriations to, .. 36–39
107. New York court of common pleas, provisions relative to, ... 8, 9
21. New York and Erie railroad, amount of Freight carried over, each year from 1851 to 1861, inclusive:
whole number of tons, ... 5–24, 38
products of the forest, number of tons, ... 5–24, 38
animals, number of tons, ... 5–24, 38
vegetable food, number of tons, ... 5–24, 38
other agricultural products, number of tons, . 5–24, 38
manufactures, number of tons, ... 5–24, 38
merchandise, number of tons, ... 5–24, 38
other articles, number of tons, ... 5–24, 38
(See "Erie Railway.")
55. New York fire department widows' and orphans' fund, appropriations to, ... 89, 91
Free Academy, appropriations to, ... 36–39

No. Doc. Page.

21. New York and Harlem railroad, amount of freight carried over, each year from 1851 to 1866, inclusive:
whole number of tons,.................... 5–34
products of the forest, number of tons, ... 5–34
animals, number of tons, ... 5–34
vegetable food, number of tons,............. 5–34
other agricultural products, number of tons,.. 5–34
manufactures, number of tons,.............. 5–34
merchandise, number of tons,............... 5–34
other articles, number of tons,.............. 5–34

54. New York, Homœopathic Dispensary, report of donations to, ... 10

55. Life Savings Benevolent Institution, appropriations to, ... 88, 90
Mechanics' Institute, appropriations to,...... 84, 90
Prison Association, appropriations to,........ 90

146. communication from, relative to government of State prisons,............... 1–6

21. New York and New Haven railroad, amount of freight carried over, each year from 1851 to 1866, inclusive:
whole number of tons, ... 5–34
products of the forest, number of tons, ... 5–34
animals, number of tons,.................. 5–34
vegetable food, number of tons, ... 5–34
other agricultural products, number of tons,.. 5–34
manufactures, number of tons, ... 5–34
merchandise, number of tons, ... 5–34
other articles, number of tons, ... 5–34

55. New York, St. Bridget's Church School, appropriations to, ... 90
St. Mary's Church and School, appropriations to, ... 90

45. State Workingmen's Assembly, petition of, relative to eight hour law,................. 1–4

54. State Lunatic Asylum, report of donations to, 14
State Womans' Hospital, report of donations to, 11
grant of land to, ... 20

107. superior court, provisions relative to,........ 8, 9

No. Doc.		Page.
65.	New York city, report of corporation counsel of, relative to suits against, ...	1, 2
68.	court of general sessions of the peace, police force detailed as attendants on, ...	4
	court of special sessions of the peace, police force detailed as attendants on, ...	4
	1st district police court, police force detailed as attendants on, ...	4
	2d district police court, police force detailed as attendants on, ...	4, 5
13.	tax payers on real estate in, ...	1
	on personal estate in, ...	1
	as stockholders in banks in, ...	1
33.	superior court of (see "Superior Court of New York").	
43.	report by clerk of last Assembly of titles of bills relating to, ...	1–23
54.	report of comptroller of, relative to donations to charitable institutions in, ...	1–23
	fire department, report of donations to, ...	45
	Dispensary, report of donations to, ...	4, 5
	Magdalene Society, report of donations to, ...	7
	Juvenile Asylum, report of donations to, ...	7
	Volunteer Association, report of donations to,	7
	Female Assistance Society, report of donations to, ...	11
	Prison Association, report of donations to, ...	11
	Infirmary for Women and Children, report of donations to, ...	13
	Asylum for Lying in Children, report of donations to, ...	13
	Infant Asylum, report of donations to, ...	13
	Women's Infirmary, report of donations to, ...	13, 16
	Medical College, report of donations to, ..	16
55.	Eye and Ear Infirmary, appropriations to, ...	76–79
	Homœopathic Dispensary, appropriations to, ..	79
	Ophthalmic Hospital, appropriations to, ...	77–79
	College of Physicians and Surgeons, appropriations to, ...	80–83
	Industrial Temperance Home, appropriations to,	84, 90

No. Doc. Page.

55. New York city, Colored Home, appropriations to, ... 58, 59
Colored Orphan Asylum, appropriations to, .. 56–59
Ladies' Educational Union, appropriations to,. 63
Orphan Asylum, appropriations to, ... 60–63
Nursery and Childs' Hospital, appropriations to, ... 61–63
Home and Orphans' Asylum of the Protestant Episcopal Church, appropriations to, ... 61–63
Protestant Half Orphan Asylum, appropriations to, ... 60–63
Roman Catholic Orphan Asylum, appropriations to, ... 60–63
Half Orphan Asylum, appropriations to,. 60–63
Society for Protection of Destitute Roman Catholic Children, ... 63
Society for Relief of Children of Poor Widowers and Widows, appropriations to, ... 64–67
St. Joseph's Orphan Asylum, appropriations to, 66, 67
Union Home and School, appropriations to,.. 71
Hospital, appropriations to, ... 72–75
Infirmary for Indigent Women and Children, appropriations to, ... 74, 75

68. 3d district police court, police force detailed as attendants on, ... 4, 5
4th district police court, police force detailed as attendants on, ... 4, 5

77. value of property belonging to religious denominations in, exempt from taxation, ... 1

101. police in, expense of each year from 1849 to 1866, inclusive, ... 4
commissioners exercising jurisdiction in, ... 5
expenditures by State commissioners or boards in, for 1867, ... 6, 7
expenditures by city government of, for 1867,. 7–9

112. legislative power of, to be vested in a common council, ... 2
board of aldermen of, their election, classification and term of office, ... 2
to choose their own officers, ... 3

No. Doc.		Page.
112.	New York city, board of assistant aldermen, election and term of office of, ...	2
	to choose their own officers, ...	3
	comptroller, election and term of office of, ...	3, 4
	to appoint subordinate officers, ...	3
	removal of, ...	3, 4
	receiver of taxes, election and term of office of,	3, 4
	to appoint subordinate officers, ...	3
	removal of, ...	3, 4
113.	taxes raised in, for each year from 1857 to 1867, inclusive, ...	9, 10
	report of minority of committee on powers and duties of Legislature relative to government of, ...	1–11
124.	comptroller of, report by, of expenses of courts in, ...	1–8
	Supreme Court in, expenses of, ...	5
	fees received from, ...	5
	superior court, expenses of, ...	5
	fees received from, ...	6
	court of common pleas, expenses of, ...	6
	fees received from, ...	6
	marine court, expenses of, ...	6
	fees received from, ...	6
	court of general sessions, expenses of, ...	7
	fees received from, ...	7
	court of special sessions, expenses of, ...	7
	fees received from, ...	7
	police courts, expenses of, ...	7, 8
	amount received from fines imposed by, .	8
	district courts, expenses of, ...	8
	fees received from, ...	8
125.	comptroller of, report by, relative to city debt and certain revenues, ...	1–37
	sinking fund for redemption of city debt, statement of revenues applied to, ...	6–21
	pawnbrokers in, revenues derived from, ...	6, 7
	second hand dealers in, revenues derived from,	6, 7
	hackney coaches in, revenues derived from, ..	6, 7
	market fees and rents in, amount received from,	6–10

No. Doc.		Page.
125.	New York city, market cellar rents, amount received from,	10–13
fines and penalties in, amount received from,	14, 15
mayoralty fees in, amount received from,	14, 15
court fees and fines in, amount received from,	16–21
revenues, expenses of collecting certain,	22–37
126.	citizens' association, communication from, relative to commissions for government of city,	1–26
141.	rights and franchises of, communication from clerk of common council, relative to,	1, 2
115.	Ney, Henry, statement of lands sold to,	358
Ney, Mary M., statement of lands sold to,	365
Ney, N. B., statement of lands sold to, 349,	360
28.	Nichols, Charles, extra compensation paid to,	11
40.	testimony of, relative to letting canal contracts, 28th December,	679–82
testimony of, relative to points taken in declaring bids informal,	673–76
refusal of, to answer certain questions,	677–79
115.	Nicholas, David, statement of lands sold to,	58
40.	Nichols, Lorain L., testimony of, relative to award to Charles J. De Graw, 28–44,	133–38
115.	Nichols, N. & J., statement of lands sold to,	343
Nicholas, Rowland, statement of lands sold to,	369
Nicholson & Reamer, statement of lands sold to,	92
Nickerson, Elisha, statement of lands sold to,	101
Noble, B., statement of lands sold to,	291
Noble, Charles, statement of lands sold to, 101,	136
Noble, Charles & Henry R., statement of lands sold to,	40, 47
Noble, H. R., statement of lands sold to,	354
Noble, Harmon, statement of lands sold to,	309
Noble, Hiram J., statement of lands sold to,	163
Noble & Williams, statement of lands sold to,	176
28.	Noone & Fitzgerald, extra compensation paid to,	9
55.	Normal School at Albany, appropriations to,	3–7, 92
North Granville Female Seminary, appropriations to,	38, 39
North Hebron Institute, appropriations to,	38, 39
North Salem Academy, appropriations to,	36–39
North Eastern Dispensary, N. Y., appropriations to,	79

No. Doc. Page.

54. North Eastern Dispensary, N. Y., report of donations to, ... 14
grant of land to, ... 23
North Western Dispensary, N. Y., report of donations to, ... 4, 5
55. appropriations to, ... 77–79
54. Northern Dispensary, N. Y., report of donations to,.. 4, 5
55. appropriations to, ... 76–79
21. Northern railroad (of New Jersey), amount of freight carried over during the year 1866:
whole number of tons, ... 34
products of the forest, number of tons, ... 34
animals, number of tons, ... 34
vegetable food, number of tons,............. 34
other agricultural products, number of tons,.. 34
manufactures, number of tons,.............. 34
merchandise, number of tons, ... 34
other articles, number of tons,............. 34
Northern (Ogdensburgh) railroad, amount of freight carried over each year, from 1851 to 1864, inclusive:
whole number of tons,.................. 5–30, 43
products of the forest, number of tons, ... 5–30, 43
animals, number of tons, ... 5–30, 43
vegetable food, number of tons, ... 5–30, 43
other agricultural products, number of tons, 5–30, 43
manufactures, number of tons, ... 5–30, 43
merchandise, number of tons,............ 5–30, 43
other articles, number of tons,............ 5–30, 43
(See "Ogdensburgh & Lake Champlain Railroad.")
40. Northrup, Edwin R., testimony of, relative to management of Champlain canal, ... 462–69
12. Northrup, M. H., reporter, Onondaga, ... 9
55. Norwich Academy, appropriations to,.............. 36–39
115. Noxon, B. D., statement of lands sold to,........... 324
Nugent, Thos., statement of lands sold to,.......... 321
55. Nunda Literary Institute, appropriations to,......... 36–39

No. Doc. Page.

37. Nursery and Child's Hospital, petition of, relative to claims for Foundling Hospital, ... 1–5
54. grant of land to, ... 21
report of donations to, ... 9
Nursery of Poor Children, N. Y., report of donations to, 7

O.

40. O'Brien, James, testimony of, relative to management of Champlain canal, ... 555–57
28. O'Connor & Sullivan, extra compensation paid to,.... 9
115. Odell, Benjamin, statement of lands sold to, ... 278
15. Office, none but electors qualified to hold, ... 3
4. Offices, resolution relative to abolition of certain, ... 1
98. Official acts, special laws for legalization of, prohibited, 14
150. Official corruption, article reported by committee on,. 1–4
explanatory report of committee on,......... 4–11
testimony taken by committee on, ... 13–51
minority report of Mr. M. I. Townsend on,... 1–3
177. article on, as amended and referred to committee on revision, ... 1, 2
98. Official misconduct, provisions for removal in case of,. 9, 10
15. Official oath,.................................. 3
28. Ogden & Durphy, extra compensation paid to, ... 6
55. Ogdensburgh Academy, appropriations to,.......... 36–39
Educational Institute, appropriations to,...... 38, 39
21. Ogdensburgh and Lake Champlain railroad, amount of freight carried over, each of the years 1865 and 1866:
whole number of tons, ... 32, 35, 43
products of the forest, number of tons, ... 32, 35, 43
animals, number of tons,............... 32, 35, 43
vegetable food, number of tons, ... 32, 35, 43
other agricultural products, number of tons, 32, 35, 43
manufactures, number of tons, ... 32, 35, 43
merchandise, number of tons,........... 32, 35, 43
other articles, number of tons, ... 32, 35, 43
115. Ogle, Geo., statement of lands sold to,.............. 307
O'Hara & Milton, statement of lands sold to,.... 133, 142

No. Doc. Page.
115. Olcott, Lebbeus, statement of lands sold to, ... 239
Olcott, Thos. W., statement of lands sold to, ... 308, 309
55. Olean Academy, appropriations to, ... 37–39
115. Olmsted, Chas, statement of lands sold to, ... 361
Olmsted, H. L., statement of lands sold to, ... 361
55. Oneida Conference Seminary, appropriations to, ... 36–39
14. Oneida Indians, number and residence of, ... 2
agricultural statistics of, ... 4–8
23. Oneida Lake canal, income from and disbursements for, ... 28, 29, 38
cost of, over revenues, ... 39
Oneida river improvement, income from and disbursements for, ... 32, 33, 38
revenues of, over cost, ... 39
42. report of unsettled claims for damages on, ... 4
55. Oneida Seminary, appropriations to, ... 38, 39
Onondaga Academy, appropriations to, ... 36–39
Onondaga County Orphan Asylum, appropriations to, 60–63
14. Onondaga Indians, population of, on reservation, ... 2
annuities paid to, ... 2
agricultural statistics of, ... 4–8
159. Onondaga Salt Company, dividends made by, ... 11, 16, 17
surplus revenues of, ... 11
profits of, in purchase of coal, ... 11, 12
price lists of, ... 17–26
Onondaga salt springs (see "Salt Springs").
55. Ontario County Orphan Asylum, appropriations to, .. 63
Ontario Female Seminary, appropriations to, ... 36–39
1, 12. Opdyke, George, delegate at large, New York county, 1, 5
54. Ophthalmic Hospital, N. Y., report of donations to, .. 6
9. Organization of Legislature, committee on, ... 1
55. Orphan Asylums, &c., appropriations to, from 1847 to 1866, inclusive, ... 92
54. Orphan Asylum of the Protestant Episcopal Church, N. Y., grant of land to, ... 22
Orphans' Home, N. Y., report of donations to, ... 13
and Asylum, N. Y., report of donations to, .. 13
28. Osborn, Abijah, extra compensation paid to, ... 6
115. Osborne, Asa, statement of lands sold to, ... 109, 110

No. Doc.		Page.
115.	Osborne, Fred. P., statement of lands sold to, ...	135
	Osborne, Joseph, statement of lands sold to, ...	231
	Osborne, Walter, statement of lands sold to, ...	99
	Osborne, Wm., statement of lands sold to, ...	249
	Osgood, Iddo, statement of lands sold to, ...	132
28.	Oswald & Van Valkenburgh, extra compensation paid to, ...	9
23.	Oswego canal, income since 1826 from, and disbursements for, ...	12, 13
	proportion chargeable to, for repairs and maintenance of Erie and Champlain canals, .. 11,	13, 38
	tolls contributed by, to Erie canal, ...	12
	property passed through, to and from Welland canal, ...	14
	salt passed through, to Welland canal, ...	15
	property from other states passed through, ...	15
	revenues of, over cost, ...	39
42.	report of number of unsettled claims for damages on, ...	4
57.	notice for proposals for repairs of, 99, 102, 104,	144
64.	cost of enlarging locks on, ...	12
88.	average cargo of boats on, ...	14, 15
115.	Oswego Canal Company, statement of lands sold to, ..	19
	Oswego Cemetery, statement of lands sold to, ...	17
55.	Oswego High School, appropriations to, ...	38, 39
	Oswego Hospital, appropriations to, ...	73–75
	Oswego Orphan Asylum, appropriations to, ...	61–63
21.	Oswego and Syracuse railroad, amount of freight carried over, each year from 1851 to 1866, inclusive:	
	whole number of tons, ...	5–35
	products of the forest, number of tons, ...	5–35
	animals, number of tons, ...	5–35
	vegetable food, number of tons, ...	5–35
	other agricultural products, number of tons, ..	5–35
	manufactures, number of tons, ...	5–35
	merchandise, number of tons, ...	5–35
	other articles, number of tons, ...	5–35
115.	statement of lands sold to, ...	17

No. Doc. Page.
115. Otis, John, statement of lands sold to, ... 78
164. Ottawa ship canal, report of survey of, ... 75–191
61. Overseers of the poor, election and term of office of, .. 2, 3
removal of, ... 3
55. Ovid Academy, appropriations to, ... 36–39
42. Owasco Lake improvement, report of number of unsettled claims for damages on, ... 4
55. Owego Academy, appropriations to, ... 36–39
115. Owen, Leonard, statement of lands sold to, ... 164
40. Owens, Ephraim, testimony of, relative to letting canal contracts, 28th December, ... 602–11
28. Owens & Holman, extra compensation paid to, ... 9
55. Oxford Academy, appropriations to, ... 36–39
107. Oyer and Terminer (see "Courts of Oyer and Terminer").

P.

55. Packer Collegiate Institute, appropriations to, ... 37–39
115. Paddock, Joseph W., statement of lands sold to, 118, 140
Paddock, L., statement of lands sold to, ... 338, 339
Paddock, Ora F., statement of lands sold to, ... 126
Paddock, Wm. S., statement of lands sold to, ... 337
Paddock & Cheney, statement of lands sold to, ... 74
Padrick, C., statement of lands sold to, ... 205
28. Page, Daniel, extra compensation paid to, ... 6
115. Page, Eli, statement of lands sold to, ... 210
Page, Wm., statement of lands sold to, ... 209
1, 12. Paige, Alonzo C., delegate at large, Schenectady county, ... 1, 5
55. Palatine Bridge Union Free School, appropriations to, 42, 43
115. Palmer, Alanson, statement of lands sold to, ... 257
Palmer, Benjamin, statement of lands sold to, ... 50
Palmer, Joseph, statement of lands sold to, ... 341
28. Palmer, Noah, extra compensation paid to, ... 6
115. Palmeter & Ames, statement of lands sold to, ... 143
55. Palmyra Classical Union School, appropriations to, .. 38, 39
115. Parcell, Samuel, statement of lands sold to, ... 98
3. Pardoning power, provision for committee on, ... 2
9. committee on, ... 4

No. Doc.		Page.
76.	Pardoning power, report of committee on, ...	1–5
78.	supplemental report of committee on, ...	1
99.	article reported by committee on, and referred to committee on revision, ...	1, 2
48.	Pardons, list of applications to Governor for, from 1849 to 1867, inclusive, ...	1–8
76.	Governor empowered to grant, except in cases of treason and impeachment, ...	4
	Governor required to report cases of, ...	5
115.	Paris, Jno. D., statements of land sold to, ...	124
1, 12.	Parker, Amasa J., delegate 13th district, Albany county, ...	2, 5
1, 12.	Parker, Charles E., delegate 24th district, Tioga county,	3, 5
115.	Parker, C. G., statement of lands sold to, ...	362
	Parker, Jno., statement of lands sold to, ...	332
	Parker, Marvin, statement of lands sold to, ... 331,	332
	Parkhurst, Alice A., statement of lands sold to, ...	121
	Parkhurst, Jabez, statement of lands sold to, ...	126
	Parkhurst, Nathan, statement of lands sold to, ...	206
	Parkhurst, Sarah M., statement of lands sold to, ...	119
	Parkhurst, Stephen, statement of lands sold to, 119,	120 121
	Parks, B., statement of lands sold to, ...	207
	Parmelee, Sheldon, statement of lands sold to, .. 208,	211
54.	Parochial School in 14th street, New York, report of donations to, ...	15
115.	Parsell, Elvira, statement of lands sold to, ...	248
	Parsons, H., statement of lands sold to, ...	361
	Partridge, Stephen, statement of land sold to, ...	143
	Pasco, Leonard, statement of lands sold to, 331, 332,	333
	Patchin, John, statement of lands sold to, .. 85, 117,	118 130
	Patrie, Conrad, statement of lands sold to, ...	212
	Patten, Albert, statement of land sold to, ...	119
28.	Patten, A. & F. J., extra compensation paid to, ...	6
115.	Patten & Willard, statement of lands sold to, ...	120
	Patterson, David, statement of lands sold to, ...	208
	Patterson, M., statement of lands sold to, ...	327
	Patterson, Thomas, statement of lands sold to, ...	135
	Patterson, Thomas & Elias, statement of lands sold to, 89,	145

No. Doc. Page.
15. Paupers, to be deprived of suffrage, ... 2
115. Pavier, Jabez, statement of lands sold to, ... 361
Payne, Benjamin W., statement of lands sold to, ... 153
Payne, Joshua, statement of lands sold to, ... 337
Payne, Levi, statement of lands sold to, ... 337
Payne, Samuel H., statement of lands sold to, 123, 125, 284
95. Payn, Samuel N., testimony of, relative to management of canals, ... 21–24
115. Peabody, H. O., statement of lands sold to, ... 353
Peabody, Oliver D., statement of lands sold to, ... 349
12. Peart, John, doorkeeper, Saratoga, ... 8
115. Pease & Holt, statement of land sold to, ... 101
28. Peck, A., & Co., extra compensation paid to, ... 11
115. Peck, David, statement of lands sold to, ... 143, 264
28. Peck, George H., extra compensation paid to, ... 9, 10
40. testimony of, relative to points taken in declaring bids informal, ... 231–38
115. Peck, Joel, statement of lands sold to, ... 60–62
95. Peck, Linus Jones, testimony of, relative to management of canals, ... 32–37
115. Peck, Stephen, statement of lands sold to, ... 160
Peck, Percy & Betsey, statement of lands sold to, ... 307
Peckham, Cyrus, statement of lands sold to, ... 358
Peckham, Rufus, statement of lands sold to, ... 381
Peckham, L. T., statement of lands sold to, ... 258
55. Peekskill Academy, appropriations to, ... 40–43
115. Peffers, Wm., statement of lands sold to, ... 117
Peffers, W. & M., statement of lands sold to, ... 147
Pendell, Elisha, statement of lands sold to, ... 332
Penfield, Henry F., statement of lands sold to, ... 230
55. Penfield Seminary, appropriations to, ... 42, 43
28. Pennock & Skinner, extra compensation paid to, ... 6
55. Penn Yan Academy, appropriations to, ... 42, 43
47. People's College, failure of, to comply with act relative to college land scrip, ... 3
115. Perkins, Stephen, statement of lands sold to, ... 156, 189
Perry, Amos, statement of lands sold to, ... 44, 201
Perry, A. W., statement of lands sold to, ... 338
55. Perry Academy, appropriations to, ... 41–43

No. Doc. Page.

55. Peterboro Academy, appropriations to, ... 41–43
28. Peterson, Gilbert, extra compensation paid to, ... 9
149. Petition, abridgment of right of, prohibited, ... 4
115. Petrie, H. B. & L., statement of lands sold to, ... 361
Pettibone, Silvester, statement of lands sold to, ... 205
115. Petts, James, statement of lands sold to, ... 107
Pharis, Chas. E., statement of lands sold to, ... 293
Pharis, Isaac R., statement of lands sold to, ... 307
Pharis, M. P., statement of lands sold to, ... 392
Phelps, Aaron, statement of lands sold to, ... 68
Phelps, Bishop, statement of lands sold to, ... 238
150. Phelps, Edward R., testimony of before committee on official corruption, ... 38, 41
115. Phelps, Elihu, statement of lands sold to, ... 200
Phelps, Homer R., statement of lands sold to, ... 178
Phelps, Oliver, statement of lands sold to, ... 276, 279
Phelps, Theoditus, statement of lands sold to, ... 59
55. Phelps Union School, appropriations to, ... 41–43
115. Phillips, Asa, statement of lands sold to, ... 236
Phillips, Benjamin, statement of lands sold to, .. 232, 277, 285, 290, 337
Phillips, James W., statement of lands sold to, ... 105
Phillips, Jefferson, statement of lands sold to, .. 342, 349
28. Phillips & Moore, extra compensation paid to, ... 6
55. Phipps Union Seminary, appropriations to, ... 40–43
1, 12. Pierrepont, Edwards, delegate 7th district, New York county, ... 2, 5
115. Pierson, Aaron, statement of lands sold to, ... 182
Pierson, Eliphalet, statement of lands sold to, ... 301
12. Pierce, Charles S., sergeant-at-arms, Monroe, ... 8
115. Pickett, Wm., statement of lands sold to, ... 307
Pike, Simeon, statement of lands sold to, ... 96
55. Pike Seminary, appropriations to, ... 42, 43
115. Piper, S. B., statement of lands sold to, ... 321
Pitcher, Alfred, statement of lands sold to, ... 99
Platt, James, statement of lands sold to, ... 30
Platt, Starr, statement of lands sold to, ... 82
55. Plattsburgh Academy, appropriations to, ... 40–43
73. Police, public, to provide for boards of, ... 2

No. Doc.		Page.
73.	Police, public, secretary of boards of, to be member of executive council, ...	2
122.	districts, division of the State into, ...	20
	State (see "State Police").	
95.	Pomfret, James E., testimony of, relative to management of canals, ...	51
55.	Pompey Academy, appropriations to, ...	40–43
1, 12.	Pond, Alembert, delegate 15th district, Saratoga Co.,	2, 5
115.	Poole, Samuel & William, statement of lands sold to,	92
	Pool & Lester, statement of lands sold to, ...	238
	Pope, Martin, statement of lands sold to, ... 161,	310
	Poppleton, Geo. S., statement of lands sold to, ...	322
55.	Port Byron Free School and Academy, ...	42, 43
115.	Porteous, Andrew, statement of lands sold to, ...	72, 73
	Porter, Augustus, statement of lands sold to, ...	237
	Porter, James, statement of lands sold to, ...	141
	Porter, Jno. F., statement of lands sold to, ...	249
	Porter, Nathan, statement of lands sold to, ...	205
	Porter, Wm., statement of lands sold to, ...	209
	Post, Abram, statement of lands sold to, ...	211
	Post, Asa, statement of lands sold to, ...	174
	Post, Asa H., statement of lands sold to, ...	177
	Post, Lewis, statement of lands sold to, ...	134
1, 12.	Potter, Allen, delegate 31st, district, Erie county, ...	3, 5
95.	Potter, David H., testimony of, relative to management of canals, ...	17, 18
115.	Potter, Wm. C., statement of lands sold to, 72, 73, 91,	189
	193, 315, 327, 330, 331, 332, 334, 343,	388
21.	Potsdam & Watertown railroad, amount of freight carried over each year from 1855 to 1864, inclusive:	
	whole number of tons, ...	12–24
	products of the forest, number of tons, ...	12–24
	animals, number of tons, ...	12–24
	vegetable food, number of tons, ...	12–24
	other agricultural products, number of tons, ..	12–24
	manufactures, number of tons, ...	12–24
	merchandise, number of tons, ...	12–24
	other articles, number of tons, ...	12–24

No. Doc. Page.
55. Poughkeepsie Academy, appropriations to, ... 40–43
Poughkeepsie Home of the Friendless, appropriations to, ... 57–59
115. Powers, David, statement of lands sold to, ... 209
Powers, Heman, statement of lands sold to, ... 141
Powers, Hiram, statement of lands sold to, ... 361
Powell, Oran, statement of lands sold to, ... 113
Pratt, Hiram, statement of lands sold to, ... 38
Pratt, Orsamus, statement of lands sold to, ... 264
Pratt, Stephen, statement of lands sold to, ... 51, 86, 87
117, 147, 285, 286
Pratt & Bartlett, statement of lands sold to, ... 87
Pratt & Wells, statement of lands sold to, ... 375
55. Prattsville Academy, appropriations to, ... 40–43
149. Preamble and Bill of Rights (see "Bill of Rights").
4. Preamble, resolution for amendment of, ... 3
149. Press, liberty of secured, ... 4
55. Princetown Academy, appropriations to, ... 41–43
1, 12. Prindle, Elizur H., delegate 23d district, Chenango Co., 3, 6
28. Pringle & Claffy, extra compensation paid to, ... 9
3. Printing, provision for committee on, ... 2
9. committee on, ... 6
115. Printup, Wm. J., statement of lands sold to, ... 134
Pritchard, David J., statement of lands sold to, ... 132
Pritchard, Nathan, statement of lands sold to, ... 206
98. Private bills, notice of application for, to be published, 13
Private claims against the State, Legislature prohibited, 7
149. Private property taken for public use, provision relative to, ... 3
3. Privileges and elections, provision for committee on, 2
9. committee on, ... 5
107. Probate courts, establishment of, ... 14
147. Prohibitory liquor laws, enactment of, forbidden, ... 1
55. Prospect Academy, appropriations to, ... 40–43
1, 12. Prosser, Erastus S., delegate at large, Erie county, ... 1, 6
115. Pruyn, Casparus F., statement of lands sold to, ... 249
73. Public buildings, parks and water fronts, to provide for boards of, ... 2
secretary of, to be member of executive council, 2
55. Pulaski Academy, appropriations to, ... 42, 43

No. Doc.		Page.

115. Pulver, H., statement of lands sold to, ... 376
149. Punishment, cruel or unusual prohibited,........... 3
115. Purmort, James H., statement of lands sold to,...... 352
Purmort, John, statement of lands sold to,......... 54, 289
Purmort, John, Jr., statement of lands sold to, ... 55
Purmort, Nathaniel, statement of lands sold to,.. 49, 53, 55, 56
Putnam, H. A., statement of lands sold to, ... 373
Putnam, Hiram, statement of lands sold to,......... 382
Putnam, Jonas, statement of lands sold to, ... 117
Putnam & Marshall, statement of lands sold to, ... 261
Putnam, Williams & Abel, statement of lands sold to, 357, 373, 387
Putney, Sylvester, statement of lands sold to,....... 135

Q.

115. Quackenboss, Charles, statement of lands sold to, 250, 304
98. Quorum of the Legislature, provision relative to,.... 4
115. Quackenboss & Noah, statement of land sold to,..... 73

R.

115. Raddie, Alex. T., statement of lands sold to,........ 16, 25
21. Railroad freight, report of State Engineer, relative to amount of, ... 1–43
amount carried over all in State, each year, from 1851 to 1866, inclusive:
whole number of tons, ... 36
products of the forest, number of tons, ... 36
animals, number of tons,.................. 36
vegetable food, number of tons, ... 36
other agricultural products, number of tons,.. 36
manufactures, number of tons, ... 36
merchandise, number of tons,.............. 36
other articles, number of tons,............. 36
115. Ranney, Eli, statement of lands sold to, ... 209
Randall, Asa C., Jr., statement of lands sold to, ... 13
28. Randall, H. W., extra compensation paid to, ... 11
115. Randall, J. S., statement of lands sold to, ... 33

No. Doc.		Page.
115.	Randall, Nelson, statement of lands sold to, ...	38
55.	Randolph Academy Association, appropriations to, ..	41–43
115.	Ransom, Ira, statement of lands sold to, ...	287
	Ransom, J., Jr., statement of lands sold to, ...	361
28.	Ransom, Jerome B., extra compensation paid to, ...	6
19.	Ransom, P. H., superintendent of salt springs, ...	4
115.	Rathbun, Benjamin, statement of lands sold to, ...	36, 37
	Rathbun, Daniel, statement of lands sold to, ...	103
1, 12.	Rathbun, George, delegate 25th district, Cayuga Co.,.	3, 6
115.	Rathbun, W., statement of lands sold to, ...	258
28.	Ray, James, extra compensation paid to, ...	10
115.	statement of lands sold to, ...	102
	Raynor, Richard, statement of lands sold to, ... 383,	384
	Raynor, Willet, statement of lands sold to, . 279, 300,	306
	Raynor, W. & H., statement of lands sold to, ...	289
	Reagles, Winther, statement of lands sold to, ... 112,	113
	Rechtmeyer, Jno., statement of lands sold to, ...	212
	Rechtmeyer, S. & P. J., statement of lands sold to, ...	212
55.	Red Creek Union Academy, appropriations to, ...	40–43
115.	Reddington, Geo., statement of lands sold to, ...	287
	Reed, David, statement of lands sold to, ... 159, 318,	319
	Reed, Ephraim, statement of lands sold to, ...	23
	Reed, Harry D., statement of lands sold to, ...	314
	Reed, Isaac, statement of lands sold to, ...	178
	Reed, Jesse, statement of lands sold to, ...	68
157.	Regents of the University, communication from, relative to the proposed abolition of that body, ...	1–12
15.	Registry law, provision for, ...	3
16.	argument against, ...	2
15.	Registry of voters, time for completion of, ...	3
65.	Reinhardt, Emil, judgment in favor of, against city of New York, ...	2
149.	Religious profession and worship, free exercise of secured, ...	2
115.	Remington, Richard, statement of lands sold to, ...	369
	Remington, R., statement of lands sold to, ... 377, 380,	378, 387
55.	Rensselaer Institute, appropriations to, ...	40–43
	Rensselaer Polytechnic Institute, appropriations to, ..	83

No. Doc. Page.

21. Rensselaer and Saratoga railroad, amount of freight carried over, each year (excepting 1862), from 1851 to 1866, inclusive:
whole number of tons, ... 5-35
products of the forest, number of tons, ... 5-35
animals, number of tons, ... 5-35
vegetable food, number of tons, ... 5-35
other agricultural products, number of tons, . 5-35
manufactures, number of tons,.............. 5-35
merchandise, number of tons, ... 5-35
other articles, number of tons, ... 5-35
55. Rensselaerville Academy, appropriations to, ... 40-43
115. Rent, Chauncey G., statement of lands sold to, ... 28
107. Reporter of Court of Appeals, provision relative to appointment and removal of,.................... 3
76. Reprieves, Governor empowered to grant, ... 5
4. Resolution, of Mr. Graves, relative to female suffrage, 1
of Mr. Colahan, for appointment of committee on educational interests,................. 1
of Mr. Lawrence, relative to abolition of useless offices,......................... 1
of Mr. Duganne, for appointment of committee on industrial interests, ... 2
of Mr. T. W. Dwight, for appointment of committee on public and private charities,..... 2
of Mr. S. Townsend, relative to payment of taxes in specie, ... 2
of Mr. Field, for appointment of committee on claims against the State,................. 2
of Mr. Van Campen, for appointment of committee on the relations of the State to Indians therein,.......................... 2
of Mr. Clarke, for amendment of the preamble of the Constitution, ... 3
of Mr. McDonald, relative to distribution of verbatim reports,...................... 3
7. of Mr. Graves, for appointment of committee on the subject of intoxicating liquors, ... 1, 2
11. of Mr. Smith, relative to bribery at elections,. 1

No. Doc.		Page.
29.	Resolution, of Mr. Wales, relative to uniform system of suffrage in all the States,	1, 2
38.	of Mr. Sherman, relative to local legislation by boards of supervisors,	1–3
39.	of Mr. Sherman, relative to general laws,	1, 2
115.	Reynolds, Jno. D., statement of lands sold to,	125
	Reynolds, Newell J., statement of lands sold to,	50
1, 12.	Reynolds, Wm. A., delegate 28th district, Monroe Co.,	3, 6
55.	Rhinebeck Academy, appropriations to,	40–43
19.	Rhoades, Hervey, superintendent of salt springs,	5
115.	Rhoades, William P., statement of lands sold to,	90
	Rice, David, statement of lands sold to,	107
	Rice, Henry, statement of lands sold to,	213
	Rice, Joshua H., statement of lands sold to,	25
	Rich, Jonathan, statement of lands sold to,	125
	Richards, Hoel S, statement of lands sold to,	81, 83
40.	Richards, Orson, testimony of, relative to management of Champlain canal,	531–33
115.	Richards, Pelatiah, statement of lands sold to,	269
	Richardson, James, statement of lands sold to,	123
19.	Richardson, John, superintendent of salt springs,	4
150.	Richardson, Wm., testimony of, before committee on official corruption,	41–43
55.	Richburgh Academy, appropriations to,	40–43
28.	Richman, Jacob, extra compensation paid to,	8
90.	Richmond, Van R., testimony of, relative to improvements of Erie canal,	52–56
115.	Richmond & Kendall, statement of lands sold to,	212
	Richmond & Smith, statement of lands sold to,	69
28.	Riddle, Cook, Magee & Co., extra compensation paid to,	6
55.	Ridgbury Academy, appropriations to,	44–47
	Riga Academy, appropriations to,	44–47
115.	Riley, Jno., statement of lands sold to,	141
	Riley, Wait & Harris, statement of lands sold to,	138
	Ripley, J. H., statement of lands sold to,	337
	River, Eustis, statement of lands sold to,	231
39.	Roads, to require general laws for laying out and opening,	1

No. Doc. Page.

98. Roads, public or private, special laws relative to, prohibited, ... 14
115. Robbe, Theron, statement of lands sold to, ... 202
Roberts, Charles, statement of lands sold to,..... 86, 118, 263, 292
Roberts, Jonathan, statement of lands sold to, 50, 51, 164, 167
Roberts, Wm., statement of lands sold to, ... 367
40. Robertson, Alexander, testimony of, relative to contracts for repairs of section one of Erie canal, and dredging Albany basin,...... 664–67
1, 12. Robertson, Anthony L., delegate 7th district, New York county,...... 2, 6
115. Robinson, Geo. W., statement of lands sold to,...... 306
Robinson, Hugh, statement of lands sold to, ... 128, 309
40. Robinson, John A., testimony of, relative to award to Charles J. DeGraw,...... 274–83
115. Robler, Luther, statement of lands sold to, ... 202
55. Rochester, Collegiate Institute, appropriations to, ... 44–47
Female Academy, appropriations to, ... 44–47
Free Academy, appropriations to,........... 47
Home of the Friendless, appropriations to,.... 62, 63
Industrial School, appropriations to,......... 63
Orphan Asylum, appropriations to, ... 60–63
St. Joseph's Orphan Asylum, appropriations to, 67
St. Mary's Boys' Orphan Asylum, appropriations to,...... 67
St. Patrick's Female Orphan Asylum, appropriations to, ... 64–67
City Hospital, appropriations to,............ 73–75
St. Mary's Hospital, appropriations to,....... 75
University, appropriations to, ... 80–83
21. Rochester and Genesee Valley railroad, amount of freight carried over, each year from 1855 to 1862, inclusive:
whole number of tons,.................... 13–27
products of the forest, number of tons,....... 13–27
animals, number of tons, ... 13–27
vegetable food, number of tons,............. 13–27

No. Doc. | Page.

21. Rochester and Genesee Valley railroad—*Continued.*
other agricultural products, number of tons,.. 13–27
manufactures, number of tons,.............. 13–27
merchandise, number of tons, ... 13–27
other articles,............................ 13–27
(See "Erie Railway").
Rochester, Lockport and Niagara Falls railroad, amount of freight carried over, each of the years 1852 and 1853:
whole number of tons,.................... 6, 8
products of the forest, number of tons,........ 6, 8
animals, number of tons,.................. 6, 8
vegetable food, number of tons,............ 6, 8
other agricultural products, number of tons,.. 6, 8
manufactures, number of tons, ... 6, 8
merchandise, number of tons, ... 6, 8
other articles, number of tons,.............. 6, 8
Rochester and Syracuse railroad, amount of freight carried over, each year from 1851 to 1853, inclusive:
whole number of tons,.................... 5–8
products of the forest, number of tons,....... 5–8
animals, number of tons,.................. 5–8
vegetable food, number of tons, ... 5–8
other agricultural products, number of tons,.. 5–8
manufactures, number of tons,.............. 5–8
merchandise, number of tons,.............. 5–8
other articles, number of tons,.............. 5–8
115. Rockwell, George, statement of lands sold to,....... 89
Rockwell, Thomas, statement of lands sold to,.. 210, 211
Rockwell, Wm. W., statement of lands sold to, ... 376
Rodemore, H. H., statement of lands sold to, ... 378
28. Rogers, Daniel, extra compensation paid to,......... 6
115. Rogers, David S., statement of lands sold to,........ 139
Rogers, Elias B., statement of lands sold to,......... 353
1, 12. Rogers, Henry, delegate 5th district, New York Co.,. 2, 6
115. Rogers, H. W., statement of lands sold to,.. 320, 321, 324
331, 351
Rogers, James, statement of lands sold to,.......... 326

No. Doc.		Page.
115.	Rogers, James & John, statement of lands sold to, 52,	128 309
28.	Rogers, Patrick, extra compensation paid to,........	6
115.	Rogers, Buttrick & Powers, statement of lands sold to,	76, 77 308
28.	Rogers & Layton, extra compensation paid to,.......	6
55.	Rogersville Union Seminary, appropriations to, ...	45–47
1, 12.	Rolfe, John P., delegate 2d district, Kings county,...	1, 6
54.	Roman Catholic Orphan Asylum, N. Y., report of donations to,........................	10
	grant of land to,....................	22
	Children, Society for protection of destitute, N. Y., report of donations to, ...	12
55.	Rome Academy, appropriations to, ...	44–47
21.	Rome, Watertown & Ogdensburgh railroad, amount of freight carried over, each year, from 1862 to 1866, inclusive:	
	whole number of tons,....................	27–35
	products of the forest, number of tons, 27–35,	42
	animals, number of tons............ 27–35,	42
	vegetable food, ... 27–35,	42
	other agricultural products, number of tons,..	27–35 42
	manufactures, number of tons,....... 27–35,	42
	merchandise, number of tons,........ 27–35,	42
	other articles, number of tons,....... 27–35,	42
1, 12.	Root, Elias, delegate 21st district, Oswego county,...	2, 6
115.	Rosboro, A. G., statement of lands sold to,..........	355
	Rose, Nathaniel, statement of lands sold to,.........	269
54.	Rose Hill Ladies' Relief Association, New York, report of donations to, ...	13
115.	Ross, Daniel, statement of lands sold to,.... 80, 174,	176
	Ross, Henry H., statement of lands sold to, ... 373,	386
	Ross, John, statement of lands sold to, ...	124
	Ross, Leonard G., statement of lands sold to, ...	47, 268
	Ross, R. L., statement of lands sold to, 370, 373, 375, 380, 381, 386, 389,	379 391
	Ross, Wm. D., statement of lands sold to,.. 128, 139,	174 176

No. Doc.		Page
115.	Rosseau, A. J., statement of lands sold to,.. 308, 309,	326
		343
	Rosseter & Knox, statement of lands sold to,........	97
	Roth, Jno., statement of lands sold to, ...	309
	Rowe, Thomas F., statement of lands sold to, ...	17
1, 12.	Roy, James, delegate 13th district, Albany county, ..	2, 6
40.	Rozelle, Peter, testimony of relative to management of Champlain canal, ...	443–53
2.	Rules, reported by committee on,..................	1–10
6.	as adopted by convention, ...	1–11
50.	reprint of,...........................	1–12
131.	amendments to, reported by committee on, ...	1
179.	supplementary report of committee on, ...	1
12.	Rulison, Herman, doorkeeper, Jefferson, ...	8
1, 12.	Rumsey, David, delegate 27th district, Steuben county,	3, 6
115.	Rumsey, Stephen, statement of lands sold to, ...	115
54.	Ruptured and crippled, society for, New York, report of donations to,............................	17
55.	Rural Seminary, appropriations to, ...	45–47
	Rushford Academy, appropriations to, ...	45–47
1, 12.	Russell, Abraham D., delegate 6th district, New York county, ...	2, 6
115.	Russell, Daniel, statement of lands sold to, ...	272
	Russell, George L., statement of lands sold to, ...	121
	Russell, Humphrey, statement of lands sold to, ...	124
	Russell, Jno., A., statement of lands sold to,........	374
	Russell, Joseph, statement of lands sold to, 40, 41, 42,	128
	133, 134, 142, 262, 330, 344,	374
1, 12.	Russell, Leslie W., delegate 17th district, St. Lawrence county, ...	2, 6
115.	Russell, Nathan, statement of lands sold to, ...	89
	Russell, Samuel, statement of lands sold to, ... 103,	262
	Russell, Wm., statement of lands sold to, ...	124
	Rust, C. G., statement of lands sold to, ...	237
	Rust, Richard, statement of lands sold to, ...	283
55.	Rutger's Female Institute, appropriations to, ...	44–47
21.	Rutland & Washington railroad, amount of freight carried over during the year 1853:	
	whole number of tons, ...	9
	products of the forest, number of tons, ...	9

No. Doc. Page.

21. Rutland & Washington railroad—*Continued.*
animals, number of tons, ... 9
vegetable food, number of tons, ... 9
other agricultural products, number of tons,.. 9
manufactures, number of tons, ... 9
merchandise, number of tons, ... 9
other articles, number of articles, ... 9

28. Ryan, John, extra compensation paid to, ... 10

115. Rykert, Jno., statement of lands sold to, ... 277

S.

115. Sacketts Harbor railroad company, statement of lands granted to,...... 140, 158, 179, 180, 181, 182, 190, 191
192, 193, 194, 195, 196, 197, 198, 201, 316, 317, 318
319, 346, 347, 348, 352, 374

21. Sacketts Harbor & Ellisburgh railroad, amount of freight carried over each year from 1853 to 1856, inclusive:
whole number of tons,.................... 9–15
products of the forest, number of tons, ... 9–15
animals, number of tons, ... 9–15
vegetable food, number of tons, ... 9–15
other agricultural products, number of tons,.. 9–15
manufactures, number of tons, ... 9–15
merchandise, number of tons, ... 9–15
other articles, number of tons, ... 9–15

Sacketts Harbor, Rome & New York railroad, amount of freight carried over during each of the years 1860 and 1861:
whole number of tons,.................... 22, 24
products of the forest, number of tons, ... 22, 24
animals, number of tons, ... 22, 24
vegetable food, number of tons, ... 22, 24
other agricultural products, number of tons,.. 22, 24
manufactures, number of tons, ... 22, 24
merchandise, number of tons, ... 22, 24
other articles, number of tons,............. 22, 24

74. Sacketts Harbor & Saratoga railroad company, report of State Engineer, relative to lands sold by, 1–3

97. report by Commissioners of Land Office of lands granted to or acquired by,.......... 1–12

No. Doc.		Page.
28.	Sage, Albert G., extra compensation paid to,........	10
95.	testimony of relative to management of canals,	11–16
115.	Sage, C. H., statement of lands sold to,.... 381, 382,	387
	Sage, Elisha M., statement of lands sold to,.........	245
28.	Sage, Hezekiah, extra compensation paid to, ...	6
115.	Sage, Nathan, statement of lands sold to,...........	304
28.	Sage, Walrath & Dunham, extra compensation paid to,	6
55.	Sag Harbor Institute, appropriations to,............	44–47
19.	Salt, amount produced from 1797 to 1866, each year, and aggregate,.........................	4–6
	average amount produced in periods of 10 years,	7
	duties on, amount received by State, ...	8
	price of for 20 years,......................	9, 10
23.	amount of, passed through Welland canal,....	15
156.	duty to be imposed on,.....................	20
159.	tolls on, each year from 1837 to 1866, inclusive,	27
19.	Salt blocks, number, value and owners of, ...	11–17
	Salt lands, quantity of rented or leased, and lessees thereof,..............................	19, 20
	quantity of granted for manufacture of salt, and names of grantees,..................	20, 21
27.	description of, reserved by Constitution of 1826,	3, 4
	amount of reserved, ...	4
	purchased or exchanged since 1848, ...	4
	sold since 1848, ...	4
	reclaimed by lowering Onondaga lake,.......	4
	sold in 1828, statement of,................	26, 27
	sold and exchanged since 1846, statement of,.	9
	sold in 1849, statement of,................	10–13
	sold in 1850, statement of,................	14, 15
	sold in 1852, statement of,................	18, 19
	sold in 1853, statement of,................	16, 17
	sold in 1855, statement of,................	20–23
	sold since December, 1866, statement of, ...	24, 25
	amount paid for, since 1846, and for damages,	28–30
	statement of exchanges of, ...	31
9.	Salt springs, committee on,.......................	5
156.	report of committee on,.....................	1–20
	sale of, authorized, ...	20
158.	minority report of Mr. Comstock relative to,..	1–16

No. Doc.		Page.
159.	Salt springs, testimony taken by committee on,......	1–34
162.	minority report of Mr. McDonald relative to,.	1–39
178.	article on, as amended and referred to committee on revision, ...	1
98.	Legislature prohibited from authorizing sale or lease of,.............................	8, 9
19.	report of superintendent of,................	1–22
	superintendents of, from 1797 to 1866, ...	4–6
	cost of superintendence, structures, repairs, &c.,	7–9
27.	receipts from, and expenditures for,.........	8
	Salt reservation, report of commissioners of land office relative to,.............................	1–31
19.	Salt reservoirs, pumps, conduits and machinery, statements relative to, and value of,................	7, 8
	Salt wells, number of,...........................	1, 2
	capacity of, for production of salt, ...	2, 3
	strength of water from,....................	2
115.	Sampson, Moses, statement of lands sold to, 49, 129, 121,	277
	Sanders, Eliphalet, statement of lands sold to, ...	125
	Sanders & Rogers, statement of lands sold to,.......	125
	Sanford, George, statement of lands sold to, ... 73,	129
	Sanford, Reuben, statement of lands sold to, ... 101, 106, 143, 264, 292, 301,	326
	Sanford, Simeon, statement of lands sold to, ... 87,	143
	Sanford & Linsey, statement of lands sold to, ...	81
28.	Sanford & Eggleston, extra compensation paid to,....	6
115.	Sandford, Joseph, statement of lands sold to,........	26, 27
55.	Sand Lake Academy, appropriations to,............	44–47
21.	Saratoga and Washington railroad, amount of freight carried ever during each of the years 1852, 1853 and 1854:	
	whole number of tons,.......................	6–11
	products of the forest, number of tons, ...	6–11
	animals, number of tons,..................	6–11
	vegetable food, number of tons, ...	6–11
	other agricultural products, number of tons,..	6–11
	manufactures, number of tons,..............	6–11
	merchandise, number of tons,..............	6–11
	other articles, number of tons,..............	6–11

No. Doc. Page.

21. Saratoga and Whitehall railroad, amount of freight carried over, from 1855 to 1864, inclusive:
whole number of tons,.................... 13–30
products of the forest, number of tons,...... 13–30
animals, number of tons,.................. 13–30
vegetable food, number of tons,............ 13–30
other agricultural products, number of tons,.. 13–30
manufactures, number of tons,............. 13–30
merchandise, number of tons,............... 13–30
other articles, number of tons,............. 13–30
55. Saugerties Academy, appropriations to,............ 46–47
Sauquoit Academy, appropriations to,............. 44–47
115. Sawyer, Meltón, statement of lands sold to,..... 390, 391
Sax, Jacob, statement of lands sold to,............. 69
Saxby, Henry, statement of lands sold to,.......... 92
28. Schaub & Rohrbacker, extra compensation paid to, .. 10
1, 12. Schell, Augustus, delegate at large, New York county, 1, 6
55. Schenectady Lyceum and Academy,................ 44–47
Union School, appropriations to,............ 45–47
21. Schenectady & Troy railroad, amount of freight carried over, during each of the years 1851, 1852 and 1853:
whole number of tons,.................... 5–9
products of the forest, number of tons,...... 5–9
animals, number of tons,.................. 5–9
vegetable food, number of tons,............ 5–9
other agricultural products,................ 5–9
manufactures,............................ 5–9
merchandise, number of tons,.............. 5–9
other articles, number of tons,............. 5–9
115. Schermerhorn, John F., statement of lands sold to, .. 15, 25
Schermerhorn, John L., statement of lands sold to,... 14
55. Schoharie Academy, appropriations to,............. 44–47
39. School districts, to confer exclusive power on Supervisors for consolidation of,...................... 2
115. School lands, report relative to sale of............. 1–396
total receipts from sale of,................. 393
amount of principal due on,................. 393
statement of receipts from and sales of each year from 1823 to 1866, inclusive,.... 394, 395

No. Doc.		Page.
1, 12.	Schoonmaker, Marius, delegate 14th district, Ulster county,	2, 6
12.	Schram, C. V., doorkeeper, Oneida,	8
1, 12.	Schumaker, John G., delegate 3d district, Kings county,	2, 6
28.	Schuyler & Gay, extra compensation paid to,	6
55.	Schuylerville Academy, appropriations to,	44–47
115.	Scott, Cyrene, statement of lands sold to,	259
	Scott, Robert G., statement of lands sold to,	64
	Scott, Thomas, statement of lands sold to,	57
	Scott, Wm., statement of lands sold to,	313
	Scott, Wm. J., statement of lands sold to,	120
	Scoville, Jonah, statement of lands sold to,	113
	Scoville, Cynthia, statement of lands sold to,	247
	Scoville, Seymour, statement of lands sold to,	246
	Segar, James, statement of lands sold to,	69
55.	Seamen's Fund and Retreat, appropriations to,	85, 91
115.	Searles & Goodrich, statement of lands sold to, .. 38,	257
1, 12.	Seaver, Joel J., delegate 17th district, Franklin county,	2, 6
152.	Secretary, report by, concerning condition of business of Convention,	1–4
172.	report by, of condition of business of Convention on the 30th of January,	1–6
14.	Secretary of State, report of, relative to Indian tribes and reservations,	1–8
73.	to be member of executive council,	1
116.	to be member of State board of education,	3
84.	election and term of office of,	2, 3
	compensation and powers and duties of,	4
115.	Seely, L. C. P., statement of lands sold to,	344
95.	Seeley, Sidney, testimony of, relative to management of canals,	1–4
28.	Selye, Lewis, extra compensation paid to,	9, 10
	assignee of Byron M. Hanks, extra compensation paid to,	10
40.	testimony of, relative to letting canal contracts, 28th December,	238–41
88.	letter from, relative to capacity of Erie canal locks,	5
115.	Sellew, Thos., statement of lands sold to,	139

No. Doc. Page.

30. Senate, president pro tem. of, to be chosen, ... 4
49. amendment of Mr. Greeley, relative to organization of, ... 1, 2
to provide for minority representation in, ... 1, 2
districts, amendment of Mr. Greeley, relative to number and apportionment of, ... 1, 2
60. Governor may call special sessions of, ... 5
Lieutenant-Governor to be president of, ... 6
95. committee on management of canals, testimony taken by, ... 1–86
40. Senate committee to investigate management of canals, report of testimony taken by, ... 1–928
30. Senators, number, classification and term of office of,. 2
election of, ... 3
1. Senatorial district delegates, ... 1–3
30. districts, number and apportionment of, ... 1, 2
no county to be divided in formation of, ... 2
enumeration of inhabitants for subsequent apportionments, ... 2
55. Seneca Falls Academy, appropriations to, ... 44–47
14. Seneca Indians (see "Allegany Reservation").
23. Seneca river towing path, income from and disbursements for, ... 34, 35, 38
revenues of, over cost, ... 39
38. Separate road districts, to vest power for creation of, in boards of supervisors, ... 1
55. Seward Female Seminary, appropriations to, ... 44–47
55. S. S. Seward Institute, appropriations to, ... 48–51
1, 12. Seymour, David L., delegate at large, Rensselaer Co., 1, 6
86. and Mr. Bergen, minority report of, on canals, 1–6
115. Seymour, Henry, statement of lands sold to, ... 14, 23
Shannon & Malony, statement of lands sold to, ... 307
Shapley, A. B., statement of lands sold to, ... 22
Shapleigh, Wm., statement of lands sold to, ... 240
Shares, Nathan, statement of lands sold to, ... 391
Sharpe, Peter G. and Henry, statement of lands sold to, 103
Shattuck, Burton, statement of lands sold to, ... 49–51
Shaw, John, heirs of, statement of lands sold to, ... 368
Shaw, Daniel J., statement of lands sold to, ... 242
Shaw, Samuel, statement of lands sold to, ... 328

No. Doc. | Page.
115. Shedd, Marshall, statement of lands sold to, ... 97
Sheldon, Ambrose H., statement of lands sold to,... 49, 327
Sheldon, Oscar F., statement of lands sold to,....... 64
Sheldon, Walter, statement of lands sold to, ... 166
1, 12. Sheldon, Wilson B., delegate, 11th district, Dutchess county, ... 2, 6
115. Shepard, E., Jr., statement of lands sold to,......... 210
Shepard, Leonard, statement of lands sold to,... 34, 35, 246 247
Shepard, Luther, statement of lands sold to, ... 258
Sherburn, Milton, statement of lands sold to, ... 48, 146
55. Sherburne Union Academy, appropriations to, ... 44–47
61. Sheriffs, election and term of office of,.............. 1
removal of, by Governor,.................. 2
ineligible to hold other office, ... 2
ineligible for re-election for succeeding term,.. 3
relative to security to be given by,.......... 3
counties not responsible for their acts,....... 3
115. Sherman, Augustus, statement of lands sold to, 374, 375
Sherman, Isaac, statement of lands sold to, ... 283
1, 12. Sherman, Richard U., delegate 19th district, Oneida county, ... 2, 6
38. resolution of, relative to local legislation by boards of supervisors,.................. 1–3
39. resolution of, relative to general laws, ... 1, 2
115. Sherman & Breese, statement of lands sold to, ... 283
40. Sherrill, James H., testimony of, relative to management of Champlain canal, ... 538, 545
28. Sherrill & Doty, extra compensation paid to,........ 6
115. Sherwood, J. C., statement of lands sold to,.... 362, 381
Sherwood, Wm. C., statement of lands sold to,.. 320, 321
12. Shields, David L., doorkeeper, Wyoming county, ... 8
14. Shinnecock Reservation, number of acres in, ... 3
population on, ... 3
115. Shipman, Menton & Fuller, statement of lands sold to, 125
28. Shippey, Caswell & Co., extra compensation paid to,.. 7
115. Shirley & Parker, statement of lands sold to,........ 103
Shuart, J. D., statement of lands sold to,........... 20
28. Shuler, James D., extra compensation paid to,....... 7

No. Doc. | | Page.
54. Sick Assistance Society, N. Y., report of donations to, 8
115. Sill, Theodore, statement of lands sold to, ... 258
Silsby, W. H., statement of lands sold to, ... 237
1, 12. Silvester, Francis, delegate 11th district, Columbia Co., 2, 6
12. Simmons, Edward N., assistant secretary,........... 8
115. Simpson, A., statement of lands sold to, ... 295, 298
Simpson, Geo. D., statement of lands sold to,........ 139
Simpson, William, statement of lands sold to,....... 97
Singer, James M., statement of lands sold to,........ 73
66. Sinking fund to pay State debts, provision for, ... 2
54. Sisters of the Good Shepherd, N. Y., Community of, report of donations to, ... 9
Sisters of Mercy, N. Y., report of donations to, ... 11
115. Sittser, Willis W., statement of lands sold to,....... 357
Skidmore & Matthewson, statement of lands sold to,.. 207
Skinner, Eli, statement of lands sold to,............ 131
95. Skinner, William I., testimony of, relative to management of canals, ... 78, 82
115. Slattery, Matthew, statement of lands sold to, ... 33
Sloan, James, statement of lands sold to,........... 23
Sloan, L. G., statement of lands sold to,............ 207
Smalley, David, statement of lands sold to, ... 301
Smith, A. J., statement of lands sold to,............ 337
Smith, Abner, statement of lands sold to,...... 201, 258
Smith, Abijah, statement of lands sold to,.......... 386
Smith, Abijah, Jr., statement of lands sold to, ... 83, 139
140, 343
Smith, Arabert B., statement of lands sold to,....... 238
28. Smith, Asa T., extra compensation paid to, ... 7
12. Smith, Charles E., reporter, Albany,............... 9
115. Smith, Christopher, statement of lands sold to,...... 312
Smith, Crawford C., statement of lands sold to,...... 150
Smith, E. E., statement of lands sold to, ... 337
40. Smith, Ezekiel, testimony of, relative to management of Champlain canal,..................... 298, 305
115. Smith, Ezra B., statement of lands sold to, ... 42
Smith, Gerrit, statement of lands sold to, ... 14, 15, 16, 19
20, 21, 22, 23, 24, 25, 26, 27, 29, 30, 31, 32, 323, 340
343
Smith, H. H., statement of lands sold to, ... 343

No. Doc.		Page.
115.	Smith, Hiram, statement of lands sold to,...... 293,	309
1, 12.	Smith, Horace E., delegate 15th district, Fulton Co.,.	2, 6
11.	resolution of, relative to bribery at elections,..	1
115.	Smith, Ira, statement of lands sold to, ...	210
	Smith, Isaac, statement of lands sold to,..... 89, 90,	386
	Smith, Israel, statement of lands sold to, ...	105
	Smith, Jacob, statement of lands sold to, ...	55
	Smith, Joel, statement of lands sold to, ...	211
	Smith, John, statement of lands sold to,............	54
28.	Smith, John P., extra compensation paid to, ...	7, 11
	Smith, John P. & Co., extra compensation paid to,...	7
115.	Smith, J. M., statement of lands sold to, ...	355
12.	Smith, J. Wesley, reporter, Albany, ...	9
115.	Smith, Lemuel, statement of lands sold to, ...	210
	Smith, Luke, statement of lands sold to,............	378
	Smith, Mary Ann, statement of lands sold to,.......	259
	Smith, Mary M., statement of lands sold to, ...	241
	Smith, Newton, statement of lands sold to, ...	211
	Smith, Othniel, statement of lands sold to,..........	54
	Smith, Owen, statement of lands sold to,...........	94
	Smith, Peter, statement of lands sold to,.. 12, 40, 41,	42, 43
	47, 48, 49, 50, 51, 52, 53, 54, 55, 56, 57, 58, 59,	60, 61
	62 63, 64, 65, 66, 73, 74, 75, 76, 77, 78, 82,	83, 86
	107, 108, 109, 112, 113, 114, 116, 118, 119, 120,	121
	125, 128, 129, 131, 132, 133, 134, 135, 136, 137,	138
	140, 142, 143, 145, 146, 149, 151, 152, 153, 155,	156
	157, 160, 162, 163, 164, 165, 166, 167, 168, 169,	170
	171, 172, 173, 175, 176, 177, 199, 201, 214, 215,	216
	217, 218, 219, 220, 221, 222, 223, 224, 225, 226,	227
	228, 229, 230, 243, 244, 246, 250, 252, 253, 254,	255
	262, 263, 265, 266, 267, 268, 269, 270, 271, 272,	273
	274, 275, 276, 277, 278, 279, 280, 281, 282, 283,	284
	285, 286.	
	Smith, R. P., statement of lands sold to, ...	292
	Smith, Sampson, statement of lands sold to, ...	174
	Smith, Samuel P., statement of lands sold to, ...	248
	Smith, Simon, statement of lands sold to, ...	238
	Smith, Solomon L., statement of lands sold to,......	147
	Smith, Timothy, statement of lands sold to, 323, 348,	359
	363,	364

No. Doc. | | Page.
115. Smith, Thomas, statement of lands sold to, ... 248
19. Smith, Vivus W., superintendent of Salt Springs,.... 5
115. Smith, William, statement of lands sold to, 94, 210, 319
Smith, Wm. H., statement of lands sold to,......... 211
Smith & Derby, statement of lands sold to, ... 354
Smith & Harrison, statement of lands sold to,....... 35
Smith & Merrill, statement of lands sold to, ... 258
28. Smith & Norton, extra compensation paid to, ... 7
115. Smith & Richards, statement of lands sold to,........ 344
Smyth, Charles, statement of lands sold to,..... 264, 273
Snell, A. J., statement of land sold to,............. 27
Snody, William, statement of lands sold to,........ 85, 199
40. Snook, Clark, testimony of, relative to Snook & Beebe award,.................................. 740–51
28. Snooks & Beebe, extra compensation paid to,........ 10
115. Snow, Freeman, statement of lands sold to,......... 68
Snow, Joseph W., statement of lands sold to,....... 137
40. Snyder, Herman R., testimony of, relative to management of Champlain canal, ... 385–90
115. Snyder, Philip, statement of lands sold to, ... 129, 145
Snyder, Wm., statement of lands sold to,........... 141
54. Society for the relief of poor widows and poor children, New York, report of donations to,......... 7
55. Sodus Academy, appropriations to,................ 45–47
19. Solar salt, amount produced from 1841 to 1866, each year and aggregate,...................... 5, 6
vats or covers, number, value and owners of,.. 18, 19
duties received from, since 1845,............ 22
98. Solicitor of Claims, provisions relative to, ... 8
40. Southwick, Henry C., testimony of, relative to letting canal contracts, 28th December,................ 886–88
115. Southwick, Solomon, statement of lands sold to,..... 215
Sparrow, Erastus, statement of lands sold to, ... 39
Sparrow & Burt, statement of lands sold to,......... 256
Spaulding, Gilbert R., statement of lands sold to,.... 54
Spaulding, Jno., statement of lands sold to,......... 357
40. Spaulding, John D., testimony of, relative to repairs of section 9 of Erie canal, ... 45–7
115. Spaulding, Reuben, statement of lands sold to, ... 233
Spaulding, R. C., statement of lands sold to,........ 234

No. Doc. Page.

115. Spears, Timothy, statement of lands sold to, ... 281
98. Special county judges, election of may be authorized, 13
Special laws, prohibited where general laws are applicable, ... 14
25. Special or local legislation, resolution of Mr. E. Brooks, relative to, ... 1, 2
98. Special surrogates, election of may be authorized, ... 13
4. Specie, to provide for payment of taxes, tolls, &c., with, 2
53. Specie payments, laws authorizing suspension of, prohibited, ... 2
98. Legislature prohibited from sanctioning suspension of, ... 12, 13
149. Speech, liberty of, secured, ... 4
115. Speers, Ebenezer, statement of lands sold to, ... 377
1, 12. Spencer, Geo. T., delegate 27th district, Steuben Co., . 3, 6
115. Spencer, H. D., statement of lands sold to, ... 354
Spencer, James B., statement of lands sold to, ... 126
Spencer, Joseph, statement of lands sold to, ... 108, 111
Spencer, Joshua A., statement of lands sold to, ... 282
19. Spencer, Thomas, superintendent of salt springs, ... 5
28. Spencer, Hubbs & Curtis, extra compensation paid to, 7
55. Spencertown Academy, appropriations to, ... 44–47
115. Sperry, Isaac O., statement of lands sold to, ... 123
28. Sponenbergh, William, extra compensation paid to, .. 7
115. Sprague, Alvin, statement of lands sold to, ... 110
Spraker, David, statement of lands sold to, . 108, 109, 280
Spraker, Spencer & Cornue, statement of lands sold to, 113
55. Spring Mills Academy, appropriations to, ... 51
Springville Academy, appropriations to, ... 48–51
115. Squire, Levi, statement of lands sold to, ... 201
Squires, Norman, statement of lands sold to, ... 104
Squires, N. B., statement of lands sold to, ... 353, 354
54. St. Bridget's School, N. Y., report of donations to, ... 16
St. Gabriel's School, 37th street, N. Y., report of donations to, ... 16
115. St. John, Stephen, statement of lands sold to, ... 97, 98
55. St. John's College, Fordham, appropriations to, ... 80–83
54. St. Joseph's Orphan Asylum, N. Y., report of donations to, ... 10
55. St. Lawrence Academy, appropriations to, ... 48–51

No. Doc.		Page.
55.	St. Lawrence University, appropriations to,.........	82, 83
54.	St. Luke's Hospital, N. Y., report of donations to, ...	10
	St. Mary's school, 6th and 13th wards, New York, report of donations to,.........................	17
	St. Nicholas Orphan Asylum, New York, report of donations to,............................	9
	St. Peter's church school, New York, report of donations to,....................................	17
14.	St. Regis Indians, number and residence of,.........	2
	quantity of lead on reservation, ...	2
	annuities paid to,.......	2
	agricultural statistics of,..................	4-8
54.	St. Stephen's school, 28th street, New York, report of donations to, ...	16
	St. Teresa's school, Rutgers street, New York, report of donations to,............................	17
	St. Vincent's Hospital, New York, report of donations to, ...	11
115.	Stacy, Joseph, statement of lands sold to,...........	264
	Stafford, J. R. & J., statement of lands sold to, ...	235
	Stafford, Thomas, statement of lands sold to,........	47
	Stafford & Griswold, statement of lands sold to,......	18
	Stanford, Sylvanus, statement of lands sold to, ...	49, 137
	Stanford, Sylvanus, Jr., statement of lands sold to,..	64, 136 137
	Stanley, Frederick, statement of lands sold to, ...	17
	Stark, Argalus, statement of lands sold to,..........	114
55.	Starkey Seminary, appropriations to,...............	48-51
115.	Starr, Thomas, statement of lands sold to,..........	232
	Starr & Hawley, statement of lands sold to,.........	141
116.	State board of education, provisions relating to, ...	3
66.	State credit or property, loan or gift of, prohibited, ..	6
98.	legislature prohibited from authorising loan or gift of,............................	6, 7
66.	State debts, for which canal revenues are pledged, ...	1
	provision for payment of,..................	2, 3
	may be contracted in certain cases,..........	6, 7
34.	State engineer, report of, relative to cost of enlarging locks on Chemung canal, ...	1-8

Doc. No. Page.

70. State engineer, report of, relative to state of work on and cost of completing extension of Chenango canal, ... 1–6
74. report of, relative to lands sold by certain railroad companies, ... 1–3
84. election and term of office of, ... 2, 3
compensation and powers and duties of, ... 4
176. State medical board, report of select committee on, .. 1–3
provisions for creation of, ... 1, 2
3. State officers, provision for committee on, ... 2
9. committee on, ... 2
84. report of committee on, ... 1–4
104. article reported by committee on, as amended and referred to committee on revision, ... 1, 2
3. State prisons, provision for committee on, ... 2
9. committee on, ... 4
122. report of majority of committee on, ... 1–18, 21–27
article reported by majority of committee on,. 19–21
superintendent of, provisions relative to, ... 19–21
wardens of, provision relative to, ... 19
clerks of, how appointed, ... 19
chaplains of, how appointed, ... 19
physicians of, how appointed, ... 19
subordinate officers of, how appointed, ... 19
local visitors of, provision relating to, ... 19
123. minority report of Mr. C. C. Dwight relative to, 1, 2
146. communication from New York Prison Association relative to government of, ... 1–6
174. article on, as amended and referred to committee on revision, ... 1, 2
122. State police, provision relating to, ... 20, 24–27
superintendent of, appointment and term of office of, ... 20
21. Staten Island railroad, amount of freight carried over, during each of the years 1860 and 1861:
whole number of tons, ... 23, 25
merchandise, number of tons, ... 23, 25
98. Statute laws, publication of, to be provided for, ... 13
Statute of limitations in court of claims, provision relative to, ... 8

No. Doc. Page.

115. Stearns, Chas., statement of lands sold to,........... 345
Stearns, T. T., statement of lands sold to,........... 368
Stedman, L. & J., statement of lands sold to,........ 337
Steele, W. S., statement of lands sold to, ... 21
21. Sterling Mountain railroad, amount of freight carried over, during the year 1866:
whole number of tons, ... 35
products of the forest, number of tons, ... 35
manufactures, number of tons,............... 35
merchandise, number of tons, ... 35
115. Stevens, Chester, statement of lands sold to, ... 326
Stephens, Ebenezer, statement of lands sold to,...... 125
Stevens, Geo. L., statement of lands sold to, ... 387
Stevens, Horatio, statement of lands sold to,..... 39, 298
Stevens, J., Jr., statement of lands sold to,.......... 210
Stevens, Reuben, statement of lands sold to, ... 69
Stevens, Samuel, statement of lands sold to, ... 334, 345
Stephens, Seth, statement of lands sold to,.......... 68
19. Stevens, William, superintendent of salt springs, ... 4
115. Stevens, Wm., statement of lands sold to, ... 374
Stevens, Wm., 2d., statement of lands sold to, .. 297, 302, 329, 345, 376, 384, 389
40. Stevens, William C., testimony of, relative to letting canal contracts 28th Dec.,..................... 81–100
115. Stevenson, Geo., statement of lands sold to,......... 370
Stevenson, J. L., statement of lands sold to, ... 349, 362
Stevenson, James, Jr., statement of lands sold to,. 81, 83, 84, 87, 139, 200, 308
Stevenson, Jno., Jr., statement of lands sold to,...... 274
Stewart, Daniel, statement of lands sold to,......... 332
28. Stewart, James, extra compensation paid to, ... 7
115. Stewart, John A., statement of lands sold to, ... 205
Stewart, Jno. D., statement of lands sold to, ... 346
19. Stewart, Nathan, superintendent of salt springs,..... 4
115. Stewart, Oliver, statement of lands sold to,..... 211, 212
Stickney, David, statement of lands sold to,.... 163, 164
Stickney, Geo. W. & Daniel, statement of lands sold to, 75
Stickney, Jonathan, statement of lands sold to,...... 162
Stickney, Joseph, statement of lands sold to,........ 161

No. Doc. Page.

115. Stickney, Moses, Jr., statement of lands sold to,..... 40
Stiles, A., statement of lands sold to, ... 289
Stiles, Elijah, statement of lands sold to, ... 55
Stiles, Silas, statement of lands sold to, ... 100
55. Stillwater Academy, appropriations to,............. 48–51
115. Stocker, Samuel, statement of lands sold to, ... 164
Stockholm, D. B., statement of lands sold to,........ 201
Stocking, Samuel, statement of lands sold to,. 14–17, 19–21
24, 27
Stockwell, Joshua, statement of lands sold to,....... 125
Stoddard, Erastus, statement of lands sold to,... 120, 121
Stoddard, Preston, statement of lands sold to,........ 362
Stone, Hiram A., statement of lands sold to,........ 234
Stone, Samuel, statement of lands sold to, ... 209
Stoneburner, Leonard, statement of lands sold to,.... 232
Storrs, Lucius, statement of lands sold to,.......... 262
Stout, Aaron, statement of lands sold to, ... 241
1, 12. Stratton, Norman, delegate 5th district, New York county,.. 2, 6
39. Streets, to confer powers on supervisors relative to, .. 2
98. Street railroads, provisions relative to, ... 11
special laws for, prohibited,................ 11
consent of local authorities and property owners to be obtained for,.................. 11
franchises of, to be sold at auction,.......... 11
115. Striker, John, statement of lands sold to, ... 212, 273
Stryker, B. W., statement of lands sold to,.......... 292
Stringham, Joseph, statement of lands sold to, ... 258
Strobeck, Cornelius, statement of lands sold to,. 108, 146
Strong, Elisha B., statement of lands sold to,........ 97
Strong, James, statement of lands sold to, 87, 88, 114, 134
176, 215, 216, 217, 225, 226, 227, 228
Strong, Salmon, statement of lands sold to, ... 364
1, 12. Strong, Selah B., delegate 1st district, Suffolk county, 1, 7
28. Stroup, John, extra compensation paid to, ... 7
90. Stuart, Charles B., testimony of, relative to improvements of Erie canal,.......................... 35–41
115. Sturges, Ebenezer, statement of lands sold to,....... 96

No. Doc. Page.

40. Sturtevant, Daniel, testimony of, relative to management of Champlain canal, ... 577–80
180. Submission of the constitution to the people, report of select committee on, ... 1–4
3. Suffrage, provision for committee on, ... 2
9. committee on, ... 2
15. report of committee on (article), ... 1–3
report of committee on (explanations), ... 4–9
qualifications necessary for, ... 1–3
causes for exclusion from, ... 2
11. minority report on, ... 1–4
29. resolutions of Mr. Wales in favor of uniform system of, in all the States, ... 1–2
41. report of committee on, as amended in committee of the whole, ... 1–4
44. report of committee on, as amended in committee of the whole and Convention, ... 1–4
80. article on, as amended and adopted, ... 1–4
115. Sumner, Uri, statement of lands sold to, ... 47, 49, 52, 101
19. Superintendent of Onondaga salt springs, report of, .. 1–22
116. Superintendent of public education, appointment and term of office of, ... 23
powers and duties of, ... 3
to be member of State board of education, ... 3
71. Superintendent of public instruction, report of, relative to statistics of common schools, ... 1–8
63. Superintendents of public works, report of minority of committee on canals relative to, ... 1–7
67. appointment and term of office of, ... 2, 3
powers and duties of, ... 1, 3
suspension or removal of, ... 3
86. to provide for election of, by people, ... 5
general provisions of minority report relative to, 5, 6
107. Superior Court of Buffalo (see "Buffalo").
33. Superior Court of New York, report of clerk of, relative to state of business of, ... 1–4
general terms of, ... 1, 2
special term and chambers of, ... 2, 3
trial terms of, ... 4
number of persons naturalized in, ... 4

No. Doc. Page.

107. Superior Court of New York, provisions relative to (see "New York").
38. Supervisors, plan for conferring power of local legislation on, in certain cases, ... 1–3
61. election and term of office of, ... 2–3
removal of, ... 3
75. provision for boards of, and their election, ... 2
provision relative to local legislation by, ... 2
82. plan of Mr. Sherman relative to local legislation by, ... 1–3
98. Legislature required to grant power of local legislation to boards of, ... 9
61. boards of (see "Boards of Supervisors").
107. Supreme Court, provision for, ... 4, 5
general and special terms, ... 7
justices of (see "Justices of Supreme Court").
140. sections relative to, proposed by Mr. Hale, ... 1, 2
107. Surrogates may be elected in counties of certain population, ... 10
duties of, to be performed by county judges in counties where no surrogate is elected, ... 9
55. Susquehanna Seminary, appropriations to, ... 50, 51
115. Sutton, Wm. A., statement of lands sold to, ... 256
38. Swamp lands, to confer exclusive power on supervisors relative to draining of, ... 3
90. Sweet, Sylvanus H., testimony of, relative to cost of improvements on Erie canal, ... 1–6
115. Sweet, Wm. A., statement of lands sold to, ... 367, 383
Sweetland, James, statement of lands sold to, ... 69
Swift, Sanford H., statement of lands sold to, ... 202
Symond, Wm., statement of lands sold to, ... 301
55. Syracuse, High School, appropriations to, ... 50, 51
Home Association, appropriations to, ... 70, 71
St. Vincent de Paul Orphan Asylum, appropriations to, ... 67
21. Syracuse and Binghamton railroad, amount of freight carried over, each year (excepting the year 1856), from 1855 to 1866, inclusive:
whole number of tons, ... 13–35, 41
products of the forest, number of tons, ... 13–35, 41

No. Doc. Page.

21. Syracuse and Binghamton railroad—*Continued.*
animals, number of tons,............... 13–35, 41
vegetable food, number of tons,......... 13–35, 41
other agricultural products, number of tons, 13–35, 41
manufactures, number of tons,.......... 13–35, 41
merchandise, number of tons, ... 13–35, 41
other articles, number of tons,.......... 13–35, 41

115. Syracuse and Oswego Railroad Company, statement of lands sold to,.............................. 338

21. Syracuse and Utica railroad, amount of freight carried over, during each of the years 1851, 1852 and 1853:
whole number of tons,.................... 5–9
products of the forest, number of tons,...... 5–9
animals, number of tons,.................. 5–9
vegetable food, number of tons, ... 5–9
other agricultural products, number of tons,.. 5–9
manufactures, number of tons, ... 5–9
merchandise, number of tons, ... 5–9
other articles number of tons,.............. 5–9

T.

115. Taber, Chas. F., statement of lands sold to,.......... 353
Taber, L. C., statement of lands sold to,............ 383
Tafft, Amariah, statement of lands sold to,.......... 117

12. Tanner, James, doorkeeper, Schoharie,............. 8

115. Tanner, John, statement of lands sold to,........... 117

1, 12. Tappen, Abraham B., delegate 9th district, Westchester county,................................ 2, 7

115. Tarbill, Jonathan statement of lands sold to,........ 301
Tarbell, Peter, statement of lands sold to,........... 87

98. Taxation, exemption of property from, prohibited except in certain cases,................. 10

118. section relating to, reported by Mr. A. F. Allen, 1, 2

139. section proposed by Mr. McDonald relative to, 1, 2

4. Taxes, tolls, &c., to provide for payment of, with specie, 2

13. Tax payers of New York city, report of number of,.. 1

115. Taylor, Daniel, statement of lands sold to,.......... 325

No. Doc.		Page.
	Taylor, Israel, Jr., statement of lands sold to, ...	142
90.	Taylor, William B., testimony of, relative to improvements of Erie canal, ...	56–60
55.	Teachers' institutes, appropriations to,..............	85–90
115.	Teall, Oliver, statement of lands sold to,............	340
	Teeter, Henry, statement of lands sold to, ...	241
	Ten Eyck, Jacob H., statement of lands sold to, ...	249
	Thayer, Delight, statement of lands sold to,.........	358
	Thayer, Gardner, statement of lands sold to, ...	344
	Thayer, G., Jr., statement of lands sold to, ... 329,	330
	Thomas, Ambrose, statement of lands sold to,.......	237
28.	Thomas, Chester B., extra compensation paid to, ...	11
115.	Thomas, Joseph, statement of lands sold to,. 239, 296,	297
28.	Thomas & Worden, extra compensation paid to,.....	7
55.	Thomas Asylum for Indian Children, appropriations to,	69–71
115.	Thompson, Cyrus, statement of lands sold to, ...	324
	Thompson, David, statement of lands sold to,........	205
	Thompson, Dyer, statement of lands sold to,........	59
	Thompson, Eli, statement of lands sold to,..........	206
	Thompson, J M., statement of lands sold to,........	380
	Thompson, J. & A., statement of lands sold to,......	355
	Thompson, James E., statement of lands sold to, 369,	380
	Thompson, Jno., statement of lands sold to, ... 210,	211
65.	Thomson, Peter, judgment in favor of, against city of New York,..................................	2
115.	Thompson, Roswell, statement of lands sold to,......	328
	Thompson, Thos., statement of lands sold to,........	232
28.	Thompson & Beebe, extra compensation paid to,.....	7
115.	Thompson & Dodge, statement of lands sold to,......	320
	Thompson & Rice, statement of lands sold to, ...	46
28.	Thompson & Utley, extra compensation paid to,.....	7
115.	Thurman, James L,. statement of lands sold to,......	142
	Thurman, Jno. & James, statement of lands sold to,..	203
	Thurman & Patterson, statement of lands sold to,....	203
28.	Tibbitts & Forsyth, extra compensation paid to, ...	7
1, 12.	Tilden, Sam'l J., delegate 7th district, New York Co.,	2, 7
115.	Tillotson & Hamlin, statement of lands sold to, ...	111
	Tipple, Jno., statement of lands sold to, ...	361
	Titus, Seymour, statement of lands sold to, ...	244

No. Doc.		Page.
28.	Tobee, Glatt & Glatt, extra compensation paid to,....	7
115.	Tobey & Rogers, statement of lands sold to, ...	13
	Tomlinson, T. A., statement of lands sold to, 365, 369,	370
	Tomlinson & Smith, statement of lands sold to,. 283,	284
	Tompkins, Elijah, statement of lands sold to, ...	292
	Tompkins, Joel, statement of lands sold to,.........	241
54.	Tompkins Square Homœopathic Dispensary, N. Y., report of donations to, ...	14
14.	Tonawanda Indians, number of,....................	3
	quantity of land on reservation, ...	3
	agricultural statistics of, ...	4–8
28.	Tousley & James, extra compensation paid to,.......	7
75.	Town bonds in aid of corporations (see "Bonding of Towns").	
38.	Town and county buildings, to vest power for location and erection of boards of supervisors,...........	1
3.	Town and county officers, provision for committee on,	2
9.	committee on, ...	2
61.	report of committee on, ...	1–11
81.	report of committee on, as amended in committee of the whole, ...	1, 2
83.	article on, as amended in committee and referred to committee on revision,...........	1–4
38.	Town meetings and town officers, to empower supervisors to legalize informal acts of,..............	2
115.	Townsend, Jacob, statement of lands sold to,........	246
1, 12.	Townsend, Martin I., delegate at large, Rensselaer Co.,	1, 7
151.	minority report of, on official corruption,.....	1–3
1, 12.	Townsend, Solomon, delegate 1st district, Queens Co.,	1, 7
4.	resolution of, relative to specie payments, ...	2
115.	Townsend, W. & C., statement of lands sold to, ...	112
	Tracy & Love, statement of lands sold to, ...	36, 37
54.	Transfiguration Church School, report of donations to,	17
67.	Treasurer, to be one of commissioners of canal fund,.	1
84.	election and term of office of, ...	2, 3
	provision for suspension or removal of, ...	3
	compensation, and powers and duties of, ...	4
28.	Treat & Cromwell, extra compensation paid to,......	7
115.	Tripp, Wm. W., statement of lands sold to,.... 306,	307
	Troop, Robert, statement of lands sold to,....... 68,	213

No. Doc. Page.

55. Troupsburgh Academy, appropriations to,.......... 51
Troy Academy, appropriations to,................. 48–51
Troy Catholic Male Orphan Asylum, appropriations to, 68–71
Troy Female Seminary, appropriations to,.......... 48–51
Troy High School, appropriations to, ... 51
Troy Hospital, appropriations to,.................. 72–75
Troy Orphan Asylum, appropriations to,........... 68–71
Troy St. Vincent's Female Orphan Asylum, appropriations to,.................................... 67
Troy University, appropriations to,................ 82, 83
21. Troy and Boston railroad, amount of freight carried over, each year (excepting 1862), from 1852 to 1865, inclusive:
whole number of tons,.................... 7–33
products of the forest, number of tons, ... 7–33
animals, number of tons,.................. 7–33
vegetable food, number of tons, ... 7–33
other agricultural products, number of tons,.. 7–33
manufactures, number of tons,.............. 7–33
merchandise, number of tons,.............. 7–33
other articles, number of tons,.............. 7–33
21. Troy and Greenbush railroad, amount of freight carried over, each year from 1851 to 1855, inclusive:
whole number of tons,.................... 5–13
products of the forest, number of tons, ... 5–13
animals, number of tons,.................. 5–13
vegetable food, number of tons, ... 5–13
other agricultural products, number of tons,.. 5–13
manufactures, number of tons, ... 5–13
merchandise, number of tons, ... 5–13
other articles, number of tons,.............. 5–13
115. Truax, Henry, statement of lands sold to, ... 362
True, Jno., statement of lands sold to, ... 208
55. Trumansburgh Academy, appropriations to, ... 50, 51
115. Trumbull, Ira, Horace & Simeon, statement of lands sold to, ... 75
Trumbull, Ira, Levi & Simeon, statement of lands sold to, ... 75

No. Doc.		Page.
115.	Trumbull, Ira, Simeon & Thomas, statement of lands sold to,	75
	Trumbull, Levi & Simeon, statement of lands sold to,	75
	Trumbull, J. & S., statement of lands sold to,	325
	Trumbull, T. D., statement of lands sold to,	369
	Tryon, Amos S., statement of lands sold to, 247, 331,	335
	Tryon, Eber, statement of lands sold to,	124
	Tryon, Jno., statement of lands sold to,	125
	Tubbs, Geo., statement of lands sold to,	298
1, 12.	Tucker, Gideon J., delegate 6th district, New York county,	2, 7
115.	Tucker & Howland, statement of land sold to,	20, 32
	Tucker & Williams, statement of lands sold to,	122
	Tuke, Polly, statement of lands sold to,	212
	Turner, Cornelius, statement of lands sold to,	248
	Turner, Jno., statement of lands sold to,	321
	Turner, Sternburg, Joy, Congdon & Munson, statement of lands sold to,	103
	Turrill, J., statement of lands sold to,	16, 17
	Turrill & Varick, statement of lands sold to,	16
14.	Tuscarora Indians, number of,	3
	quantity of land on reservation,	3
	agricultural statistics of,	3
115.	Tuttle, Phineas, statement of lands sold to,	120
	Tuttle & Stevens, statement of lands sold to,	46
	Tyler, J. & R. C., statement of lands sold to,	69
	Tyler, Richard C., statement of lands sold to,	69
	Tyler, William & Sprague, statement of lands sold to,	68
	Tyrrell, Wolcott, statement of lands sold to, 82,	132

U.

	Ulrich, Martin, statement of lands sold to,	258
55.	Unadilla Academy, appropriations to,	49–51
26.	Unanimous verdicts by jurors, memorial of Dr. Francis Lieber, relative to,	1–4
12.	Underhill, Edward F., stenographer, New York,	8
115.	Underwood, Amos, statement of lands sold to,	257
12.	Underwood, Cornelius S., assistant secretary, Auburn,	8

No. Doc. Page.

115. Underwood, David, statement of lands sold to,...... 42
Underwood, Oliver, Jr., statement of lands to, ... 42
Underwood, Samuel, statement of lands sold to,..... 354
55. Union Academy of Belleville, appropriations to, ... 50, 51
55. Union Hall Academy, appropriations to, ... 48–51
Union Literary Society, appropriations to,.......... 48–51
Union Village Academy, appropriations to,......... 48–51
54. Union Home and School, New York, report of donations to,.................................... 12
116. Union schools, instructions in to be free,............ 3
United States deposit fund, capital of, to be paid into treasury,............................. 1
investment of, ... 2
application of revenues of,................. 1, 2
55. University of Buffalo, appropriations to, ... 83
University of New York, appropriations to, ... 83
72. Upper Hudson and Wilderness railroad, report of Comtroller, relative to stocks deposited to secure payment of taxes on lands donated to,..... 1
4. Useless offices, resolution of inquiry, relative to abolition of, ... 1
55. Utica Academy, appropriations to, ... 48–51
Utica Female Academy, appropriations to, ... 48–51
Utica St. John's Catholic Orphan Asylum, appropriations to, ... 64–67
Utica St. Vincent's Male Orphan Asylum, appropriations to, ... 67
Utica Orphan Asylum, appropriations to,........... 68–71
21. Utica & Black River railroad, amount of freight carried over each year, from 1862 to 1866, inclusive:
whole number of tons, ... 27–35
products of the forest, number of tons, ... 27–35
animals, number of tons, ... 27–35
vegetable food, number of tons, ... 27–35
other agricultural products, number of tons,.. 27–35
manufactures, number of tons, ... 27–35
merchandise, number of tons,.............. 27–35
other articles, number of tons,.............. 27–35

No. Doc. Page.

21. Utica & Schenectady railroad, amount of freight car ried over during each of the years 1851, 1852 and 1853:
whole number of tons, ... 5-9
products of the forest, number of tons, ... 5-9
animals, number of tons, ... 5-9
vegetable food, number of tons, ... 5-9
other agricultural products, number of tons,.. 5-9
manufactures, number of tons, ... 5-9
merchandise, number of tons, ... 5-9
other articles, number of tons,.............. 5-9
115. Utley, Elisha, statement of lands sold to,........... 211

V.

98. Vacancies in office, provisions to be made relative to,. 9
115. Valentine, James, statement of lands sold to,........ 237
Valleau & Allen, statement of lands sold to, ... 257
Van Antwerp, J. D., statement of lands sold to,. 113, 114
Van Benthuysen, A. & G., statement of lands sold to, 200
Van Benthuysen, Barent, statement of lands sold to,. 82
140, 200, 201, 273
Van Benthuysen, Jno., H., statement of lands sold to, 189
363
Van Buskirk, L., statement of lands sold to, ... 345
1, 12. Van Campen, George, delegate 32d district, Cattaraugus county, ... 3, 7
4. resolution of, relative to Indians, ... 2
12. Van Campen, James K., messenger, Cattaraugus, ... 8
1, 12. Van Cott, Joshua, M., delegate at large, Kings Co., .. 1, 7
28. Van Debogart & Marselis, extra compensation paid to, 7
Van Demark, John, extra compensation paid to,..... 7
115. Vandenburgh, C., statement of lands sold to,........ 368
Vandenburgh, Cornelius W., statement of lands sold to, 123
Vandenburgh, G. G., statement of lands sold to,..... 107
109, 110
40. Vanderberg, Solon, testimony of, relative to management of Champlain canal..................... 357-66
Vanderkar, Charles, testimony of, relative to letting canal contracts, 28th December, ... 8-11

No. Doc.		Page.
115.	Vandewerker, David, statement of lands sold to,.....	250
	Van Duzer, H., statement of lands sold to,..........	277
	Vane, John, statement of lands sold to, ...	92
28.	Van Evera & Burdick, extra compensation paid to,..	7
115.	Van Hoesen, Jno., statement of lands sold to,.......	210
	Van Loan, Joshua, statement of lands sold to,.......	362
	Van Patten, P. J., statement of lands sold to, ...	339
	Van Rensselaer, Jno. S., statement of lands sold to,..	147
	Van Rensselaer, Rensselaer, statement of lands sold to,	108
	109, 111, 112, 113, 114, 138, 146, 261, 267, 270,	280
	Van Rensselaer, Richard, statement of lands sold to,	107
	108, 121, 129,	146
	Van Rensselaer, Schuyler, statement of lands sold to,	111
		271
	Van Sevall, G. W., statement of lands sold to, ...	359
	Van Schaick, William H., statement of lands sold to,	81
	Van Schoonmaker, Jno. C., statement of lands sold to,	167
	Vantyne, Charles H., statement of lands sold to,.....	15
	Van Valkenburgh, John, statement of lands sold to,..	93
	Van Vechten & Davis, statement of lands sold to, 281,	289
159.	Van Vleck, James, testimony of, before committee on salt springs, ...	3–5
115.	Van Wormer, J. H., statement of lands sold to, ...	331
	Varick, Abram, statement of lands sold to,...... 14,	15, 16
	17, 19, 20, 22, 23, 24, 26, 27, 28, 31, 32,	138
	Varnum, Jaquays & White, statement of lands sold to,	209
	Vaughn, Alanson B., statement of lands sold to, 254,	288
	Vaughan, David, statement of lands sold to, ...	143
	Vaughn, D. & R., statement of lands sold to,........	287
	Vedder, Jno. H., statement of lands sold to,.........	360
1, 12.	Veeder, William D., delegate 3d district, Kings county,	2, 7
28.	Veeder & Harmon, extra compensation paid to,......	7
115.	Vee, Francis, statement of lands sold to,............	231
28.	Vernam, A., estate of, extra compensation paid to, ...	9, 10
	Vernam & Merrill, extra compensation paid to,......	7
55.	Vernon Academy, appropriations to,...............	48–51
1, 12.	Verplanck, Isaac A., delegate 31st district, Erie county,	3, 7
60.	Veto power, relative to,..........................	7, 8
98.	Vetoes, legislative proceedings in case of,..........	12

No. Doc.		Page.
115.	Vickery, Claudius, statement of lands sold to, ...	85
	Videta, Justus, statement of lands sold to, ...	122
	Videto, Stephen, statement of lands sold to, ...	124
107.	Villages, judicial officers of, provision relative to, ...	11
115.	Vischer, John E., statement of lands sold to, ...	110
	Voorhees & Leitch, statement of lands sold to, ...	325
	Vose, Franklin, statement of lands sold to, ...	89
15.	Voters, relative to taxation of, ...	7
115.	Vredenburgh, Wm., statement of lands sold to, ...	239
	Vrooman, Edward, statement of lands sold to, ...	13

W.

No. Doc.		Page.
115.	Waddell, W. C. H., statement of lands sold to, ...	345–47
	Wager, Henry, statement of lands sold to, ... 178,	179
1, 12.	Wakeman, Seth, delegate 29th district, Genesee Co., ..	3, 7
115.	Walden, Ebenezer, statement of lands sold to, ...	37
40.	Waldron, Cornelius A., testimony of, relative to letting canal contracts 28th Dec., ...	11–15
115.	Waldron, William J., statement of lands sold to, ...	63
1, 12.	Wales, Gideon, delegate 10th district, Sullivan county,	2, 7
29.	resolutions of, in favor of uniform system of suffrage in all the States, ...	2
115.	Wales & Baker, statement of lands sold to, ...	206
	Walker, Edward, statement of lands sold to, ...	116
	Walker, John H., statement of lands sold to, ...	73, 74
	Walker, Obadiah, statement of lands sold to, ...	240
55.	Walkill Academy, appropriations to, ...	48–51
115.	Wallace, Jonathan, statement of lands sold to, ...	125
	Walter, Phineas, statement of lands sold to, ...	92
	Walter, Geo. B., statement of lands sold to, ...	342
	Walton, Oliver, statement of lands sold to, ... 47,	309
	Walton, Rufus, statement of lands sold to, ...	48
	Walton, William B., statement of lands sold to, .. 45, 64, 66, 90, 91, 145, 222, 224,	225
	Walton & DeGraff, statement of lands sold to, ...	236
55.	Walton Academy, appropriations to, ...	49–51
	Walworth Academy, appropriations to, ...	48–51
115.	Ware, Daniel, statement of lands sold to, ...	49

No. Doc. Page.

115. Ward, Henry, statement of lands sold to, ... 149
Ward, James B., statement of lands sold to, ... 237
Ward, Martin, statement of lands sold to, ... 116
Ward, Wm., statement of lands sold to, ... 117, 133
Ward, Zael, statement of lands sold to, ... 78
28. Ward & McVickar, extra compensation paid to, ... 11
115. Ward & Pray, statement of lands sold to, ... 163
Warner, Jonathan, statement of lands sold to, ... 240
Warren, Nelson J., statement of lands sold to, ... 134
Warren, Samuel, statement of lands sold to, ... 107
Warren, Walter, statement of lands sold to, ... 114
55. Warrensburgh Academy, appropriations to, ... 54, 55
Warsaw Union School, appropriations to, ... 54, 55
Warwick Institute, appropriations to, ... 53–55
21. Warwick Valley railroad, amount of freight carried over, each of the years from 1862 to 1866, inclusive:
whole number of tons, ... 27–35
products of the forest, number of tons, ... 27–35
animals, number of tons, ... 27–35
vegetable food, number of tons, ... 27–35
other agricultural products, number of tons, .. 27–35
manufactures, number of tons, ... 27–35
merchandise, number of tons, ... 27–35
other articles, number of tons, ... 27–35
115. Washburn & Andrews, statement of lands sold to, ... 302
55. Washington Academy, appropriations to, ... 52–55
County Seminary and Collegiate Institute, appropriations to, ... 53–55
21. Washington and Saratoga railroad, amount of freight carried over, during the year 1851:
whole number of tons, ... 5
products of the forest, number of tons, ... 5
animals, number of tons, ... 5
vegetable food, number of tons, ... 5
other agricultural products, number of tons, .. 5
manufactures, number of tons, ... 5
merchandise, number of tons, ... 5
other articles, number of tons, ... 5
115. Wasson, James D., statement of lands sold to, ... 287

No. Doc. Page.

55. Waterford Academy, appropriations to, ... 52–55
Waterloo Academy, appropriations to, ... 52–55
Union School, appropriations to, ... 53–55
Watertown Home for Destitute and Orphan Children, appropriations to, ... 58–59
21. Watertown and Rome railroad, amount of freight carried over, each year from 1851 to 1861, inclusive:
whole number of tons, ... 5–25, 42
products of the forest, number of tons, ... 5–25, 42
animals, number of tons, ... 5–25, 42
vegetable food, number of tons, ... 5–25, 42
other agricultural products, number of tons, 5–25, 42
manufactures, number of tons, ... 5–25, 42
merchandise, number of tons, ... 5–25, 42
other articles, number of tons, ... 5–25, 42
(See "Rome, Watertown and Ogdensburgh railroad.")
115. Waters, Howard, statement of lands sold to, ... 290
Waters & Priest, statement of lands sold to, ... 134
40. Watkins, Julian A., testimony of, relative to management of Champlain canal, ... 395–421
55. Watkins Academy, appropriations to, ... 54–55
115. Watrous, John B., statement of lands sold to, ... 92
Watrous, John P., statement of lands sold to, ... 65, 137
Watson, Ralph, statement of lands sold to, ... 87
Watson, S., statement of lands sold to, ... 340
Waverly Institute, appropriations to, ... 54–55
28. Way & Mack, extra compensation paid to, ... 7
115. Weaver & Hazen, statement of lands sold to, ... 254
Webb, Henry L., statement of lands sold to, ... 218, 221, 224, 225
Webb, Thomas J., statement of lands sold to, ... 125
Weber, Christina, statement of lands sold to, ... 123
Webster, Geo., statement of lands sold to, .. 271, 281, 289
Webster & Beekman, statement of lands sole to, ... 81–84, 130, 132, 140, 151, 153, 155, 156, 271
Webster, Rich & Sanborn, statement of lands sold to, 124
55. Webster Academy, appropriations to, ... 54–55
115. Weed, George, statement of lands sold to, ... 37

No. Doc. Page.

115. Weed, Samuel C., statement of lands sold to, ... 253
1, 12. Weed, Smith M., delegate at large, Clinton Co., ... 1, 7
8. Weed, Parsons & Co., provisions of contract with, for printing, ... 1, 2
115. Weeks, Geo. S., statement of lands sold to, ... 338
Weeks, Jacob R., statement of lands sold to, ... 128
Weisser & Brunck, statement of lands sold to, ... 350
95. Welch, Alanson, testimony of, relative to management of canals, ... 4–11
115. Welsh, Geo. W., statement of lands sold to, ... 178
Welch, Harry F., statement of lands sold to, ... 100
Welden, Abram, statement of lands sold to, ... 293
23. Welland canal, property from and to, passed through Oswego canal, ... 14
salt passed through from Oswego canal, ... 15
115. Wellington, R. G., statement of lands sold to, ... 33
Wells, Benjamin, statement of lands sold to, ... 105, 115
40. Wells, Benjamin F., testimony of, relative to letting canal contracts, 28th December, ... 76–81
115. Wells, Benjamin T., statement of lands sold to, ... 142
Wells, Gardner, statement of lands sold to, ... 240
Wells, John S., statement of lands sold to, ... 133
28. Wells, Joseph, extra compensation paid to, ... 7
115. Wells, Joseph S., statement of lands sold to, ... 41
Wells, R. & J., statement of lands sold to, ... 233
Wells, Reuben, statement of lands sold to, ... 89
Wells, William, statement of lands sold to, .. 51, 101, 171, 173
40. Wendell, Nathan D., testimony of, relative to award to Charles J. De Graw, ... 661–64
115. Wendover, Peter, statement of lands sold to, ... 244
West, Wm. C., statement of lands sold to, ... 201
West, J. S., statement of lands sold to, ... 210
55. Western House of Refuge, appropriations to, ... 3–7, 92
115. Westfall, Henry, statement of lands sold to, ... 239
Westfall, Lewis, statement of lands sold to, ... 366
55. Westfield Academy, appropriations to, ... 52–55
115. Westcott, Darius, statement of lands sold to, ... 46
Westcott, Selah, statement of lands sold to, ... 128

No. Doc.		Page.
115.	Weston, James D., statement of lands sold to, ...	345
	Weston, Marcellus, statement of lands sold to, ...	108
55.	Westtown Academy, appropriations to, ...	52–55
	West Winfield Academy, appropriations to, ...	52–55
115.	Wetherly, David, statement of lands sold to, ... 128,	139
	Wetherbee, Jonathan, statement of lands sold to, 161,	226
	Wetherbee, Oliver, statement of lands sold to, .. 136,	139
	Wetmore, Seth, statement of lands sold to, 107, 108, 110, 111, 112, 113,	109, 267
	Whaley, Jonathan, statement of lands sold to, ...	25
	Whallon, James L., statement of lands sold to, ...	309
	Whalon, Reuben, statement of lands sold to, ...	85
	Wheat, Jonathan, statement of lands sold to, ...	236
	Wheat & Doolittle, statement of lands sold to, ...	235
	Wheaton, Joseph, statement of lands sold to, ...	114
	Wheeler, Moses, statement of lands sold to, ... 208,	211
	Wheeler, Wm., statement of lands sold to, ...	325
1, 12.	Wheeler, William A., delegate at large, Franklin Co.,	1, 1
115	Whipple, William W., statement of lands sold to, ...	77, 78
	Whitaker, John, statement of lands sold to, ...	95
	Whitcomb, Preston S., statement of lands sold to, ...	177
	White, Ebenezer, statement of lands sold to, ...	117
	White, Hans, statement of lands sold to, ...	336
	White, Jacob, statement of lands sold to, ...	213
	White, James, statement of lands sold to, ...	122
	White, Jno., statement of lands sold to, ...	325
	White, Luther, statement of lands sold to, .. 208, 210,	211
65.	White, M. A., judgment in favor of, against city of New York, ...	2
115.	White & Bedell, statement of lands sold to, ...	297
	White & Oliver, statement of lands sold to, ...	292
55.	Whitehall Academy, appropriations to, ...	52–55
	Whitehall Hospital, appropriations to, ...	75
115.	Whitehead, Jno., statement of lands sold to, ...	211
55.	Whitesboro Academy, appropriations to, ...	52–55
	Whitestown, Seminary, appropriations to, ...	52–55
115.	Whitlock, Hezekiah, statement of lands sold to, ...	142
	Whitman, George, statement of lands sold to, ...	105
	Whitman, Jno., statement of lands sold to, ...	283

No. Doc.		Page.
115.	Whitney, Arad, statement of lands sold to,..... 125,	126
	Whitney, James F., statement of lands sold to,.. 178,	249
	Whitney, Jno., statement of lands sold to,..........	213
	Whitney, Peter, statement of lands sold to, ... 45,	107
	264,	268
	Wickes, Ambrose, statement of lands sold to, ...	92
1, 12.	Wickham, William, delegate 1st district, Suffolk Co.,	1, 7
115.	Wickham, Wm., statement of lands sold to, ...	241
	Wiggins & Conger, statement of lands sold to, ...	69
28.	Wilbur, Briggs & Richardson, extra compensation paid to,..................................	7
40.	Wilcox, Hiram C., testimony of, relative to management of Champlain canal, ...	570–76
12.	Wilder, Alexander, reporter, New York, ...	9
115.	Wilder, Alanson, statement of lands sold to, ... 75,	234
28.	Wiles, John J., extra compensation paid to,.........	8
115.	Wiley, T. B., statement of lands sold to, ...	308
	Wilkison, Samuel, statement of lands sold to,.... 36,	37, 38
	Willard, M. & J. E., statement of lands sold to,......	300
	Willard & Lewis, statement of lands sold to, ...	122
	Willard & Patten, statement of lands sold to,........	121
	Willard & Williams, statement of lands sold to, ...	119–122
55.	Willard Insane Asylum, appropriations to, ...	7, 92
115.	Willett, Thomas, statement of lands sold to,.........	26, 28
	Willey, Ephraim, statement of lands sold to,........	325
	Williams, B. F., statement of lands sold to, ...	238
	Williams, Daniel D., statement of lands sold to, ...	241
	Williams, Edmund F., statement of lands sold to,. 47,	174
	264, 265, 268, 284, 309, 327,	340
	Williams, Elisha, statement of lands sold to, ...	69
1, 12.	Williams, George, delegate 19th district, Oneida Co., .	2, 7
115.	Williams, Gibson T., statement of lands sold to,.....	256
	Williams, Isaac, statement of lands sold to,...... 97,	161
	Williams, Lucy A., statement of lands sold to, ...	383
28.	Williams, William H., extra compensation paid to, ..	8
	Williams, Butts & Williams, extra compensation paid to, ...	9
115.	Williams & Young, statement of lands sold to, ...	79
55.	Williamsburgh Dispensary, appropriations to,.......	76–79

No. Doc. Page.

55. Williamsburgh Industrial School, appropriations to, 71
98. Wills, informal, special laws for legalization of, prohibited, ... 14
115. Wilson, Andrew L., statement of lands sold to,...... 287
Wilson, Benjamin, statement of lands sold to,....... 239
Wilson, David, statement of lands sold to,.. 357, 369, 373
379
Wilson, Elias, statement of lands sold to,........... 114
Wilson, Hiram, statement of lands sold to, ... 231, 330
150. Willson, Hugh B., testimony of, before committee on official corruption,.......................... ... 13–34
115. Wilson, James, statement of lands sold to,.......... 140
Wilson, John, statement of lands sold to,........... 27
Wilson, Lyman G., statement of lands sold to, ... 303
Wilson, Norman, statement of lands sold to, ... 206
Wilson, Stillman, statement of lands sold to,........ 168
Wilson & Lund, statement of lands sold to, ... 270
55. Wilson Collegiate Institute, appropriations to,....... 52–55
54. Wilson Industrial School, N. Y., report of donations to, 7
55. Windsor Academy, appropriations to,.............. 52–55
115. Wing, Daniel W., statement of lands sold to,........ 302
Winne, James, statement of lands sold to, ... 331
Winne, Jellis, Jr., statement of lands sold to,........ 178
Winner, Henry, statement of lands sold to, ... 110
Winter, Asa C., statement of lands sold to, ... 290
Withey, Erastus, statement of lands sold to,......... 360
149. Witnesses, unreasonable detention of, prohibited, ... 3
55. Women's Hospital, New York, appropriations to,.... 73–75
Infirmary, Washington Heights, appropriations to, ... 79
Prison Association, N. Y., report of donations to, ... 8
115. Wood, Henry, statement of lands sold to,...... 143, 162
Wood, Horatio N., statement of lands sold to, ... 243
Wood, Isaac, statement of lands sold to,....... 107, 141
Wood, James, statement of lands sold to, ... 369
Wood, Jonathan, statement of lands sold to,........ 209
Wood, T. M., heirs of, statement of lands sold to,.... 307
Woods, J. L., statement of lands sold to,........... 239
Woodburne, Lewis, statement of lands sold to, ... 308

No. Doc. Page.

115. Woodruff, A. J., statement of lands sold to, ... 366
Woodruff, Gideon H , statement of lands sold to,.... 15, 21
Woodward, Jonathan, statement of lands sold to,.... 199
Woodworth, John, statement of lands sold to,... 98, 104
Woodworth, L., statement of lands sold to,......... 209
Woolson, A. G., statement of lands sold to,......... 324
Woolson, A. & G., statement of lands sold to, 293, 307, 324
Woolson & Clift, statement of lands sold to,........ 342
Woolson & Wheeler, statement of lands sold to,.... 324
Woolworth, David, statement of lands sold to,.. 114, 260
Wooster & Smith, statement of lands sold to,... 108, 189
150. Worcester, Edwin D., testimony of, before committee on official corruption, ... 43–51
40. Wormley, William, testimony of, relative to award to Charles J. DeGraw,.......................... 271–74
115. Wormath, Wm. C., statement of lands sold to, ... 360
Wray, Chas., statement of lands sold to,............ 339
Wright, David S., statement of lands sold to,....... 121
Wright, Jno., statement of lands sold to,........... 258
Wright, Josiah, statement of lands sold to, ... 206
Wright, Lucein, statement of lands sold to,......... 49
Wright, Luther, statement of lands sold to, ... 30, 325
19. Wright, Real, superintendent of salt springs, ... 5
115. Wright, Samuel, statement of lands sold to,..... 13, 121
Wright, Thomas, statement of lands sold to,........ 265
Wright, Thomas M., statement of lands sold to,..... 145
40. Wright, Wm. W., testimony of, relative to repairs of section 9 of Erie canal, ... 15–17, 20, 21
testimony of, relative to Parker's contract for repairs on section 1, Chenango canal,...... 17, 18
testimony of, relative to manner of letting contracts by contracting board,.............. 19, 20
testimony of, relative to contract for repairs of section 1, Erie canal, and dredging Albany basin, ... 710–15
90. testimony of, relative to capacity of Erie canal, 32–34
115. Wyckoff, Cornelius P., statement of lands sold to,... 14, 16
Wyman, John, statement of lands sold to,.......... 81
Wyman, J. F., statement of lands sold to,.......... 392
Wynkoop, Augustus, statement of lands sold to, ... 101

No. Doc. | Page.

Y.

115. Yates & McIntyre, statement of lands sold to, ... 230
55. Yates Academy, appropriations to, ... 52–55
Polytechnic Institute, appropriations to, ... 53–55
115. Yaw, Elisha, statement of lands sold to, ... 295
Yon, Charles B., statement of lands sold to, ... 160
54. Yorkville Dispensary, N. Y., report of donations to, . 16
115. Young, Alexander, statement of lands sold to, ... 76, 77, 87
Young, James G., statement of lands sold to, ... 249
1, 12. Young, Solomon G., delegate 14th district, Ulster county, ... 2, 7
54. Young Men's Christian Association, N. Y., report of donations to, ... 13